SO-CBQ-985

INSPIRATION AND
REVELATION IN THE
OLD TESTAMENT

INSPIRATION AND REVELATION IN THE OLD TESTAMENT

BY

H. WHEELER ROBINSON, D.D.

LATE PRINCIPAL EMERITUS OF REGENT'S PARK COLLEGE
OXFORD, AND SPEAKER'S LECTURER IN THE
UNIVERSITY OF OXFORD

GREENWOOD PRESS, PUBLISHERS
WESTPORT, CONNECTICUT

Library of Congress Cataloging in Publication Data

Robinson, Henry Wheeler, 1872-1945.
   Inspiration and revelation in the Old Testament.

   Reprint of the ed. published by Clarendon Press,
Oxford.
   Lectures delivered before the University of Oxford,
1942-1945.
   Includes bibliographical references and indexes.
   1. Bible. O.T.--Theology. 2. Prophets.
3. Revelation--Biblical teaching. I. Title.
BS1192.5.R62 1979   221.6   78-9891
ISBN 0-313-21068-3

Reprinted in 1979 by Greenwood Press, Inc.
51 Riverside Avenue, Westport, CT 06880

Printed in the United States of America

10 9 8 7 6 5 4 3 2 1

EDITORIAL NOTE

THIS volume, which Dr. Wheeler Robinson had himself hoped to publish, contains the lectures which he delivered before the University of Oxford as Speaker's Lecturer from 1942 to 1945. The two final chapters were not read as lectures but were written to furnish a conclusion to the series of lectures, when published, and were left in typescript. Dr. Robinson was unable, through the illness from which he died in May 1945, to make the final revision of the typescript, and this has been done, according to his wish, by his two former colleagues, the Rev. L. H. Brockington and the Rev. E. A. Payne. A memoir of Dr. Robinson by Mr. Payne will be published shortly.

Had he been able to fulfil his plans a chapter on the growth of the Canon would also have been included, as indicated in his introduction to the lectures which is printed below. Chapter III, in full, and part of Chapter XII with some rewording, have already appeared as articles in the *Journal of Theological Studies* and are reprinted here with the permission of the Delegates of the Clarendon Press.

Dr. Robinson had for several years been planning to write a volume on the *Theology of the Old Testament*. The Speaker's Lectures would have constituted the prolegomena, setting out in detail the *form* of the revelation whose *content* would have supplied the material for the theology. The last two paragraphs of the present volume indicate to some extent what Dr. Robinson had in mind.

L. H. B.
E. A. P.

REGENT'S PARK COLLEGE,
  OXFORD

AUTHOR'S INTRODUCTION

THE general subject of these lectures will be approached through three subordinate topics, viz. God and Nature, God and Man, God and History, dealing respectively with the physical world considered as a manifestation of God, with the psychical world of human nature, involving a study of Hebrew psychology and some relevant topics, and with the capacity of history, especially the history of Israel, to be made a revelation of God.

In the second part of the main subject the nature of prophetic inspiration will be central, though this will involve consideration of the Hebrew language as a vehicle of inspiration, the alliance of poetic form to prophetic oracle, the general psychology of prophecy and apocalyptic, and the relation of prophecy to history and ritual.

In the third part of the main subject attention will be given to the other great parallel line of revelation, the priestly oracle and the sacred or secular decisions which grew up around or alongside it, ultimately to constitute the legislative codes of the Torah. This will lead on to the growth of the Canon of the Old Testament as a whole, and the nature of the authority attached to it by early Judaism and primitive Christianity.

H. W. R.

CONTENTS

ABBREVIATIONS

*ATAO*² *Das Alte Testament im Lichte des Alten Orients*, A. Jeremias, 2nd ed.

*ATAT*² *Altorientalische Texte zum Alten Testament*, 2nd ed. (ed. H. Gressmann).

BDB   Brown, Driver, Briggs, *A Hebrew and English Lexicon*.

BZAW Beihefte zur Zeitschrift für die alttestamentliche Wissenschaft.

E.Bi.   *Encyclopedia Biblica.*

ERE   *Encyclopedia of Religion and Ethics.*

HDB   Hastings, *Dictionary of the Bible.*

ICC   International Critical Commentary.

JBL   *Journal of Biblical Literature.*

JTS   *Journal of Theological Studies.*

*KAT*³ *Die Keilinschriften und das AT.*, 3rd ed.

*RGG*² *Die Religion in Geschichte und Gegenwart*, 2nd ed.

SOED *The Shorter Oxford English Dictionary.*

ZAW   *Zeitschrift für die alttestamentliche Wissenschaft.*

ZDMG *Zeitschrift der deutschen morgenländischen Gesellschaft.*

PART I

GOD AND NATURE

I

THE HEBREW CONCEPTION OF NATURE

§ 1

THE Hebrew vocabulary includes no word equivalent to our term 'Nature'. This is not surprising, if by 'Nature' we mean 'The creative and regulative physical power which is conceived of as operating in the physical world and as the immediate cause of all its phenomena'.[1] The only way to render this idea into Hebrew would be to say simply 'God'.[2] We should have to describe a particular physical activity through anthropomorphic phrases, such as the 'voice' of God, heard in the thunder; the 'hand' of God, felt in the pestilence; the 'breath' of God, animating the body of man; the 'wisdom' of God, ultimately conceived as His agent in creation.[3] In fact, we may say that such unity as 'Nature' possessed in Hebrew eyes came to it through its absolute dependence on God, its Creator and Upholder. It has been said that 'Greek philosophy began, as it ended, with the search for what was abiding in the flux of things'.[4] The Hebrew found that in God. Modern conceptions of natural law find a partial analogue in the Babylonian astrology which dominated the thought of the Near East for so long a period. The regular rising and setting of the sun, moon, and constellations, together with planetary movements amongst the signs of the zodiac, supplied a pattern of fixed order. This was believed to impose itself upon both natural phenomena and human actions, because of the cardinal premise of astrology, that the world above supplies the key to the conduct of the world below. It is true that the Babylonians also personified natural phenomena, where we should use abstract terms, and that the stars were conceived by them as gods. Of such beliefs there are

---

[1] *SOED*, s.v.

[2] Just as the only way to express 'victory' is to say 'salvation'.

[3] e.g. Ps. xxix. 3, 5, 7, 9; 1 Sam. v. 6; Gen. ii. 7 and Ps. civ. 29, 30; Prov. viii. 22 ff.

[4] J. Burnet, *Early Greek Philosophy*[2], p. 15.

B

not a few echoes and survivals in the Old Testament, as when, at the foundation of the earth,

> the morning stars sang together,
> And all the sons of God shouted for joy.[1]

or, again, when apocalyptic described the punishment, not only of the kings of the earth, but also of the host of the height, the star-deities who have rebelled with them, or have even inspired their rebellion.[2] In fact, the familiar phrase 'Yahweh of hosts' which flourished to so marked a degree in the Babylonian period[3] seems to have been extended from earthly to heavenly armies, and to have become the memorial of Yahweh's absorption of these star-rivals into his retinue. Yet Yahweh was far more than a victor over them on their own plane. They were nature-deities, with all the ethical limitations which this implies; He was above Nature, as its Creator and Controller according to a moral purpose. The prophetic conception of Yahweh is quite explicit in contrasting Him with this astrological background, as in Deutero-Isaiah:

'Declare the things that are to come hereafter, that we may know that ye are gods. . . .

'I am Yahweh that maketh all things; that stretcheth forth the heavens alone; that spreadeth abroad the earth; who is with me? That frustrateth the tokens of the boasters and maketh diviners mad. . . .

'Let now the astrologers, the star-gazers, the monthly prognosticators, stand up and save thee (Babylon) from the things that shall come upon thee.' (Isa. xli. 23; xliv. 24, 25; xlvii. 13)

It is by the conflict of ideas that truth chiefly develops, and we may be sure that the conception of Yahweh owed no little of its enlargement to the clash with that of the star-gods of Babylon. The primary conception of Yahweh which made such progress possible cannot have been itself a development from natural phenomena. Its inspiration was derived from the very different realm of human history. Yahweh's ultimate relation to things is a derivative from His primary relation to men.

A parallel contrast is afforded by Canaanite mythology, now so strikingly illustrated by the Ugaritic (Ras Shamra) docu-

---

[1] Job xxxviii. 7; cf. Pss. ciii. 21; cxlviii. 2, 3; 1 Kings xxii. 19, and Bertholet's comment on Neh. ix. 6: 'Das Himmelsheer wird als belebtes gedacht.'
[2] Isa. xxiv. 21.
[3] Köhler, *Theologie des A.T.*, pp. 31 ff.; but see BDB, s.v.

ments. The related mythology of Babylon will concern us when dealing with the doctrine of creation. The Ugaritic sources illustrate the myth of the dying and rising god as the explanation of seasonal vegetation. Thus Baal and his son, Aliyan, the gods of autumn and winter, are overthrown each spring by Mot, the god of summer heat.[1] Before Aliyan follows his father to the underworld he has union with his sister-mistress Anath, in the form of a heifer.[2] After the death of Aliyan, Anath avenges him, and the description of her vengeance portrays the harvest customs:

> Anath seized Mot, the divine son,
> With a sickle she cut him,
> With a winnow she winnows him,
> With a fire she scorches him,
> With a mill she crushes him,
> She scatters his flesh in the field to be eaten by birds
> So that his destiny may be fulfilled. (Schaeffer, p. 72)

We should notice here the forthright identification of the god with the product of the harvest, which takes us much farther than personification. We may compare the Babylonian ritual as noted by C. J. Gadd: 'The miller is charged to deliver flour for the loaves to the appropriate priest, and must chant over his mill an incantation beginning, "The astral Ploughman has yoked in the plain (of Heaven) the seed-sowing Plough", and likewise the baker has to say over his bread "Nisaba, luxuriant plenty, pure food", and the butcher, as he slaughters his beasts, exclaims, "The son of Shamash, lord of cattle, has created fodder in the plain".'[3]

There can be little doubt that such ideas underlay much of the Israelite religion as denounced by the prophets, and especially its sexual features.[4] Sacred prostitution, for example, was a form of symbolic magic, promoting the fertility of the earth, whilst giving intensity of self-expression and conscious participation in the religious cult. It will be remembered that in the Elephantine form of Jewish religion, doubtless continuing the belief of an older Israel, the divine name Anathya'u implies that

[1] Schaeffer, Schweich Lectures, *The Cuneiform Texts of Ras Shamra Ugarit*, p. 69.
[2] Cf. Exod. xxii. 19; Lev. xviii. 23, xx. 15 f.
[3] *Myth and Ritual* (ed. by S. H. Hooke), p. 43. Nisaba was the consort of one of the agricultural gods (Jastrow, *The Religion of Babylonia and Assyria*, p. 102).
[4] Deut. xxiii. 17, 18; 1 Kings xiv. 24; Amos ii. 7; Hos. iv. 14; Deut. xxii. 5; Isa. xvii. 10, 11.

Anath the queen of heaven is a consort of Yahweh.[1] Isaiah
refers to the Adonis-plants, by which the growth of the corn
was promoted through a plant identified with the god and
forced into rapid growth.[2] The vintage festival of Yahweh at
Shiloh,[3] when the Benjaminites seized women for themselves,
illustrates the combination of agricultural and sexual features
and supplies a link with the regularized agricultural festivals,
which Yahwism appropriated from the Canaanites and assimilated to itself. But in regard to these very festivals, it is highly
significant that the historical *motif* more and more prevails over
what was originally a purely nature-celebration. One by one
the great feasts came to celebrate the deliverance from Egypt,
the giving of the Torah on Sinai, the dwelling in tents of Israel's
nomadic days. Such transformation is typical of all the higher
religion of Israel. History supplied a revelation of God which
Nature, notwithstanding all its rich content and variety, could
never afford. Yet the conception of the God who works in
history is inseparably linked to His manifestation in natural
phenomena. He is what Nature, as well as history, reveals Him
to be,[4] and Nature is His peculiar language.

§ 2

Because of the outstanding emphasis in the Old Testament
on the religious aspects of Nature in relation to Yahweh, it is
not easy for us to recover the Hebrew way of regarding Nature
itself. We can be sure that it was very different from our own
attitude, in spite of much common ground. The Song of Songs
is the one originally secular book in the Old Testament, and
fortunately it is also a Nature-book. Its anthology of love-lyrics
is partly set in descriptions of natural scenery. It names a score
of plants or trees and a dozen animals.[5] The erotic use of some
of these references to Nature accompanies a real appreciation of natural beauty,[6] such as the coming of the flowers and
the singing of the birds in the spring, the dove in the clefts of the
rock or by pools of water, the sheaf of yellow wheat in its circle

[1] Cowley, *Aramaic Papyri*, p. xix.
[2] xvii. 10, 11.   [3] Judges xxi. 19 ff.
[4] Cf. P. Kleinert, *Die Naturanschauung des Alten Testaments* (Studien und Kritiken,
1898, p. 13).   [5] Ranston, *The O.T. Wisdom Books*, p. 227.
[6] Cf. Ecclus. xliii. 11, l. 6 ff. Note also the twofold *motif*, aesthetic and erotic,
in Egyptian love-songs of which examples are given by Erman, *Literature of the
Ancient Egyptians*, E.T. by A. M. Blackman, pp. 242 ff.

of henna flowers, and the red hyacinths against a background
of thistles, the flock of goats streaming down the mountain-side,
the shorn and newly washed sheep in their white freshness, the
young gazelles pasturing amongst the hyacinths, the spring of
water in the garden, the waving fronds of the palm-tree, the
horizontal foliage of the cedars of Lebanon, the blossom of the
pomegranate, the scented apples and the pleasant shade of
the apple-tree, the greenness of the nut-garden, the budding of
the vines and their full clusters, the glory of the dawn and the
beauty of the moon, the sky-line of Carmel, the grace and beauty
of the human body in man and woman. Such appreciation of
the beauty of Nature does not, as is sometimes suggested, belong
to the romanticism of the modern world alone. It goes back
at least to 1100 B.C., when the Egyptian Unamun, visiting the
prince of Byblos, found him by a window with the tossing waves
of the Syrian sea as his background.[1]

But there is a difference of emphasis, even in such aesthetic
appreciation. This is illustrated by the many references in the
Song of Songs to the scents and perfumes of natural objects.[2]
A Western poet would hardly have given us so much of these
any more than he would have written, like one of the Wisdom
writers, 'oil and perfume gladden the heart'.[3] On this appreciation of natural beauty there is superimposed the erotic imagination of the poets of the Song of Songs, just as the religious
imagination of poet and psalmist incorporated the wonder and
majesty of Nature in their very different view of the world. In
both realms the aesthetic response is to particular objects,
rather than to Nature as a whole. This is a characteristic
difference from our own outlook. We miss a general appreciation of landscape, whilst the sea is for the Hebrew rather an
enemy to be overcome than the majestic setting of the land. It
is characteristic of Hebrew interests also that his Old Testament
vocabulary deals much more with birds than with fishes.[4]

It is the Wisdom writers who display the most marked interest

---

[1] 'The Voyage of Unamun', Erman, op. cit., p. 178.
[2] C. Doughty, *Arabia Deserta*, i. 210, ascribes Bedouin hyperaesthesia to smell to
the pure air of the desert.   [3] Prov. xxvii. 9.
[4] There are ten specialized names of birds in the O.T., and none of fishes,
according to H. Weinheimer (*Hebräisches Wörterbuch in sachlicher Ordnung*, pp. 9, 10).
Cf. Gen. ii. 20 where Adam names birds and beasts, but not fishes: cf. also Milton,
Par. Lost, viii. 345 ff., and *ERE*, 'Fish'. There is no specific name for fish, apart
from the generic ἰχθύς, even in the New Testament.

in Nature, and this accounts for the reference to the traditional wisdom of Solomon:

'He spoke concerning trees, from the cedar which is in Lebanon even to the hyssop that springs out of the wall; he spoke also of beasts, of birds, of reptiles and of fish.'[1]

But this interest is not what we should call scientific.[2] Its aim is to draw a moral, as when the labours of the ant become a pattern of thrifty industry, and the thistles and nettles a warning against its opposite. The trapped gazelle becomes the type of easy-going suretyship, the tree planted by the waters that of the Torah-nurtured man, the leech that of insatiable greed. It is the concentrated and concrete wisdom of ant, rock-badger, locust, and lizard that explains their efficiency. The proud-stepping lion, cock, and he-goat are made to point on to the haughty mien of a king. The mystery of the vulture's path through the air, the serpent's on the crag, the ship's through the sea, lead on to the greatest mystery of all—that of sex, which fascinated the ancient Israelite no less than the modern psycho-analyst.[3]

§ 3

Certainly the mystery of Nature's ways is one of its outstanding features in Hebrew eyes. George Adam Smith comments on their Syrian environment, in contrast with the monotony of the desert, by saying: 'Syria is a land of lavish gifts and oracles—where woods are full of mysterious speech, and rivers burst suddenly from the ground. . . . The spirit and the senses are equally taken by surprise.'[4] In both the Wisdom book known as Ecclesiastes and the apocalyptic book known as 4 Esdras, the mystery of Nature teaches that God's ways in other realms also are inscrutable. This, too, is the immediate lesson drawn in the greatest and most comprehensive account of natural phenomena which the Old Testament affords, viz. the speeches of Yahweh in the Book of Job.[5] Here the descriptions of particular objects are intended to show that Nature is full of

---

[1] 1 Kings iv. 33.

[2] On the pragmatic character of the Hebrew knowledge of Nature, see Nowack, *Lehrbuch der hebräischen Archäologie*, i. 297.

[3] Prov. vi. 6 f., xxiv. 30 f., vi. 5; Ps. i. 3, cf. Jer. xvii. 8; Prov. xxx. 15, xxx. 24 ff., xxx. 18 ff.

[4] *Historical Geography of the Holy Land*, ed. 7, p. 88.   [5] xxxviii ff.

mysteries which are beyond man's achievement, mysteries which point to a divine activity that is beyond man's comprehension. Thus we are told of the foundation of the earth upon its columns in their sockets,[1] the vast measurements of the earth, the imposition of strict limits on the rebellious cloud-wrapt sea,[2] the marvellous coming of the dawn to displace darkness and its attendant evils, the deep-lying springs of the sea and the portals of death that lead to Sheol, the dwelling of light and darkness, conceived as concrete entities, not as mere consequences of the presence or absence of light, the heavenly storehouses of snow and hail, the motion of wind and thunderbolt, the ever-renewed miracle of the rain and of the fertilizing night-mist ('dew'), the formation of ice-crystals, the control of star-constellations such as the Pleiades, Orion, the Northern Crown, the Great and Little Bear, the path of the lightnings, the ordering of the clouds, the tilting of the great water-skins of heaven.

After this brilliant review of what we systematize as cosmology, meteorology, and astronomy, we pass to the biological mysteries of the animal world. Here it is the variety of God's activities which impresses us.[3] The lion and the raven alike find their food; the pregnancy and parturition of mountain-goat and doe have their proper times and seasons. We look on the free wanderings of the wild-ass, the unfettered strength of the wild-ox, the strange behaviour of the ostrich, the majesty and élan of the battle-horse, the journeyings of the migratory hawk, the swoop of the vulture on the carcases. The second speech of Yahweh is wholly devoted to the hippopotamus and the crocodile and stresses their invincible strength, rather than their mystery, and is probably a later addition to the book.

Rudolf Otto, in the chapter of his well-known book, *Das Heilige*, which is devoted to 'The Numinous in the Old Testament', singles out these chapters from 'Job' as a pure example of the *mysterium tremendum*. He argues that we have here not simply a reduction of the hero to silence before God's incomprehensibility, but also a positive revelation of the non-rational element in the divine being. There is certainly a truth here, for the revelation of God in Nature can never be purely negative

---

[1] According to Job xxvi. 7, the earth hangs on nothing. In Ps. xxiv. 1, 2 it is said to be founded on the seas.

[2] Cf. Jer. v. 22; Prov. viii. 29.

[3] In the late Wisdom book, Ecclesiastes, it is the *monotony* of Nature's endless cycles which impresses the writer, e.g. i. 4–9.

and the Old Testament conception of holiness gathers up into
itself much besides rational righteousness. But it should also
have been pointed out by Otto that the rationality of Nature
is implied in its exhibition of Yahweh's Wisdom, and that the
Prologue to Job supplies a vision of the rational purpose of God
to vindicate disinterested religion through the sufferings of His
true servant Job, though the very nature of the challenge of
the Adversary required that this purpose should be hidden
from the sufferer. Job is a martyr-witness that men will serve
God for naught. The physical catastrophes that bring this about
are themselves 'rationalized' by being taken up into the divine
purpose. In fairness to Otto, it should be realized that he does
in general regard the numinous as assimilated by the larger
prophetic religion; for him, the Allah of Islam, rather than the
Yahweh of Israel, is the exemplification of the *numen*. But
whether we take the lower or higher manifestations of Israel's
religion, the contribution made by Nature to revelation is of
wide range and of great importance; through Nature are known
the mystery, majesty, and wisdom of God's ways which raise
Him above man, yet serve His moral and religious revelation
of Himself.

If the first speech of Yahweh in the Book of Job gives us the
fullest Old Testament review of Nature's mysterious details, the
best picture of Nature as a going concern is to be gained from
Psalm civ, even though this is partly borrowed from the Egyptian 'Hymn to the Sun'.[1] The psalmist shows, in co-ordinated
presentation, the immovable earth on its mountain pillars, the
giant beams of Yahweh's abode above amidst the waters of
heaven, the waters beneath driven back from the habitable
earth, and their bounds unalterably fixed, the raising of the
mountains and the lowering of the valleys, the springs from
which the wild creatures drink, the produce of the earth providing for man and beast, the cedars of Lebanon and its birds, the
stork with her home in the cypress, the wild-goats of the mountains, the rock-badgers. The point of view is here a different
one from that of 'Job'. It is not the incomprehensible mystery
of these items in the catalogue of Nature that attracts the eye
of the psalmist, but the harmonious order which rules them all,

---

[1] Erman, op. cit., pp. 288 ff. We may regret that the psalmist did not include
the delightful detail that the Sun-god gives breath to the chick in its egg and
strength to break its shell with a triumphant chirp.

through the moon and the sun, so that the night is made for the wild creatures and the day for man. Man is indeed central in the picture, though at first sight he seems to take so small a place.[1] The sea also is viewed with more friendly eye in Ps. civ than in the Book of Job, and the fearsome crocodile has become a playful beast. The dependence of all living things upon the continuous activity of God is emphasized in an important passage (verses 27–30):

These all wait upon thee,
To give them their food in due season.
What thou givest them, they gather up;
When thou openest thy hand, they are satisfied with good things,
When thou hidest thy face, they are disturbed;
When thou takest away their breath, they die,
And turn again into dust.
When thou sendest forth thy breath, they are created,
And thou renewest the face of the earth.

For Vedantist thought the divine breath blows the bubble of Maya, the illusory cosmos; for the Hebrew, it gives the activity of life to all creatures. Clearly this implies a much more personal and immediate control of Nature than that which 'natural law' would suggest, even to a theist.

§ 4

Yet we must not exaggerate this difference into neglect of the Hebrew recognition of order in Nature. Such recognition was inevitable, even though its explanation was much more obviously anthropomorphic than our own. In the covenant with Noah after the Flood, the rainbow becomes the permanent pledge or 'sacrament' of the fixed order henceforth to prevail:

'As long as the earth endures, seedtime and harvest, cold and heat, summer and winter, day and night, shall never cease.' (Gen. ix. 13 ff., viii. 22; cf. Jer. v. 24.)

Jeremiah[2] appeals to the fixed order of movement of sun, moon,

---

[1] It is a serious misreading of the psalm to say with Professor D. B. Macdonald (*The Hebrew Literary Genius*, p. 28, cf. 161), 'According to it man was simply a part of the world and had no special pre-eminence in it'. This ignores the culmination of the psalm in the praise of God by man—the one earthly creature in whom praise can be articulate. The psalm really illustrates the thought of Isa. xlv. 18 which says that God formed the earth that it might be inhabited, and the thought of Psalm viii, which sets man in the supreme place amongst the creatures of God.

[2] xxxi. 35, 36; xxxiii. 25, 26; xxxiii. 20.

and stars and the orderly succession of day and night, as both
the standard and the pledge of Yahweh's consistent preservation of Israel. Yahweh speaks to Job of the 'ordinances' (*huqqoth*)
of the heavens, and similarly the rain has its 'ordinance' (*hoq*).[1]
God's steadfast rule of the sea is often named,[2] though for the
Hebrew conception of it we must of course eliminate our own
knowledge of the tides and of topographical levels. The
apparently unruly conduct of the horse, plunging headlong into
battle, is contrasted with the orderly migrations of the stork,
the turtle-dove, the swift, and the swallow.[3] Yahweh in fact
has His 'covenant' with Nature, which means that His effective
command is laid upon it in its several details. The renewal of
that covenant 'with the beasts of the field, the birds of the air,
and the reptiles of the ground' becomes part of the promise of
security in the future given through Hosea.[4] According to an
apocalyptic writer, this covenant involved an oath taken by
the different elements of the order of Nature.[5] Eliphaz promises
to an upright Job a covenant with the stones of the field, i.e. the
removal of their threat to its fertility, whilst the beasts of the
field will be at peace with him.[6] The proper treatment of
the land is that in which God instructs the farmer, so that all
may be done in due order.[7] Every part of Nature has its own
min or category, and this, as we learn from the first chapter
of Genesis, was given to it at its creation.[8] But all this detail
of Nature is unified not simply or chiefly by intrinsic qualities,
such as we group under physics, chemistry, and biology, but by
the universal dependence on God who made them what they
are and sustains them in it.

The nearest approach to any philosophical unification, such
as that of early Greek philosophy, is supplied by the conception
of 'Wisdom' as a mediating and quasi-personalized entity, and
this significantly appears for the first time in the Greek period.[9]
This Wisdom is subjective, in the sense that it is God's and proceeds from Him, yet it is also objective, in the sense that He

---

[1] Job xxxviii. 33, cf. xxviii. 26.
[2] e.g. Job xxxviii. 8–11; Prov. viii. 29; Jer. v. 22; Ps. civ. 8, 9; Ps. cxlviii. 6.
[3] Jer. viii. 6, 7.   [4] ii. 18.
[5] 1 Enoch lxix. 16 ff.; cf. Gressmann, *Der Ursprung der isr.-jüdischen Eschatologie*,
p. 206.
[6] Job v. 23.   [7] Isa. xxviii. 26.
[8] Gen. i. 11; cf. Pedersen, *Israel I–II*, p. 485.
[9] Prov. viii. 12 ff.; Ecclus. xxiv; Wisdom of Solomon, vii. 22 ff.

employs it in the creation and conservation of both Nature and human life. Wisdom was the first product of God's creative activity, for it is the condition and instrument for the creation of all things. Before there were the deeps and their fountains, before the mountains were sunk into their places, before the earth and its fields existed, Wisdom was present to assist in fixing the heavens and in tracing the great circle of the farthest horizon, in setting the fountains of the deeps, in giving to the sea its appointed boundary, in tracing out the foundations of the earth. Wisdom was to Yahweh an intimate friend, as well as the agent and overseer in all this work, finding delight in the creation of all things. The other great mediating conception of the Old Testament, that of the Spirit of God, is concentrated on activity in and through human nature. The reference in Gen. i. 2 to the wind-spirit of God as hovering[1] over the face of the waters stands alone, and is probably due to Babylonian mythology. Some phenomena ascribed to the Spirit coincide with some that might equally be derived from Wisdom, such as technical skill and judicial efficiency,[2] but Wisdom included in addition all the natural phenomena whilst practical usage confined Spirit to the personal realm. Even so, we must not identify Wisdom with such conceptions of immanence as we encounter in the Stoic doctrine of the Logos, at any rate for native Hebrew thought, to which the idea of divine immanence is foreign.

The precise origin of the figure of Wisdom in Hebrew usage is obscure and disputable. Here it must be sufficient to say that its appearance suggests outside influence, possibly Iranian.[3] Its unifying function in regard to Nature is obvious. The world becomes a revelation of the divine wisdom, and Nature is a unity in the sense that it exhibits the wisdom of its divine Creator and Upholder. Whilst the mystery of Nature, and still more its numinous qualities, tended to separate God from man, this revelation of the divine Wisdom constitutes a bond of union between them, capable of further development in the Logos background of the Incarnation, to which Wisdom was an important tributary.

---

[1] The conception of the cosmic world-egg may have given rise to the use of this participle (*ERE*, iv. 147 f.).

[2] e.g. Exod. xxxv. 31; Isa. xi. 2.

[3] So O. S. Rankin, *Israel's Wisdom Literature*, pp. 228f.

§ 5

In what has so far been said, we have approached Nature rather from without than from within. What are we to say further of Nature in its intrinsic qualities? How did the Hebrew conception of it differ from that which underlies our own physics, chemistry, and biology? It is natural enough that the modern mind should treat the survivals of primitive mythology in the language of prophet and psalmist as merely poetical figures. It is, of course, perfectly true to say that the psalmist has risen far above such myths as that of Marduk's conflict with Tiamat, when he says of Yahweh:

> Thou rulest over the raging of the sea,
> When its waves rise thou stillest them;
> Thou hast crushed Rahab like one that is slain,
> With thy strong arm thou hast scattered thy foes.
> (Ps. lxxxix. 9, 10; cf. Job ix. 13, xxvi. 12; Ps. lxxiv. 12–17.)

So also with the prophet who thus addresses 'the arm of Yahweh':

> Was it not thou that didst hew Rahab in pieces,
>   that didst pierce the dragon? (Isa. li. 9.)

Yet both the Accadian and Hebrew writers, at their different religious levels, were dealing with familiar realities of Nature, in which they found something suggesting a quasi-independent entity that needed restraint. This quasi-independence was interpreted in psychical terms where the modern physicist would use symbols of electronic energy, and the modern biologist would make use of organic chemistry. This indication of a different underlying conception is reinforced when we recall the place taken by fountains, trees, and stones in the religion of Israel. At Kadesh there was a 'spring of Judgment'.[1] In a song preserved from Israel's nomadic period a well is addressed as a living thing—'Spring up, O well!'[2] There were oracle-giving trees, such as the balsams in which the wind gave to David the sound of marching as the signal for attack.[3] The stone of Bethel, which Jacob made his pillow, was the medium through which came his dream-vision of the ladder reaching the sky and the angels going up and down on their missions. Such phenomena suggest that the material objects of Nature were conceived as having a psychical life of their own, making them capable on occasion

---

[1] Gen. xiv. 7.   [2] Num. xxi. 17, 18.   [3] 2 Sam. v. 23f.

of more special manifestations of life.[1] A particularly instructive
passage comes from the prophet Hosea, which describes the
responsive life of Nature:

I will answer the heavens,
And they shall answer the earth;
And the earth shall answer the grain, the wine and the oil;
And they shall answer Jezreel. (ii. 21, 22.)

Here we have a sequence of hungry people, the food they need,
the soil in which alone it can grow, the rain from heaven which
makes that soil fertile, and the ultimate control of the rain, as
a miracle of grace, by Yahweh. Certainly we have here more
than a poetical personification of natural processes. Each
element of the sequence has a life of its own which must be
duly elicited to make the chain complete. For the general idea
of such a sequence we may compare the Babylonian:

'When Anu made heaven, heaven made earth, earth made the
rivers, rivers made the ditches, the ditches made the marsh, and the
marsh made the worm.'[2]

The attribution of psychical life, not only to animals and
plants, but also to what we should call inanimate objects, does
in fact point us back to the realm of 'prelogical' thinking, the
realm of *mana*[3] or animatism, rather than that of animism. This
was already seen by Robertson Smith, and is confirmed by the
comparative evidence which has accumulated since his time.
In *The Religion of the Semites* he remarks that primitive minds,
'habitually ignore the distinctions, which to us seem obvious,
between organic and inorganic nature, or within the former
region between animals and plants . . . all things appear to
them to live . . . the unseen life that inhabits the plant, tree
or sacred stone makes the sacred object itself be conceived as a
living being'.[4] More recently Pedersen has emphasized this in
regard to Israel, saying: 'earth itself is alive. . . . The earth has
its nature, which makes itself felt and demands respect',[5] and

[1] Cf. F. Lundgreen, *Die Benutzung der Pflanzenwelt in der alttestamentlichen Religion*,
p. 155: 'Irgendwie beseelt dachte man sich gewiss die Flora.'
[2] 'The Legend of the Worm', quoted by C. J. Gadd, in *Myth and Ritual*, p. 66.
[3] On this conception see R. R. Marett, *The Threshold of Religion*, pp. 101 ff.
[4] 3rd. ed., pp. 85 ff. The very fact that Hab. ii. 19 rebukes those who say, 'Awake'
to the image of wood or stone shows the popular belief. The Bedouin swear by
the life of even inanimate things (Doughty, *Arabia Deserta*, i. 269).
[5] *Israel*, p. 479.

he goes on to quote aptly Job's protest that his land has not cried out against him or its furrows complained of ill-treatment (xxxi. 38–40). Francis of Assisi could enter into this consciousness of Nature's kinship with man, as when he summons all its elements to join him in praising God and calls them his brothers and sisters, or preaches to the birds. We may sometimes hear a keen farmer to-day speaking of the land much as a Hebrew would have done, and successful farmers have to be realists. Indeed modern science appears to be returning to a recognition of the truth that underlies this earlier mode of thought. Professor A. M. Low remarks that 'if the old division between organic and inorganic substance is no longer true, the word "living" can perhaps be applied to everything that is found in our world'.[1]

The Hebrew mode of thought is revealed indirectly in many passages which we are apt to pass over without recognition, as, for example, in Joseph's dreams. The future acknowledgement of his supremacy is seen by him in the obeisance of his brothers' sheaves of corn to his own, and that of sun, moon, and stars to himself. This is certainly not the kind of imagery which would occur to-day to a youth full of his own self-importance; it is suggested by psychical life in these inanimate objects. The ancient fondness for fable, illustrated by Jotham's fable of the trees,[2] is explained when we remember that a fable would have much more cogency for those who saw psychical life in a plant and tree.[3] A psalmist can conceive the many-peaked Bashan cherishing envy because God has chosen the much smaller Zion for His dwelling, or can call on sun, moon, and stars to praise God.[4] The prophets summon the hills to hear Yahweh's cause against His people.[5]

We can get a little farther into this far-reaching conception of Nature if we replace our own psychology by that of the Hebrews. For them, personality was essentially the body of flesh and bones, animated by a transient breath-soul, which ceased to have independent existence at death. That is why Eve was created from one of Adam's bones, and not from his *nephesh* or breath-soul. Adam expresses the kinship of his per-

---

[1] *Science Looks Ahead*, 1942, p. 242.　　　　[2] Judges ix. 7 ff.
[3] Lundgreen, op. cit., p. 150, calls attention to the acute nature-observation which underlies Jotham's fable. Cf. Gressman, *Ursprung*, p. 121, whose concern, however, is with the related mythology.
[4] Ps. lxviii. 15, 16; cxlviii. 3.
[5] e.g. Mic. vi. 1 ff.; cf. Ezekiel's prophesying to the hills of Israel (xxxvi).

sonality with hers, in contrast with his relation to the animals, by saying, 'bone of my bones and flesh of my flesh', not 'soul of my soul'.[1] The different parts of the body, whether inner or peripheral, possess what we may call a diffused consciousness. Their qualities are psychical as well as physical, which is why Job can say,

> Is there perversity in my tongue,
> Or does my palate not discern calamities? (vi. 30.)

Just because the Hebrew habitually distributed consciousness to hand, foot, eye, mouth, ear, heart, liver, bowels, and kidneys, he could the more easily conceive of a psychical life in Nature. After all, our bodies are the one part of Nature of which we can get an inside view. The body seemed to show how Nature felt and acted when viewed from within, and it was natural to extend this psychology to the external world. The whole body consists of a number of *mana*-bearing parts, hair and nails, eye and heart, and all the rest in their several degrees.[2] Again we note that such ascription accords much more with the stage of preanimistic thinking than with animism proper. It is not so much a 'soul' that is ascribed to natural objects as a potential *mana*, a diffused consciousness with its own psychical (including ethical) possibilities, and its own capacity to be indwelt or made instrumental by yet higher powers, and finally by the activity of Yahweh Himself.[3] To remember this gives much more meaning to such a passage as the blessing of Joseph:

> God Almighty, who blesses you
> With the blessings of the heavens above,
> The blessings of the abyss couching below;
> The blessings of breast and of womb . . .
> The blessings of the eternal mountains (LXX) . . .
>   and of the everlasting hills. (Gen. xlix. 25 f.)

Here the intrinsic attributes of the natural objects are taken up into the divine blessing, with that pregnant sense of *berakah* which Pedersen, in particular, has taught us to feel. We may similarly understand the opposite of such blessing in the curse of the (*tillable*) ground which will henceforth refuse sustenance

---

[1] Gen. ii. 23.

[2] Cf. A. Bertholet, *Das Dynamistische im Alten Testament*. The magic staff is itself an extension of the *mana* of the hand (ib., pp. 10, 27).

[3] The fruit of the forbidden tree in Eden shows the transition from potential to actual *mana* (Bertholet, ib., p. 31).

to Cain.[1] By the divine creation of natural objects, each with its appropriate nature, and each capable of its own response to its Creator and Upholder, He ministers to men and administers the world. He employs each object according to its intrinsic capacity and fitness, so that clouds become His chariot and winds His messengers.[2] He gives His special orders to each, as in the words of Deutero-Isaiah:

> Drop down, ye heavens, from above,
> And let the skies pour down righteousness
> Let the earth open, that they may bring forth salvation.
>
> (Isa. xlv. 8.)

Thus we may say that there is a realistic extension of anthropomorphism to Nature as well as to God, and both types, the lower as well as the higher, are much more than arbitrary figures of speech or mere poetic licences. Nature is alive through and through, and therefore the more capable of sympathy with man, and of response to the rule of its Creator and Upholder, on whom it directly depends.

In the recently published *Legacy of Egypt* (p. 18) it is admitted that the Old Testament stands alone, even as literature, among the records of the historical experience of the ancient Near East, those of Egypt and Babylonia being 'as a rule dry reading'. The explanation of this indubitable fact lies largely in the Hebrew conception of Nature, which inspires the vocabulary, shapes the imagery, and supplies no small part of the material. We often feel, when reading Milton, that he was a classical scholar before he was a poet, and we wonder what he could have made of the fallen angels without his storehouse of classical lore. But when we are reading the Old Testament we are never made to feel that metaphor and simile are an artificial embellishment of prophetic truth. Whether as velvet glove or steel gauntlet, they fit closely to the hand of God. The conception of Nature which underlies them can thus unite with the highest ethical conception of God because both are constituted in terms of life. So the Old Testament, in literary form as well as in substantial content, remains a living book to set forth the glory of the ever-living God.

Gen. iv. II.   [2] Ps. civ. 3, 4.

II

CREATION, CONSERVATION, AND
TRANSFORMATION

In the previous chapter we saw that the varied life of Nature found its unity in a common dependence on God. The dependence of Nature on God is represented in the Old Testament under three aspects, which together cover the whole of the divine activity in this realm, viz. creation, conservation, and transformation. First, God created the physical world; without Him it would not have come into being, but He is in no way dependent on it.[1] Second, God conserves the world, maintaining it either by the energies imparted to it in creation or by some new influx of power, exercising constant and complete control of it. Third, God will eventually transform Nature to its ideal state, in fulfilment of His persistent purpose. These three aspects of Nature will concern us in the present chapter, and it will be found that they comprehend the whole of the divine activity in this realm. The Nature-miracles, which will form the subject of the next chapter, are no real exception to this statement; they are properly *extensions* of the constant and normal activities of Yahweh.

§ 1

Different as are the two Creation-stories of Genesis i and ii, in origin, detail, and general atmosphere, they agree in ascribing the creation of the world to the free initiative of a personal God. In the second chapter of Genesis, the earlier of the two, the present form of the narrative begins with a rainless and therefore infertile earth, from whose substance Yahweh shaped man, as a potter does his clay, and animated the lifeless figure by His own breath. Yahweh then planted a garden containing all sorts of trees, to provide a home and a task for man. In order to relieve Adam's loneliness Yahweh experiments in similarly moulding beasts and birds, which Adam successively names, though none of them proves adequate to the original purpose of its creation. Consequently, Yahweh takes the new line of building up a new creature, woman, from a bone taken out of

[1] Forcibly expressed in Jeremiah's comparison of the potter and the clay (xviii. 6).

C

man. This origin explains the peculiar attraction of sex, though
sex-consciousness was absent before the forbidden fruit was
eaten.

In the later story of Genesis i this mechanism of detail in the
creation of man is eliminated, and a much more transcendent
God creates, by His bare word, first light amid the darkness
of primitive chaos, then the massive firmament to divide the
upper from the lower waters. . He orders these lower waters to
be gathered away from the earth, which then produces plants
and trees in all their fixed varieties. Three complete recurrences
of night and day have passed before God sets lamps in the
firmament, the sun, moon, and stars, not only to give light, but
even more to rule day and night, and to mark the calendar.
The fifth day sees the creation of fishes and birds, which are
commanded to propagate their kinds. On the sixth day the
earth produces its animals domestic and wild, and also its
reptiles. Only after their creation (not before, as in the earlier
creation-story) is man created. He is made uniquely in God's
image, male and female, with similar command to propagate
his species. He is to rule other creatures, but, like the animals,
he is to find his food only from plants and trees. The only
crudely anthropomorphic feature of this narrative is the statement that God 'rested' from His work on the seventh day. If
we are tempted to treat this statement as merely figurative, we
should note the stronger statement at a later stage of the same
source,[1] again to establish the Sabbath: 'on the seventh day He
rested and refreshed Himself'—literally, 'took breath' (שָׁבַת
וַיִּנָּפַשׁ). We have only to contrast this conception of creation
with that of the Babylonian and other ethnic stories to see how
clear-cut is the Hebrew separation of divine personality from
Nature. In the classical *Enuma eliš* of the Babylonians the gods
themselves emanate from the primeval elements of chaos.

There has been much theological debate as to whether, in the
story of Genesis i, God is conceived as the creator of chaos itself,
so that we have a *creatio ex nihilo*. This view has recently been
taken by Eichrodt, but rather in a theological interest than on
sound exegetical grounds. The concurrent view of the chief commentators on Genesis—Dillmann, Gunkel, Holzinger, Driver,
Skinner, Procksch—is that God worked on a pre-existent chaos.[2]

---

[1] Exod. xxxi. 17; cf. 2 Sam. xvi. 14.
[2] See Gunkel, *Psalms*, p. 397, for a variation of the creation story.

This is much more probable, nor does it detract from the absolute sovereignty of God, which the Hebrew writer is naturally concerned to maintain. The explicit issue has not yet arisen;[1] creation is the antithesis of the *tohu wa bohu* of chaos, which forms its background. We may compare the quite independent statement of Deutero-Isaiah:[2]

> The creator of the heavens, *He* is God,
> The former of the earth and its maker, He established it;
> Not chaos (*tohu*) did He create it, for dwelling did He form it.

On purely grammatical grounds, the natural rendering of the opening verses of Genesis is: 'In the beginning of God's creation of the heavens and the earth—the earth being chaos and darkness over the deep, and a wind of God hovering over the waters —then God said, "Let there be light".'

Another point in the later Creation-story which has claimed an important place in theology lies in the statement, 'Let us make man in our image, after our likeness'. There has been, and still is, a tendency to settle the meaning by *a priori* considerations of what an adequate idea of God is supposed to require. Physical resemblance of God and man is ruled out on the ground that a late Priestly writer could not have been guilty of such a crude anthropomorphism. But historical exegesis must be guided by the actual use of terms, and this appears decisive. The same writer in Genesis v. 3 says that Adam begat Seth 'in his likeness, according to his image', employing the same terms as here. But there the only possible meaning is physical resemblance; the deliberate use of identical terms implies that the resemblance of man to God in the initial creation was continued in successive births; in fact the previous verses there recall that resemblance in order to emphasize this point, saying, 'When God created man, it was in the likeness of God that He made him'.[3] On the other hand, physical reference, for genuine Hebrew psychology, does not exclude reference to the psychical or spiritual qualities of man's nature; it was, in fact, the only way to express them which Hebrew idiom possessed.

As we saw in the first chapter, the physical members of the

---

[1] The earliest statement of the belief appears to be that of 2 Macc. vii. 28, cf. Heb. xi. 3.   [2] xlv. 18.

[3] This interpretation is rejected by Hempel, *Das Ethos des Alten Testaments*, 1938, p. 201.

body have these psychical qualities, and the body is the essential
personality. In no intelligible way could a Hebrew writer of
this period have expressed the kinship of human nature with
the divine other than by asserting bodily resemblance. We
should express this by using the common term 'personality', but
there was no Hebrew word corresponding to this.[1] Both the
upright posture of man and his outstanding mental and moral
qualities distinguished him from the animal world, and justified
that supremacy over it which was divinely assigned to him. A
psalmist does not shrink from saying that man is made but
little lower than God,[2] and the visions of God from the early
stories of the Pentateuch down to the late book of Daniel show
Him in human form,[3] even if with attributes of awe-inspiring
majesty. The essential difference of nature between God and
man is beyond question; but that difference belongs to substance rather than to form in the Old Testament period. Isaiah
came nearest to an expression of this difference when pouring
scorn on an alliance with man against God:

> Now the Egyptians are men and not God;
> And their horses are flesh and not spirit. (xxxi. 3.)

Man, too, is essentially flesh, with all the limitations which this
implies. God's essence is Spirit, though 'Spirit' in the Old
Testament is still conceived as that which could be 'poured out'
or 'divided',[4] i.e. it is the sublimation of the material rather than
the non-material. This is corroborated by the references to the
visible glory of God, His fire-like presence on which none can
endure to gaze.[5] But, however much created man stands below
His creator, as flesh and not spirit, we need not demand that the
difference, as conceived by the Hebrew, should also be one of
form. The living personality of God was, as Gressmann rightly
says,[6] conceived in all periods after the image of man, and had
to be so conceived. Indeed, the necessity still remains, however
greatly spiritualized.

The story of Creation fitly stands on the opening pages of the
Bible, for it is fundamental to all the subsequent history as
the Hebrew conceived it. It marks the dawn of history, just as the

---

[1] Cf. Procksch, *Genesis*, 2, 3, p. 449; an analogy for its content is found in God.
[2] Ps. viii. 5.
[3] Exod. xxxiii. 23; Dan. vii. 13. Note such passages as Exod. xxiv. 10, 11 where
the hand and feet of God are mentioned.
[4] e.g. Isa. xxxii. 15; Num. xi. 17.
[5] Exod. xxxiii. 18 ff.   [6] *Ursprung*, p. 120.

story itself in Genesis i may have been partly shaped by observation of the dawn of day, from the first twilight slowly revealing the outlines of the earth, to the emergence of the sun, and the going forth of man to take his place amongst the other creatures.[1] The combined stories set forth the personal activity of a Person who is above Nature, a Person who will control it through all the successive generations of men until His purpose is accomplished and His will is fully done. For this, He must be its Master, and nothing could so forcibly express this mastery as to show Him as the Creator of Nature. Both dualism and pantheism are excluded by this conception.[2] The creation is so closely linked to the conservation and control that all dualistic deism is irrelevant, whilst there can be no pantheistic absorption of such a Person in the immanent energies of Nature. The subsequent history was destined to bring out, in ever-increasing fullness and richness of quality, the personal relations of this divine Being with mankind in general and with His chosen people in particular, relations which find their favourite expression in the terms of a 'covenant'. Therefore it was fitting and consonant with this future development that the Creation-stories should emphasize the free and spontaneous initiative of the divine activity, leaving room for the essentially divine quality of 'grace'. Already we notice that the Priestly narrative records the divine verdict, passed on the successive stages of creation, 'good, very good', which the Septuagint not unjustifiably renders by *kalon*, 'fine'.[3] We are not at this stage concerned with the consequences

> Of man's first disobedience and the fruit
> Of that forbidden tree,

but we see divine grace in the trouble God takes to remove the loneliness of Adam in Genesis ii, as well as in the more methodically conceived forethought for animal and human needs in the Priestly narrative. Nature is taken up into history as a constant revelation of both the goodness and wisdom of God, on which psalmists and prophets are never weary of insisting:

> The heavens keep on telling the glory of God,
> And the sky keeps on declaring the work of His hands.[4]

---

[1] The suggestion is due to Procksch, *Genesis*, p. 455.
[2] Cf. Eichrodt, *Theologie des Alten Testaments*, ii. 49.
[3] So Kleinert, op. cit., p. 18.
[4] Ps. xix. 1; note the present participles.

Hosea reproaches Israel for attributing corn and wine and oil
to the Baalim, whereas it was Yahweh who had been constantly
giving these.[1]

> What more could have been done for my vineyard
>   (asks Yahweh through Isaiah)
> Than that which I have done for it? (Isa. v. 1 ff.)[2]

It is not possible, or necessary for our immediate purpose, to
discuss in much detail the question of the date at which the
creation of the Universe was first attributed to Yahweh. The
question is important rather for the history of the development
of Israel's religion than for the theological issues of revelation.
It is clear that by the time of Deutero-Isaiah the creative work
of Yahweh could be taken for granted, since it is one of the
chief grounds on which the prophet bases confidence in a future
restoration:

> Lift up your eyes on high,
> And see! who created these? . . . (Isa. xl. 26.)

> I, Yahweh, the maker of all,
> Who stretched out the heavens alone,
> Who laid out the earth—who was with me? (xliv. 24.)

In our present Book of Amos there are three doxologies,[3] which,
if original, would take us three centuries back in the ascription
of full creatorship to Yahweh. But the connexion of these three
passages with their contexts is doubtful, and they should probably be regarded as later interpolations. We should also note
the marked difference in scope between the earlier and later
Creation-stories. The earlier, in Genesis ii, does not explicitly
ascribe all things to Yahweh, though it recognizes His power
over Nature. That power is manifest from the beginnings of
Israel's history in the Exodus and at Sinai, and Isaiah of Jerusalem already in the eighth century can speak of all that fills the
earth as Yahweh's glory.[4] The conception of creatorship is

---

[1] Hos. ii. 7–10.

[2] Isaiah's parable of the vineyard of course covers more than material gifts, but
it does include the intrinsic beneficence of God in Nature. The vine and the fig-
tree under the ample shade of which the Hebrew dreamed of sitting in peace
(1 Kings iv. 25; Mic. iv. 4) became sacraments of God to the devout Israelite.

[3] iv. 13, v. 8f., ix. 5f. For an interesting theory of their true nature, see F. Horst,
ZAW, 1929, pp. 45ff. They are probably the three strophes of a single hymn (note
the similar refrain).

[4] Cf. Jer. xxiii. 24, 'Do not I fill heaven and earth?', but, as Duhm remarks, this
denotes ubiquity rather than 'omnipresence'.

bound up with that of monotheism, and in both conceptions that which was more or less implicit in earlier centuries first becomes explicit in Deutero-Isaiah. In earlier days certain phenomena of Nature are closely associated with Yahweh, as we shall see when we turn to the theophanies. In the earliest document which we possess, the Song of Deborah, Yahweh is pictured as coming from His original home in the south in a storm which discomfited the Canaanites:

> From the heavens fought the stars;
> From their courses they fought with Sisera,
> The wady Kishon swept them away. (Judges v. 20, 21.)

In such a belief that natural phenomena became subservient to Yahweh's purpose, there is already a nucleus ready to be developed into the larger belief in Yahweh's universal control of Nature and ultimately the assertion of this in the explicit doctrine of His creatorship. But this development seems to have been dependent on that of the history. Yahweh had to conquer the Baalim before He could be conceived as absolute Lord over them, and the conquest had to be achieved realistically in the visible and material realm to make fully apparent and explicit the inner victory of ideas. It was the exile which sealed the truth of prophecy and exterminated for ever the Baalized Yahwism which reduced Yahweh to the level of a Nature-god. It was the prophet of the exile who first clearly shows Him to be the Creator of all Nature, and to this period the first chapter of Genesis belongs.

§ 2

Creation is integrally linked to conservation, and each throws light on the other. The penitential psalm, in Nehemiah ix, which illustrates what has been called 'the birth-hour of Judaism'[1] opens with the words:

'Thou art Yahweh, thou alone: thou hast made the heavens, the heavens of heavens and all their host, the earth and all that is upon it, the seas and all that is in them, and thou art giving life to all of them.' (verse 6)

The present participle of the final verb here has its full force in expressing *continuity* of action, in contrast with the perfect tense

---

[1] The phrase is Bertholet's, in his commentary, ad loc. Neh. viii and ix belong to Ezra's work, not Nehemiah's.

of 'thou hast made'. The initial creative activity of Yahweh is continued without break in the conservation, the regular maintenance, of the world. Many passages describe this continuous activity of 'the unwearied God',[1] unwearied though represented as 'resting' after the unique outflow of His energy in the week of creation:

> He causes vapours to rise from the ends of the earth;
> He maketh lightnings for the rain,
> And brings out the wind from His storehouses. (Jer. x. 13.)

> He gives snow like wool,
> He scatters hoarfrost like ashes,
> He casts forth His ice like crumbs. (Ps. cxlvii. 16f.)

> He covers the heavens with clouds,
> He prepares rain for the earth,
> He makes grass spring forth upon the hills. (Ps. cxlvii. 8.)

> Thou preparest their grain . . .
> Thou dost saturate its furrows,
> Thou dost settle its ridges;
> With showers thou dost soften it:
> Its young growth thou dost bless. (Ps. lxv. 9, 10.)

> He gives to the cattle their food,
> And to the young ravens when they cry. (Ps. cxlvii. 9.)

> The eyes of all wait upon thee,
> And thou givest them their food in due season.
>   (Ps. cxlv. 15; cf. civ. 27.)

No doubt this continued maintenance of Nature is effected through established ordinances and inherent energies, as the reference to the seed-containing fruit of Genesis i implies.[2] But these ordinances and energies are nowhere conceived as in any sense rivals of God, or limitations of His will; they remain wholly dependent on His constant support. It is of interest to note that this conception of a continued creation is in full harmony with what both the science and the philosophy of the modern world can accept. Thus Professor Whittaker, as a scientist, in the Riddell Memorial Lectures of 1942, on *The Beginning and End of the World*, remarks:

'It is necessary to guard against the deistic conception of a God

---

[1] Isa. xl. 28.   [2] Cf. Pedersen, op. cit., p. 204.

who, having constructed the world, left all subsequent happenings
to be determined by invariable scientific laws, much as a watch-
maker might construct a watch and leave it to run by its own
mechanism. The Christian doctrine is that all evolution is creation,
though all creation is not evolution.' (p. 64)

In modern philosophy, Pringle Pattison says, 'the idea of
creation tends to pass into that of manifestation. . . . God
exists as creatively realizing himself in the world.'[1] Thus the
Old Testament conception of continued divine activity is intui-
tively more modern than much theology and philosophy. The
Canaanite religion, as illustrated by the Ras Shamra tablets,
had not moved past the magical or quasi-magical stage in which
ritual controls the gods and their activities. In Israel's higher
religion, God controls Nature, and ritual is sublimated to His
worship.

This close dependence of Nature upon God for its maintenance
is specially marked in regard to the life of animals and men.
The greatest of the Nature psalms, after speaking of their sustenance by the divine provision of food in due season, goes on to
refer to their very existence:

> When thou takest away their breath, they die
> And turn again into dust.
> When thou sendest forth thy breath, they are created,
> And thou renewest the face of the earth. (Ps. civ. 29, 30.)

This is parallel with the thought of the 90th psalm, in which
God turns back each generation to its native dust, or of Elihu
in the Book of Job:

> If He were to withdraw His Spirit to Himself,
> And to gather His breath to Himself,
> All flesh would expire at once,
> And man would return to the dust. (Job xxxiv. 14, 15.)

We are naturally led to ask how this conception of a breath-
soul, inbreathed by Yahweh into the human body in continued
creation, is related to the formation of the body itself, as known
through the growth of the embryo in the womb and the birth
of offspring. This is an instructive line of inquiry for the Hebrew
idea of the relation of God to Nature, and the data are not
scanty. The creative fatherhood of God in regard to individual

---

[1] *The Idea of God*, pp. 308, 312.

man is declared when Malachi protests against the divorce of
Jewish wives:

> Have we not all one father?
> Did not one God create us?[1]

Job extends this appeal to make it a ground for the just treatment of the slave by his master:

> Did not He who made me in the womb make him?
> And did not One prepare us in the womb? (xxxi. 15.)

The creation of the embryo within the womb is thus described:

> Thy hands did form me and make me. . . .
> Didst thou not pour me out like milk,
> And curdle me like cheese?
> With skin and flesh thou didst clothe me,
> And with bones and muscles thou didst knit me together.
>
> (x. 8 ff.; cf. Wisdom vii. 2.)

Here we may compare Ezekiel's vision of the Valley of Dry
Bones (xxxvii) as illustrating Hebrew ideas of anatomy. The
dryness of the bones shows that they have lost the vitality they
once possessed. The prophet sees first the articulation of the
separate skeletons, bone to his bone, then the placing of sinews
and tendons upon the bones; over this framework of the body
muscular tissue, the flesh, is brought up, and the outer skin is
then drawn over the flesh. The mechanism is complete; they
are now men, but dead men; it still needs the animating breath-
soul supplied by the wind-Spirit of God, before each is able to
rise and stand upon his feet, as a living man. This shows the
permanence of the idea expressed in Gen. ii. 7.

Another striking passage relating to the embryo is found in
Psalm cxxxix. 13 ff.

> For it was thou that didst create my kidneys,
> Thou wast weaving me together in my mother's belly. . . .
> Not hidden was my bony frame from thee,
> Made as I was in secret,
> Embroidered in the depths of the earth;
> Thine eyes saw my embryo
> And upon thy book are all of them written.

The enigmatic phrase 'in the depths of the earth' has been
taken[2] to refer to the widespread conception of the earth as the

---

[1] ii. 10; cf. Isa. lxiv. 8.   [2] As by Gunkel, ad loc.

mother of mankind.[1] We have similar echoes of primitive mythology in Job i. 21:

> Naked did I come forth from my mother's womb,
> And naked shall I return thither,

and in Ecclus. xl. 1:

> From the day of their coming forth from their mother's womb,
> Until the day for their burial in the mother of all things.

The psalmist's use of the phrase, 'in the depths of the earth', was perhaps prompted by the implicit comparison of the womb with the teeming and fruitful earth.[2] His real emphasis falls on the mystery of man's fearful and wondrous creation seen in each new birth. This sense of mystery is prominent also in Eccles. xi. 5:

> Even as you know not what is the way of the spirit
> Into the bones in the pregnant womb,   (So many MSS. and Targ.)
> So you know not the work of God,
> Who makes everything.

There the mystery is characteristically mentioned as checking inquiry, whereas for the psalmist (verse 14) it summons to the praise of God. For the mother of the seven Maccabean martyrs the mystery becomes a ground of faith in the other mystery of the resurrection from the dead:

> 'I know not how ye came into my womb, neither was it I that bestowed on you your spirit and your life, and it was not I that brought into order the first elements of each of you.' (2 Macc. vii. 22.)

The passages we have noticed are illuminative because they show that a partial knowledge of biological process in the growth of the embryo did not preclude its ascription to divine activity, any more than did the parallel knowledge of agricultural growth.[3] In fact the peculiar mystery of the womb called the more attention to it as a sphere in which God was continually at work. This is seen in numerous references to the blessing of human fertility or to the curse of barrenness. It becomes

---

[1] With which we may compare Gen. i. 11 and 24, and Milton, *Paradise Lost*, vii. 453:

> Opening her fertile womb teem'd at a birth
> Innumerous living creatures . . .

though the true Hebrew equivalent of this is the creation of man by Yahweh out of the dust of the earth.

[2] So Calès, ad loc.; cf. Procksch, *Genesis*, p. 444.   [3] Isa. xxviii. 23-9.

explicit in the detailed birth-stories of the Old Testament. To study these is an instructive lesson in the exercise of God's creative activity, in the wombs of Eve, Hagar, Sarah, Rebekah, Leah, Rachel, Ruth, the Shunnamite woman, Manoah's wife and Hannah. Of Jeremiah it is said:

'Before I formed thee in the belly I knew thee, and before thou camest forth out of the womb I sanctified thee: I have appointed thee a prophet unto the nations.' (Jer. i. 5; cf. Isa. xlix. 1; Ps. xxii. 9, &c.)

Jeremiah was, as Duhm aptly remarks, a thought of God before his birth. The Hebrew would have fully sympathized with the Chinese reckoning of the months of conception as the first year of life.

§ 3

The eschatological transformation of Nature is a further continuation of its creation and conservation, a further illustration of its fluidity and responsiveness according to the Hebrew conception of it. Nature is an essential part of eschatology, and indeed supplies many of its principal ingredients.[1] Jeremiah, in one of his most impressive visions, saw the world deprived at God's word of its light and life and stability, and returning to its primitive chaos:

> I looked at the earth, and lo! it was chaos;
> At the heavens, and their light was gone.
> I looked at the mountains, and lo! they were quaking;
> And all the hills swayed to and fro.
> I looked, and lo! there was no man,
> And all the birds of the air had flown.
> I looked, and lo! the garden land was desert,
> And all its cities were pulled down before Yahweh,
> Before His fierce anger. (iv. 23–6.)

The prophet saw all the lights of life going out because Yahweh in His anger had withdrawn His normal support of them; that is very significant for the relation of Nature to God. But, obviously, such a relation of dependence implies that, at any time, there may be a crescendo of the life of the world to reveal more of the divine energy, for man's good or ill. This is the right way to regard the many pictures of the world as restored to more than its former well-being, when once the judgement

[1] Cf. Gressmann, *Ursprung*, p. 38.

of God upon the evil of the world has been accomplished. These pictures are to be taken realistically, not allegorically; if they seem strangely impossible to us, it is partly because we come to Nature with an inveterate prejudice in favour of its fixity and virtual independence of God. But, if we look closely at the details, we shall often find unmistakable hints of the underlying realism, proofs that the whole is to be taken as more or less literal expectation, and not merely as poetic imagery. Thus, when Deutero-Isaiah describes the return from exile through the desert, he proclaims that its physical difficulties will be overcome for the travellers, and that the objective transformation will convince the Gentiles that the hand of Yahweh has wrought this quickening of the life of Nature, always sustained by Him:

> When the poor and needy seek water in vain,
> And their tongue is parched with thirst,
> I, Yahweh, will answer them,
> I, the God of Israel, will not forsake them.
> I will open rivers on the bare heights,
> And wells in the midst of the valleys,
> I will make the wilderness a pool,
> And the parched land fountains of water
> I will plant in the wilderness the cedar,
> The acacia, the myrtle and the olive;
> I will set in the desert the cypress,
> The plane and the larch as well,
> That men may see and know,
> May consider and also understand
> That the hand of Yahweh has done this,
> That the Holy One of Israel has created it.
>
> (Isa. xli. 17 ff.; cf. xliii. 19 ff.)

Elsewhere[1] it is said that these transformations of Nature will be a memorial and everlasting sign, i.e. they will be literally fulfilled. Similarly, when Ezekiel describes[2] the life-giving stream that flows from under the restored temple (instead of the precarious supply of water hitherto given by Jerusalem's one spring) we are told that the stream will bring life to the Dead Sea, and will create a vigorous fishing industry on its banks, but that the marshes and swamps will not become fresh, because their supply of salt will still be necessary. Yet again, in the closing chapter of the Book of Zechariah,[3] when the

[1] Isa. lv. 13.   [2] xlvii. 1–12.   [3] xiv. 4 ff.; cf. Isa. ii. 2, Mic. iv. 1.

enemies of Jerusalem have been overthrown, there will be a
permanent change in the topography of the area. The Mount
of Olives, blocking in the city from the east, will be split in two
by a very wide valley, and half of the mountains will move
northwards and half southwards, so blocking out the accursed
valley of Hinnom, and leaving Zion supreme in its now unchallenged height over the other mountains. Such details belong
to a gigantic town-planning programme, though one not to
be carried out by human hands. They are to be interpreted
realistically.

We can understand, therefore, how easily apocalyptic expectation could look for a changed order of Nature, in which the light
of sun and moon would be multiplied or become unnecessary,
because the light-glory of God's presence would far more than
replace them.[1] The length of human life would be extended so
that a mere centenarian would be held to die young.[2] Yahweh's
new 'covenant' with the animal world would result in the wild
creatures losing all their ferocity, or being restrained from any
invasion of the roads along which the ransomed of Yahweh
would henceforth travel in security.[3] Egypt and Edom would
lie waste and barren,[4] and the people who did not come up to
Jerusalem to worship would have their rain-supply cut off by
a divine 'blockade',[5] but Israel's land would break forth into
unexampled fertility:

> Then will the steppe become garden-land
> And the garden-land be counted an orchard.
>
> (Isa. xxxii. 15.)

The influence of an earlier mythology, foreign or native, on this
conception of a golden age, is beyond question, apart from any
difference of opinion about the date of its emergence.[6] But such
influences must not conceal from us one that is earlier still, i.e.
the primitive conception of Nature as itself alive, and able to
respond even psychically to God's demands, in the past, the
present, and the future.

In this connexion we must notice the interrelation of Nature
with the moral life of man, though fuller discussion of moral
issues belongs to a later part of our subject. In Gen. iii. 14 ff.

[1] Isa. xxx. 26; lx. 19.   [2] Isa. lxv. 20 f.; Zech. viii. 4.
[3] Hos. ii. 18; Isa. xi. 6 ff., xxxv. 9.   [4] Joel iii. 18, 19.   [5] Zech. xiv. 17.
[6] Cf. Gressmann, *Ursprung*; Gunkel, *Schöpfung und Chaos*; Mowinckel, *Psalmenstudien*, ii, passim.

the sin of Adam and Eve has for its sequel a triple curse, i.e.
on the serpent, which in future must crawl and feed on dust; on
the woman, who will suffer in childbirth, and live in sexual
servitude; on the ground, which will produce thorns and thistles,
and compel man to win his food from it only by hard toil. All
these curses are mythical explanations of observed facts, viz.
the peculiar movements of the serpent, the pangs of travail, the
hard life of a peasant on Palestinian soil. The influence of
Genesis iii on Jewish and Christian theology[1] falls outside the
Old Testament, on which it has had little, if any, effect. Our
immediate point of interest is the way in which the phenomena
of Nature are correlated with human history. There is no
suggestion of any intrinsic moral evil in Nature, as in the
Gnostic view of matter, nor does St. Paul suggest this in his use
of this passage in Romans viii. In fact, he explicitly declares
that Nature was made subject to corruption, not of its own will,
but by the ordinance of God. This applies to similar curses
elsewhere, as in the long catalogue of Deuteronomy xxviii, or
the curse of the ground for Cain's sake. In all such passages[2]
the evils of Nature are instrumental to God's purpose concerning man, and spring from an inherent sympathy with man. So
also St. Paul can speak of the *apokaradokia* of Nature, its straining
forward, as with outstretched neck, towards a deliverance from
its present bondage. Nature is destined, he says, to share at long
last in the redemption for which Christians themselves eagerly
wait. As it has participated in the evil, so it will participate in
the good of man. This is a recognition of quasi-consciousness
in Nature, which now groans and travails in pain, because of
the frustration of its true aims through man's fault. The moral
evil is man's alone, but Nature and man are so closely inter-
linked that one can hardly suffer without the other. The
apocalyptic renovation of Nature is therefore not a mere condition of man's well-being, it is also an act of justice. As Pedersen
has said of the curse,[3] 'there is an intimate connection between
the nature of the land and the men who dwell in it. . . . The
curse entails the nature of the desert . . . if, through their sin,
the people have become penetrated with the curse, then this
must act throughout and consume the blessing of the country.'

---

[1] See Strack-Billerbeck, *Kommentar zum Neuen Testament* iii. 245 ff., and N. P.
Williams, *The Ideas of the Fall and of Original Sin*, passim.
[2] Cf. Job xix. 21; Hos. xiii. 14.   [3] *Israel I–II*, pp. 458 ff.

Conversely, we may say that the living sympathy, the sympathy of a shared life between land and people, will bring such a removal of the evils suffered by Nature as to make a land fit for the heroes of God. This unity of land and people[1] for weal and woe derives from their common dependence on God as their creator, upholder, and future transformer.

To discuss the origin of this eschatological hope, and its relation to mythological, cultic, and nationalistic ideas would take us far beyond our present scope. All these have contributed to the formulation of the eschatology, both in the Old Testament and in the apocalyptic literature which continues it. But, as we have already seen, creation and conservation themselves point forward with real continuity to a final transformation of the physical conditions of human life. Such a hope springs directly from the characteristic conception of Israel's God. With truth it has been claimed that 'Apart from the Jews, there was no nation in the Mediterranean world which consciously hoped.'[2] The Epistle to the Ephesians[3] speaks of the Gentile world as 'not having hope and without God'.[4] That significant collocation gains new point in view of both Jewish and Christian eschatology. There is no sure ground for hope in a future, whether for mankind or for its individual members, which does not involve faith in a God who reveals Himself in history, and is the guarantor that the revelation will be vindicated. Such a God was Yahweh in the faith of Israel, and such a conception was unique in pre-Christian times.

In the pre-exilic period this hope was sustained (though not created) by the observance of a New Year's festival, celebrated in the autumn. At this annual observance, it is highly probable that the ark was brought in procession into the temple, and that the future blessing of Yahweh and His continued presence with king and people were invoked. It is probable, also, that Yahweh's creative work was celebrated at this festival, just as the liturgy of the Babylonian New Year's festival celebrated

---

[1] The animals of Nineveh, as well as the people, were arrayed in the sackcloth of repentance. 'The association of the animal world and even the inanimate world with man in his suffering is an idea widely held among the prophets (Amos viii. 8; Isa. xvi. 8, xxiv. 3–6; Zeph. i. 2, 3; Jer. xii. 4; Joel i. 10, 18; cf. Rom. viii. 22) and is based upon the early belief that land and man and animal were in some way closely connected' (Harper, *Amos and Hosea*, p. 251).

[2] T. R. Glover, *Vergil*, p. 331.   [3] ii. 12; cf. Rom. ix. 4, 5.

[4] ἄθεοι, the only occurrence of the word in the New Testament.

the victory of Marduk over Tiamat.[1] Thus the Israelite worshipper was encouraged to look both backwards and forwards. Mowinckel has argued that this cultic observance of the New Year not only ensured the recall of the mythology but also originated the eschatology. But it should be remembered that, whatever the eschatological influence exerted by the festival, of the observance of which we have no direct record, there is no real parallel in the Babylonian ritual or indeed elsewhere to the characteristic hope of Israel.[2] This hope is expressed in the prophetic confidence that the Day of Yahweh would vindicate His control of both Nature and history, and finally establish His kingly rule. The Biblical conception of the Kingdom of God is unique because it springs from a unique conception of God Himself.[3]

[1] For this liturgy, so far as preserved, see Gressmann, *ATAT*², pp. 295–303.
[2] Eichrodt, op. cit., vol. i, p. 269.   [3] Eichrodt, op. cit., vol. i, p. 272f.

III

THE NATURE-MIRACLES OF THE
OLD TESTAMENT

THE Nature-miracles of the Old Testament have a twofold significance. They illuminate the Hebrew conception of Nature, and they are an important feature in the method of divine revelation. But if they are to be understood they must be approached in their proper historical environment, and with the thought-forms of the age that felt their cogency. We must not make them more difficult to understand by imposing on the Hebrew mind a modern view of Nature. 'The fundamental principle in the world-outlook of the primitive man is that everything is possible.'[1]

§ 1

It follows from this that any attempt to classify the Nature-miracles statistically as supernatural events would be futile, if not impossible. We should have to include ordinary rain amongst the 'miracles', whilst angelic visitation or possession by good or evil spirits is a normal explanation of certain physical or psychical phenomena. But a contemporary approach to the whole subject can be made through the three chief terms used in the Old Testament to denote 'miracle'. These are *'oth* or 'sign', *mopheth* or 'portent', and *niphla'oth* (with related forms) or 'wonders'.

(*a*) The first of these, *'oth*, occurs 79 times, of which 25 relate to the plagues of Egypt. As a material 'sign' the term is used of the tribal mark on Cain, the scarlet cord by which Rahab's house was indicated, the ensign marking particular family groups in the Israelite camp, the stone memorials of the crossing of the Jordan, the blood of the passover sacrifice smeared on Israelite dwellings, the metal censers of Korah and his company when beaten out to cover the altar as a memorial of their penalty.[2] From these examples the general meaning of the term is apparent; it can denote any physical object to which some special meaning has been given. In more extended use it can refer to circumcision as a sign of the covenant with

---

[1] S. Mowinckel, *Psalmenstudien*, ii. 224.

[2] Gen. iv. 15; Joshua ii. 12; Num. ii. 2; Joshua iv. 6; Exod. xii. 13; Num. xvi. 38.

Abraham, or the Sabbath as a sign of that with Israel at Sinai, or the rainbow as a sign of that with Noah.[1] The application of this term to the rainbow is particularly instructive; it shows how 'miraculous' meaning could be given to what is for us a purely natural phenomenon. We inevitably regard the rainbow as a permanent result of the refraction of light; we can no more believe that it was put in the sky as a covenant sign than we can regard it in the earlier way as the battle-bow of Indra or of Marduk hung up there when the divine battle was over. In the Priestly narrative of creation, the sun, moon, and stars are 'for signs and for seasons', the reference being to the ecclesiastical calendar as ruled by the movements of the heavenly bodies.[2] On the other hand, Jeremiah bids Israel not to be perturbed by those 'signs of the heavens' (such as eclipses) which dismay the heathen.[3] For the sign given to Hezekiah of the turning back of the shadow on the steps of Ahaz,[4] there is no natural explanation; it may be due, like the standing still of the sun during Joshua's victory over the Amorites,[5] to the prosaic interpretation of a poetic metaphor describing Hezekiah's recovery from sickness.

The use of 'oth for events in human lives to which some special meaning is given does not directly belong to a study of Nature, but it should be noted as forming a parallel to the interpretation of ordinary phenomena as 'signs'. Thus Jonathan makes the reaction of the Philistines to his climbing attack the sign that will warrant or forbid further advance; Samuel makes the meeting of Saul with a company of prophets a sign of the divine co-operation with him; the death of Eli's two sons on the same day will be a sign of the divine judgement on his house.[6] Once more we see that it is not the abnormality of the event that makes the sign, but its interpretation in a particular pattern of divine control. This is probably the right view to take of the Immanuel sign given by Isaiah; it was a normal birth which would acquire prophetic meaning.[7] Sometimes, as in the symbolic acts of the prophets, the event itself is arbitrarily created in order to be a miniature of that larger activity of God

[1] Gen. xvii. 11; Exod. xxxi. 13, 17; Gen. ix. 12.
[2] So Skinner, ad loc., as against Gunkel; cf. Driver, ad loc.
[3] Jer. x. 2.   [4] Isa. xxxviii. 7, 22; cf. 2 Kings xx. 8, 9.
[5] Joshua x. 12, 13.
[6] 1 Sam. xiv. 10; x. 7, 9; ii. 34.
[7] Isa. vii. 11, 14; cf. G. B. Gray, ad loc.

which it initiates.[1] Isaiah goes about Jerusalem 'naked and barefoot' as 'a sign and a portent' of the future captivity of the Egyptians and Ethiopians on whom Israel is tempted to rely.[2] Such usage throws the emphasis of the *'oth* very strongly on the meaning assigned to it, and again warns us that the sign is not essentially and intrinsically anything opposed to the normal phenomena of Nature. Indeed, the very names that Isaiah and his children bear are 'signs and portents'.[3] Nor were men to think that the announcement of a sign afterwards fulfilled proved the giver of it to be a true prophet;[4] God may allow such a fulfilment in order to test the loyalty of Israel, who must disregard even accomplished signs if the prophet's message was contrary to the true national tradition. Thus miracles were not necessarily a proof that a particular prophecy was true.[5]

(*b*) The parallel and often associated term, *mopheth* or 'portent', occurs 36 times, and in 19 of these refers to the plagues of Egypt. Etymologically it has been connected with an Arabic root, meaning 'to suffer harm',[6] and the usage seems to support this, and to justify the English rendering 'portent', with its predominant suggestion of 'calamity'. The future destruction of the altar at Bethel on which Jeroboam proposed to make an illegitimate offering was such a portent.[7] The Deuteronomic curses against disloyalty are signs and portents.[8] A psalmist speaks of his sufferings as having made him a portent to many.[9] Joel pictures the great and terrible day of Yahweh as ushered in by:

> portents in the heavens and on the earth,
> blood and fire and columns of smoke.
> The sun shall be changed to darkness
> And the moon to blood. (iii. 3, 4; Eng. ii. 30, 31)

Such a description is obviously drawn from an eclipse, raised to its eschatological degree. Ezekiel's acted symbolism of exile from Jerusalem is spoken of as a portent, as is his conduct at the death of his wife; for the calamity the customary laments were

---

[1] See my article on 'Hebrew Sacrifice and Prophetic Symbolism' in *JTS.* July–Oct., 1942.   [2] Isa. xx. 3; cf. Ezek. iv. 3.

[3] Isa. viii. 18.   [4] Deut. xiii. 2, 3 (E.T. 1, 2).

[5] At an earlier time the inspiration of a false prophecy could be accepted as genuine, but its contents were ascribed to a lying spirit commissioned by Yahweh; this is illustrated by Micaiah's vision (1 Kings xxii. 22).

[6] إيف, Kazimirski, *Dictionnaire Arabe-Français*, i. 88; so Gesenius, *Thesaurus*, i. 143, s.v. אפס.

[7] 1 Kings xiii. 3, 5.   [8] Deut. xxviii. 46.   [9] Ps. lxxi. 7.

inadequate.[1] That the word *mopheth* could connote good as well as evil we may see from Zechariah's reference to the chief priest and his companions as 'men of *mopheth*';[2] they are a promise and prophecy of the Messianic kingdom which is to be. The frequent use of the term together with '*oth* shows that they are close synonyms. The chief difference between them may be put in S. R. Driver's words,[3] '*Mopheth* is a portent, an occurrence regarded merely as something extraordinary, '*oth* is a sign, i.e. something ordinary (Exod. xii. 13, xxxi. 13; Isa. xx. 3, &c.) or extraordinary, as the case may be, regarded as significant of a truth beyond itself, or impressed with a Divine purpose'. We may illustrate the difference by the fact that '*oth* is used in the first chapter of Genesis of the regular course of the sun, whilst we have just seen that the eclipse of the sun can be described as a *mopheth*. But neither term necessarily implies what 'miracle' suggests to us, i.e. 'a marvellous event exceeding the known powers of Nature, and therefore supposed to be due to the special intervention of the Deity or of some supernatural agency'.[4] There is no such Hebrew separation between the natural and the supernatural as that definition implies; Nature is already supernatural, though it can be raised to new meaning.

(c) The third term, *niphla'oth*, occurs 43 times,[5] whilst there are a certain number of verbal and nominal derivatives from the same root, *pala'*, which also have to be taken into account. The plural participle used as a noun, *niphla'oth*, is, however, central, and can be rendered 'wonders'. Such a rendering brings it nearer to the etymology of our English word 'miracle', though not to its implication in our usage of a sharp division between natural and supernatural. The cognates of the Hebrew term suggest that the root meaning is the quite general one of distinction or separation.[6] An allied form of the verb (פלה) occurs in the words of Moses: 'If thou goest with us, then we shall be *separated*, I and thy people, from all the people that are upon the face of the earth.'[7] Israel is itself a miracle, a wonder, through the divine providence. 'Wonders' are outstanding events to be distinguished from ordinary occurrences. Those

---

[1] Ezek. xii. 6, 11; xxiv. 24, 27.   [2] iii. 8.
[3] On Deut. iv. 34.   [4] *SOED*, s.v.
[5] In my article (*JTS*. Jan.–Apr. 1944) the number is given as 51, but this wrongly included the derivatives.
[6] The Arabic *fala* (Hebrew *palah*) means 'wean'; the Ethiopic *falaya* 'divide'.
[7] Exod. xxxiii. 16.

who go down to the sea in ships see Yahweh's wonders when His storm-wind drives up the waves of the sea.[1] The rain is elsewhere ranked as an outstanding example of His wonders.[2] The miracle of the rain is strikingly brought out in Deuteronomy,[3] which contrasts Palestine with Egypt. The irrigation of Egypt is carried out by mechanical means (from the Nile), but Palestine is watered by rain directly from heaven, because Yahweh has it under His special care. That is a very instructive commentary on the interpretation of natural phenomena. Elihu names 'the balancings of the clouds' as amongst the supreme wonders of God (*miphla'ah*).[4] God's voice in the thunder is wonderful; Nature's ways as a whole are too wonderful for Job to understand.[5] The heavens, by their very constitution, praise the wondrousness of Yahweh; in Jeremiah's words,[6] 'thou hast made the heavens and the earth by thy great power and by thy outstretched arm; nothing is too wondrous for thee'. These statements about the ordinary course of Nature, as we reckon it, give us the Hebrew approach also to what we should account 'miracles', such as the crossing of the Jordan under Joshua, or the child-bearing of Sarah in advanced years.[7] These are to be regarded as extensions of the divine power which is being constantly exercised in more normal occurrences—the wonders of the deep, the mystery of all childbirth.[8] Some divine wonders, however, pass beyond this, as when the angel of Yahweh—the visible manifestation of Yahweh—ascends in the flame of sacrifice before the eyes of Manoah and his wife. The angel's very name is *pil'i*, 'wonderful', beyond human comprehension.[9]

Wonders will mark the apocalyptic future, as at the overthrow of the city of Chaos in the Isaianic apocalypse or of empires in Danielic visions;[10] only Sheol is regarded (at earlier periods) as out of bounds for Yahweh's activity:

> Is it for the dead that thou wilt do wonders?
> Will the *repha'im* arise to thank thee? . . .
> Will thy wonders be made known in the darkness,
> Or thy righteousness in the land of oblivion?
>
> (Ps. lxxxviii. 11, 13; Eng. 10, 12)

---

[1] Ps. cvii. 24. [2] Job v. 9. [3] xi. 10–12.
[4] Job xxxvii. 16. [5] xxxvii. 5; xlii. 3. [6] xxxii. 17.
[7] Joshua iii. 5; Gen. xviii. 14. [8] Ps. cvii. 24; cxxxix. 14.
[9] Judges xiii. 18 f.; cf. Ps. cxxxix. 6, where the use of the same adjective for the growth of the embryo is significant.
[10] Isa. xxv. 1; Dan. xii. 6.

God's wonders, seen in their providential aspects, become His 'mighty acts' (*g^eburoth*, Deut. iii. 24) and His 'righteousnesses' (*z^edakoth*, 1 Sam. xii. 7). Nature and history alike serve to reveal Him, for they are equally under His control, and are closely linked as the common sphere of *'oth*, *mopheth*, and *niphla'oth*. Nature and history are simply different aspects of the continued activity of God, and miracles are the representative occasions on which that activity specially impresses human consciousness.

§ 2

The Nature-theophanies, the manifestations of God through physical phenomena, deserve particular attention. They bring to a focus the general miracle of all Nature as the handiwork of God. But the theophany is a transient manifestation of deity, and, as such, to be distinguished from the continuous revelation of Him in all Nature. This may be illustrated from Isaiah's inaugural vision. The antiphonal song of the seraphim is 'the fulness (the full content) of all the earth is His glory'.[1] This manifestation of Him in all created things forms the background to the momentary manifestation of the divine being given to the prophet. The characteristic of the Nature-theophany is rather its intensity than any peculiarity of essence. The thunder is always the voice of God, even though its articulate interpretation is only occasional. The theophany is essentially 'more of the same thing'.

One of the earliest theophanies, that of the Burning Bush,[2] is also one of the simplest. We find Moses in the neighbourhood of 'the mountain of God', Horeb: 'And the angel of Yahweh appeared unto him in a flame of fire from the midst of the (bramble) bush (*hass^eneh*),[3] and he looked, and behold! the bush was burning with fire and the bush was not consumed.' Here, as elsewhere, the term 'angel of Yahweh' denotes a temporary manifestation of Yahweh, to be regarded as His presence in human form, and not an angel in the ordinary sense of an independent heavenly being. As a Nature-theophany, the

---

[1] Isa. vi. 3. As Duhm points out (ad loc.), we must not exclude Nature from this 'glory', even though it is not until Deutero-Isaiah that we get the fuller and more explicit appeal to God's revelation in Nature.   [2] Exod. iii.

[3] Cf. Lundgreen, *Pflanzenwelt*, p. 47: 'Dass hier der Baum nur ein סְנֶה, ein Stachelgewächs, ist, erklärt sich daraus, dass man solche am Horeb besonders häufig fand.'

interest of the bush is that it links with primitive ideas of the life
in all vegetation, and of fire as peculiarly associated with deity.
The reference to vegetation is brought out more clearly in the
phrase of Deut. xxxiii. 16, 'the good will of Him who dwells in
the bush', which suggests a more permanent connexion, such
as we often see in the Old Testament references to sacred trees.
All life had its mystery, but to the desert-dweller the vegetation
of the oasis had peculiar significance. The flame of fire which
is here associated with the bush is a familiar feature of theophanies and may be regarded as the physical phenomenon
manifesting Yahweh beyond all others.

Fire-theophanies may be illustrated by the references to the
pillar of fire and cloud which figures in the stories of the Exodus
and desert wanderings, manifesting the divine presence and
veiling His 'glory'. Indeed, 'the glory of Yahweh' is pre-
eminently a fiery manifestation of His being, as when at Sinai
'the appearance of the glory of Yahweh was like devouring fire
on the top of the mount',[1] and the face of Moses afterwards sent
out rays of derived light.[2] On Carmel, it was the fire of Yahweh
that consumed the offering,[3] and the (later) conception of the
Shechinah was of a fiery presence. Such descriptions are not
to be regarded as a figure of speech; the glory *is* fire, though
charged with the added mystery of the divine activity. Thus
Abraham sees God passing between the divided sacrifice (according to the ritual of primitive covenant-making) in the form of
'a smoking furnace and a flaming torch'.[4] A prophet asks,
'Who among us shall dwell with the devouring fire? who among
us shall dwell with everlasting burnings?'[5] Similarly with the
word *ruach*, which denotes both the wind of the desert and the
'Spirit' of God; the physical wind *is* a divine activity, and
the Spirit acts like a blast of wind. The hot blast of the sirocco
is regarded as a form of the fiery activity of Yahweh, just as fire
and wind are associated at Pentecost. Another parallel to this
significant evidence of identical vocabulary is supplied by the
word *ḳol*, which means both 'thunder' and 'voice'. The thunder
was as much the voice of God as the wind was His breath and
the fire His consuming activity. Every thunderstorm was a
potential theophany.[6]

---

[1] Exod. xxiv. 16, 17.   [2] Exod. xxxiv. 29 ff.   [3] 1 Kings xviii. 38.
[4] Gen. xv. 17.   [5] Isa. xxxiii. 14; cf. x. 17; Mal. iii. 2; Num. xi. 1; Deut. ix. 3.
[6] Cf. Duhm on Ps. xcvii. 4–6.

At Sinai occurred the cardinal theophany which set the pattern for so many others, experienced or imagined. Sinai, wherever it lay, was, until Zion usurped its place, the mountain of God, *par excellence*, the mountain of which Yahweh could say, 'I brought you unto myself'.[1] The present narrative in Exod. xix, xx, xxiv is confused, owing to the combination of three different documents. Of these, the Elohistic gives most detail of the method of revelation. On the morning of the third day 'there were thunders and lightnings and a heavy cloud upon the mountain and the sound of a horn very loud. . . . Moses used to speak and God used to answer him by thunder'.[2] Thus, as S. R. Driver has said, 'the repeated thunderings were interpreted as God's part in a dialogue with Moses'.[3] All the three narratives make Moses the unique channel of the revelation, the essential interpreter of whatever physical phenomena mediated it. In J, whilst the elders also are called up the mountain, they prostrate themselves afar off, and Moses alone draws near to God.[4] But a theophanic vision is given to them: 'They saw the God of Israel; and under His feet was a sort of sapphire pavement, like the heart of heaven for brightness.'[5] In P, the 'glory' rests on the mountain, the cloud covering it for six days; the glory is like devouring fire. On the seventh day Moses is called up alone into the midst of the cloud.

Some[6] have found volcanic as well as storm phenomena in the happenings at Sinai, e.g. in the pall of smoke resting on the mountain.[7] The combination is not impossible; if accepted, it would affect the question of the geographical position of Sinai.[8] But the evidence is not so clear as is sometimes alleged,[9] and we have always to remember the marked syncretistic tendencies

---

[1] Exod. xix. 4.   [2] Exod. xix. 16, 19; the tenses are frequentative.

[3] On Exod. xix. 19. We may compare John xii. 28, where the voice from heaven is regarded by the multitude as thunder. For O.T. passages showing thunder to be God's voice, see 1 Sam. xii. 18; Job xxxvi. 33—xxxvii. 5; also cf. Ps. xviii. 13; xxix. 3–9; 1 Sam. vii. 10; Exod. ix. 28.   [4] Exod. xxiv. 1 f.

[5] xxiv. 9 f. A covenant meal follows in this independent narrative.

[6] Most fully W. J. Phythian-Adams, *The Call of Israel*, Part III. Against the attribution, see Kittel, *Geschichte des Volkes Israel*, ed. 5/6, i. 348, n. 2; Mowinckel, *Psalmenstudien*, ii. 215 n.   [7] xix. 18 (J); xx. 18 (E).

[8] The Sinai tradition of J and P seems to place the mountain near Kadesh; the Horeb tradition of E on the east of the Gulf of Akabah. Cf. McNeile, *Exodus*, pp. cii ff.

[9] In xix. 18, the quaking of the earth in MT disappears in LXX, where, with more probability, in view of the verb used, it is the people who 'quake', as in verse 16.

of theophanic descriptions. The account of any theophany, whether actually experienced or poetically imagined by prophet or psalmist, would tend more and more towards conventionalized language, to which features of storm, earthquake, and volcanic activity would all contribute. We can see this in the 'literary' theophanies.

For the 'literary' theophanies Sinai naturally supplied a pattern, for it was the classic example. Besides their greater elaboration of detail in the repeated descriptions of storm-phenomena we often find mythological elements, such as references to the victory won by Marduk over Tiamat:

Awake, awake, put on strength, O arm of Yahweh. . . .
Art thou not it that cut Rahab in pieces, that pierced the dragon?
(Isa. li. 9.)

That is not from the description of a theophany actually experienced, as at Sinai, but from a prayer for one in the future, though after the pattern of the deliverance from Egypt. In the great theophany of the 18th psalm (from verse 10), Yahweh comes in the storm, riding upon a cherub and flying swiftly on the wings of the wind, to lay bare the foundations of the world.[1] In Habakkuk iii, the rhetorical repudiation of the ancient mythological attack on monsters leads up to the new occasion for a theophany directed against human foes:

> Was thine anger against the rivers,
>   Or thy wrath against the sea,
> That thou didst ride upon thine horses,
>   Upon thy chariots of salvation? (verse 8.)

In some instances the storm enters realistically into the battle by bringing panic on the foe, or otherwise helping in their overthrow. This is noticeably true of the victory celebrated in the Song of Deborah, when the stars in their courses fought against Sisera, and the storm-filled wady Kishon swept them away. Prophetic speakers naturally emphasize the divine part in the battle; but this is not to be taken to exclude human co-operation with God.[2] In the classical description of the Day of Yahweh given by Zephaniah (i. 14 ff.) the culminating point

---

[1] For the reference to Sinai, cf. Gunkel, *Schöpfung und Chaos*, p. 106; and note Ps. lxxvii. 16 ff.

[2] Cf. Isa. xiii. 13, 'I will make the heavens to tremble', &c., with verse 17, 'I will stir up the Medes against them'; also Exod. xvii. 8 ff., where the uplifted hands of Moses secure divine help to the Israelites fighting against Amalek.

is the sound of the horn and the battle-shout of attacking enemies. But in the theophanic storm which is to bring about the overthrow of Assyria, according to Isa. xxx. 27 ff., there is no mention of Judah's warriors, and the suggestion is of panic falling upon the enemy.[1]

The use of primitive mythology in Nature-theophanies and related passages need not imply that the historic belief in Yahweh ever passed through a phase comparable with that of the Babylonian creation myths, or the Ugaritic mythology. To some extent, at least, the elaboration of mythology outside Israel, and the literary usage within Israel, form parallel lines of development, both of them going back to the *mana* of earlier days, pre-polytheistic and pre-Yahwistic. Just as the biologist regards man as a parallel, though far higher, development to that of the apes, rather than as a direct descendant from them, so we may speak of the henotheism of Israel, whilst admitting its partial kinship with the polytheism and crude mythology of Babylonia and Canaan. But both go back to the primitive cradle of a belief that all nature is alive with the mystery of superhuman power.

§ 3

To say this, of course, affords no explanation of the peculiar quality of the development within Israel. For this we must look to the prophetic interpretation of both Nature and history. We may, like an early narrator, ascribe the actual deliverance of the Israelites from the Egyptians to the timely blowing of an east wind that made possible a passage through the waters: 'Yahweh caused the sea to go back by a strong east wind all the night.'[2] But the merely physical event would not become a miracle of deliverance until it found an interpreter in Yahweh's prophet. Interpretation is inseparable from miracles of the Old Testament pattern. We begin at the wrong end if we try first to rationalize them, and to reduce them to their smallest nucleus of historical event. We should begin rather with the faith of both prophet and people, by which the events of the physical world, normal or abnormal, were interpreted in a

---

[1] So Procksch, ad loc.

[2] Exod. xiv. 21 (J); cf. x. 13 (J), where the east wind brings up the locusts, and xv. 25 (J), where a tree is used to sweeten bitter water. For a possible theory of the contribution of sand and tide to the Israelite crossing of the Red Sea, cf. T. H. Robinson, *ZAW*, 1933, pp. 170 ff.

particular context of history. All nature, as we have seen, is potentially miraculous, and continually manifests the wonders of God. At particular points of time and space this wonder may be intensified, or given a new meaning by its incorporation in a new context. The prophetic interpretation creates the *religious* fact, just as the relation to God transforms moral evil into the religious fact of 'sin'. The psychical factor in the religious fact is of primary importance, both for the proper exegesis of the Old Testament literature, i.e. the recovery of the original Hebrew emphasis, and also for any right conception of miracle. It is only when the event is lifted into the realm of the personal relation between God and man, the realm of faith, that the triple sequence of prayer, providence, and miracle becomes intelligible, without losing its profound mystery. Prayer, providence, miracle, alike depend on the reciprocity of God and man in the unity of the religious fact. The glory of sunrise and sunset depends on the atmosphere of earth as much as on the sun's relation to it. The commonest act of perception is a complex unity of the subjective and objective factors. Why then should not this be true of the act of religious perception which constitutes faith?

When we come to our study of the prophetic consciousness we shall see how vital and important this interpretative element becomes. Meanwhile we may note the preparation for this complex unity in the religious appreciation of Nature. Perhaps the rather enigmatic incident of Elijah's experience at Horeb bears on this, and marks a transition to fuller consciousness of the psychical factor: 'Behold! as Yahweh was passing, there was a great and powerful wind tearing away mountains and breaking up rocks before Yahweh; but Yahweh was not in the wind. After the wind there was a shaking, but Yahweh was not in the shaking. After the shaking there was fire, but Yahweh was not in the fire. After the fire there was a sound (coming) from thin silence.'[1] Prophecy was in process of becoming more consciously psychical in its medium, hearing the articulate word, in place of seeing the physical event.

The Elijah and Elisha stories provide a further main group of Nature-miracles in the Old Testament, as distinct from the

---

[1] 1 Kings xix. 11, 12; or (cf. Burney and BDB) 'the sound of a light whisper'. As Hempel rightly emphasizes (*Gott und Mensch*[2], p. 9, n. 3) 'hearing' involves a much less close contact with God than 'seeing' Him. Cf. Deut. iv. 12.

much more important Exodus stories. In these prophetic stories
the accretion of the legendary element is obvious, being such
accretion as will always gather round forceful personalities in
all generations, though the categories of explanation will differ.
The psychical factor is here prominent in the making of the
event, as well as in its interpretation.[1] It is useless to inquire
exactly what happened on Carmel, and what might have been
seen by a cool and dispassionate spectator of scientific temper;
there were no such people there. But Elijah is obviously a man
of dominating personality, quite apart from his use of symbolic
magic when he crouched on Carmel in the semblance of a
rain-cloud, and of his super-normal frenzy in running as fast
as could the chariot-horses of Ahab. We certainly cannot hope
to analyse out the physical and psychical factors in whatever
happened, and we must leave room for a ministry of illusion.[2]
Yet it is perfectly clear to the student of Israel's religion that the
event on Carmel was of great importance for the future, and
marked the victory of Yahwism over Baalism as a rival religion.
The providence of God is seen in the unity of the religious fact,
whatever its components. The supreme miracle of the Old
Testament is the historical development of the religion of Israel,[3]
and that is inseparable from the religious interpretation of
Nature.

§ 4

The close relation of the Nature-miracles to the history is
apparent from the outset. Both the Exodus and its interpretative complement at Sinai-Horeb depend on 'miracle' in the
large sense implied in this discussion. Israel's religion of the
higher, i.e. the prophetic kind, is as truly a redemptive religion
as that which springs from the Christian faith. But the Exodus,
like the Cross, has no religious value apart from its interpretation as an act of God. The integrated religious fact takes its
own place in the history; compared with it, the precise details
of the event, even if recoverable, are of secondary importance.
Dr. Phythian-Adams, in his suggestive book, *The Call of Israel*,
distinguishes three aspects of the miracle of this call—that of
'Material Coincidence', by which he means the physical pheno-

[1] Thus Elisha's curse can evoke two bears to devour forty-two little children.
[2] On this, see *Redemption and Revelation* by H. Wheeler Robinson, ch. ii.
[3] Cf. J. A. MacCulloch, in the *ERE*, viii. 679, and note especially Exod. xxxiv. 10
where what Yahweh does with Israel = His *niphla'oth*.

mena of the time and place, that of 'Spiritual Coincidence', the
presence of a competent interpreter, viz. Moses, and that of
'Sacramental Coincidence', viz. 'that there was in the nature
of the phenomena themselves a reservoir of inexhaustible
spiritual significance'.[1] By this last statement is meant the
possibility of the continued and ever larger interpretation of the
redemptive work of God which the subsequent religion of Israel
actually displays. This analysis of the miracle can be accepted
as true both for the religion of Israel and for those who inherit
its faith in the God of Israel. The use of the term 'coincidence'
is justified, because the events can be viewed on the lower level
of mere event, where coincidence is ascribed to chance, as well
as to the higher level at which an explanation is found in the
divine purpose. The virility of Biblical religion is partly due
to this realism, which always keeps close to the event. Hebrew
theology, like Hebrew metaphor, emphasizes the end, rather
than the means; thus in Ps. cvii the escape of the lost traveller,
the prisoner, the sick man, the storm-tossed sailor are all
reckoned as *niphla'oth* of God, for which men should praise Him.
There is no concern with the means by which escape was made.
Our modern analysis of Biblical miracles so far as it accepts
them as historical events of some kind or other, shows a longer
and more complex chain of cause and effect than the Hebrews
recognized; yet it still leaves open the equal possibility of faith
in a divine Agent. But our desire to share the idealism of Israel
must not blind us to its characteristic realism. There are perils
in the higher interpretation of the data which may have very
misleading consequences. It may lead to the arbitrary use of
allegory as if it were dogmatic truth instead of more or less
interesting 'Midrash'. It may ensnare us in a surreptitious
dualism of shadow and substance which may explain the
Epistle to the Hebrews, but is more Platonizing than Hebraic.
It may, worst of all, lead to the distortion of the history itself
as in timidly conservative or fundamentalistic formulations of
it, which ask us to believe more than Hebrews themselves ever
believed. The true approach is to maintain that the things
which really happened to the Hebrew might still happen, or
rather, that they do happen. But the faith that can interpret
them, as they are interpreted in the Bible, is not of every age.
Even when present, it will necessarily change its intellectual

[1] pp. 180–3.

forms and theories from generation to generation, if its spiritual continuity is to be maintained. The essential truth for Biblical faith is that Nature, like history, is wholly under God's control; the manner of that control, which means the way in which successive generations formulate it for themselves, is of much interest, but in the long run of secondary importance.

If we glance back over the ground we have traversed in these three chapters, some general features of the Old Testament conception of Nature will be apparent.

1. Nature is alive, not only in animal and tree and plant, but also in spring and river, in star and stone. In various degrees this life has psychical as well as physical qualities, comparable with those of the human body, and in close and quasi-conscious sympathy with man.

2. All this varied life was created by God and is continuously sustained by Him; the 'living waters' of a running stream mirror the 'living God' without whom they would not be.[1]

3. Nature therefore reveals God in several ways:

(a) It is the unique utterance of a unique Being. If we say of human language that 'the style is the man', then we may say of Nature that 'the style is the God'. The majesty of Nature and its 'numinous' qualities impressed the Hebrew more than its beauty,[2] but he was very conscious of the wisdom as well as of the power of God which Nature revealed. 'Shall the planter of the ear not hear? shall the shaper of the eye not discern?' (Ps. xciv. 9; cf. Exod. iv. 11). The established order of Nature becomes itself a pledge of God's steadfastness, as the bounty of Nature reveals His grace.

(b) Nature is made to be the arena of history, and becomes its instrument; a prophet's voice reminds us that the earth was made to be inhabited (Isa. xlv. 18). Nature is taken up into history as an essential part of it; the line between them, so far as it exists at all, is a wavy one, running up and down. Storm and pestilence and locust-plague are made part of history: 'Shall evil befall a city and Yahweh hath not done it?' (Amos iii. 6; cf. Isa. xlv. 7). The deeds of men, on the other hand, bring blessing or curse on Nature also.

---

[1] Cf. Gen. xvi. 14, בְּאֵר לַחַי רֹאִי

[2] The appreciation of Nature's beauty in Wisdom xiii. 1–7 illustrates the Greek, as distinct from the Hebrew emphasis. Cf. Hempel, *Gott und Mensch²*, p. 50, n. 5.

(c) Finally, the very limitations and defects of Nature carry the mind of the Hebrew up to the God on whom Nature wholly depends. Life is cut off by death like a web on the loom (Isa. xxxviii. 12), and even its pride is but trouble and sorrow (Ps. xc. 10). Pestilence walketh in darkness, and sickness wasteth at noon-day (Ps. xci. 6). If the harvest is reaped with joy, yet it has to be sown in tears (Ps. cxxvi. 5, 6). The heavens withhold their rain; wild beasts ravage the flock. Yet He on whom all Nature depends is more than sufficient to recreate it, and to give to it the perfection which man's happiness requires. So Nature enters into the hope of Israel. Its manifest limitations point beyond themselves to the unlimited resources of its Creator and Upholder, who shall finally be its Redeemer (Ecclus. xliii. 28). As ben Sira says, 'He is greater than all His works'. Nature's supreme word to the Hebrew mind is that to understand her we must go beyond her; the fear of the Lord is the beginning of wisdom.

PART II

GOD AND MAN

IV

THE CHARACTERISTIC INTERRELATIONS

IN previous discussion of 'God and Nature' we were dealing with man's outer environment. The relation of 'God and Man' to which we now turn supplies the corresponding inner environment of revelation. The inner is the necessary complement of the outer, but it is also more than this, since it supplies the interpretation of the outer. A useful illustration may be drawn from physiology. It was pointed out by a distinguished French physiologist of the last century, Claude Bernard, that the life of the human body has not only its outer environment, but also an inner one, formed by the blood, and he remarks that 'all the vital mechanisms, varied as they are, have only one object, that of preserving constant the conditions of life in the internal environment'.[1] We have a parallel to this in the Old Testament view of man and his well-being. This concentrates upon the maintenance of an adequate inner environment, reflected in the human consciousness. Only by the right relation of God and man can man be spiritually healthy. The Old Testament word for the 'completeness' of well-being is *shalom* (שָׁלוֹם).[2] This originally emphasized security from outer disturbance, but moves towards fuller recognition of that inner 'peace' which is even more essential to well-being.

Any study of the relation of God and man requires some analysis of its various factors. But there is always the danger that such abstractions should become remote from anything actually experienced in concrete life. The great formative ideas of both God and man have constantly to be brought back to their *Sitz im Leben*, their functioning in actual experience, in order to retain their vital truth. The Old Testament habitually shows man in his relation to God, not in himself as a detached unit. It also shows God in His relation to man, not in the

---

[1] *Claude Bernard*, by J. M. D. Olmsted (1939), pp. 290–1.
[2] Cf. Pedersen, *Israel I–II*, pp. 263 ff.

E

philosophical interests of 'ethical monotheism'. We shall therefore approach our subject by thinking of some of the most
characteristic contrasts of God and man as mutually related,
before passing in later chapters to some particular aspects of
man's nature, conduct, and destiny.

A classical statement, which may be usefully kept in mind
throughout, is that of the 8th psalm:

> When I see thy heavens, the work of thy fingers,
> The moon and the stars which thou hast established,
> What is man that thou rememberest him,
> And the son of man that thou art concerned with him?[1]

Here we get the contrast between the greatness of God, as seen
in His supreme works of Nature, with the littleness of man. But
the psalmist goes on to draw another contrast, that between
man himself and all the other inhabitants of the earth, air, and
sea,[2] over which man rules *Dei gratia*, lacking little of the status
of a god (*elohim*) and wearing a crown[3] of royal authority over
them. This sense of a dignity bestowed on man, combined
with humility before God's inherent majesty, runs all through
the religion of Israel, and helps to give us the 'stereoscopic'
portrait of man which characterizes it. It finds many and
diverse expressions, some of which we may now proceed to
notice.

§ 1. Spirit and Flesh

The most fundamental of all these contrasts is that between
Spirit and flesh as characterizing the respective natures of God
and man. Here the cardinal passage is Isa. xxxi. 3:

> The Egyptians are men (אָדָם) and not God (אֵל),
> And their horses flesh (בָּשָׂר) and not spirit (רוּחַ).

Though the direct reference is to 'horses', the famed Egyptian
chariotry, and not to men, the poetic parallelism shows that man
also is flesh, being made as he is,[4] of the same substance as the

---

[1] Verses 4 and 5; cf. Job vii. 17 (a deliberate parody, suggesting that God has
reared man only to torture him) and Ps. cxliv. 3 (an appeal for help in helplessness)
with the serene confidence of Ps. viii. Kant's famous aphorism, in which the moral
law within man matches the majesty of the starry heavens above him, shows the
characteristically modern emphasis on man himself.

[2] Cf. Gen. i. 28 and Ecclus. xvii. 1–9.

[3] Note the force of תְּעַטְּרֵהוּ. Cf. Job's confidence that he could go 'prince-
like' into God's presence (xxxi. 37) with the abasement of xl. 3 ff., xlii. 1 ff.

[4] Ezek. xxxvii. 8, &c.

THE CHARACTERISTIC INTERRELATIONS 51

animals, and often included with them in the familiar phrase, 'all flesh'.[1] It is equally implied by the parallelism that the essential substance of the divine is 'spirit', ethereal substance charged with dynamic energy, something like what was once erroneously conceived as 'the electric fluid'. The comment of Duhm on Isaiah's words is instructive and important. He says:

'Yahweh and His sway represent for Isaiah the spirit-element; all else is אדם and בשר. Foreign gods are ignored; the spiritual world is claimed for Yahweh alone. In the struggle of nations for dominion and freedom on the arena of world-history, the spirit-principle and the flesh-principle stand over against each other, and it is the spirit-principle that will win the final victory. This is the supreme formula of the universalism of the older prophets, urged without theological polemic. This is the driving force of the subsequent development of religion down to 1 Cor. 15.'[2]

Another striking example of the original contrast of Spirit and flesh is supplied by the unfortunately mutilated passage, Gen. vi. 1–4:

'When men began to multiply on the surface of the ground, and daughters had been born to them, the sons of God saw the daughters of men to be goodly, and took in marriage all they chose. And God said, My spirit shall not remain in these men forever,[3] because[4] they are flesh; and their days shall be 120 years.'[5]

The most natural explanation of this difficult passage is, I think, still that which Wellhausen gave half a century back.[6] Spirit, *ruach*, is the essential substance of the superhuman beings denoted by the 'sons of God', or, as we might say, the 'angels'. By their union with 'flesh', of which the offspring were the giant races of the mythical past, this divine substance passed into human nature, and its further operation had to be checked; hence the new age-limit for man. Here, then, there is a parallel to the risk that Adam might partake of the tree of life, and thereby acquire immortality;[7] to prevent this he was expelled from Eden. A remoter parallel may be seen in the measures taken against the builders of Babel.[8] This view of *ruach* as

---

[1] Gen. vi. 17, &c.   [2] *Das Buch Jesaia*, ed. 3, p. 205.
[3] So LXX.   [4] Cf. the Vss.
[5] A possible reference to the giants; cf. Hempel, *Gott und Mensch*, p. 199 n. (following Lods).
[6] *Composition des Hexateuchs*[3], pp. 307–10.
[7] Gen. iii. 22; see the discussion of this passage in Ch. VII.
[8] Cf. Gunkel, Com. on Gen. vi. 1–4.

divine essence and power is confirmed by the history of the development of the term, for it never denotes a permanent element in man's constitution, like *nephesh*, before the exilic period.[1] In support of this view, also, we have the probable etymology of *'el('elohim)* as 'power'.[2] At first the Elohim, as supernatural beings, were found everywhere; later their powers were gathered up in the Elohim *par excellence*, and finally the term became a proper name, identified in Israel with Yahweh. To remember the contrast between divine power and the weakness of human flesh gives new point to such words as those of Ps. lvi. 4:

> In Elohim have I trusted; I will not fear;
> What can flesh do to me?

or those of Job, indignantly addressing God (x. 4, 5):

> Are eyes of flesh thine,
>   Or with human vision dost thou see?
> Are the days of a man thy days,
>   Or thy years as the days of a human being?

It will be seen that the divine immortality here again enters into the contrast with man's relatively brief life. In this respect, as in so many others, man as flesh is grouped with all creatures. He is utterly dependent on God, so that his supreme virtue is that of humility, as his supreme sin is that of rebellious pride.[3]

Professor Hempel, in his important book *Gott und Mensch im Alten Testament*, thinks that the relation of man to God is best expressed by the formula of repulsion and attraction, somewhat along the lines of Otto's conception of the numinous as both *mysterium tremendum* and *mysterium fascinans*. In 1865, half a century before Otto published the first edition of *Das Heilige* (1917), John Henry Newman expressed this central combination of the 'numinous' in his 'Dream of Gerontius'. He speaks of the soul's agony before the judgement-seat as torn between

> these two pains, so counter and so keen—
> The longing for Him, when thou seest Him not;
> The shame of self at thought of seeing Him.

---

[1] See p. 70. In Gen. ii. 7 *ruach* is *not* used by J of the breath of Yahweh which animates man's body; it is, however, so used by P some four centuries later in this connexion ('the breath of the *ruach* of life', vii. 22).

[2] E. Dhorme, *L'Evolution religieuse d'Israel I*, p. 339. His conception of the course of development in the use of the term (pp. 347–8) is accepted above.

[3] Isa. ii. 5 ff.; cf. Mic. vi. 8.

Hempel discusses much of the Old Testament material under this thesis, and shows how instructive a line of presentation it can be. Naturally he insists on our regarding 'repulsion' and 'attraction' not as mutually exclusive opposites, but as polar elements of one and the same emotional experience, and he claims that as such they interpenetrate the whole of Israel's piety. Though we have started from the more ontological duality of Spirit and flesh, we shall see that it brings us to the similar result of a duality within an experienced unity.

§ 2. HOLINESS AND SIN

A second contrast, that of 'Holiness' and 'Sin', follows closely from that which has been indicated between 'Spirit' and 'Flesh'. Holiness is the attribute of the divine; sin is a characteristic product of the human. They are alike in the fact that originally they are both non-moralized conceptions. This fact naturally colours their subsequent developments and serves to explain some of the peculiarities in the use of the terms.

'Holiness', ḳodesh (קֹדֶשׁ), has no convincing etymology, but usage shows clearly enough that it belongs to the class of ideas which anthropologists explain from tabu-mana conceptions. Dr. Marett defines tabu as 'the negative mode of the supernatural, to which mana corresponds as the positive mode'.[1] The holy object is that which is separated from common or profane use,[2] such as the shewbread which Ahimelech hesitated to give to David and his men. We find a closely parallel idea in the term ḥerem (חֵרֶם), as applied to objects 'devoted' to the deity and 'banned' to common use.[3] The difference between ḳodesh and ḥerem is clearly defined by G. F. Moore:

'both denote inviolability, and in a religious sense, withdrawal from common use or contact. But in the further development of this idea in Heb. they go in opposite directions: קדשׁ applies to things which God appropriates to himself because he chooses them for his pleasure or service; חרם to things which he prohibits to men because he hates them with peculiar hatred.' (ICC, Judges, p. 36.)

The mana which resides in the holy object according to primitive ideas may be illustrated from the 'ordeal of jealousy' in Numbers v, where the potion given to the suspected woman is

---

[1] The Threshold of Religion[3], p. 110.
[2] The antithesis is with ḥol (חֹל) as in Lev. x. 10.
[3] W. Robertson Smith, The Religion of the Semites[3], p. 150.

composed of 'holy' water, in which is mingled dust from the floor of the sanctuary, whilst a written curse is washed off into it. This 'water of bitterness' is supposed to descend into the womb, and to produce, apparently, an abortive birth in case of the woman's infidelity.[1] Here we have a crude survival of primitive ideas of 'holiness', preserved as a sort of fossil in the strata of the later ritual.

The non-moral character of the original conception of holiness is forcibly illustrated also by the term for temple-prostitutes, male or female, viz. *ḳedesh* and *kᵉdeshah*, as being 'holy' persons, attached to the local sanctuaries[2] and even to the temple in Jerusalem.[3] The inherent danger of contact with a holy object is shown by the fate of Uzzah, when he grasped the ark on its way to Jerusalem to save it from falling through the stumbling of the draught-oxen:

The anger of Yahweh was kindled against Uzzah, and God smote him there . . . and he died. (2 Sam. vi. 7.)

The later ritual took meticulous pains to prevent unauthorized and therefore dangerous contact with holy things. Ezekiel's programme for the reconstruction of the temple and its ordinances has this separation for its dominating principle.

It is in connexion with the ark that we find the earliest recorded application of the term 'holy' to God.[4] When the men of Beth-shemesh had suffered through looking into the ark on its way back from the Philistines, they said:

Who is able to stand before Yahweh, this holy God? (1 Sam. vi. 20.)

Here, evidently, we are still in the realm of non-moralized ideas; Yahweh is a dangerous being to approach. But it is obvious that the higher religion of Israel could not assimilate such a conception of 'holiness' without profoundly modifying it. The concept of holiness had to develop with that of the divine personality. To see this we have only to compare the use of the term in the account of the Beth-shemesh incident with its use in the story of Isaiah's temple-vision where the prophet's reaction is fully moralized. Yet even there the term retains from its older history the sense of the mystery and majesty of

---

[1] See the note contributed by me to G. B. Gray's *Numbers*, p. 48.
[2] 1 Kings xiv. 24, xv. 12, xxii. 46; Job xxxvi. 14; Deut. xxiii. 18 (17); cf. Hos. iv. 14; Amos ii. 7.
[3] 2 Kings xxiii. 7.   [4] Smend, *Alttestamentliche Religionsgeschichte*², p. 150.

the divine, the sense explicit also in a well-known passage of Trito-Isaiah, alongside the newer consciousness of Yahweh's moral character:

Thus hath said the high and exalted One, dwelling forever, and
    'Holy' is his name:
On high and as a holy One do I dwell, but (also) with the crushed
    and lowly of spirit. (Isa. lvii. 15.)

Most impressively we see this in Isaiah's temple-vision, where the holiness of Yahweh, still terrible and dangerous, awakens first and foremost the profound sense of moral unworthiness:

Woe is me, for I am ruined, for a man unclean of lips am I,
And in the midst of a people unclean of lips am I abiding.
                                      (Isa. vi. 5.)

Thus we have the sin of man set in contrasted relation with the holiness of God, and this interrelation is of the highest significance for the religion of Israel.

Though there is but one Hebrew term for 'holiness', as applied to God, there are many terms for sin, which is what we might have expected from the disunity of man over against the unity of God. These terms may be conveniently grouped into four classes, according as they denote (1) *deviation* from the right way, (2) the changed *status* (guilt) of the agent, (3) *rebellion* against a superior or unfaithfulness to an agreement, (4) some characterization of the *quality* of the act itself.[1] It is sufficient for our present purpose to note that the concept of sin has passed through a development comparable with that of 'holiness'. There was an earlier phase at which the moral emphasis belonging to the prophetic conception of sin was not yet present. One marked limitation in the earlier idea is seen in the group conception of moral responsibility; it is not until Jeremiah and Ezekiel that we reach an adequate sense of the relation of the individual within the group to Yahweh. To this, however, we shall return in the discussion of Hebrew morality. Here we may note two other limitations of what we should regard as a true conception of sin. One of these is the treatment of the sinful act as purely objective, without regard to motive or intention; the other is the placing of a purely ritual offence on the same

[1] The Hebrew terms under each of these heads are given in H. Wheeler Robinson, *The Christian Doctrine of Man*, p. 43. Cf. Hempel, *Das Ethos des Alten Testaments*, pp. 185–9, and C. H. Dodd, ch. iv, in *The Bible and the Greeks*.

level as one involving strictly moral condemnation. Both may be illustrated from the early narrative of a victory won by Saul over the Philistines.[1] It was reported to Saul that the people, hungry because he had set a taboo on all food during the battle, were now eating the flesh of captured animals without draining out the blood to offer it to the deity. He condemned this in the strongest terms as a sin against Yahweh, and forthwith improvised an altar on the battlefield, in accordance with the primitive Semitic rite of sacrifice.[2] But when Saul consulted the oracle of divination, Urim and Thummim, as to a further night attack, there was no response. Ultimately this was traced to a breach of Saul's taboo on food during the fighting, a breach committed by Jonathan in entire ignorance of it. This brings Jonathan so near to death that none but a favourite of the people to whom victory was largely due would have been spared. The people insisted on 'ransoming' Jonathan, which doubtless means that someone was put to death under the ban in his place. We see here that absence of intention on Jonathan's part makes no difference to the offence or its penalty.

This narrative, then, shows us the *mana* or 'holiness' of the blood on the one hand, a conception which runs all through the later ritual, and on the other we see 'sin' as simply a breach of taboo, a conception also retained in the later religion, alongside of the higher and more spiritual conception learnt from the prophets. Montefiore speaks quite frankly of what he calls the drawback or misfortune of his national code of law, 'its equal accentuation of the ceremonial and the moral. More precisely, the evil lay', he says, 'in that mournful relic of outworn paganism—the conception of external holiness and pollution, of clean and unclean'.[3] To agree with this judgement need not prevent us from recognizing that the ritual as a whole could become a highly important and influential discipline in holiness of the moral kind, and not least when approached as obedience to the divine command. The proof of this fruit of the Law may be seen in the Book of Psalms which came into being largely through the training of the temple ritual and to give expression

---

[1] 1 Sam. xiv. 33 ff.; ib. 24, 27 ff., 37 ff.

[2] The word for 'sacrifice', *zebaḥ*, is shown by the Arabic cognate (ذبح) to mean cutting the throat of the animal. See Wellhausen, *Reste Arabischen Heidentums*[2], p. 114.

[3] Hibbert Lectures on the *Origin and Growth of Religion as illustrated by the Religion of the Ancient Hebrews*, p. 478.

to its spirit. At all stages of the religion there were higher and lower levels. But in one form or another, holiness and sin remained polar elements, and constitute one of the most important and characteristic of the interrelations between God and man.

§ 3. GRACE AND REPENTANCE

If we were analysing the conception of God for its own sake, rather than His characteristic interrelation with man, we should naturally be led for one member of our third contrast to His 'righteousness', as denoting the moralization of the concept of holiness through the great prophets and most explicitly through Isaiah. His teaching in this respect is epitomized in the words:

Yahweh Zebaoth is exalted in judgement (*mishpaṭ*),
And the holy God shows Himself holy[1] in righteousness (*zᵉdaḳah*)
(v. 16.)

The Hebrew word translated 'righteousness' is, however, chiefly forensic in its primary associations, and had to share in the same process of prophetic moralization as the term 'holiness'. As Robertson Smith says,[2]

'the Hebrew always thought of the right and the wrong as if they were to be settled before a judge. Righteousness is to the Hebrew not so much a moral quality as a legal status.'

Probably Kautzsch is correct in deriving the term from the fundamental idea of conformity to a norm, an idea developed in the juristic, ethical, and theocratic realms.[3] We need something more positive and intimate to characterize the interrelation of God and man than the implication of 'righteousness' that He will conform to the true standard of that relation. Now the outstanding word to describe its content rather than its form is *ḥeṣed* (חסד), which when ascribed to God may often be rendered 'grace' rather than 'loving-kindness' or 'mercy'. But even the rendering 'grace' does not suggest the element of loyalty, of moral obligation, of social bond, which the Hebrew word includes, an element finding parallel expression in the quite different word translated 'redeemer', properly kinsman-

---

[1] The verb is from the same root as 'holy', and in the reflexive form. R.V. 'sanctified' obscures the point of the phrase.

[2] *The Prophets of Israel²*, p. 71.

[3] *Die Derivate des Stammes* צדק *im Alttestamentlichen Sprachgebrauch* (1881), pp. 54 ff.

vindicator.[1] The root-meaning of *ḥesed* is brought out very
effectively in the Arabic equivalent (حسد), which means
promptitude to help, or, as a verb, 'to gather with a view to
help'.[2] Thus in Hosea ii. 19, 20 (Heb. 21, 22), where the
prophet is characterizing Yahweh's future and lasting betrothal
to Israel, its qualities are given as those of righteousness (צֶדֶק),
justice (מִשְׁפָּט), grace (חֶסֶד), compassion (רַחֲמִים), and fidelity
(אֱמוּנָה). The spontaneous character of Yahweh's grace, which
springs from His deep-seated loyalty to Israel, is seen in
Jeremiah's striking anticipation of the parable of the Prodigal
Son:

> The people found favour[3] in the desert—
> A people escaped from the sword.
> While Israel marched to his rest,
> From afar did Yahwe appear.
> 'With a love from of old I love thee;
> Therefore in *ḥesed* I draw thee. (xxxi. 2, 3.)

In the parable the penitent son is already returning, 'But while
he was yet afar off, his father saw him, and was moved with
compassion and ran and fell on his neck and kissed him'.[4] The
spontaneous loyalty of the father to his son is even more marked
in the prophecy than in the parable, for there God takes the
initiative.

If, then, we take *ḥesed* as best denoting the deep-seated relation of God to Israel, which it is His 'righteousness' to carry into
effect, we are at once pointed to 'repentance' as the corresponding attitude in man, which it is the purpose of God's *ḥesed* to
arouse and maintain. The fundamental idea of 'repentance'
in the Old Testament is expressed by the verb *shub* (שׁוּב),
which means to 'turn' or 'return'. It is unfortunate that the
Authorized and Revised Versions should have used the term
'repent' in a now archaistic sense, to express regret or sorrow
without any moral connotation, as when we read that 'it
repented the Lord that he had made man on the earth, and it
grieved him at his heart'.[5] Here and elsewhere, 'repent' renders

---

[1] Job xix. 25; Pss. xix. 14, lxxviii. 35; Prov. xxiii. 11; Isa. xli. 14, &c.

[2] Kazimirski, i, p. 549. So Robertson Smith, *The Prophets of Israel*[2], p. 408:
'friendly combination . . . in Hebrew חסד is the virtue that knits together
society.'

[3] Skinner, whose translation in *Prophecy and Religion*, p. 300, is here followed,
renders *ḥen*, a related term, by 'grace', and *ḥesed* by 'kindness'.

[4] Luke xv. 20.   [5] Gen. vi. 6.

another Hebrew word meaning 'be troubled';[1] but we are concerned with the verb rendered 'turn'[2] or 'return'[3] in repentance. This occurs very frequently, although it is actually rendered 'repent' only three times in our Authorized Version,[4] and even these three disappear in favour of 'turn again' or 'return' in the Revised. It may seem a little curious that there is no corresponding noun in the Old Testament with the meaning 'repentance'; the derived word *t'shubah*, so frequent and important in later Judaism,[5] has not yet acquired that meaning. We may see in the use of the verb a characteristic emphasis on action, the volitional emphasis of Hebrew morality, which clings to the verb 'turn' in preference to an abstract noun.[6] Repentance does not mean simply the passive state of being sorry about sin (or its consequences); it denotes a positive turning away from it with new resolution and direction. This, of course, is the ultimate demand made by the prophets, even when they are simply announcing a divine judgement on sin. We think of Amos as the outstanding prophet of judgement and little else; yet we find as the repeated refrain to one of his utterances which reviews the disciplinary judgements of God, 'Yet ye have not returned unto me, saith Yahweh'.[7] Such judgements and such warnings were already an exhibition of grace; apart from Yahweh's *ḥeṣed*, why should He trouble any more with a rebellious people, or raise up prophets at all? But the grace which was for the most part implicit in pre-exilic prophecy[8] became explicit in the religion of the exilic[9] and post-exilic periods,[10] and repentance becomes more definitely the proper response to that grace, as sin now becomes the churlish refusal of it. The ultimate definition of sin is always in terms of grace.

---

[1] *Naḥam* (נחם), apparently connected with an Arabic root having the fundamental meaning 'breathe heavily' (cf. Kazimirski, iv, p. 468, 'groan deeply' as under a heavy burden). Hence the two apparently inconsistent meanings of the root in Hebrew, viz. 'be grieved' and 'be comforted', i.e. draw a deep breath either of distress or of relief (so König, *Heb. Wörterbuch*, s.v.).

[2] e.g. 2 Kings xvii. 13: 'Turn ye from your evil ways.'

[3] e.g. Deut. i. 45: 'Ye returned and wept before Yahweh.'

[4] 1 Kings viii. 47; Ezek. xiv. 6, xviii. 30.

[5] Cf. Moore, *Judaism*, i, pp. 507 ff.

[6] LXX regularly translates by ἐπιστρέφειν, but in later Jewish writers and translators we find μετανοεῖν, 'giving a somewhat different turn of meaning to an established idea' (Dodd, op. cit., p. 181).   [7] Amos iv. 6, 8, 9, 10, 11.

[8] It becomes explicit in Hos. xiv, which can claim to be a genuine outcome of his personal experience.

[9] e.g. Isa. xliii. 25.   [10] e.g. Ps. ciii. 3, 4, 8 ff.

The *locus classicus* for repentance is the 51st psalm. Here we find the appeal from the inevitable frailty of flesh, prone to sin, to the Holy Spirit of God, thus incorporating our two previous antitheses of Spirit and flesh, Holiness and sin. But the psalmist reaches a new level of insight in his conceptions of Grace and repentance. Doubtless he would not have been able to realize the grace of forgiveness without the removal of the physical penalty for sin, as we may see from the words, 'that the bones which thou hast broken may rejoice'. But his repentance is moral and spiritual, and his appeal for forgiveness is primarily to the *ḥeṣed* of God, and not to his own merits or to ritual sacrifices. So he begins:

Be gracious unto me (חָנֵּנִי), O God, according to thy *ḥeṣed*.

He also reaches the profound truth that man's right relation to God must be initiated by God Himself:

Create in me a clean heart, O God,
And renew a right spirit within me.

That is the thought of Jeremiah's 'new covenant' of God with Israel, in which God will write His *torah* on the hearts of individual Israelites;[1] it is also the thought of Ezekiel's more drastic remedy for sin:

A new heart will I give you
and a new spirit will I put within you. (xxxvi. 26)

The significant thing here is that grace and repentance are not separate abstractions; they are unified in the living experience of the penitent believer, which overcomes the sharp antithesis of holiness and sin by its transformation of both. It is this inwardness of the new relation which characterizes the higher levels of Israel's religion, and enables us to understand something of the height to which the close of the 73rd psalm reaches—the Old Testament equivalent to the close of Romans viii—or the paradox of the Shema' in Deut. vi when the impossible command to love God is made possible by the disclosure of a God whom to know is to love, since He is a Redeemer.[2] By the same inwardness, the apparent externalism of Torah-religion was transcended for the devout Jew, the Jew who learnt to say, 'Thy statutes have become my songs in the house of my pil-

---

[1] Jer. xxxi. 33.   [2] Ch. V.

grimage'.[1] Obedience and the routine which directs it and trains for it must have its essential place in every religion that outlives its early enthusiasms. But its fulfilment is reached only in the love that finds its perfect freedom in service.

The three contrasts which we have considered—Spirit and flesh, Holiness and sin, Grace and repentance—as characterizing the Old Testament interrelation of God and man thus supply a general pattern or framework of that relation, much more important and permanent than the mythological or any other external pattern. We have approached it through its salient antitheses. Professor Albright, in his most recent book,[2] remarks that 'In no religion of antiquity was there such a strong tendency to bring opposites together as in Canaanite and Phoenician belief and practice'. The religion of Israel, owing so much to these, went far beyond them, transcending their external antitheses in the unity of man's experience of Yahweh.

It is fitting that this unity of experience should be emphasized at the end, as it was at the beginning, of this chapter. The simplest act of perception in general is a unity of consciousness, although it has to reconcile the activities of two such disparate entities as body and mind. At each new level we may expect to find the same process of assimilation and unification, and not least at the level of the highest religious experience. Here, for the Israelite, nature and history both made their great contributions to the revelation of the God who controlled both. But these external contributions were assimilated in the personal response of individual faith. In this 'challenge and response'[3] we reach the innermost of unities in which, as the Hebrew phrase goes, man 'sees the face of God'.

To remember and constantly to emphasize this ultimate unity of the experience of God in its concrete and ultimately simple form for the ordinary worshipper will protect us from the peril of acquiescence in abstractions, which it is often the fate of 'revelation' to encounter. In any discussion of revelation it is easy to fix on natural phenomena and historical events which may be charged with revelatory significance, and to abstract them from the personal response of faith, though without it they would never have become data for religion. These

---

[1] Ps. cxix. 54; cf. Ch. VI.   [2] *Archaeology and the Religion of Israel*, p. 80.

[3] Represented in the reputed words of Jesus, 'He that hath ears to hear, let him hear'.

phenomena and events were not for the worshipper, as they are for the analyst of his experience, detachable from it; they belonged to it and largely constituted it. All this should be borne in mind, not only in the consideration of such contrasts as we have noted, but also in regard to the special aspects of Israelite experience with which subsequent chapters will be concerned, viz. the divine control of human personality, the moral element in religion, and such hope as was reached in the Old Testament times concerning the ultimate destiny of man.

V

HUMAN NATURE AND ITS DIVINE CONTROL

GOETHE used the metaphor of 'the roaring loom of time'[1] on which the Time-spirit weaves the garment by which God is made visible. Our aim should be to learn as much as we can of the very shape and texture of that garment, as it was woven by Hebrew hands and minds. For this is what gives the peculiar quality of the 'revelation' constituted by the Old Testament.

In the previous chapter the general relation of God and man was characterized by three salient contrasts, viz. those of Spirit and flesh, Holiness and sin, Grace and repentance. But we saw that such generalizations, however necessary and convenient for study, must be replaced by the concrete situation of the individual man at any given moment, if we are really to know his relation to God.

§ 1. THE CONSCIOUSNESS OF GOD

How are we to think of the consciousness of God in the daily life of the ordinary Israelite?[2] Perhaps the most useful line of approach to this difficult inquiry is to compare with it the normal experience of a believer to-day, measuring off the agreements and differences so far as we are able. First, we may say that both now and then the greater part of life consists of routine, without any particular thought of God in it at all. Whatever may be a man's prayers or reflections at the beginning and end of the day, the day itself for most of us is fitly described by the psalmist's words: 'Man goeth forth to his work and to his labour until the evening.'[3] Most Israelites were peasants, and their dominant interests are well set out in a psalm which has been aptly called 'The Peasant's Paradise' (cxxviii). Here we find the well-being of the loyal Israelite whom God rewards described

---

[1] *Faust*, Erster Theil, ll. 508–9:
> So schaff' ich am sausenden Webstuhl der Zeit,
> Und wirke der Gottheit lebendiges Kleid.

[2] Lord David Cecil (*Hardy the Novelist*, p. 78) has reminded us that 'It is extremely difficult to give a convincing account of people in a past age—that is why there are so few good historical novels. An imaginative world is real to us because we feel the people to be living. But the only sort of people we know intimately enough for us to be able to make a living portrait of them are the sort of people we have known ourselves.'　　　　[3] Ps. civ. 23.

as consisting primarily in two conditions—that he gather in his harvest and eat its fruit (instead of seeing it carried off by marauders), and that his wife be a fruitful vine and his sons as many as the shoots of an olive-tree. Field and family are thus his dominant interests, whilst Zion and all it means form the permanent background of life. To-day there is for us much more variety of occupation, and probably there are many to complain with Koheleth that the routine of life is no more than a treadmill, whilst the religious background, so far as it exists at all, finds very different expression. Yet, when we have allowed for these differences, there is a broad measure of agreement in the *proportions* of life. Most of it is necessarily a routine, leaving little opportunity for any direct consciousness of God.

Further, in such a routine there is equally little consciousness of any exercise of free choice; men are committed to a defined course of action and follow it more or less mechanically. But from time to time particular occasions would arise in Israel calling for personal initiative, such as the barter of a crop, the bride-price of a daughter, the valiant defence of the homestead against robbers. Whilst the greater part of life is controlled by its circumstances, there is, as there was, a smaller part of it in which the ordinary man is conscious of freedom to choose and act and of the necessity for this. The progress of civilization tends to lessen this element, and to protect men from the unexpected, at least in times of peace. The religious man, then or now, might seek for guidance as to his choice and action, but in general he would accept responsibility for it as his own, and distinguish it from any act of God.

But in all lives, whether ancient or modern, there will be a third and very varied group of events which are neither colourless, like the routine of life, nor colourful with the intimate exercise of a man's own will-power on great or small affairs. This third group consists of the events which are both unusual, and also beyond man's apparent control. They range widely, from national calamities, through individual crises of fortune, down to the trivial happenings which can be transformed into signs and omens of the activity of God. It is in this group that the chief differences between the ancient and the modern man are likely to emerge, for the premisses from which the two start are different.

(*a*) As an example of national calamities, we may take that series of them which Amos reviews.[1] Famine, drought, failure of crops, pestilence and defeat in battle, earthquake—all these, which we should explain from 'natural' causes, are directly explained by the prophet as divine warnings and preliminary judgements. Even when, on other occasions, some kind of secondary causation is recognized, the process as a whole goes back to God or is controlled by Him, and the nature of the causation is often quite differently conceived. Thus a divine oracle discloses that three years of famine in David's time are due to the failure to carry out blood-vengeance against the house of Saul; the famine does not cease until seven of Saul's descendants are hung up before Yahweh.[2] Or again, Yahweh is said to have incited David to take a census;[3] this breach of a widely occurrent taboo (quite apart from its divine instigation in this instance) calls for a penalty, and the prophet Gad offers to David the choice from seven years of famine, three months of defeat, and three days of pestilence. He chooses the last, not because of its brevity, but because it is felt to be more directly than the others the act of God: 'Let us fall now into the hand of Yahweh ... and let me not fall into the hand of man' (verse 14). Thus the pestilence directly caused by the hand of Yahweh vindicates the broken taboo. This was felt to be necessary in the very nature of things, even though Yahweh Himself in His anger against Israel had moved David to take the census.[4] Such a view of Yahweh's activity naturally became repugnant after the teaching of the great prophets had been assimilated, and so we find the Chronicler many centuries later retelling the old story with Satan as the instigator instead of Yahweh.[5]

(b) It is significant that both these examples of Yahweh's corporate dealings with Israel should be drawn from the time of the early monarchy, whilst for the best illustration of the divine control of individual life we have to turn to a much later stage in the religion of Israel. Psalm xci is one of the most

---

[1] iv. 6–11. [2] 2 Sam. xxi. 1–14. [3] 2 Sam. xxiv.

[4] We may compare the similar objectivity in dealing with Jonathan's breach of a taboo. The fact of Jonathan's ignorance of it, and that of Yahweh's causation of it, do not alter the necessity that the thing done must be undone. The breach of the taboo is part of the *modus operandi* by which Yahweh is conceived to carry out His will. Cf. Ezek. xx. 25 f.: 'I gave them statutes that were not good ... that I might destroy them'; also xiv. 11.

[5] 1 Chron. xxi. 1. Satan has here become a proper name, without the article, whereas in Zech. iii. 1 and Job i. 6 ff. he is still a recognized official in Yahweh's service ('the Adversary', with the article).

striking expressions of faith in particular providence within the
general scheme of Yahweh's control of all actions and history.
In this psalm a vigorous series of metaphors describes both the
perils and the deliverances in concrete detail. The perils arise
from the plotting or attack of men, from the pestilence that
spreads at night, or the sunstroke that strikes at noon, from the
dangers of battle; or they may come from the rough path to be
trodden and the wild beasts to be encountered on it. But, no
matter what the peril is, trust in Yahweh will remove anxiety,
ward off particular 'strokes' or occasions of injury, ensure His
presence when distress does come. The psalm declares that this
divine aid is due to a ministry of angels, those usually invisible
servants of Yahweh who replace our 'laws of nature':

> He shall give His angels charge over thee,
> To keep thee in all thy ways. (verse 11.)

This interpretation of the *modus operandi* of divine providence
should be taken quite seriously and literally, and not treated as
the poetical motto for a pious Scripture text-card. We may
compare Ps. ciii. 20, 21:

> Bless Yahweh, ye angels of His,
> Ye heroes fulfilling His word . . .
> Ye servants of His, doing His will.

The pre-exilic vision granted to Elisha's servant at his master's
prayer was of horses and chariots of fire, and they were just as
real to the two men as were the Syrian horses and chariots.
The post-exilic story of Tobit illustrates very attractively faith
in divine guidance through an angel, who, if Raphael will for-
give the comparison, is as real a figure in the story as Tobit's
dog.[1] Whilst the earlier prophets and some of the psalmists
prefer to speak more directly of God, the popular religion took
kindly to a doctrine of angels, and we see its copious development in apocalyptic.[2] There can be little doubt that if we had
asked the ordinary Israelite to explain anything out of the way
that had happened to him as from God, he would have thought
of an angelic mediator of the divine command.[3] As Moore sums
up the attitude at the end of the Old Testament period,[4] 'God's
will in the world was executed by a multitude of such deputies.

---

[1] Tobit v. 4 ff., 16, xi. 4.   [2] Gunkel, *Die Psalmen*, p. 405.
[3] Cf. the interpreting angel of Job xxxiii. 23.
[4] *Judaism*, i. 403; cf. Gray, *E.Bi.*, s.v. 'Angel'.

Not only is his revelation communicated through them, not only are they his instruments in providence and history, but the realm of nature is administered by them.' Remote as this may seem from our own outlook, it is useful to remember that where Tennyson regarded the flower in the crannied wall as the epitome of the world's mystery, John Henry Newman went farther, and asks us what our thought would be, if when examining some flower we thought below us in the scale of existence, we were suddenly to discover that we were in the presence of some wondrous being whose robe it was.[1]

(c) We have been considering those corporate or individual events which broke into the daily routine, yet were not due to the conscious volition of man. Besides these more noticeable happenings, however, there were others, often of a quite ordinary or trivial kind in themselves, which were capable of some deeper reference or meaning. These played a great part in the life of the Hebrews, as of the peoples of antiquity in general, and have given rise, for example, to much of the science and art of divination which will call for later and fuller notice. Here it will be sufficient to examine the Hebrew word for 'chance', and to see how far the idea of 'chance' can properly be said to enter into the Hebrew horizon. The noun is *miḳreh* (מקרה), which denotes a happening or event. The corresponding verb *ḳarah* (קרה) or *ḳara'* (קרא) expresses an encounter or meeting, as when Amalek met Israel by the way with hostility,[2] or (in the Siloam inscription) when the two ends of a tunnel were successfully joined by the excavators.[3] Yahweh 'met' with Israel as represented by Moses,[4] and with Balaam to impart His oracles.[5] The verb is accordingly used of the happening of past or future events as that which 'meets' man.[6] That which meets man in this way can be good or evil,[7] and such 'happenings' as mere events may be under man's control to some extent.[8] The

---

[1] *Apologia*, p. 28; Oxford ed. of 1913, p. 129. I recall an able philosophical thinker breaking off a long discussion of human personality with the remark, 'For all we know, there may be an angel in each of us seeking self-expression.'

[2] Deut. xxv. 18. The Arabic cognate قرى means 'receive a guest' (Kazimirski, iii. 926).

[3] The inscription will be found in G. A. Cooke, *North Semitic Inscriptions*, p. 15; *E.Bi.* i, c. 883; S. R. Driver, *Hebrew Text of the Books of Samuel*[2], p. ix (facsimile).

[4] Exod. iii. 18.   [5] Num. xxiii. 3, 4, 15 f.

[6] Esther iv. 7, vi. 13; Gen. xlii. 29; Isa. xli. 22; Dan. x. 14; Num. xi. 23.

[7] Gen. xxiv. 12, xliv. 29.

[8] As Saul promises to the 'witch of Endor' (1 Sam. xxviii. 10).

young Amalekite who brought to David the news of the death
of Saul and Jonathan reported that he 'happened' to be on
Mt. Gilboa.[1] Sheba happens to be on the spot when there was
opportunity to provoke a revolt,[2] as Absalom happened to fall
in with David's servants in the wood, the chance encounter
leading to his death at the hand of Joab.[3] A man may happen
to find a bird's nest.[4] The element of the unexpected in such
happenings may, of course, be wholly from the human standpoint, as when Moses reports to Pharaoh that Yahweh has 'met'
Israel, the reference being to the occasion of the burning bush.[5]
Here the happening is from Yahweh's standpoint part of a
deliberate and far-reaching purpose. This may be true of any
happening. So when Jacob has brought his father's venison
with such remarkable speed, he says, 'Yahweh thy God made it
to happen before me'.[6] This reminds us that the element of
chance is only provisional, since the event could always be
referred back to Yahweh's control. Thus there will be events
of which it is uncertain whether they are to be ascribed to
'chance' or 'intention'. When the suspicious Saul notices the
absence of David from his accustomed place at the king's table,[7]
he at first thinks nothing of it; David is kept away by a taboo,
so that from the king's standpoint his absence may be traced to
chance, concealing no further intention. But the explanation
will not serve for David's absence on the next day also. The
'happening' now acquires sinister meaning and suggests disloyalty. Both Jacob's alleged hunting and David's alleged
family duty (as put forward by Jonathan on the second day)
remind us of the neutrality of the event as a mere 'happening',
until it is traced back to some divine or human intention. Such
neutrality means that the event in question is allowed to fall
into the routine of life, and really belongs to that larger portion
of life which has no significance for man's consciousness of God.
It is not the intrinsic quality of the event which lifts it out of
this, but its congruity with the pattern of human or divine

---

[1] 2 Sam. i. 6; 'it was by pure chance that I was . . .' The fact that his report
contradicts 1 Sam. xxxi. 4 ff., and that he may be lying, does not of course affect
the value of the example of usage.   [2] 2 Sam. xx. 1 (ḳara', Niph.).
   [3] 2 Sam. xviii. 9 ff.   [4] Deut. xxii. 6.
   [5] Exod. v. 3, cf. iii. 18 (both J): 'in a sudden, unexpected way' (Driver).
   [6] Gen. xxvii. 20. The A.V. 'brought it to me' is a better translation than the
R.V. 'sent me good speed', which is a paraphrase obscuring the exact point.
   [7] 1 Sam. xx. 24 ff.

purpose. Thus Koheleth, for whom life is largely a grey neutrality, can deny that there is any difference between the *miḳreh* that befalls wise and foolish, righteous and guilty, man and beast;[1] time and chance happen to all.[2] It is doubtful therefore whether we ought to say, with Eichrodt,[3] that Israel's faith in providence derived its unshakable strength and unique intensity from the grounding of all events without exception in the activity of God. We should rather say that any event *could* be so grounded, but that the average Israelite, like ourselves, probably left a good deal of his life out of any conscious relation to God. On the other hand, he was far readier than most of us would be to see a particular providence in any happening, if its context suggested this. Our inquiry therefore has brought us to a similar position in regard to the events of life as we reached in regard to the revelation of God through Nature. Here, as there, we cannot eliminate the subjective side of the religious fact; the unit of revelation is not the event but the interpreted event.

§ 2. The Constitution of Human Personality

So far we have been thinking of the external environment of man's life and of his relation to external events. It is necessary to say something also of the constitution of human personality as the Hebrew conceived it. This is important for our purpose because both inspiration and revelation are obviously conditioned by the way in which human nature is thought to be accessible to God. We are not yet concerned with the peculiar phenomena of the prophetic consciousness, or with other forms of divine oracle; our immediate task is to notice those psychological features which facilitate these more specialized developments.

(a) First of all, the Hebrew conception of personality helped to make it from birth to death directly dependent on God. The conception was concrete and religious, not metaphysical and abstract. Man comes into being through the creative activity of God, and in the discussion of 'God and Nature' we saw how that creative work was conceived, whether in the myth of Gen. ii or in the scattered references to birth and in the birth-stories of the Old Testament. Here it is important to get rid of the Greek ideas about the soul which are so often read into the quite

---

[1] ii. 14, 15, iii. 19, ix. 2, 3.

[2] ix. 11; here the word is *pegaʻ* (פֶּגַע), a synonym of *miḳreh* with verb from its root (יקרה).   [3] Op. cit. ii, p. 92.

different Hebrew conception. The Hebrew conceived man as
an animated body and not as an incarnate soul. This may be
seen from the story of the creation of the first man. Yahweh
blows into man's nostrils 'living breath' to animate the body
which He has already made.[1] The result is that man becomes
'a living being'. It is quite misleading to translate the phrase
nephesh ḥayyah (נֶפֶשׁ חַיָּה) by 'a living soul', as our English
versions do, so putting the emphasis where a Greek, but not a
Hebrew, would have done. *Nephesh* is not a spiritual entity
which enters the body at birth and leaves it as such at death;
it is simply a principle of life which makes the body effective,
and the body is the real basis of personality. As Gen. iii. 19
shows, man is essentially *'aphar* (עֲפַר), dust, and at death
becomes dust again.[2] *Nephesh* is never used in the Old Testament of a disembodied soul or spirit; the inhabitants of Sheol
are never there called 'souls'.[3] In fact, the very word *nephesh*,
in view of the Accadian *napištu*, seems originally to have meant
'throat',[4] and was extended to denote the breath as passing
through the throat, the principle of life. The Old Testament
conception of man, therefore, regards him as coming into
existence and as continuing to exist, by the grace of God, and
as ceasing to be in any real sense at death; clearly this conception emphasizes man's dependence on God as his creator and
upholder, and gives him no independence over against God,
such as a Greek view of *psyche* might suggest.[5]

(b) A second important aspect of Hebrew psychology affecting the relation of God and man is that which may be conveniently designated 'corporate personality'.[6] By this is meant
the idea of a close relation, and for some purposes, an identity
of the individual and the group to which he belongs. This
principle is, of course, familiar in Hebrew law, as when a whole
family is destroyed for the fault of one of its members,[7] or in

---

[1] Cf. Isa. ii. 22, where the animating principle is simply 'breath' (נְשָׁמָה) as
equivalent to נפש, and there is no reference to רוח.
[2] This is not brought out adequately by Pedersen, op. cit., pp. 102 ff., whose
discussion of 'soul' dwells rather on the more general use of *nephesh* as a centre of
consciousness. For fuller details see my essay on 'Hebrew Psychology' in *The
People and the Book* (ed. Peake).   [3] See below, pp. 92 ff., 'Human Destiny'.
[4] L. Durr, in *ZAW*, 1925, pp. 262 ff.
[5] *Ruach*, the later synonym of *nephesh*, is considered in § 3 of this chapter.
[6] See my essay, 'The Hebrew Conception of Corporate Personality', in *Werden
und Wesen des Alten Testaments* (BZAW, lxvi).
[7] e.g. Joshua vii. 24.

the widespread practice of blood-vengeance, when the penalty for homicide by one member of a group is exacted from some other member of it.[1] But it also runs through the whole of the life and religion of Israel, even though not always so obvious. Yahweh is described as 'visiting the sins of the fathers upon the children',[2] though Hebrew law, by the seventh century, had reached the point of decreeing that 'the fathers shall not be put to death for the children, neither shall the children be put to death for the fathers: every man shall be put to death for his own sin'.[3] Morality is sometimes ahead of religion, as it is usually ahead of law. This moral advance was undoubtedly due to prophetic teaching, Jeremiah being its pioneer. But even after the assertion by him and by Ezekiel of an individual relation between God and the Israelite, against the popular saying, 'The fathers have eaten sour grapes and the children's teeth are set on edge',[4] the idea of a corporate relation remains important and operative. We must not, as is often done, sharpen the new emphasis into an antithesis. The new covenant of Jeremiah, though individualistic in method, is still a covenant 'with the house of Israel',[5] and Ezekiel, whilst strongly individualizing retribution, describes it as a judgement on 'the house of Israel'.[6] The truth is that Israel's relation to God was throughout corporate, though it progressively developed the sense of a more individual relation to Him, within and through the group. That is why it is possible for a psalm of obviously individual experience to be consciously representative of Israel as a whole, and to pass easily backwards and forwards from the singular to the plural, or again for the conception of Israel to be so impressively individualized as in Isa. liii, so that it has often been taken to refer to a single Israelite. This fluidity or elasticity of reference is a psychological fact affecting the whole relation of God and man, and we shall have to return to it in the discussion of morality and religion.

(c) We have seen that the body, not the soul, affords the true approach to the Hebrew conception of personality. That body itself is regarded by the Hebrew very differently from our modern idea of a unified organism under the central control of the brain and nervous system. The Hebrew knew nothing of their function; to him the brain was the 'marrow' of the

---

[1] 2 Kings ix. 26. [2] Exod. xx. 5. [3] Deut. xxiv. 16.
[4] Jer. xxxi. 29; Ezek. xviii. 2. [5] Jer. xxxi. 33. [6] Ezek. xviii. 30.

head.[1] Nor did he know, any more than antiquity in general, of the circulation of the blood, another centralizing fact. He saw the body as a congeries of separate organs, central and peripheral, each with its own set of attributes and functions, which were psychical and ethical as well as physical. Not only did the heart and liver, the kidneys and the bowels, possess a quasi-consciousness of their own, but so also did the eye, ear, tongue, hand, and foot. This is why Elisha, when restoring to life the Shunammite's child, lies upon him, putting his mouth to the child's mouth, his eyes to the child's eyes, his hands to the child's hands.[2] When Job asks (vi. 30):

> Is there perversity in my tongue?
> Does not my palate discern calamities?

or again (xii. 11):

> Doth not the ear try words
> Even as the palate tasteth its meat?

or says of the poor whom he has helped (xxix. 11):

> When the ear heard me, then it blessed me;
> And when the eye saw me, it gave witness unto me,

he is not speaking in conscious metaphor; he is speaking literally in terms of the 'diffused consciousness' of Hebrew psychology. This is the explanation of the frequent references to flesh and bones as conscious. A psalmist can say, not only

> My *nephesh* thirsteth for thee,

but also

> My flesh longeth for thee; (lxiii. 1)

and not only

> My *nephesh* shall rejoice in Yahweh,

but also

> All my bones shall say,
> Yahweh, who is like thee? (xxxv. 9, 10.)

Of course, the contributions of these particular parts of the body were more or less unified in consciousness, just as the United States of America can unify its State law with federal government. Of this unification the chief organ was supposed to be

---

[1] מוֹחַ (Job xxi. 24 מֹחַ עַצְמוֹתָיו יְשֻׁקֶּה) the marrow of the bones occurs in post-Biblical Hebrew for 'brain' (Levy, *Neuheb. und Chald. Wörterbuch*, s.v.), so مُخّ, مُخَّة.

[2] 2 Kings iv. 34.

the heart alongside of the *nephesh* as the principle of life. But usage made the heart specially the seat of intelligence and volition, whilst *nephesh* predominantly centralized the emotional states, of which kidneys and bowels were the physical seats. It is evident that this distribution of psychical function made human personality much more accessible to outside influence whether good or evil. This is well brought out by an illuminating Midrash:[1]

'Man has two hundred and forty-eight limbs, and the ear is but one of them; yet even though his whole body be stained with transgressions, so long as his ear hearkens, the whole body is vivified.'

Or we may compare 2 Baruch lxxxiii. 3:

'He will assuredly examine the secret thoughts of that which is laid up in the secret chambers of all the members of man.'

Such sayings as these obviously spring from a psychology very different from our own to-day. The conception of a new heart would be taken by them much more literally than by us. God could be more easily conceived as taking possession of a particular organ in man, with or without his concurrence. Thus God puts a lying spirit in the mouths of Ahab's prophets,[2] whilst Isaiah's mouth was 'cauterized' of its uncleanness that it might speak holy things.[3] Hebrew law contemplates the case of a homicide in which the slayer does not lie in wait (i.e. has no prior intention to kill), but God brings the opportunity *to his hand*,[4] i.e. the hand is able to work out its impulse, apart from the man's heart. In this connexion we have the striking phrase, 'according to the God of my hand',[5] used by Laban in asserting his power to do hurt to his fugitive son-in-law, which apparently suggests an invasion of the hand by the demon of anger.

Such departmental accessibility, as we may term it, was a widespread conception in the ancient world, and was usually accompanied by belief in invasive spirits or demons. Frequent

---

[1] *Midrash Rabbah* on Exod. xxvii. 9.
[2] 1 Kings xxii. 23.   [3] Isa. vi.
[4] Exod. xxi. 13, וַאֲשֶׁר לֹא צָדָה וְהָאֱלֹהִים אִנָּה לְיָדוֹ. Cf. Hempel, *Gott und Mensch*, p. 54, n. 5. This is an interesting example of the way in which Hebrew psychology expresses what we might call an uncontrollable or instinctive impulse; it was the work of part of the man, not of his conscious volition.

[5] *le'el yadi* (יֶשׁ־לְאֵל יָדִי לַעֲשׂוֹת עִמָּכֶם רָע) Gen. xxxi. 29; cf. Prov. iii. 27; Mic. ii. 1; Deut. xxviii. 32. Cf. C. Brockelmann, in *ZAW*, xxvi. 29 ff. (1906), who cites some interesting ethnic parallels to this usage.

examples of this belief occur in the literatures of Babylonia and
Assyria, Egypt and Arabia, and we shall have to return to it
when we come to the nature of prophetic inspiration. We may
be sure that this belief in invasive spirits entered largely into
the popular religion of Israel, as is stated in the 'Song of Moses':
'they sacrificed unto demons, which were no God'.[1] But the
increasingly strong emphasis on Yahweh alone in the higher
religion has allowed few traces of this popular demonology to
remain in the Old Testament.[2] Phenomena which were once
referred to demonic influence, such as the sudden accession of
strength to Samson,[3] or the melancholia of Saul,[4] are now
ascribed to the Spirit of Yahweh, or to a spirit of, or from,
Elohim. The vision of Micah ben Imlah, to which reference
has just been made,[5] illustrates the transition; the once independent 'spirit of lies' is brought into the service of Yahweh to
lead Ahab through his prophets into destruction.[6]

§ 3. THE SPIRIT OF GOD

The most important of the agents or instruments by which
God controls man is undoubtedly the Spirit of God, and even
a rapid statistical survey of the use of the term 'Spirit' will
suggest some striking features of this conception.[7] The term
ruach (רוח) occurs 378 times in all, and in 131 of these (rather
more than a third) spread throughout the whole period of the
Old Testament it denotes 'wind', whether in a literal or figurative sense. In about the same number of instances (134) it
denotes supernatural influences acting on man (very rarely on
inanimate objects). The remainder of the examples (less than
a third) are divided between those in which the term denotes
the principle of life, or of its particular energies in man (39) and
those in which it refers to the normal or permanent psychical
life of man (74). The conclusions which we may draw from
detailed study of the term are as follows:

[1] Deut. xxxii. 17 (*shedim*, שֵׁדִים), cf. Ps. cvi. 37.
[2] e.g. *'aza'zel*, עֲזָאזֵל: Lev. xvi. 8 ff.; *lilith*, לִילִית, Isa. xxxiv. 14; see further
G. A. Barton, art. 'Demons and Spirits (Hebrew)' in *ERE*, iv. 594–601.
[3] Judges xiv. 6.   [4] 1 Sam. xvi. 14.   [5] 1 Kings xxii. 21 ff.
[6] Cf. the original conception of the Satan. Outside the realm of life and light,
there was another world of death and darkness: 'Mythische Motive verbinden
sich unlösbar mit der persönlichen Leidenserfahrung' (Hempel, *Gott und Mensch*,
p. 200).
[7] Cf. *The Christian Doctrine of Man*, pp. 18 ff.

(1) The original meaning was the physical one of 'wind', but often the wind regarded as exhibiting superhuman power. The wind of the desert would be one of the most conspicuous phenomena in shaping the thought and speech of the nomad as impressively as it shaped his sand-dunes.

(2) It was natural, therefore, to ascribe exceptional displays of power in man, in view of his accessibility to external influence, to a wind-like power (*ruach*), especially since the panting or deep breathing of a man under strong emotion linked itself with the blowing of the wind.

(3) The most striking fact that emerges from a statistical survey of the literature, when this is critically dated in its historical succession, is that in no pre-exilic instance (where the text is beyond suspicion) do we find *ruach* used of human breath or with psychical predicates. It is only from the exile onwards that the term becomes acclimatized as a *normal* constituent of human nature, and as a higher synonym of *nephesh*.[1]

The importance of the last-named result is that it disposes of any 'trichotomy' of body, soul, and spirit, as representing the Hebrew view of man. We have already seen that the real basis of personality is the body, animated by the *nephesh* during life. We now see that the exilic and post-exilic use of *ruach* simply parallels this, without implying any third constituent in human nature. So we find that the Priestly Code employs *ruach ḥayyim*[2] where the Yahwist had said *nishmath ḥayyim*.[3] It was natural, therefore, for the post-exilic Book of Job to use *ruach* and *nᵉshamah* (breath) in parallelism:

> There is a spirit in man,
> And the breath of the Almighty gives them understanding.
> (xxxii. 8)

But at an earlier period there was no *ruach* in man in any such psychical sense as this. So far as the term was used of man, it

---

[1] This fact was brought out by the writer in 1902, and first published in 1909 (*Mansfield College Essays*, p. 271), as again in *The Christian Doctrine of Man* (1911), p. 18. It was also established by an independent investigation carried out by E. D. Burton, in a series of articles from 1913, collected and published as *Spirit, Soul and Flesh* (Chicago, 1918).

[2] Gen. vi. 17, vii. 15; Charles (*E.Bi.* ii. 1342) is able to show a 'trichotomy' only by drawing his evidence from synonyms separated by four centuries. This mistake is corrected only in part in his *Eschatology*, p. 37. His whole account of Hebrew psychology is misleading (pp. 42 ff.). [3] Gen. ii. 7.

denoted life-energy in general which could be quickened by some new accession of *ruach*-energy from God. When *ruach*, from the exile onwards, had become 'naturalized' in human nature as a synonym of *nephesh* or *leb* (heart), it still suggested this reference to the continued use of *ruach* for some supernatural influence, and so supplied a point of contact between man and God. The importance of this becomes apparent in the New Testament, where Pauline anthropology partly turns on the identity of the permanent *pneuma* in man with the Christ-*pneuma*, the indwelling Spirit of God underlying the new creation.[1]

In the Old Testament we can see the importance of the conception of the Spirit in the reference to what may be called theologically 'pre-venient grace' in Psalm cxxxix. 7:

> Whither shall I go from thy Spirit?
> Or whither shall I flee from thy presence,

where the parallelism shows us that in effect the Spirit means the active presence of God. So we can see what theologians call *gratia infusa* suggested by Ps. li. 10, 11:

> Renew a right spirit within me. . . .
> Take not thy holy Spirit from me.

On such inner activity of the Spirit of God the prophets set their highest hopes for the accomplishment of what their own warnings had failed to do: this is explicit in Ezekiel (xxxvi. 26, 27):

'A new heart will I give you and a new spirit will I put within you, and I will take away the heart of stone out of your flesh, and I will give you a heart of flesh, and I will put my spirit within you, and cause you to walk in my statutes.'

This raises the further question for us, though apparently not for Israel, how such divine control or regeneration could still leave room for the freedom of moral responsibility. Perhaps the answer, so far as an answer is possible in such a realm, would be that the freedom of man, however affected by external influence, is still conceived as really existing and being somehow exercised within the protection of the divine control, just as when the prophet Hosea pictures Yahweh as a father teaching His child to walk, and carrying it on His arms when it is too

---

[1] Further details in *Mansfield College Essays*, 'Hebrew Psychology in relation to Pauline Anthropology', or in *The Christian Doctrine of Man*, pp. 109 ff.

tired to go farther.[1] The activity of the Spirit did not replace, but was rather thrown around the spirit of man. Thus there was no inconsistency to the Hebrew in saying 'Pharaoh hardened his heart' and in accepting Yahweh's word, 'I have hardened his heart'.[2] These were but different aspects, smaller and larger, of the same event, contributory factors in one sense, yet so that the larger, the divine, included the smaller, the human. Even the real freedom thus left to man to rebel against God's purpose could be made by Him to subserve it, so that the wrath of man could praise Him.[3] By some inherent flaw the clay might mar itself in the hand of the potter, but the potter could make even the marred clay to serve his purpose—and man from the beginning was clay in the hand of God.[4]

[1] Hos. xi. 1 ff.   [2] Exod. ix. 34, x. 1.
[3] Ps. lxxvi. 10 (11), cf. Prov. xvi. 4. Even if the text be doubtful, its application as translated above is beyond question (cf. Gen. xlv. 5 ff.).
[4] Jer. xviii. 4.

VI

THE RELATION OF MORALITY AND RELIGION

'MORALITY', as its etymology implies,[1] originates historically in the customs and manners of a society. 'Religion', of much more obscure etymology,[2] may have denoted 'binding custom' in relation to superhuman powers. Robertson Smith[3] regards religion as 'a series of acts and observances, the correct performance of which was necessary or desirable to secure the favour of the gods or to avert their anger', and argues that a man's religion 'was simply one side of the general scheme of conduct prescribed for him by his position as a member of society'. The anthropologist Westermarck, in his chapters devoted to 'Gods as guardians of morality',[4] emphasizes the place of a belief in magical forces within religion, and warns us against the assumption that from the beginning the gods were always concerned with human morality: 'It is a quality attributed to certain deities only, and as it seems, in most cases slowly acquired' (p. 663). Dr. Marett[5] considers that 'religion consecrates the Good so far as it is embodied in the rule of life imparted by each generation to the next'. Each of these typical approaches through ritual, magic, and tradition to the relation between morality and religion is open to some criticism and is obviously incomplete, but the evidence would warrant us in saying that though morality and religion originally had common ground in the customs of a social group, they relate to different realms, the seen and the unseen, the human and the super-human, and they have had separate histories. The most familiar example of the separation is afforded by the morality and religion of Greece. It was in fact the immoral character of the Olympic deities which was one of the causes of their downfall. Professor Gilbert Murray, after showing the advance made by this stage of Greek religion over the primitive beliefs which preceded it, goes on to say:[6] 'To make the elements of a nature-religion human is inevitably to make them vicious. . . . The

---

[1] *Mōres*, by which Cicero (*De Fato*, ad init.) renders ἦθος (with the same meaning of customs, manners), from which comes our 'ethics', the science of morals.

[2] *religare*, bind? (Lewis and Short).

[3] *The Religion of the Semites*[3], pp. 28, 30.

[4] *The Origin and Development of the Moral Ideas*, vol. ii, pp. 663 ff.

[5] *ERE*, v. 429.   [6] *Five Stages of Greek Religion* (ed. of 1935), pp. 67–8, 69.

unfortunate Olympians, whose system really aimed at purer morals and condemned polygamy and polyandry, are left with a crowd of consorts that would put Solomon to shame.' Western civilization has come to take for granted the interfusion of morality and religion, and to it an immoral God would be a contradiction in terms, and an immoral worshipper a hypocrite. Such assumptions are historically traceable to the teaching of the Christian faith, itself drawing on the higher religion of Israel. It was the prophetic religion that for the first time in history brought morality and religion together in a unique way, which distinguishes this religion from all others not dependent upon it. The uniqueness is not in the mere interfusion, for that has proceeded in some degree wherever religion had reached higher levels and passed beyond nature-worship. The uniqueness is in the integration of both into a new unity as when hydrogen and oxygen combine to produce water. This uniqueness can be suitably approached through the implicates of an historical revelation.

§ 1. THE IMPLICATES OF AN HISTORICAL REVELATION

There are only three religions which proclaim an historical revelation, such as we find in the Old Testament, and the other two are directly dependent upon this, and would lose much of their essential content without it. Now, when we think out what an historical revelation means, (a) the very fact that God makes use of a history to reveal Himself implies that the revelation will necessarily include both morality and religion. These are complementary functions, whatever their precise relation, functions of the social group of which the history is a record. This, of course, is as true of Christianity and Islam as of the prophetic religion of Israel. All three are ethical religions because they appeal to an historical revelation. They envisage a definite social group, with its moral customs and laws, more or less incorporated into the religion. Examples of their characteristic emphases are the Israelite demand for social justice, the Christian acceptance of suffering in the spirit of the Cross, the Muslim insistence on almsgiving, to meet particular social needs. Each of these religious duties is what it is because the religion which incorporates them was born in a particular social environment, at a particular point of its history. The religion is moral because it is historical.

(b) Further, these three are the three monotheistic religions; they agree that there is but one God, and that to Him alone belongs the worship of all mankind. The universalism which is implicit in morality of the fullest and freest kind is reinforced or elicited by the universalistic claims of monotheism. If there be but one God and Father of all, then all are under common obligations to each other within the human family, and in principle, if not in practice, the limits of class and nationality are already transcended. This step, indeed, was the great step forward taken by the eighth-century prophets of Israel. As Buchanan Gray puts it,[1] 'It is the prophets who first explicitly teach that the moral is the fundamental element in the personality of Jehovah, and that the guiding principle of His activity is righteousness, and is not the interests of a single people.' Of course, this does not mean that the eighth-century prophets invented the morality, or that they were the first to see moral elements in the divine personality. But they were the first to make explicit the truth that the worship of one God logically requires one moral relation to all men,[2] and that this is the intimate concern of Yahweh. Principal Elmslie is justified in claiming that 'it is only when the Deity is conceived monotheistically and as transcendent perfection that religion can profoundly influence ethics'.[3] That condition was achieved for the first time in the prophetic religion of Israel.[4]

(c) A third characteristic of these three religions also serves to explain the close interrelation of morality and religion which (with important differences) they all exhibit. They are not only historical and monotheistic, but are also to be traced to the will of a personal founder, Moses, Jesus, Muhammad, and bear the imprint of that will in their content. This is seen both in the conceptions of God which they entertain and in the moral demands which they make in His name upon men. Nor is it accidental to this personal origin that in all three the volitional emphasis is strongly marked throughout. They all conceive the purpose of God as the ruling fact of the history, and the duty of man as obedience to a divine command, rather than (as in the Greek emphasis) the achievement of a human ideal. This

[1] *The Divine Discipline of Israel*, p. 22.
[2] As in the moral standards applied by Amos to the surrounding peoples, c. 1.
[3] *Record and Revelation*, p. 280.
[4] On the limitations of 'neighbour' in Lev. xix. 18, and of 'stranger' in xxiv. 22, see Gray, op. cit., pp. 47, 48.

volitional emphasis, therefore, is a psychological factor that
helps to bring morality into the foreground of religion, since the
conduct of the will is the very basis of morals. Virtue, therefore,
is not, as with the Greeks, knowledge to be taught, but action
in which God is obeyed. It is, in the Hebrew phrase, a 'walking
with God',[1] in which moral obedience becomes the supreme
act of worship. The parable of the house built on the rock
of obedience[2] faithfully represents the emphasis of the Old
Testament.

Thus we have found that an historical revelation seems
necessarily to imply the inclusion of both morality and religion
within its content. The closeness of their actual relation in each
of the three connected religions which claim to offer an historical revelation is impressive. It is important, for it suggests the
right approach to the uniqueness of the Biblical revelation,
which we shall have to follow under our next main topic, viz.
'God and History'. That uniqueness consists, so far as the Old
Testament is concerned, in a remarkable integration of morality
and religion, whilst it is open to the Christian to claim that the
Incarnation itself, on its historical side, is an extension of the
same principle, the truth being presented as the life. The *form*
of a religion never fully and adequately explains its actual content, but, on the other hand, form and content can never be
wholly divorced; they develop together in mutual interaction
and organic life. Thus we are justified in claiming that a revelation of God in history will inevitably tend to bring morality and
religion into the closest unity, when both have freedom to
develop their essential natures into their highest forms and their
richest contents.

§ 2. THE SOCIAL EVOLUTION OF MORALITY

(*a*) The close interrelation of morality and religion is also promoted by that feature of the life of Israel which has already been
noticed on its psychological side, viz. the corporate emphasis.[3]
This has also important consequences for morality and religion
and for the absorption of the morality into the religion. The
primary unit for the religion is the whole Israel, not the
individual Israelite; yet the moral relation of Israelites to one
another within the group decisively affects the relation of the

---

[1] Gen. v. 22, 24, vi. 9; Mic. vi. 8; Mal. ii. 6.
[2] Matt. vii. 24 ff.; Luke vi 47 ff.   [3] See above, pp. 70 f.

group as a whole to Yahweh. The treatment of the group rather
than the individual as the unit is, of course, not peculiar to
Israel. In a course of lectures given in Oxford University,
which at first it was intended to call 'The Discovery of the
Individual',[1] the primacy of the corporate idea over the individualistic was shown for primitive society, and for Greece,
China, and India, as well as for Israel. The Old Testament is
constantly reminding us of it by its references to Israel as a unit.
Thus Amos represents God as speaking of 'the whole family
which I brought up out of the land of Egypt' (iii. 1), and
Deutero-Isaiah repeatedly speaks of Israel as 'the servant' rather
than as the 'servants' of Yahweh;[2] Zechariah describes the
representatives of Israel as asking about the observance of fasts
in such terms as these: 'Should I weep in the fifth month,
separating myself, as I have done these many years?' (vii. 3).
The messengers of Israel say to Sihon, king of the Amorites,
'Let *me* pass through thy land; *we* will not turn aside'.[3] Neither
in morality nor in religion are such references a figure of speech;
there is a sense of real unity which underlies both and colours
the conception of both. We have already seen its operation in
the legal treatment of the family as unit; it is also expressed
in the words of Abigail to David, 'the life of my lord shall be
bound in the bundle of the living, with Yahweh thy God' (that
is, under His protection).[4] It underlies the apparent individualism of the piety of the psalmists, whose prayers and praises so
easily pass from the singular to the plural, or from the plural
to the singular. In the corresponding approach of Yahweh to
Israel, the corporate conception is brought out in the series of
covenants which will be discussed when we come to the 'election' of Israel, covenants indeed made through individuals,
whether Abraham, Noah, or Moses, but with them as representatives of the whole group. Just as Eichrodt can plausibly
bring the whole theology of the Old Testament under the
conception of a covenant with Israel, so Hempel sets in the
forefront of his discussion of Old Testament ethics [5] this collec-
tiveness of Israel's moral consciousness. Morality and religion

---

[1] Published under the title, *The Individual in East and West* (ed. by E. R. Hughes),
1937.
[2] In Isa. xliii. 10, the singular 'servant' parallels the plural, 'witnesses'.
[3] Num. xxi. 22; see further BZAW lxvi, already cited.
[4] Joshua vii. 24, 25; Deut. xxv. 5 ff.; 1 Sam. xxv. 29.
[5] *Das Ethos des Alten Testaments*, 1938.

are therefore drawn the more closely together because they are dominated by a common conception of the group as primary, a conception which is by no means destroyed for either when in course of time the individual relation to Yahweh becomes more prominent. We must learn to construe all the morality and all the religion of the Old Testament more or less within the sphere of this corporate relation. To do this will bring out many points that are apt to be overlooked. Why, for example, are intercessory prayers, prayers for other men, so remarkably absent from the Psalter, when it is so rich in every other variety of prayer? Surely because even the most personal of the Psalms is potentially vicarious, because of its more or less conscious undertones and overtones—the undertones of what it involved towards the family of God to be Yahweh's guest, and the overtones of Yahweh's covenantal relation with all Israel, so that the one always represented the many, and the many prayed and praised through the one.

(b) The actual content of Hebrew morality clearly shows the influence of this corporate emphasis. By general consent the best epitome of prophetic teaching is to be found in the well-known words of the Book of Micah:

'He hath shewed thee, O man, what is good; and what doth Yahweh require of thee, but to do justice and to love mercy, and to walk humbly with thy God?' (vi. 8; cf. the similar epitome in Hos. xii. 7 (6)).

Here, the supreme virtue of religion, as the Hebrew conceived it, is grouped with the two outstanding moral virtues. The religious virtue is that humility of bearing and of conduct,[1] 'making modest the walking' before God, which alone answers properly to man's constant dependence upon Him. It has for its opposite the insolent pride of self-assertion (zadon, זָדוֹן)[2] which is a practical denial of this dependence. The two moral virtues here named are mishpaṭ, 'justice', and ḥeṣed, 'loyal helpfulness'. Both of these conceptions were formally created by the concrete conditions of Hebrew social life. Mishpaṭ is notoriously a difficult word to render with precision, because it covers so wide a range of usage. But there can be no question of its

[1] haznea' leketh (הַצְנֵעַ לֶכֶת).
[2] As in Prov. xi. 2, where the disgrace that will come to pride is contrasted with the wisdom of humility (bringing success).

primary meaning. It is the decision of the *shopheṭ*, the judge
who tries a case and passes sentence. His due judgement, distinguishing between the *ẓaddik* (צַדִּיק) as innocent, and the
rasha' (רָשָׁע) as guilty, is 'justice', the justice which awards
to every man his due. This concrete usage creates the abstract
idea of justice, the moral attribute which belongs both to God
by His nature, and to the man who obediently conforms to His
will. It is a conception which is natural to a democratic society,
keenly conscious of the rights of the individual within the group,
and bringing the freedom of the desert into the changed conditions of social life. It has been rightly said that:

> 'Israel . . . must receive the credit for one of the greatest contribu-
> tions ever made to the political thought of man. She brought with
> her from the nomad stage a conception of common brotherhood
> which she was the first to apply to the conditions of a highly organ-
> ized settled community . . . a strong sense of the value of human
> personality, and a stress on the rights of man as man.'[1]

The smaller groups of which Israel was composed, from nomadic
times and more or less always, were a form of society in which
every man's character and circumstances were well known to
his neighbours, who would closely and eagerly scan them in any
dispute. That which was known to be due to the individual
constituted 'righteousness', i.e. conformity to the norm of common knowledge and conscience. The righteousness of the
whole community, that is its standing before God, was, according to the prophets, to be measured by the degree to which
internal 'justice', the rightful due of each member of it, was
recognized and discharged.[2]

Complementary to this is the other supreme moral value,
ḥeṣed, which has already been discussed in the account of God's
grace.[3] We saw that 'mercy' is an inadequate rendering of it,
and that the other English term often used, 'loving-kindness',
is also inadequate, since it does not bring out the element of
moral obligation, the recognition of the social bond which
prompts and requires mutual helpfulness, even beyond anything which can be demanded strictly as 'justice'. It is the
quality in man which prompts him to stand by his neighbour

---

[1] T. H. Robinson, in his Schweich Lecture on *Palestine in General History*, p. 41.

[2] The bearing of this on the Pauline doctrine of 'justification' is apparent; the
centre of gravity of the new group is now found in Christ.

[3] See above, pp. 57 ff.

in his time of need; it is that larger 'justice' which no legal tribunal can exact, since it must be the spontaneous expression of an inner spirit or disposition.

(*c*) The vocabulary of a people is always an epitome of its history. These two outstanding moral qualities of *mishpaṭ* and *ḥeṣed* carry us back to the Hebrew clans of nomadic times, when the very existence of the group depended on its social solidarity, that group of the desert which must be large enough to defend itself, yet not so large as to exhaust the limited water-supply of its own area. In Canaan the settled local communities of Israel for a long time lived under similar necessities of mutual interdependence. They lived often in a hostile environment, and were always relatively small in number and usually without much permanent co-ordination with other groups. When the monarchy brought some measure of national consciousness it brought with it also economic changes which created not only class distinctions but also the perennial contrast of rich and poor, the powerful and the weak. In presence of many abuses to which these social contrasts led the way, the great prophets called for a revival of the *mishpaṭ* and *ḥeṣed* of the desert, a return to nomadic virtues, even to nomadic simplicities of life, such as the Rechabites and earlier Nazarites still retained. Though the prophets gave to these nomadic virtues a wider scope and a richer quality, they were still those which sprang from the necessities of small groups in the desert and in Canaan, and were fostered wherever the corporate consciousness was strengthened. That was strengthened most of all by the consciousness of the relation of Israel as a whole to Yahweh. The religious consciousness was the prime factor in creating the nation of Israel, as we may see from the work of Moses, from the Song of Deborah, and from the prophetic promise of a 'righteous remnant' and its partial fulfilment in post-exilic times. It is not surprising, therefore, that a strong faith in the God of Israel should be accompanied by a strong sense of the moral ties amongst those who constituted Israel. The marked emphasis on family life and its duties[1] which has characterized Jewish ethics down to the present times is itself heir to the far-off necessities of desert clans, reinforced by the sense of the divine Fatherhood.

[1] Cf. M. Lazarus, *Die Ethik des Judenthums*, pp. 336 ff., and *A Rabbinic Anthology* (C. G. Montefiore and H. Loewe), cc. xxii–xxiv.

§ 3. THE INTERACTION OF MORALITY AND RELIGION

(a) The two examples of human morality just given are of outstanding importance for the characterization of morality amongst the Hebrews, though they are of course no more than the most conspicuous examples of it. Many other features would call for consideration in a complete survey. But these are sufficient to raise the important question which underlies every doctrine of revelation, viz. the legitimacy of transferring such human attributes to God. That they are so transferred is evident when we study their use in relation to Him. 'Shall not the *shophet* of all the earth do *mishpat*?' asks Abraham.[1] Isaiah describes Him as a God of *mishpat*,[2] i.e. not simply One who passes sentence and says the last word, but One whose last word will conform to the strictest rectitude. This rectitude, moreover, is not the antithesis of 'mercy', as we are apt to think under the influence of this misleading translation of *ḥeṣed*; Isaiah's preceding sentences say that His grace culminates in this *mishpat*, and Deutero-Isaiah[3] describes Him as 'a righteous God and a Saviour', that is One whose righteousness is seen in His acts of deliverance. So also, as we have already seen, the *ḥeṣed* of God is not an attribute wholly different from the *ḥeṣed* of man; it is man's *ḥeṣed* raised to new powers and unexpected applications. God delights in *ḥeṣed*, as the bond of helpfulness which unites Him to man, and therefore will not retain His anger for ever.[4] To know Him is to know One who will carry into effect the *mishpat*, *ḥeṣed*, and *zᵉdakah* (righteousness) in which He delights.[5] Most clearly of all, Hosea transfers his own human *ḥeṣed* towards Gomer to the similar relation existing between Yahweh and Israel. We might have added to this in half apology for the anthropomorphism, 'though I am God and not man'. It is characteristic of the Hebrew idea of God that Hosea adds, 'because I am God and not man', therefore I will not abandon the holy purpose which called Israel as a son out of Egypt.

(b) But this transference of the human to the divine is accompanied by important differences. One of them is in the steadfastness of the divine purpose. The steadfastness ('ᵉmunah, אֱמוּנָה) of God[6] means that His covenant is, on His side, unbreakable, His word unalterable, His betrothal permanent.[7]

---

[1] Gen. xviii. 25.   [2] xxx. 18.   [3] Isa. xlv. 21.
[4] Mic. vii. 18.   [5] Jer. ix. 23 (24).
[6] Ps. lxxxix. 34, 35 (33, 34).   [7] Hos. ii. 22 (20).

To this permanence and unfailing character of God's *ḥeṣed* must be added the scope and power of fulfilment by which it differs from man's:

> Yahweh, in the heavens is thy *ḥeṣed*,
> And thy steadfastness is unto the clouds,
> Thy righteousness is like mighty mountains,
> Thy judgments the great deep. (Ps. xxxvi. 6, 7 (5, 6).)

Nothing could be better than Kittel's exposition[1] of these four similes:

'The greatest, widest, deepest which the eye of man beholds, and the mind of man can conceive is alone great and strong enough for comparison with God's grace, steadfastness and righteousness. The unending height of heaven and the clouds which draw to it, not to be reached by the hand of any man, which the eye can glimpse only from afar, alone reach far enough to portray the unending greatness of divine grace and fidelity to promise. The eternal, unchangeable mountains planted by God Himself in the beginning, and therefore named after (His might) are alone fixed deep enough to describe the trustworthiness and security of God's righteousness, whilst the unending ocean, the *Tehom*, which flows around heaven and earth, is alone wide enough to describe the all-extensive breadth of the judgments of God.'[2]

The 36th psalm may be called the psalm of God's *ḥeṣed*, and it admirably suggests the change wrought in the human virtue when it is ascribed to God, and blended with His unique 'holiness', the quality which separates Him from man. In spite of this inevitable separation, the identity of the attributes remains; apart from that identity the words *ḥeṣed* and *mishpaṭ* would have no intelligible application to God. The faith that these qualities did belong to God was reached by intuition, not by inference. We can defend this use of analogy on one condition only—that there is sufficient kinship between man and God to make it valid. That is the Biblical assumption, which underlies the declarations that man is made in the image of God, that Israel is the son of God, and even (in the New Testament) that Adam is the son of God, and all men His offspring.[3] Our modern way of reconciling the psychology of revelation with its result is to say that discovery and revelation are two aspects of the same

---

[1] Cf. Ruskin's panegyric of the passage in *Frondes Agrestes* (1898), p. 92.
[2] *Die Psalmen*, ad loc. Cf. the christological use of the highest categories.
[3] Gen. i. 26; Hos. xi. 1; Luke iii. 38; Acts xvii. 26-8.

process. Ezekiel made telling use of the vine as a symbol of
Israel (xv. 2 ff.), the vine whose wood is worthless in itself, the
vine whose only justification is in its fruit. We might think of
Israel as a vine in a different way—as stretching out her human
tendrils for that firm support which she needed for her faith,
and clinging to the unseen in order to realize her life in the seen.
Her religion did that explicitly; her morality did it implicitly;
the two are inseparable for the true knowledge of God.

(c) The principle of analogy, however, has subtler and rarer
applications than those which we have seen to be true of the
normal virtues of *ḥeṣed* and *mishpaṭ*. It extends to those new
conceptions of God[1] in which the wonder of His ways breaks
on some prophet with an overwhelming surprise, as we may
well suppose to be true of the author of the Songs of the Servant
of Yahweh in Deutero-Isaiah. Here the *mishpaṭ* of God has been
seen in the sufferings of exile, and their magnitude seems to
have gone beyond His righteousness. 'Israel hath received of
the Lord's hand double for all her sins.' But what if God could
redeem that undeserved margin of suffering from its futility and
apparent injustice, and make of it a new thing, a sacrificial
offering, moving the nations to penitence and providing for
them an atoning approach to the God of Israel? This great
conception, destined to become the very heart of the New
Testament doctrine of salvation when applied to the Cross of
Christ, reaches as far above the ordinary conception of sacrificial worship as did the temple vision of Isaiah of Jerusalem
above the experience of the ordinary worshipper there. Yet
even such thoughts of God are rooted and grounded in the heart
of man, though they reach up to a *mishpaṭ* and a *ḥeṣed* which
man himself has never achieved.

(d) The effect of this close and intimate union of morality and
religion is seen not only in the quickening of religious faith by
the ascription of moral attributes to God, but also in the rein-
forcement and vindication of morality by religion. It is obvious
that the practice of morality will be strengthened by the faith
that God is concerned with it, and that He has made it essential
to any approach to Him. To bring this home to Israel was the
primary task of the prophets, who appeal confidently to the
religious sanctions of morality, the judgements of God made

[1] Cf. Isa. lv. 9: 'As the heavens are higher than the earth, so are my ways higher
than your ways, and my thoughts than your thoughts.'

visible or yet to be made visible, in history. Less obvious than
this external vindication, which could and did easily become
a doctrine of exact retribution, the union of religion and morality in Israel's faith brought with it, at least for the more spiritually minded, a clarification and refinement of inner motive.
For these, obedience to the commands of God was not simply
the condition of avoiding penalties and of obtaining rewards,
issuing in a sort of utilitarian calculus, so as to attain to a *shalom*
of physical, social, and economic well-being through a powerful
ally. Because God is Himself conceived morally, and far beyond
any moral attainments of man, He becomes attractive in Himself, loved for His own sake, served gladly, and it may be without hope of any visible reward at all. No one can read Deut. vi
intelligently without perceiving this. Not only does it give the
apparently paradoxical command, 'Thou shalt *love* the Lord thy
God', but it goes on to present Him as a redeeming God, whom
to know is to love, so that love itself becomes the fulfilling of the
law. True, this chapter does expect reward for such obedience,
and there is nothing irreligious or immoral in such an expectation. Yet there are some passages of the Old Testament, as
well as of the New, in which the obedience does not depend on
such a reward, notably the close of the psalm which has been
attached to the Book of Habakkuk:

> Though the fig tree shall not blossom,
> Neither shall fruit be in the vines;
> The product of the olive shall fail,
> And the fields shall yield no food;
> (Though) the flock shall be cut off from the fold,
> And there shall be no cattle in the stalls,
> Yet I will exult in Yahweh,
> I will rejoice in the God of my salvation. (Hab. iii. 17 f.)

In such words morality has become religion by transcending
itself.

§ 4. THE WISDOM SYNTHESIS

The interrelation of morality and religion which we have so
far examined was intuitive and the product of the prophetic
insight and inspiration; there was no conscious or explicit
theory of the relation other than that which was directly
prompted by religious faith. It was the Wisdom literature
which first moved in the direction of a theory, and supplied the

nearest approach to a philosophy of religion which the Old Testament affords. This itself sprang from practical needs and the experience of life, not from intellectual presuppositions. Just as the Psalms show the synthesis of prophetic religion with the worship of the temple, and the law literature its synthesis with traditional customs and legal codes, so the Wisdom literature shows its synthesis with the daily life of the ordinary man.[1]

(a) Much of the form and content of the Wisdom literature is drawn from the large quantity of international Wisdom, especially the Egyptian and the Babylonian, which exercised so great an influence on the Wisdom writers of Israel.[2] But, whether drawn from these copious sources, or from pre-exilic elements in the life of Israel, the Israelite Wisdom has its own characteristic qualities. They are derived from Israel's unique conception of God, which the prophets had developed. Even though much of the Wisdom literature is not directly concerned with what is generally understood by religion, it must always be read with the thought of Israel's God as its background. As Fichtner[3] says, 'The fundamental significance of religion for Wisdom is here, in contrast with the rest of the ancient east, recognized and expressed from an early date, with the result that moral exhortation tends to take a religious colour'.

(b) This bears on the alleged 'utilitarianism' of Israelite Wisdom. It is true that the doctrine of retribution, so powerfully impressed on the religion of Israel by the eighth-century prophets, and with equal impressiveness confirmed by the course of history, was transferred by the Wisdom writers from the nation to the individual, and so created the most intensely felt problem in the religious life of the post-exilic community, the maladjustment of exact retribution, the prosperity of the wicked and the suffering of the innocent. But we have to remember also Job's defiant challenge of this doctrine, and his unconscious vindication of disinterested religion. It was a Wisdom writer, after all, who thus gave us the most brilliant assertion that man could serve God for naught. We are all utilitarians up to a

[1] See the essay on 'The Social Life of the Psalmists' (in *The Psalmists* (ed. by D. C. Simpson)), which presents the evidence of Proverbs and ben Sira as to the social side of the life of those who were contemporary with many of the psalmists, if not of their number.

[2] On this debt, see the extensive study by J. Fichtner, *Die altorientalische Weisheit in ihrer israelitisch-jüdischen Ausprägung* (BZAW, 1933). Cf. also 235 ff.

[3] Op. cit., p. 124.

point; the crucial test is as to what lies beyond that point for our faith and practice.

(c) As to the inner and subjective relation of morality and religion, there is an impressive verse in Proverbs (xx. 27) which says:

> The breath of man is Yahweh's lamp,
> Searching all the chambers of the belly.

That seems to be the Hebrew way of saying that conscience (for which the Hebrew vocabulary has no word, other than 'heart') is inspired by God, and becomes an inner tribunal which represents Him. But it is doubtful whether we ought to press this isolated saying beyond making it mean what is elsewhere said of God's knowledge of man's inner life:

> Sheol and Abaddon are before Yahweh,
> How much more, then, the hearts of the children of men![1]

Anything approaching to a doctrine of divine immanence is foreign to genuine Hebrew thought, since the antitheses in the conceptions of God and man considered in the fourth chapter were effective barriers to it. When Wisdom says:

> By me kings reign
> And princes decree justice (Prov. viii. 15)

we have to remember that it is the external figure of Wisdom, something outside the conscience and consciousness of man, who is speaking. The natural Hebrew development of the relation of God and man in this respect is that which we find in ben Sira's identification of Wisdom with the objective Torah:

'All these things (enumerated in the foregoing panegyric of Wisdom) are the book of the covenant of the Most High,
The law which Moses commanded us for a heritage unto the assemblies of Jacob.' (Ecclus. xxiv. 23.)

Such an identification reminds us that we must think rather of an external mediation than of an indwelling faculty. Hebrew thought has not reached the Logos doctrine of the Stoics, either in regard to Wisdom or to the Spirit of God. But the external figure of Wisdom is itself the most striking monument of that synthesis of morality and religion with which this lecture has been concerned. The fact that Wisdom deals with man as man and not as Israelite[2] also illustrates the universalistic tendencies of both the synthetized elements.

[1] Prov. xv. 11; cf. Fichtner, op. cit., p. 116.   [2] Fichtner, op. cit., p. 125.

VII

HUMAN DESTINY

IN a recent book by a well-known surgeon[1] we are asked to compare the life and death of man with the birth, growth, struggle for existence, nourishment, decay, and final absorption of one of the innumerable cells of which the living body is composed. All these processes, as he points out, can now be witnessed on the screen, with the help of cine-photography and tissue-culture. He goes on to say: 'To one of those cells, ignorant of the existence of that greater being of which it formed a tiny part, life would seem to be a meaningless struggle, a coming out of nothing and a departure into nothing. Only to us who are aware of the greater organism of which the cell is a part has the drama of its life and death any meaning.' So, he says, it is with ourselves as individual men and women: 'Our birth and death are mysteries which can only be solved by a knowledge of that greater being of which we form a tiny part.'

The analogy, within proper limits, is a true and suggestive one and points directly to a religious view of life and death, and especially to that of the particular form of religion with which we are concerned. The Hebrews, as we have seen, were possessed by a strong conviction that the individual was part of a larger whole, that of Israel, and that this larger whole was dependent on the God of Israel, and existed to fulfil His purpose.[2] The meaning of life could be known only in the light of this larger setting. How far does it illuminate the shadow cast by death?

§ 1. THE MORTALITY OF MAN

Death, like birth, and all that came between them was under God's control:

> In His hand is the life of every living thing,
> And the breath of all mankind. (Job xii. 10.)

If He gather unto Himself (man's) spirit and his breath,
All flesh shall perish together,
And man shall turn again unto dust. (Job xxxiv. 14, 15.)

---

[1] Kenneth Walker, *The Circle of Life*, p. 77.

[2] The magnitude of this purpose should be compared with that of the Babylonian Creation Epic, according to which 'Man was created to serve the gods, and his ministration was designed to free them from every kind of toil' (C. J. Gadd, in *Myth and Ritual* (ed. Hooke, p. 51)).

In the very midst of a man's natural expectation of life, he might be cut off from the thrums of the loom of life, as Hezekiah so nearly was.[1] But, sooner or later, death is the natural end of life, when it comes in the fullness of time to one already 'satisfied with days'.[2] Death is not regarded within the Old Testament in general as a penalty for sin. Its general attitude is exemplified in the words of the wise woman of Tekoa to David:

'We must needs die, and are as water spilt on the ground, which cannot be gathered up again.' (2 Sam. xiv. 14.)

It is by God's appointment that death, with nothing beyond it save a shadowy existence in Sheol, is the universal end of life:

Thou turnest man to dust (*dakka'*, דַּכָּא)
And sayest, Return, ye children of men, (Ps. xc. 3.)

which is but another way of saying,

Dust ('*aphar* עָפָר) thou art, and unto dust shalt thou return.
(Gen. iii. 19.)

It is true that, in the Yahwistic story of Eden, death was threatened as the *immediate* penalty of eating the fruit of the tree of the knowledge of good and evil:

In the day that thou eatest thereof thou shalt surely die. (Gen. ii. 17.)

But this divine threat was not carried out, and the serpent's promise to Eve was justified. Instead, there was substituted the toilfulness of man's life in future.[3]

The Old Testament makes no use elsewhere of the conception which has figured so largely in Christian theology, that death itself is the direct penalty for sin, as in the words of the apostle Paul: 'through one man sin entered into the world and death through sin' . . . 'the wages of sin is death'.[4] But there is partial justification for this connexion in the present form of the story of Eden, because of the reference to a second tree, the

---

[1] Isa. xxxviii. 10, 12.

[2] Gen. xxxv. 29 (Isaac); Job xlii. 17 (Job). Cf. Köhler, op. cit., pp. 134, 135; Eichrodt, op. cit. iii. 97 n.

[3] Gen. iii. 17, 18. For another withdrawal of a divine declaration, Gunkel compares Gen. xx. 3 (Abimelech and Sarah). Sellin (*Theol. d. A.T.*), like others, tries to reconcile the threat with the actual course of the story by saying that life became a continuous death, but this attempt at reconciliation is not justifiable exegesis. Ezek. xxxiii. 8, 14, bring out the conditionality (and beneficent purpose) of a divine threat.

[4] Rom. v. 12, vi. 23. Cf. Koeberle, *Sünde und Gnade*, p. 64; Clemen, *Die christliche Lehre von der Sünde*, p. 242. For the Rabbinic teaching cf. Moore's *Judaism*, i. 474 ff.

tree of life.[1] This had to be guarded by the Cherubim against
fallen man, which suggests that, though man was not originally
immortal, he might have attained immortality by eating the
fruit of this tree. Such an idea of a tree or plant of eternal life
is widespread,[2] and we find something very like it in the Babylonian epic of Gilgamesh. Here the hero obtains from Utnapish-
tim (the Babylonian Noah) the plant of eternal life, of which
the name is 'When old man will become young again'.[3] Gilgamesh reserves it for his delectation on return to his native
Uruk. But, in the course of the journey homewards, whilst he
is bathing, a serpent smelt and stole it. Gilgamesh could do
nothing but sit down on the bank and weep over his irreparable
loss, whilst the triumphant serpent becomes young again and
sloughs his old skin, so coming off much better than the serpent
of Genesis. There is no indication that Gilgamesh lost his chance
of immortality through disobedience to a divine command; the
only moral to be drawn would be to abstain from bathing when
in charge of something valuable. Babylonia has a Creation-
story and a Flood-story, but not a Fall-story,[4] and that is a fact
significant of the Hebrew emphasis on morality.

§ 2. SHEOL

Death itself is, in the rendering of our English Versions, a
'giving up the ghost',[5] which is literally in the Hebrew a 'breathing
out of the *nephesh*', the animating principle of bodily life, and not
any self-contained entity which continues to exist as such. Thus
Rachel's death is described as 'the going out of her *nephesh*'[6], and
Elijah stretches himself three times on the body of the dead child
at Zarephath, praying, 'Yahweh, my God, let the *nephesh* of this
child return within his inner parts (*'al ḳirbo*, עַל־קִרְבּוֹ)'.[7] Elisha,
in similar circumstances, actually puts his mouth on the child's
mouth, doubtless to breathe into it. The sneezing of the child
marks the success of this early method of artificial respiration.[8]

[1] It seems likely that the present story is composite, and that in one form of it
the tree of life was the forbidden tree. So Skinner and Gunkel, ad loc.

[2] Jeremias, *ATAO*[2], pp. 191 ff.

[3] Rogers, *Cuneiform Parallels*, pp. 101, 102 (Tablet xi); Gressmann, *ATAT*[2],
pp. 182, 183. [4] Jeremias, op. cit., p. 204.

[5] Job xi. 20, xxxi. 39. [6] Gen. xxxv. 18. [7] 1 Kings xvii. 21, 22.

[8] 2 Kings iv. 34, 35. The passages in which the *nephesh* is spoken of as 'dying'
(Judges xvi. 30; 1 Kings xix. 4; Num. xxiii. 10; Jonah iv. 8) come between *nephesh*
as the principle of life, and *nephesh* as the 'self', and express the result of the 'going
out of the *nephesh*', which is the more precise statement.

At death, therefore, there is no 'soul' or 'spirit' to continue in some future state.[1] There is no passage in the Old Testament which warrants such a statement as 'The soul went with the body into the under world or Sheol'.[2] When a psalmist, for example, says:

'thou hast brought up my *nephesh* from Sheol'

he explains it in the parallel line by saying:

'thou hast kept me alive, that I should not go down to the pit.'

(xxx. 3.)

Similarly,

'thou wilt not abandon my *nephesh* to Sheol'

is explained by

'nor wilt thou suffer thy devout one to see the pit.' (xvi. 10.)

All such passages refer to living men, whose *nephesh* remains in their bodies, though sickness may have brought them so near to death that they can speak of recovery as Yahweh's lifting them up from its gates.[3] Nowhere is the term *nephesh* applied to the actual residents in Sheol, for whom the proper designation is *repha'im* (רפאים).[4] This term is usually derived from a root *raphah* (רפה) denoting slackness or weakness,[5] and this well suits all that we are told of them in Sheol. To a fallen tyrant who joins them they say:

Art thou also become weak (חָלִיתָ) as we?
Art thou made like unto us? (Isa. xiv. 10.)

So when Isaiah contemptuously refers to the spiritualistic oracles sought from the dead, he describes the ghosts as those who chirp

---

[1] The exceptional and obscure passage, Job xiv. 22:

His flesh upon him has pain
And his *nephesh* within him mourneth

may refer to a lingering vitality and quasi-consciousness, until the body has wholly decayed.

[2] G. A. Barton, in *ERE*, xi. 750b. Pedersen, op. cit. 180, 181 and many others speak loosely of 'the souls of the dead', but strictly speaking there are no souls of the dead; the *repha'im* are not souls at all, but ghosts.

[3] Ps. ix. 13. So Jastrow, *Religion of Babylonia and Assyria*, 1898, p. 577: 'the suffering individual stricken with disease could be awakened to new life. It is this "restoration" which lies in the power of the gods, but once a man has been carried off to Aralû, no god can bring him back to earth.' See also p. 576.

[4] Their name is a synonym for the dead (Prov. ii. 18, xxi. 16), who have no future life to expect (Isa. xxvi. 14), except by a miracle (verse 19) and so will never again join in the praise of God (Ps. lxxxviii. 10) though they remain conscious of the earthly career of a new-comer (Isa. xiv. 9 ff.). Their place is in the depths (Prov. ix. 18), beneath the waters (Job xxvi. 5).

[5] So BDB, Stade, Ges.-Buhl, König.

and mutter, with evident reference to their feebleness. These *rᵉpha'im* are shadowy replicas of the whole living man, not any formerly constituent part of him. They are 'shades', as in the Latin use of *umbra* to denote a ghost.[1] So in Egyptian psychology the *ka* in the other world was constituted, in every detail, like the body of flesh which it had occupied on earth.[2] In the Babylonian story of the descent of Ishtar to the underworld, there is a well-known passage which shows the general conception of Aralû, the Babylonian equivalent to the Hebrew Sheol:

To the land whence there is no return, the land of darkness(?)
Ishtar, the daughter of Sin, turned her mind,
The daughter of Sin turned her mind;
To the house of darkness, the dwelling of Irkalla,
To the house whence no one issues who has entered it.
To the road from which there is no return, when once it has been
　　trodden.
To the house whose inhabitants are deprived of light.
The place where dust is their nourishment, their food clay.
They have no light dwelling in darkness dense.[3]

Aralû and Sheol illustrate the widespread inability of primitive belief to regard death as an absolute end to existence, though it is the end of anything that can be called life.[4]

This shadowy existence in Sheol appears to be conditioned by the circumstances of death; hence Jacob pleads that his grey hairs be not brought down to Sheol in sorrow.[5] In Ezekiel's picture of Sheol (xxxii. 22 ff.) the dead warriors (of all nations) are recognizable by their weapons, just as was the returning ghost of Samuel by his familiar mantle.[6] It was therefore important that the dead body should be properly treated. Just as mutilations of the dead were supposed to affect their ghostly replicas in this after-world below, so proper burial and due rites would conduce to the greater ease of their lot.[7] These

---

[1]　　　　　　　nos ubi decidimus
　　quo pius Aeneas, quo Tullus dives et Ancus,
　　　　pulvis et umbra sumus. (Horace, *Odes*, iv. 7.)
[2] G. Foucart, *ERE*, ii. 764.
[3] Jastrow, op. cit., pp. 565–6.　　　　　　[4] Cf. Jastrow, op. cit., p. 556.
[5] Gen. xlii. 38. Cf. xxxvii. 35, 'I will go down to Sheol to my son mourning', where אָבֵל ('mourning') means 'in garments of mourning', as is explicitly said in 2 Sam. xiv. 2. The appearance of the dead in dreams in their best-known or latest seen form, would explain this belief (so Stade, *Geschichte des Volkes Israel*², i. 419).　　　　　　　　　　[6] 1 Sam. xxviii. 14.
[7] This explains Jezebel's attention to her toilet, when she knew death awaited

conceptions, as is apparent, are an application of the principle of symbolic magic which we encounter in so many realms, and in all ages; as the body is here, so is the ghost there.

A peculiarly interesting passage deals with the punishment of Dathan and Abiram for their rebellion against Moses and Aaron.[1] Yahweh is said to have dealt with them in an entirely new way. Instead of their dead bodies remaining on earth, and their 'shades' alone going down to Sheol, the earth opens and swallows them and theirs alive and just as they are, so that they actually go down to Sheol as living men. Obviously this is intended to be a peculiarly severe penalty. The severity may consist not only in the sudden and spectacular death, but also in their entrance into Sheol with full living capacity to feel its deprivations, whereas the $r^{e}pha'im$ proper are no longer capable of feeling with the intensity of living men. This supplies a contrasted parallel to the fate of Enoch and Elijah, who are transported from earth without dying,[2] i.e. with their bodies still animated by $nephesh$, and therefore capable of enjoying heaven as no ghostly replica could do. Thus the swallowing up of Dathan and Abiram on the one hand, and the translation of Enoch and Elijah on the other, agree with the later doctrine of a resurrection of the body as the only means of bestowing adequate penalty or reward in a future life, a life at first conceived as continued on earth and under earthly conditions. But from exceptional instances no generalization can be drawn as to the fate of common men. For them, the dreary and neutral existence in Sheol is naturally repellent; Job asks what hope awaits him beyond death to strengthen his endurance of present suffering:

> If I hope, Sheol is my house,
> In the darkness I have spread my couch.
> To the pit I have said, Thou art my father,
> To the worm, My mother and my sister.[3]

her, and Jehu's trampling her body under foot. When, after a good meal, he relents so far as to order her burial, the dogs that roam about an Eastern city have left but little of it, and this is noted as a special aggravation of her fate.

[1] Num. xvi. 29-34 (JE); see Gray, ad loc., for the critical analysis of the narrative, separating it from the references to Korah (P), whose followers are destroyed by fire.　　　　　[2] Gen. v. 24; 2 Kings ii. 11.

[3] Job xvii. 13, 14, a passage which may have inspired the lines in Keats's 'Song of the Indian Maid',

> Come then, Sorrow,
> Sweetest Sorrow! . . .
> Thou art her mother,
> And her brother.

Job elsewhere expresses the intensity of his suffering and despair by longing even for this intrinsically repellent sequel to life, where existence is reduced to its lowest terms, so that the distinctions of earth are lost; the wicked cease from their turbulence and the worn-out from their toil.[1] It may be asked how this conception of Sheol as a 'congregation of the r*pha'im'[2] is related to the statements about 'being gathered to one's kindred',[3] or 'sleeping with one's fathers'.[4] The body moulders away, to common knowledge, in the tomb, until only the dry bones are left; but *they* may exceptionally retain so much of their former vitality to wake the dead by their contact, as the bones of Elisha were believed to have done.[5] The ghost, however, is relegated to the dark underworld of Sheol, which is usually explained, as by Charles, as 'a combination of the graves of the clan or nation'.[6] We can put this more exactly and more in accordance with primitive ways of thinking, if with Pedersen,[7] we apply the corporate conception:

'Sheol is the entirety into which all graves are merged. . . . All graves have certain common characteristics constituting the nature of the grave and that is Sheol . . . it belongs deep down under the earth, but it manifests itself in every single grave as *mo'abh* manifests itself in every single Moabite.'

It has frequently been argued that Sheol is relatively a late conception amongst the Hebrews, and that when adopted it belonged to a reaction from a primitive ancestor-worship in favour of the faith in Yahweh alone.[8] That the prophetic conception of Yahweh would discourage any practices and beliefs associated with a cult of the dead is obvious, just as it displaced (for those who accepted it) the tyranny of demons and spirits by the unifying and dominant power of the Spirit of Yahweh.

[1] Job iii. 17.   [2] Prov. xxi. 16.

[3] Gen. xxv. 8, 17, &c., where 'ammaw (עֲמָּיו) is to be explained from the Arabic 'amm, denoting paternal relatives as well as 'people'.

[4] 2 Sam. vii. 12; 1 Kings i. 21.

[5] 2 Kings xiii. 21, suggesting that the psychical power is the most permanent. For parallels and related customs, see my article, 'Bones', in ERE, ii. 791, 792.

[6] Doctrine of a Future Life, p. 33.

[7] op. cit., p. 462 and note on p. 542. Cf. also Lods, La Croyance à la vie future, i. 205 ff.

[8] e.g. by Oesterley and Robinson, Hebrew Religion, p. 358. Cf. Schwally, Das Leben nach dem Tode (1892), pp. 75 ff.; Stade, Geschichte des Volkes Israel², i. pp. 426, 427; Charles, Doctrine of a Future Life, pp. 19 ff.; Lods, La Croyance à la vie future, i. 57 ff.

But the evidence for any clear stage of ancestor-worship is itself doubtful and inadequate, and it is significant that there is no legislation against it.[1] On the other hand, the Sheol belief has every mark of being primitive. It doubtless belongs to the general body of Babylonian beliefs which passed over to the invading Israelites by the mediation of the Canaanites. Sheol, as we have seen, closely resembles Aralû, the Babylonian place of the dead. Appeal is often made to the story of Samuel's ghost at Endor in proof of ancestor-worship,[2] because the medium describes him as *'elohim*, but this is inadequate. Any ghost is credited with superhuman powers, and that of an outstanding man like Samuel occupies a unique position, as did Enoch and Elijah. We cannot therefore generalize about all the dead from a single instance. Moreover, the ascription of such powers to the dead as would warrant worship seems to rest on a wrong conception of Hebrew personality, with which we have already dealt. There is no evidence that the Hebrew ever believed in a disembodied entity capable of attracting worship. The stress sometimes placed on an individual eschatology in contrast with that of the nation[3] needs revision in the light of corporate personality. Anthropologists, moreover, have generally come to recognize a pre-animistic stage of *mana* belief, which would sufficiently explain some of the Old Testament prohibitions or customs in regard to the dead. On the whole, therefore, we should reject any attempt to contrast sharply the eschatology of the pre-prophetic and post-prophetic periods. The contrast is rather between a higher Yahwism, the faith of a minority, and popular religion, which at all times carried with it a large admixture of crude beliefs and practices which were inconsistent with or unrelated to, the conception of the God of Israel. In the Old Testament period, even the higher faith has not yet won sufficient extension into the realms beyond death to transform Sheol from being the apotheosis of the grave, the common destiny of the good and the evil, to become a place of differentiated retribution.

It should be clear that from so negative a conception as Sheol

[1] As is recognized by Schwally, op. cit., p. 76. Eichrodt, op. cit. ii. 115–18 may be consulted for a good recent discussion of the whole subject of ancestor-worship; he decides against its presence in Israel. Jastrow (op. cit., p. 560) remarks 'in historical times we find but little trace of such worship among the Babylonians'.

[2] e.g. by Schwally, op. cit., p. 46, on 1 Sam. xxviii. 13.

[3] Especially by Charles, op. cit., pp. 19 ff.

we could expect no positive contribution to a doctrine of life beyond death. Only when the moral ideas of the great prophets had been assimilated could their conception of a present judgement be projected into a life beyond death, and this projection lies beyond the limits of our survey, except for certain features yet to be noted. Originally, Sheol is not conceived as belonging to Yahweh's dominion at all:

In death there is no remembrance of thee,
In Sheol who shall give thee thanks? (Ps. vi. 6 (5))

Shall the dust praise thee?
Shall it declare thy truth? (Ps. xxx. 10 (9); cf. Isa. xxxviii. 18)

Is it for the dead thou workest miracles?
Shall the *repha'im* rise up and praise thee? (Ps. lxxxviii. 10; cf. verses 4 ff.)

It is true that Amos can say of fugitives from Yahweh (ix. 2):

> Though they dig into Sheol,
> Thence shall my hand take them,

whilst Isaiah offers a sign from the depths of Sheol (vii. 11). But such references simply show the gradual extension of Yahweh's power into domains originally foreign to Him, just as were those of rival kingdoms on earth. The references given are to exceptional action, like a king's temporary invasion of another's realm. Ultimately, all limits are removed:

> Sheol is naked before Him,
> And Abaddon hath no covering (Job xxvi. 6),

whilst a late psalm can describe Yahweh's omnipresent activity in the words (cxxxix. 8):

> If I ascend up into heaven, thou art there,
> If I make my bed in Sheol, behold thou art there.

§ 3. RESURRECTION

We must look elsewhere, then, than to Sheol for the possibility of a real advance in the ideas of human destiny. As we might have expected, the new hope, when it does come, springs from the belief in a continued and improved life upon earth, not a life beneath it, or even above it.[1] The very negation of any real life for man after death served to intensify all the more the

---

[1] 'According to O.T. ideas of the blessed future, man is not translated to dwell with God, but God comes down to dwell with man, and His Presence transforms earth into heaven' (G. A. Cooke, I.C.C., *Ezekiel*, p. 404).

present experience and enjoyment of life. This intensity projected itself all the more passionately under the stress of disaster
and suffering into the hope of a transformed and restored *earth*.
For a long period this new life was regarded as the prerogative
only of those whom Yahweh preserved as a 'righteous remnant',[1]
those 'written among the living', preserved to share it for an
extended season. Sooner or later, however, the fate of some
who deserved to survive, yet did not, forced the issue—could
not Yahweh bring them back even from death and Sheol? So,
for the first time, we reach the idea of a resurrection, and this
in the apocalypse now forming Isaiah xxiv–xxvii, which may
be dated about 300 B.C.[2] Here we have the words (xxvi. 19):

> Thy dead shall live,
> Their corpses shall arise,
> They that dwell in the dust
> Shall awake and give a ringing cry.
> For the dew of lights[3] is thy dew
> And the earth shall give birth to r*epha'im*.[4]

It should be noted that this is a resurrection of some only, and
these of outstanding merit, who deserve to live again and to
enjoy the new earth which Yahweh will create, when He has
overthrown the wicked. A century or so later, in the Book of
Daniel (xii. 2), we find the natural extension of this expectation
so as to include the conspicuously wicked also, since they equally
deserve retribution:

'Many of them that sleep in the dust of the earth shall awake,
some to everlasting life, and some to shame and everlasting contempt.'

These are the two, and the only two, passages in the Old Testament which clearly assert a second life after death. It is a life
on earth, however new its conditions, and it is a resurrection-

---

[1] From Isaiah's time onwards (e.g. iv. 3).

[2] The conception of a supernatural restoration of the *nation* in Ezek. xxxvii and
in Isa. liii does not posit a prior belief in individual resurrection; both these
passages are imaginative creations that posit a miracle of grace, and are not
records of an actually held hope. Job xiv discusses the possibility of individual
restoration and dismisses it as too good to be true. Koheleth bluntly denies it.

[3] טַל אוֹרֹת, i.e. from the heavenly regions, reviving the dead as the dew that
revives vegetation (cf. Hos. xiv. 6 (5)). LXX ἴαμα for אוֹרוֹת shows that it read
אֲרֻכָה = 'new flesh' (upon the bones of the dead); cf. the process of 'resurrection' in Ezek. xxxvii.

[4] See Gray, ad loc., for this translation and its justification. The change of the
suffix in n*ebelathi* (נְבְלָתִי) has the authority of the Syriac; that of tense in 'shall
awake and give' has the support of the Septuagint.

life, involving the restoration of the dead body. This form of belief is seen to have been inevitable, once we have grasped the Hebrew idea of personality; a resurrection of the body was the only form of triumph over death which Hebrew psychology could conceive for those actually dead. Even St. Paul shrinks from the thought of a bodiless existence.[1]

§ 4. THE RELIGIOUS CONTENT

The occurrence of only two references in the Old Testament to the resurrection may seem a very slender foundation for the subsequent faith which largely transformed Judaism before passing into Christianity. Montefiore, answering the question how the Judaism of 350 B.C. differed from that of A.D. 50, says that 'the fundamental and far-reaching difference would be that in 350 B.C. the average Jew believed that, so far as any bliss or happiness was concerned, whether higher or lower, death was the end; whereas in A.D. 50 he believed that, for the righteous at any rate, the higher happiness would actually not be experienced till beyond the grave'.[2] The importance of the change can hardly be overrated, either for the Jew or for the Christian. It is registered in the Jewish name for a cemetery as 'the house of life' as it is in the vast theological ramifications of Dante's *Divina Commedia*. But in fact the explicit mention of the resurrection in the Old Testament concerns form rather than substance. The real foundations of the subsequent belief are to be found in the whole of the higher religious life of Israel, and especially in its faith in God. Whilst I think it must be admitted that there is no Old Testament passage which makes this explicit, there are not a few of which a full logical development would certainly point to it. The most notable of these occurs towards the close of Psalm lxxiii, and may be rendered with Cheyne:

And yet I am continually with thee;
    Thou hast taken hold of my right hand.
According to thy purpose wilt thou lead me,
    And afterwards receive me with glory.
Whom have I (to care for) in heaven?
    And, possessing thee, I have pleasure in nothing upon earth.
Though my flesh and my heart should have wasted away,
    God would for ever be the rock of my heart and my portion.

[1] 2 Cor. v. 1 ff.
[2] *In The Beginnings of Christianity*, vol. i, p. 36 (ed. by Jackson and Lake).

The crucial point is whether the 'afterwards' falls on this, or on the other, side of death. This has to be decided by general considerations. Amongst these is the fact that the next verse but one refers to the wasting away of the body, which suggests death, and that the verb rendered 'receive' (*lakaḥ* לקח) is the same as that used of Enoch's translation.[1] On the other hand, as Gunkel points out, we should note the absence in the 73rd psalm of any of the technical terms of the later eschatological belief, and especially the fact that the problem of the psalmist—the prosperity of the wicked—would hardly have existed if he had been sure of the retribution awaiting them in another life. This powerful argument holds, of course, for the Book of Job also, and in that book life after death is explicitly rejected (xiv). We must therefore conclude that in Psalm lxxiii, and in other psalms in which the confidence of faith in God's fellowship with man is less strikingly expressed, the 'afterwards', expressed or implied, does not mean 'after death', but rather after the most overwhelming of disasters on this side of death. This holds true for other passages in which it is natural enough to read the later belief when we bring this to the strong words of faith. Thus in Psalm xvii. 15:

As for me, I shall behold thy face in righteousness;
May I be satisfied, when I awake, with thine image (Cheyne)

the figure of 'waking' does not necessitate the inference 'after the sleep of death', any more than does 'in the morning' (Ps. xlix. 14). The coming of light after darkness may be so described in any of the contingencies of life, as in Ps. xxx. 5:

Weeping may come in to lodge at eventide,
But in the morning, a ringing cry of joy!

All that we seem justified in saying, therefore, is that the faith of the Old Testament logically points forward towards a life beyond death, because it is so sure of an inviolable fellowship with God, but that it does not attain to any clear vision of the goal of its journey. Nevertheless this religious faith supplied the real content for the resurrection hope when this had been

---

[1] Gen. v. 24: וְאֵינֶנּוּ כִּי לָקַח אֹתוֹ אֱלֹהִים. But in Psalm xlix. 16 (15), where the same verb is found:

'God will redeem my *nephesh* from the hand of Sheol:
For He shall receive me,'

it does not necessarily imply death.

reached along the different line of apocalyptic, as we saw in the
two resurrection passages. The real basis of faith in the life to
come must always be religious. It springs from the relation of
the individual believer to God, and from the confidence that
the individual life has ultimate value for God.[1] This faith
showed itself first in the ever renewed expectation of providential deliverance from suffering and disasters of all kinds on
earth, and of the establishment or enrichment of personal welfare. But it was too strong not eventually to challenge 'the last
enemy' of man,[2] viz. death. A very remarkable passage which
significantly occurs in the same apocalypse from which we have
taken the first statement of the resurrection belief in the Old
Testament, tells us of Yahweh's coronation festival. All men,
not Jews only, will pass before Him in the long procession of
suffering humanity (Isa. xxv. 7, 8):

He will destroy in this mountain the face of the covering (the
mourner's garb) that is cast over all peoples, and the veil that is
spread over all nations. He hath swallowed up death for ever: and
the Lord God will wipe away tears from off all faces.

A life on earth from which death had been eliminated seemed
to the writer of the apocalypse the noblest fulfilment of human
destiny. But later faith has travelled by a better way—the individual victory of faith over death without the removal of death,
and the transformation of death into the gateway to a new
life, not to be limited by the conditions of earth.

§ 5. THE MEANING OF FAITH

Our discussion of human destiny has brought us to the same
issue as have all the other aspects of the relation of God and man
in the Old Testament, viz. that there has to be the response of
man's faith to the self-revelation of God. We saw this in regard
to man's consciousness of dependence on God, both for existence
and for the forgiveness of sin, and also in regard to the whole
control of human life by the divine providence. We saw it, also,
in regard to the sanctions of morality through divine action, as
well as in this present chapter, where we have found faith almost
passing beyond the seen into the unseen. In itself this 'faith'

[1] Cf. W. A. L. Elmslie, 'Ethics', in *Record and Revelation*, ed. H. W. Robinson,
p. 277: 'the individual has *in himself* an ultimate value for God—from which
conviction came at last the faith that death cannot be the end of all things for man.'
[2] 1 Cor. xv. 26.

is presented in the Old Testament as a very simple thing. It is
the intuitive response to the disclosure of God's reliability. It is,
in theological phrase, *fiducia*, confidence or trust, rather than
mere *assentio*, belief; it is active and volitional rather than
intellectual. It is a response that stakes something upon its
conviction; to use Pascal's famous phrase,[1] it knows the necessity to make its wager. Such a confidence is expressed in each
of the three main words expressing faith, viz. *baṭaḥ*, *he'emin*, and
ḥasah. *Baṭaḥ* or 'trust' comes from a root suggesting firm support
such as the ground gives to the man who lies on it.[2] *He'emin*[3]
means reliance on that which is firm as a pillar supporting a
building,[4] or as the devotion of foster-parents,[5] steadfast dependence on that which itself is steadfast.[6] *Ḥasah* means seeking
refuge, whether under the shadow of a tree from heat, or under
the wings of Yahweh from evil of any kind,[7] just as the conies
seek refuge in the rocks.[8] Such faith is elicited by the grace of
the divine self-revelation; it is man's ultimate and sufficient
response to God.

[1] 'Il faut parier': *Pensées*, Brunschvicg, p. 210.

[2] Arabic بَطَحَ 'lie prostrate'.

[3] e.g. Gen. xlv. 26, where the 'coldness' of the irresponsive heart describes
unbelief.   [4] 2 Kings xviii. 16.

[5] Cf. the use of the participle to denote this (Num. xi. 12; Isa. xlix. 23; Ruth
iv. 16; 2 Sam. iv. 4).

[6] Isa. vii. 9 (note the play on words: 'If ye will not be firm in faith, ye shall not
be confirmed in life and well-being by God' (אִם לֹא תַאֲמִינוּ כִּי לֹא תֵאָמֵנוּ).

[7] Judges ix. 15; Pss. xxxvi. 8 (7), lvii. 2 (1).   [8] Ps. civ. 18.

PART III

GOD AND HISTORY

VIII

TIME AND ETERNITY

As a realm of revelation, history includes the potentialities of both physical and psychical nature,[1] and passes beyond them. *Physical nature* is the necessary arena of history, and when it is conceived to be under the control of God, it reveals something of His ways, whilst its events can contribute to the working out of His purposes. *Human nature* by its self-consciousness and in its social relations offers new channels of revelation to which physical nature, despite all its magnitude and majesty, cannot attain. But *history*, gathering the story of many generations, can show the depth of meaning in the divine will and at the same time its dynamic force. It can show the inner and outer worlds in their ceaseless interaction,[2] creating the very values by which history will eventually pass judgement upon itself. History can show the working out of a divine pattern of which Nature is the warp and man the woof. It is no local accident and no provincial or racial idiosyncrasy that the revelation which holds the greatest place in history should itself have been made through history.

We must not, however, come to this ancient history with the standards of judgement which its fuller developments alone have taught us. We must expect to find it but half-conscious of its own significance and often making presuppositions which are no longer our own. There will be a difference of texture in its consciousness of itself, which we ought at least to feel, even if we cannot fully explain. Something of this will be apparent if we try to realize what the Hebrew meant by time and eternity, which are the ultimate constituents of history.

Throughout the ancient world in general, the sense of time originated in the changes of a succession of concrete events, as the early vocabulary of time-measurement sufficiently shows. The measurements of time were primarily and inevitably

---

[1] The subjects of earlier chapters.   [2] Amos iv. 13.

derived from the phenomena of Nature which were so closely linked to the common life of men. The nearest and most familiar were the constant succession of night and day. This could not be explained, as it is by us, as the product of the earth's rotation; indeed the Hebrew story of creation in the first chapter of Genesis suggests that darkness and light are conceived as concrete 'somethings', accompanying rather than caused by the apparent movement of the sun through the heavens. First of all, we read, light was created in antithesis to the darkness of chaos. It was not until the fourth day that the great 'lights', the sun and moon, were added to the independently existing light; before they existed, the characteristic sequence of the evening and the morning had already constituted the 'day'. The sun and moon, when they were created, were there not only to shed additional light or to add beauty to the heavens, but to be signs and sky-marks 'for fixed times and for days and years'.[1] That the sun had some connexion with the day was obvious from the outset;[2] but observation of the sky needed to become systematic before the conception of an exact solar year could be reached, and even then, as is shown by the problems of the calendar amongst many ancient peoples, the year had no definite and fixed beginning, other than the general return of the seasons.[3] On the other hand, the waxing and waning of the moon easily suggested the monthly period and supplied a measurement of time which was as definite, if not as obvious, as that of night and day. The systematic astronomy of Babylonia and Egypt learnt to fix the year with more precision than from the seasons, through the observation of the sun's changing path through 'the signs of the zodiac'. But the problem of correlating the solar year with the monthly periods was one not easily solved in ancient calendars.

Classical Hebrew had no word for 'hour', and the term *sha'ah* (שעה) assimilated from the Aramaic in post-Biblical Hebrew denoted a brief space of time, rather than an arithmetical fraction of the day. As Pedersen has said,[4] 'the colourless idea of "hour", measuring time in a purely quantitative way, is far from the old Israelite conception'. The Hebrew divisions of the

---

[1] Gen. i. 14.

[2] Orelli, *Die hebräischen Synonyma der Zeit und Ewigkeit genetisch und sprachvergleichend dargestellt*, p. 60.

[3] Cf. J. K. Fotheringham, in *ERE*, iii. 61.   [4] *Israel I–II*, p. 489.

day were of a quite general kind—morning, noon, evening—as in the cries of those pictured as attacking Jerusalem:

> Up! let us storm her at noon!
> Woe to us! the day declines,
> The shadows of evening lengthen. (Jer. vi. 4.)

Thus Job compares his days with those of a hireling, a slave panting for the shadow, when work will be done and wages received (vii. 2). The night was divided into three 'watches' (אשמורה, perhaps modelled on the triple division of the day), as we learn from a reference to the 'middle' watch.[1]

The point of interest in these rough-and-ready divisions of the day and night is that they are characterized by their content, such as the lengthening shadows of the evening, the night duty of the watchman or sentinel.[2] Thus a Hebrew could not have said, with Macbeth,

> Come what may,
> Time and the hour run through the roughest day.

But he might have said,

> Come what might,
> The roughest day runs through its time till night.

Similarly, the earliest division of the year was made by its seasons, and their relation to agriculture, as we may see from the promise to Noah:

'While the earth remaineth, seed-time and harvest, and cold and heat, and summer and winter, and day and night shall not cease.' (Gen. viii. 22, J.)

Another example of the same kind is such a phrase as 'spring-rain time' (Zech. x. 1). The supreme importance of the seasons to an agricultural people is illustrated in the elaboration of their mythology, as seen for Canaan in the Ras Shamra cult, or by the agricultural festivals of pilgrimage (ḥag) which marked off

---

[1] Judges vii. 19; cf. the 'morning' watch, Exod. xiv. 24; 1 Sam. xi. 11. In New Testament times the division was fourfold (Mark vi. 48, xiii. 35), after the Roman pattern (vigiliae).

[2] The reference to the 'steps' (not 'dial') of Ahaz, in Isa. xxxviii. 8 (cf. 2 Kings xx. 9–11 in more developed form) is the only one in the Old Testament to 'clock-time'. We are apparently to think of a double flight of steps, east and west, with a pillar at the top casting its shadow upon them (so Procksch, Com., ad loc.). This device may have been derived from Assyria; according to Herodotus (ii. 109) the Greeks derived the sun-dial and gnomon and the twelve divisions of the day from the Babylonians.

the divisions of the Hebrew year. The three chief times of resort to the sanctuaries[1] ultimately gained an historical interpretation: the Feast of Unleavened Bread (united with the Passover) commemorated the Exodus, Tabernacles the nomadic wanderings, and the Feast of Weeks, at the end of the spring harvest, was associated with the giving of the Torah on Sinai.[2]

§ 1

A more detailed and systematic knowledge of the Hebrew sense of time is best gained by an examination of the common term to denote 'time', which is *'eth* (עֵת). The etymology of the term is generally agreed. In view of the cognates,[3] it seems to denote 'occurrence', that which runs across us, meets us. This suggests what the actual usage confirms, that the Hebrew mind conceives time in the concrete, in its filled content, and not as an abstract idea. 'Time' is that which meets you on your path through life.

Of the 297 instances of the word *'eth*[4] nearly a third are of a formal character, as in the familiar phrase 'at that time' in narrative,[5] and in the designation of an event ('when'), which may be past, present, or future.[6] The loose phrase, 'about this time to-morrow'[7] serves to remind us of the absence of clock-time, and of that different 'feel' in the texture of time given by this absence.

The phenomena of nature, forming a second group of the uses of *'eth*, have already been mentioned in general and apart from their combination with עֵת. In that combination we are

---

[1] Exod. xxiii. 14; Deut. xvi. 16. The wider term *mo'ed* denotes the 'appointed time' for such festivals.

[2] This came only in the post-canonical period. Moore, *Judaism*, ii. 48, cites Pesachim 68*b* as assuming the currency of the association. The old Hebrew (Canaanite?) names for some of the months illustrate the same reference to content, e.g. הָאָבִיב, fresh ears of barley (1st m.), אֵיתָנִים, steady flowing of wadies (7th).

[3] The Hebrew root is *'anah* (עָנָה), 'answer'; the *n* of the root appears in the Aramaic *'antha* (עַנְתָא) and the Accadian *anu* (*ittu*), both in the sense of 'time'; see König, *Syntax*, II. i, p. 177. The Syriac use of *'unaya* (ܥܢܝܐ), *'unitha* of antiphonal and choral 'response', brings out the idea of 'occurrence'.

[4] Six of these are probably due to a corrupt text, viz. Judges xiii. 23, xxi. 22; 2 Sam. xxiv. 15; Ezek. xvi. 57, xxvii. 34.   [5] e.g. Gen. xxi. 22.

[6] Neh. xiii. 21; Num. xxiii. 23; Job xxxix. 18. The plural can denote a period (Dan. xi. 14) as does *bekol-'eth*, Esther v. 13, a phrase usually equivalent to our 'always' (Lev. xvi. 2, &c.).

[7] Exod. ix. 18; Joshua xi. 6; 1 Sam. ix. 16, xx. 12; 1 Kings xix. 2, xx. 6; 2 Kings vii. 1, x. 6.

further reminded that the regular recurrence of day and night
through God's 'covenant' with them becomes a sign and seal
of the permanence of the covenant with David.[1] The specified
times of the day are those of noon, sunset, and evening.[2] It may
be simply an accident that '*eth* is not linked with the dawn,
sunrise, or morning; or it may suggest that these were already
sufficiently definite by their nature as points of time.[3]

The year has its fixed return, as have the stars.[4] Those who
are versed in astrology know these fixed times.[5] An interesting
phrase is that which speaks of the 'revival' of the time, meaning
the corresponding time next year,[6] a reminder of the Hebrew
idea of time as a living entity.[7]

Natural phenomena linked to the term '*eth* and bringing out
the concreteness of the Hebrew time-sense are those of rain,[8]
harvest,[9] threshing,[10] pruning,[11] fruitage,[12] bringing the cattle
home,[13] the regular migration of birds,[14] the drying up of wadies,[15]
the birth of mountain-goats and does,[16] and the breeding-heat
of flocks.[17] Phases of human life linked with the term '*eth* are
birth,[18] adolescence,[19] menstruation,[20] old age,[21] death,[22] and
the forty-three specifications to be found in the third chapter
of Ecclesiastes, a book which might almost be described as a
treatise on time, though it is by no means characteristic of the
Hebrew valuation of it.[23]

These specifications of time are by physical phenomena

[1] Jer. xxxiii. 20f.; *berith* here means a binding ordinance (cf. the Accadian *biritu* (*birtu*) 'fetter').

[2] Jer. xx. 16; Joshua x. 27; 2 Chron. xviii. 34; Gen. viii. 11, xxiv. 11; 2 Sam. xi. 2; Joshua viii. 29; Isa. xvii. 14.

[3] Cf. Doughty, *Arabia Deserta*, i. 72, 302, but note also Job vii. 4, of the morning twilight. The peculiar phrase *ben ha'arbaim* (בֵּין הָעַרְבָּיִם) is usually taken to mean 'between sunset and dark' (so BDB). The phrase *liphᵉnoth 'ereb* (Gen. xxiv. 63; Deut. xxiii. 12) is, however, matched by *liphᵉnoth (hab)boḳer* (Exod. xiv. 27; Judges xix. 26; Ps. xlvi. 6).   [4] 1 Chron. xx. 1; Job xxxviii. 32.

[5] Esther i. 13 and probably 1 Chron. xii. 32.

[6] So Pedersen, op. cit., p. 488; *ka'eth ḥayyah* (Gen. xviii. 10, 14; 2 Kings iv. 16, 17).

[7] So König, *Syntax*, ii. 557, instead of 'spring' (Burney on 2 Kings iv. 16). Skinner's explanation of Gen. xviii. 10, 'according to the time of a pregnant woman', is quite unsatisfying in view of verse 14.

[8] Lev. xxvi. 4; Deut. xi. 14, xxviii. 12; Jer. v. 24; Ezek. xxxiv. 26; Zech. x. 1; Ezra x. 13; the last named is in the striking appositional form, 'the time was rains'.

[9] Jer. l. 16, li. 33; Hos. ii. 11 (9); Job v. 26.

[10] Jer. li. 33.   [11] Cant. ii. 12.   [12] Ps. i. 3.   [13] Gen. xxix. 7.

[14] Jer. viii. 7.   [15] Job vi. 17.   [16] Job xxxix. 1, 2.   [17] Gen. xxxi. 10.

[18] Gen. xxxviii. 27; Hos. xiii. 13.   [19] Ezek. xvi. 8.

[20] Lev. xv. 25.   [21] 1 Kings xi. 4, xv. 23; Ps. lxxi. 9.

[22] Job xxii. 16; Eccles. vii. 17, ix. 12.   [23] See Appendix B.

wholly or largely beyond human control. But we have another
group springing from social convention or appointment, viz.
meal-time,[1] campaigning,[2] audit of accounts,[3] weekly or yearly
periods,[4] and fixed or appointed times in general.[5] There is
also developed the sense of what is fitting and proper at a particular time, as in the well-known 'saying of the wise' (Prov.
xv. 23):

'A word in due season (lit. 'in its time'), how good!'

and in Haggai's scornful reproach of those who found it a fitting
time to build houses for themselves but not a house for God
(i. 2, 4).[6]

There remains the considerable (seventy-five) group of more
or less explicit references to God's control of man's time-
experience. These are of particular importance for the Hebrew
time-consciousness, since they point to its characteristic view of
history. They range from seeking God and calling upon Him,[7]
to finding Him[8] in His time of favour,[9] and not when He is
angry.[10] God has His appointed times[11] of activity, as seen in the
career of His anointed servant, Cyrus,[12] or in the future of God's
people,[13] even as He has helped and delivered them in the past.[14]
The conditioning of such deliverance by human activity is
forcibly expressed in Mordecai's words to Esther, 'Who knows
whether for such a time as this thou hast been brought to the
kingdom?'[15] The times of divine visitation,[16] whether on Israel
or on her enemies, are often times of vengeance,[17] and judgement;[18] such visitation is seen in many calamities befalling Israel
or other nations as divine penalty.[19] These visitations may seem

---

[1] Ruth ii. 14; Ezek. iv. 10, 11; Eccles. x. 17; including animals, Ps. civ. 27,
cxlv. 15.   [2] 2 Sam. xi. 1.
[3] 2 Kings v. 26.   [4] 1 Chron. ix. 25; Neh. x. 35.
[5] Ezra x. 14; Neh. xiii. 31; 1 Chron. xx. 1; 2 Chron. xxix. 27; Dan. ix. 21.
[6] Dr. Robinson had intended adding a paragraph or a long note on the Calendar
(cf. Lev. xxiii) as illustrating the measurement of time by *content*. [Ed.]
[7] Hos. x. 12; Jer. xi. 14.   [8] Ps. xxxii. 6.   [9] Isa. xlix. 8; Ps. lxix. 14 (13).
[10] Jer. xviii. 23; cf. x. 24, where contrasted with *b^emishpaṭ*.
[11] In Job xxiv. 1 we should probably omit *lo'* with LXX (so Dhorme, ad loc.).
Cf. Dan. xi. 24.
[12] Isa. xlviii. 16.   [13] Isa. lx. 22; Ps. cii. 14 (13), cxix. 126; Zeph. iii. 20.
[14] Jer. ii. 27; Neh. ix. 28.   [15] Esther iv. 14.
[16] *pakad* (Jer. vi. 15, viii. 12, x. 15, xlvi. 21, xlix. 8, l. 27, li. 18).
[17] Jer. li. 6; Deut. xxxii. 35; Ps. xxi. 10 (9).   [18] Ezek. xxii. 3; Eccles. viii. 5, 6.
[19] Judges x. 14; Isa. xiii. 22; Jer. ii. 27, 28, xi. 12, xv. 11, xxvii. 7; Ezek. vii. 7,12,
xxx. 3, xxxv. 5; Mic. ii. 3; Job xxxviii. 23; Neh. ix. 27; 2 Chron. xxviii. 22. The
reference in Ps. lxxxi. 16 (15) *wiyhi ʿittam leʿolam* (וִיהִי עִתָּם לְעוֹלָם) is better
taken as a time of doom (Kittel) than of prosperity (Cheyne).

remote,[1] but for the prophets they are assured. The definiteness
of concrete event which is implied is expressed by the reference
to Zedekiah's doom in 586 as 'the time of the iniquity of the
end'.[2] Such an event brings trouble to many others also,[3] but
at such times God is the stronghold or deliverer of His people.[4]
This confidence reaches full expression in such a phrase as that
of Ps. xxxi. 16, 'my times are in thy hand', or of Isa. xxxiii. 6,
'the steadfastness of thy times'. For God to withhold such help
is itself a penalty.[5] On the other hand, the un-Hebraic Koheleth regards an evil time as the casual net or snare that catches
men unawares as though they were fishes or birds.[6] Many of
the references to good or evil times in the future could be
claimed as bordering on apocalyptic and the Messianic age.[7]
This becomes obvious in such descriptions as of the evening
without sunset[8] in that future, when Nature will undergo so
many transformations, or in the Danielic references to 'the
time of the end',[9] which, as Charles says, is 'always used
eschatologically in our author and refers definiteyl to the advent
of the kingdom'.[10]

The considerable number of the references to 'time' which
we have reviewed justifies us in some generalizations. (a) The
first is, as we were led to expect at the outset, that there is a
constant emphasis on the concrete aspect, the actual content
and quality of time, and an absence of anything that might be
called a mathematical or philosophical interest in it. (b) The
second is that God is intimately connected with time, and that
His relation to men itself requires the time-order for the fulfilment of His purposes. Time, as the necessary category of those
purposes, acquires a specific quality by its very relation to God,
when man's times become God's times. (c) The third point to
notice is that God's intervention in the affairs of this world to
establish His kingly rule does not involve the suspension of the
time-order; this continues into every future contemplated by
the Old Testament. The quality of time may be modified, but
it is always time, since the kingdom is always on earth.[11]

---

[1] Ezek. xii. 27; cf. Jer. xvii. 15.   [2] Ezek. xxi. 30, 34 (25, 29).
[3] Jer. xxx. 7; cf. Amos v. 13.
[4] Isa. xxxiii. 2; Jer. xiv. 8; Pss. ix. 10 (9), x. 1, xxxvii. 19, 39.
[5] Jer. viii. 15, xiv. 19: 'a time of healing'.   [6] Eccles. ix. 12; cf. viii. 9, ix. 11.
[7] e.g. Mic. v. 2 (3).   [8] Zech. xiv. 7; cf. Isa. lx. 20.
[9] xi. 35, 40, xii. 4, 9; cf. viii. 17, xii. 1.   [10] Comm., p. 394 n. 4.
[11] Study of the time-vocabulary in general ('year', 'month', 'day', &c.) of which

§ 2

The other primary term requiring detailed examination is 'olam (עוֹלָם), the chief word used to denote 'eternity'. It has usually been derived from 'alam, 'hide', in the sense of something hidden, but a more attractive derivation links it with the Accadian ullânu, which means that which is 'remote', either in time or place.[1] That which is remote from the present can be either the past or the future, and both are amply illustrated amongst the 438 (?) occurrences of the word 'olam in the Old Testament. Of the past, in the sense of 'ancient', it is used to designate the prehistoric giants,[2] or the ancestors of Israel,[3] or her prophets;[4] so also, the mountains and hills,[5] the gates of the sanctuary,[6] landmarks,[7] ruins,[8] old ways of righteousness or wickedness,[9] often with the suggestion of permanence,[10] as well as of antiquity. The quasi-hypostatic 'Wisdom' was present and active from the remotest beginnings of the world.[11] In regard to the future, 'olam connotes the permanence of the earth,[12] of Sheol,[13] of the sun and moon,[14] of destructions and ruins,[15] of Israel's hostility to her enemies,[16] and of their shame,[17] (the permanence of Israel's future welfare will be noticed later).[18]

a list is given in Appendix A, would be found to confirm the general conclusions which can be derived from the central term עֵת.

[1] Exx. in Delitzsch, *Assyrisches Handwörterbuch*, p. 65. This derivation was suggested by Barth in *ZDMG*, 1890, p. 685 (cf. Zimmern, *KAT*[3], p. 403, n. 5 in 1903) and criticized by König, *Syntax*, ii. 87, and is endorsed by Prof. G. R. Driver (cf. F. H. Brabant, *Time and Eternity in Christian Thought*, p. 235). Orelli (op. cit.) writing in 1871 accepted the derivation from 'alam without question. If the Accadian derivation be accepted, the *m* is a substantial suffix (so Barth, *Die Nominalbildung in den semitischen Sprachen*[2], 1894, pp. 351 ff.) or the Accadian 'mimation' (Brockelmann, *Kurzgefasste Vergleichende Grammatik der sem. Sprachen*, 118b, where חִנָּם, רֵיקָם, אָמְנָם, יוֹמָם are cited as other Hebrew examples).

[2] Gen. vi. 4.   [3] Joshua xxiv. 2.   [4] Jer. xxviii. 8.

[5] Gen. xlix. 26; Deut. xxxiii. 15; Hab. iii. 6; Ezek. xxxvi. 2.

[6] Ps. xxiv. 7, 9.   [7] Prov. xxii. 28, xxiii. 10.

[8] Isa. lviii. 12, lxi. 4; Jer. xxv. 9, xlix. 13.

[9] Jer. vi. 16, xviii. 15; Ps. cxxxix. 24; Job xxii. 15.   [10] As in Jer. v. 15.

[11] Prov. viii. 23.   [12] Pss. civ. 5, cxlviii. 6, lxxviii. 69; Eccles. i. 4.

[13] Jonah ii. 6.   [14] Ps. lxxxix. 37, 38 (36, 37).

[15] Exod. xiv. 13; Deut. xiii. 17 (16); Isa. xxv. 2; Jer. xxv. 12, &c.

[16] Deut. xxiii. 7 (6); Ezek. xxv. 15, xxxv. 5; Ezra ix. 12.

[17] Jer. xviii. 16, xx. 11, xxiii. 40; Ps. lxxviii. 66.

[18] I am inclined to put the enigmatic use of עוֹלָם in Eccles. iii. 11 here, as continuity in contrast with the עֵת of the earlier part of the verse (cf. Lukyn Williams, 'everness') and in parallelism with the מֵרֹאשׁ וְעַד סוֹף of the latter (cf. i. 4: permanence). See Appendix B.

In such applications as these there is a virtual transition from that which is very remote to that which is permanent, 'forever'.[1] But 'olam can be used to express this in a purely relative sense, as when the reference is to human lives and their extent. Thus we find it applied to life-bondage or life-service,[2] to the blood-guilt resting on Joab and his sons,[3] to the leprosy falling on Gehazi and his seed,[4] to the wrongful prosperity of the wicked,[5] to the duration of the Rechabite vow.[6] It is of course recognized that ancestors and even the prophets did not live for ever,[7] and Job rejects life 'for ever', if spent under his present conditions.[8] God in fact took measures against the risk of man living for ever,[9] and Koheleth laments the impermanence of even human remembrance.[10] It was natural, however, that the Oriental court-greeting should wish the king life 'for ever', by hyperbole for 'a long life'.[11] We are in a different realm, however, when 'olam is applied to God. A standard form of doxology[12] described Him as min ha'olam 'adh ha'olam (מִן הָעוֹלָם עַד הָעוֹלָם), which means 'from the most ancient time to the remotest future'. Strictly speaking, of course, that does not remove God out of time but makes Him contemporaneous, coextensive, with it. The 90th psalm, which might be called the psalm of time and eternity,[13] carries back His being beyond creation, and so lifts Him above all that is temporal:

> Before the mountains were brought forth
> And thou didst travail[14] with earth and world,
> Even from the most ancient time to the remotest future,
> Thou art God.

If God is not explicitly stated to be timeless, He is certainly set

---

[1] Orelli, p. 86, compares the *via eminentiae* of theology. We do not need to go far back in the oral tradition of a community to get the sense of antiquity (cf. village memories).

[2] Exod. xxi. 6; Lev. xxv. 46; Deut. xv. 17; 1 Sam. i. 22, xxvii. 12; Job xl. 28 (xli. 4).   [3] 1 Kings ii. 33.   [4] 2 Kings v. 27.

[5] Ps. lxxiii. 12; cf. Prov. xxvii. 24 and Isa. xlvii. 7.   [6] Jer. xxxv. 6.

[7] Zech. i. 5.   [8] Job vii. 16.   [9] Gen. iii. 22, vi. 3.   [10] Eccles. ii. 16.

[11] 1 Kings i. 31; Neh. ii. 3; cf. Pss. xxi. 5 (4), xlv. 3 (2), lxi. 8 (7), lxxxix. 5 (4), and, of perpetual remembrance, Ps. xlv. 18.

[12] Neh. ix. 5; cf. 1 Chron. xvi. 36, xxix, 10; Pss. xli. 14 (13), cvi. 48, cxv. 18.

[13] It is worth while to compare the way in which its studied repetitions, both of phrase and idea, create their effect with the similar artistry of Walter de la Mare's poem, 'Very old are the woods'.

[14] If, with Gunkel, we take earth and world as subject of the verb, we have a remnant of a creation mythology (Job xxxviii. 8 ff.) in which the earth gives birth to the mountains.

above the limitations of time, as well as of space, as we may see from Deutero-Isaiah (xl. 28):

> God of eternity is Yahweh,
> Creating the ends of the earth,
> Unwearied and unfatigued,
> Unsearchable in His understanding.

The divine energy is there brought out by contrast with the strength of the young man and of the vulture; as is elsewhere suggested, His arms are ageless in the support they can give.[1] His strength and permanence are brought out also by the figure of 'the rock of ages';[2] in the future of Jerusalem He will be an 'eternal light' replacing that of sun and moon.[3] A similar limitless outflow of energy is suggested by the phrase, 'the living God',[4] and by His own oath, with uplifted hand, 'As I live forever'.[5] His kingdom extends over all the ages;[6] the plural is significant as a parallel to 'in every generation'. Of Him, Deutero-Isaiah can say, 'Before me no God was formed and after me, none shall be' (Isa. xliii. 10). A challenging phrase is the *'el 'olam* (אֵל עוֹלָם) describing the pre-Yahwistic local numen of Beersheba,[7] possibly to be linked with a Phoenician god of 'ageless time'.[8] We should hardly be justified in reading into the Hebrew phrase more than 'God of antiquity', with which we might compare and contrast Daniel's 'ancient of days'.

The agelessness of God is brought out in numerous references to His manifestations or attributes, such as His 'name',[9] His word,[10] His counsel,[11] His glory,[12] His power,[13] His righteousness,[14] His steadfastness,[15] His love,[16] and especially His loyalty (*ḥeṣed*),[17] which underlies so many of His activities[18] and deliverances.[19]

---

[1] Deut. xxxiii. 27; cf. Isa. li. 9.   [2] Isa. xxvi. 4.
[3] Isa. lx. 19, 20.   [4] Jer. x. 10, &c.   [5] Deut. xxxii. 40, cf. Dan. xii. 7.
[6] Ps. cxlv. 13; Exod. xv. 18; Ps. x. 16, &c.
[7] Gen. xxi. 33, where linked with Abraham (cf. Alt, *Der Gott der Väter*, pp. 7, 28, 55 ff.); Gunkel on Gen. xvi. 13.
[8] Eichrodt, op. cit. i. 88: χρόνος ἀγήραος (Damascius Princ. 123).
[9] Exod. iii. 15; 2 Kings xxi. 7; 1 Chron. xvii. 24; 2 Chron. vii. 16, xxxiii. 4, 7 (*le'olam* for *le'elom*); Isa. lxiii. 12, 19; Pss. cxiii. 2, cxxxv. 13.
[10] Isa. xl. 8; Ps. cxix. 89; 1 Chron. xvii. 23; cf. Isa. xxx. 8.
[11] Ps. xxxiii. 11.   [12] Ps. civ. 31.
[13] Ps. lxvi. 7.   [14] Ps. cxix. 142, 144.
[15] Pss. cxvii. 2, cxlvi. 6; Hos. ii. 22 (20).   [16] Jer. xxxi. 3.
[17] Pss. lxxxix. 3 (2), ciii. 17, &c. There are 44 references, if we include the perhaps accidental repetition of the refrain, 'forever His *ḥeṣed*' in Ps. cxxxvi.
[18] Hab. iii. 6; Eccles. iii. 14; Ps. cxxi. 8, cxxv. 2.   [19] Isa. xlv. 17, li. 6.

It was natural that something of God's eternity or permanence should be thought to have passed over to His institutions for Israel. In the forefront of them stands the 'berith', the covenant which is to endure 'for generations of eternity',[1] 'to a thousand generations'.[2] Within it are His ordinances, such as those of the Passover,[3] or the Sabbath,[4] the Temple, with its priesthood and ritual,[5] the Davidic kingship.[6] Palestine is given into Israel's possession for ever,[7] though the prophets warn her of the conditionality of this permanent ownership.[8] But shall Israel herself not endure,[9] seeing that God dwells in her midst,[10] making Zion a pride for ever, a joy for all generations?[11] To this divine grace, Israel's dual response is in her worship and her loyal obedience, and many passages remind her that both are to be permanent.[12] The Chronicler represents David as praying (1 Chron. xxix. 18):

'Keep this forever in the imagination of the thoughts of the heart of thy people, and establish their heart unto thee.'

On such terms, Israel and the upright Israelite can trust firmly in the permanent protection of God.[13]

§ 3. The Interrelation of Time and Eternity

Whilst the institutions of Israel thus reflect the eternity of Israel's God, they also, by their own enduring nature, throw back their light on His permanence. The agelong ritual, like the agelong mountains, makes more real to men the eternity of God. He who has learnt to say in worship, 'I love the Lord because He has heard my voice and my supplications' will hear with new depth of meaning the prophet's word, 'I have loved thee with an everlasting love'.[14] In our study of religious terminology we should always allow for this mutual give and take, as well as for the more direct and obvious derivation of meaning and quality. It holds true both for the visible institutions and

---

[1] Gen. ix. 12, xvii. 7, &c.; see further pp. 153 ff.   [2] Ps. cv. 8.
[3] Exod. xii. 24.   [4] Exod. xxxi. 16, 17.
[5] 1 Kings viii. 13; Num. xxv. 13; 2 Chron. ii. 3 (4).
[6] 2 Sam. vii. 29.   [7] Gen. xvii. 8, xlviii. 4; Exod. xxxii. 13.
[8] Jer. vii. 7, xxv. 5.   [9] 2 Chron. ix. 8.
[10] Ezek. xliii. 7, 9.   [11] Isa. lx. 15.
[12] Worship, Ps. v. 12 (11) et passim; obedience, Deut. v. 26 (29); Isa. lix. 21; Ps. cxix. 44, 52, 93, 98, 111, 112; Mic. iv. 5.
[13] Pss. xxxi. 2 (1), xxxvii. 27, xii. 8 (7); Prov. x. 30; Joel ii. 26 f., &c.
[14] Ps. cxvi. 1; Jer. xxxi. 3.

for the inner relation to God experienced through them and beyond them. When, as so often in the Psalms, a permanent relation to God is asserted, we must neither exaggerate nor minimize its meaning. In Ps. lxi. 7 there is the familiar prayer that the king's years may be for generations and generations, and we rightly treat it as a court hyperbole. But surely there is more than this when the same psalmist says (5), 'Let me be a guest in thy tent for ages' ('*olamim*). Here we encounter a religious experience which, as we should say in our own terminology, transcends time, even though it has not yet learnt the formula in which to express itself adequately. There is a recurrent urge in man's consciousness to find supra-temporal support for his temporal experience even without the proper formula. For the Hebrew that support was naturally found in Yahweh. So, when another psalmist (xli. 12 (13)) has prayed for recovery from sickness, he goes on, 'Thou settest me before thy face for-ever'. This cannot mean, in view of its context, deathless life, or another life beyond death. Yet we are justified in saying with Cheyne (on Ps. xi. 7) that the psalmist 'is close upon St. John's conception of "eternal life" as a present possession'. We ought to regard in the same way the great passage towards the end of the 73rd psalm (26) with its assertion 'my portion is God for-ever'. The psalmist has already spoken (verse 12) in similar terms of the wicked as seemingly prosperous for ever, which cannot mean 'eternally' in our sense of the word. But the consciousness of fellowship with God can lift man above the accepted limitations of life, just because God is felt to be above them. So in Ps. cxxxiii. 3, where the peace of human fellowship is traced to fellowship with God and described as 'life for ever-more'. In all such experience we approximate to the sense of eternity underlying 'With thee is the fountain of life', itself prepared for at a more primitive stage of thought by Abigail's confidence that David's 'life will be bound in the bundle of the living with Yahweh thy God'.[1]

The development here from quantity to quality may be compared to the similar development in the meaning of the Greek term αἰών. This also seems to get its sense of eternity from its later religious associations. It is defined by Aristotle[2]

---

[1] Ps. xxxvi. 10 (9); 1 Sam. xxv. 29.
[2] *De Caelo*, i. 9, 15: τὸ γὰρ τέλος τὸ περιέχον τὸν τῆς ἑκάστου ζωῆς χρόνον .. αἰὼν ἑκάστου κέκληται.

as that portion of (the unlimited) χρόνος which makes an individual lifetime. 'The bridge leading from the different and much narrower Greek conception to the Hellenistic was [presumably] in the fact that the god's or the heaven's or the cosmos' life lasts for "ever" '.[1] It has been said with truth that both the Hebrew and the Greek terms for 'eternity' in Scripture show the remarkable phenomenon that they combine two antitheses—the eternity of God and the time of the world. 'This doubled meaning which αἰών shares with עוֹלָם points back to a conception of eternity in which eternity and the duration of the world were identified.'[2]

We must not, however, confuse the inarticulate and undefined sense of a transcendent life which is implicit in any real fellowship with God with definite belief in a life after death. That could find no expression until a formula for it had been discovered, and this was not until the late apocalyptic period. The formula had to be that of the resurrection of the body, just because the body was the real personality for Hebrew thought. If, then, the righteous were to share in a Messianic age *on earth*, it could be only through a resurrection into bodily life. This finds expression in Dan. xii. 2, 3:

'And many of them that sleep in the dust of the earth shall awake, some to everlasting life and some to shame and everlasting contempt. And they that be wise shall shine as the brightness of the firmament; and they that turn many to righteousness as the stars for ever and ever.'[3]

Apart from this late development, however, death sets the limit to life, and until this formula was found, the inherent sense of victory over death, which the consciousness of fellowship with God always tends to generate, had to remain unexpressed because unattained. The tomb is man's eternal home, his dwelling for generation after generation,[4] and it is the ill fate of the tyrant to have no such memorial.[5] Koheleth laments that the dead are forgotten without any discrimination.[6] In contrast

[1] Dr. G. Zuntz, in a private communication. He emphasizes the difference between philosophical speculations in Plato and Aristotle and popular usage and adds: 'a new inspiration was needed from outside before αἰών could be used as it is used in Philo, Plotinus and the Hermetica.'

[2] Sasse in Kittel's *Theol. Wört.* i, s.v. αἰών, p. 202.

[3] In the only other reference to such resurrection life (Isa. xxvi. 19), the term '*olam* does not occur. See further, pp. 100 f. above.

[4] Eccles. xii. 5; Ps. xlix. 12 (where read *ḳibram* for *ḳirbam*, with the Versions).

[5] Isa. xiv. 20; cf. Ps. ix. 6.   [6] Eccles. ix. 6.

to the tomb or other earthly memorial, Sheol has its own shadowy permanence beneath, one of darkness and desolation and inaction.[1]

Besides *'olam*, there are two other terms expressing eternity, viz. *'adh* (עַד) and *nezah* (נֶצַח), but a detailed examination of their much more limited use would add little, if anything, to what has been learnt from the principal term.[2] In general we can safely accept Orelli's conclusion concerning the three terms, viz. 'In content, the three words resolve themselves ultimately into one. *'olam* is time, whose borders are not perceptible or not existent; *'adh* is time which extends to the remotest conceivable borders; *nezah* is time rising above all borders.'[3] As he points out, Hebrew lacks any word to express time in general,[4] apart from its concrete content, time in the abstract, as we should say, and does not attain to any purely intellectual characterization of it.[5] Time is not a general entity or an abstract and subjective form, but something as individual and concrete as possible, always '*a* time', rather than 'time'. The conception of eternity is reached by piling up limited time-periods,[6] as with the reference to a thousand generations in equivalence to *'olam*.

The bearing of all this on our study of God and History is easily apparent. In Pedersen's words:[7] 'History consists of *doroth* each with its special stamp, but all the generations are fused into a great whole, wherein experiences are condensed. This concentrated time, into which all generations are fused and from which they spring, is called eternity, *'olam*.'

If, then, we combine the results of our examination of the two cardinal terms in which the Hebrew time-consciousness finds expression, we shall summarize in such terms as these:

(a) Time and eternity stand in close relation, not in any sharp contrast; eternity implies remoteness of time.

---

[1] Lam. iii. 6; Ps. cxliii. 3; Jer. li. 39, 57; Ezek. xxvi. 20. The curious phrase in Jer. xx. 17, 'forever pregnant' (Duhm), seems to refer to the wraith in Sheol.

[2] Dr. Robinson had intended to develop more fully what he has written here about נצח [Ed.].

[3] Op. cit., p. 98; Orelli, it will be remembered, derived *'olam* from 'hide', not 'be remote'. [4] p. 64.

[5] Much the same could be said of the Hebrew sense of space. The differences of Hebrew cosmology alone would make their sense of space very different from ours.

[6] Orelli, p. cit., p. 100. [7] *Israel I–II*, pp. 490, 491.

(b) A growing difference of *quality* is, however, reached through the transcendence of time in religious experience.

(c) This interrelation is of particular importance for the eschatology in which history finds its consummation, since this is timeless in content, though compelled to use a time-vocabulary.

(d) The Hebrew time-consciousness is much less interested in the causal relation of events, since these are referred more directly to God; hence the emphasis is taken off exact chronology and the precise time-sequence.

The aspects of history which will concern us in the following three chapters are first the prophetic interpretation of the time-process as a unity which manifests God's purpose; second, the Day of Yahweh, as the culminating point of time at which Yahweh will make Himself manifest to all men; third, the election of Israel, as the central instrument for the fulfilment of that purpose.

APPENDIX A
The Vocabulary of Time

שָׁנָה   √ change (from changing seasons).

חֹדֶשׁ   √ renew (the new moon, and so month).

חֹדֶשׁ יָמִים   Gen. xxix. 14; cf. יְ׳ יָמִים Deut. xxi. 13; 2 Kings xv. 13.

יֶרַח   (יָרֵחַ moon) month. ? √ ארח 'the wanderer'.

שַׁבָּת   (? √ cease).

יוֹם   [cf. חם הי׳ Gen. xviii. 1, רוח הי׳ Gen. iii. 8 for qualities.]

שַׁחַר   dawn (used with עָלָה Gen. xix. 15 &c.) [Ps. lvii. 9 = cviii. 3 'at dawn'.]

נֶשֶׁף   (√ blow Exod. xv. 10) twilight (breeze); cf. לרוח היום.

צָהֳרַיִם   (√ mount ظَهْر) highest point of sun.

בֹּקֶר   *point* of time (never of 'morning' = forenoon) √ split (plough).

עֶרֶב   (√ go in, set) (sunset, so) evening.

מָחָר   (√ be in front) to-morrow (time in front).

אֶתְמוֹל   (תְּמוֹל) yesterday (? لَا forms II and IV, prolong) (long time).

אֶמֶשׁ   (yesterday) ? √ last night Gen. xix. 34.

לַיְלָה   ? √

קֶדֶם   that which is before, = ancient Deut. xxxiii. 15 (mountains); Ps. lv. 20 יֹשֵׁב קֶדֶם (God); Prov. viii. 22, 23 (wisdom).

עַד   perpetuity BDB √ $\overline{\text{advance}}$ Job xxviii. 8 (past and
future) [much as עוֹלָם on small scale.]

נֶצַח   √ shine, be pre-eminent (and so enduring?).

תָּמִיד   s.v. מוד BDB 556 } 'continuity'.
       √ = stretch ـَـ }

רֶגַע   (√ move) a movement, so 'moment'.

שָׁבוּעַ   week as a 'seven' of days [from *any* day].

חֹדֶשׁ הָאָבִיב   month of fresh ears (of barley) = April.

זִו   2nd month April–May 1 Kings vi. 1, 37; brightness
(cf. flowers) (Targ.).

אֵיתָנִים   7th month. Steady flowings of wadies, 1 Kings viii. 2.

בּוּל   8th month ? יְבוּל produce.
     < √ יבל stream.

Appendix B

The Time-consciousness of Koheleth

This is as un-Hebraic as we should expect to find in a book from
which the sense of history is absent. Koheleth has no concern with
a redemptive past, and no vision of a Messianic future; in fact he
rules out of account both the memory[1] and the hope that would
make these possible. His time-consciousness, therefore, is useful as
a check on that of the Old Testament in general, by its very unlike-
ness to this. His use of עת shows that there is no progress to any
revealed goal; time consists of endless cycles of repetitions with
nothing new.[2] There is an appointed time for everything[3] and a
right method for dealing with it[4] but 'time and chance' happen to
all[5] and man does not know his (evil) time (i.e. that of his death).[6]
Long life and ample posterity are futile without satisfaction, which
none can get. The permanent earth supplies the background to the
successive generations of men.[7]

As for עוֹלָם the predominant sense is of the permanent or continuous in contrast with the fragmentary 'times'. We have just
noted this contrast for the earth and the generations that come and
go[8] and the opinion that past ages have already witnessed that which
we call new.[9] The wise and the foolish are alike in finding no
permanent remembrance;[10] forever are the dead without any share
in the life of earth;[11] and man at death goes to his agelong house;[12]
the only enduring thing is that which God does.[13]

[1] ii. 16, ix. 5.   [2] i. 2–11, vi. 10; cf. i. 10.   [3] iii. 1–8, x. 17.
[4] viii. 5, 6.   [5] ix. 11.   [6] ix. 12, cf. xii. 5.
[7] i. 4.   [8] i. 4.   [9] i. 10.   [10] ii. 16.
[11] ix. 6.   [12] xii. 5.   [13] iii. 14.

Thus עת and עולם stand in contrast more than elsewhere in the
Old Testament and this contrast forms perhaps the best approach
to the enigmatic passage in iii. 11 which reads in the R.V.: 'He
hath made everything beautiful in its time; also he hath set[1] the
world (*mg.* eternity) in their heart, yet so that man cannot find out
the work that God hath done from the beginning even to the end.'
But עולם never means 'world' in Ecclesiastes or anywhere else
in the Old Testament, whilst 'eternity' suggests too much, as is
shown by the temporal limits of the final clause of the verse. The
point seems to be the permanence or continuity of God's work (of
which man is conscious iii. 14) in contrast with the transitory beauty
of the time-content. Is בלבם here used in the figurative sense 'in
their midst', referring to the things of time? Cf. this use in Exod.
xv. 8, 2 Sam. xviii. 14, &c.

[1] Cf. iii. 10 for the use of נתן.

IX

THE PROPHETIC INTERPRETATION OF HISTORY

§ 1. HEBREW HISTORIOGRAPHY

THE Old Testament is formally a history, into which other kinds of literature have been incorporated. Thus extensive codes of law, such as we see in Leviticus and in the second half of Deuteronomy, have been inserted at convenient places, whilst writings traditionally ascribed to David, Solomon, and the prophets form a sort of appendix to the historical books. But the history itself is both incomplete and different in nature from what we mean by history. Its constituent books fall into two main groups, viz. Joshua, Judges, Samuel, and Kings on the one hand, dealing with events in Canaan in the pre-exilic period, and on the other Chronicles, Ezra, and Nehemiah dealing with the post-exilic, but only down to about 400 B.C. Thus we have no history of the exilic period, 586–539, or of the four centuries before the Christian era. To compensate for these lacunae we have the Pentateuch, which is professedly a continuous history from the Creation until the entrance into Canaan. But this and the subsequent narratives, to which it serves as preface, are not in the scientific form of history as we know it to-day, with criticism of the sources, documentation of the statements, analysis of the causative factors. There appears to be much patchwork, with narratives that are repetitive or inconsistent, and general statements that are didactic and strongly propagandist. Narratives and documents are not infrequently used in a way remote from their original intention. Thus the Book of Judges presents stories of early heroes told for their own sake originally, but now set in a framework of doctrinal writing which enforces the divine retribution of evil. The Books of Kings in similar fashion offer a selection of events under the monarchy largely dictated by moral and religious judgements on the character and conduct of the respective kings.[1]

Critical study of the literature has shown us the source from which this point of view is derived. It comes chiefly from the teaching of moral and religious retribution by the prophets of the eighth century, and especially as this was formulated in the

---

[1] Cf. also Ezra iv.

seventh-century Book of Deuteronomy. At the same time, it should be recognized that the historical books contain elements prior to prophecy, though allied to it in substance. The earlier (JE) Pentateuchal narratives can be described by a modern critic[1] as 'a monument of old-prophetic thought', and indeed, it was at one time customary to call them 'the prophetical narratives of the Hexateuch'.[2] We have also to remember that there were outstanding prophets before those of the eighth century, even though we have little, if any, contemporary record of their teaching; such are Moses, Nathan, Samuel, Elijah. We are always in danger of being misled in our historical judgements by the 'chance' element in literary record, the accident that a recorder was at hand, or that the record has escaped destruction. There is little doubt, for example, that we tend to over-emphasize the contrast between the eighth-century prophets and their predecessors, and that we do not sufficiently recognize a real continuity in the moral and religious teaching from the earliest times; the figure of Elijah is a notable reminder of this. Having said this, however, we turn necessarily to the prophets from the eighth to the sixth century, who were the earliest to find literary record for their teaching (through their disciples); we turn to them inevitably for the clearest statement of the principles of the prophetic interpretation of history. It is these principles which have actually shaped the presentation of history in the historical books.

§ 2. THE CREATIVE PROPHETS

The really creative period of Hebrew prophecy extends from Amos in the eighth century to Deutero-Isaiah in the sixth. There is considerable variety in their respective contributions, whether this is to be traced to personal idiosyncrasy or to difference of historical environment. All generalizations about their principles of interpretation can be no more than rough approximations. But three main principles at least can be asserted. The prophetic interpretation of history was (*a*) theocentric, (*b*) constitutive, (*c*) unifying.

[1] Procksch, *Isaiah* (1930), p. 14.

[2] So S. R. Driver, *Introduction*[9], pp. 116–25. The justification for the name can be seen in the account of the differences and agreements of JE, as compared with the prophets given, e.g. by Gunkel, *Genesis*, pp. lxi–lxiv; Carpenter and Harford Battersby, *The Hexateuch*, I. p. 107; Kent, *The Growth and Contents of the Old Testament*, pp. 35, 36.

(*a*) In the first place, they are agreed in the emphatic demand that history should be interpreted from the standpoint of God, since it is God who effectively controls it. This is what is implied in the cardinal and characteristic demand of Isaiah of Jerusalem for faith: 'if ye will not be firm in faith, ye shall not be confirmed in life'; 'he who is firm in faith shall not be shamed.'[1] Such faith requires the clear vision of the world as God sees it, looking down from His serene height. Above the coming and going of the Ethiopian embassy, and all the pro-Egyptian diplomacy against Assyria,[2] Isaiah hears Yahweh saying, 'I quietly behold in my dwelling-place' (verse 4)—not because He can do nothing or is indifferent, but because He controls the harvest of the future and awaits His appointed hour. The believer in Him will share that quiet confidence, as does the prophet:

> By returning and rest shall you be saved,
> In quietness and confidence shall be your strength. (xxx. 15)

Of Isaiah's theocentric interpretation of world affairs, Procksch rightly claims that 'it is the grandest view of history in the ancient world which we know down to the middle of the first millennium, B.C.'.[3] But we can see the same principle at work, if not on quite the same scale, in Amos. He names a number of effects which all point to their sufficient cause, and says, as a culminating word, 'shall evil befall a city, and Yahweh hath not done it?'[4] He interprets a whole series of recent disasters, famine, drought, blasting and mildew, pestilence and the sword, earthquake, as all due to the direct activity of Yahweh. They are disciplinary penalties intended to bring repentance: 'yet ye have not returned unto me, saith Yahweh' is the repeated refrain (iv. 6–11). So, even beyond the borders of Israel, it is Yahweh's judgement that falls on Moab for the wrong done to Edom, and it is Yahweh's hand that controls the movements of the peoples: 'Have not I brought up Israel out of the land of Egypt and the Philistines from Caphtor and the Syrians from Kir?'[5] So also Isaiah, facing a more potent Assyria than Amos

---

[1] vii. 9; xxviii. 16, where read with LXX *yebosh* (יֵבוֹשׁ) for *yaḥish* (יָחִישׁ).

[2] Isa. xviii. 1–7.   [3] Op. cit., p. 13.   [4] iii. 6.

[5] ii. 1–3; ix. 7. The wide horizon of Amos is shown by the fact that some 38 names of lands and places occur in it (J. Rieger, *Die Bedeutung der Geschichte für die Verkündigung des Amos und Hosea*, p. 25). Köhler (op. cit., p. 62) makes the interesting suggestion that the presence of visitors from the surrounding peoples at the Bethel festival was the occasion of the opening prophecies of Amos.

could have known, contemptuously dismisses the great empire
as but the rod of Yahweh's anger and the staff of His indignation, and sees the prescribed limit to its insolent and aggressive
pride (Isa. x. 12, 15). So Jeremiah hears Yahweh speaking of
'Nebuchadnezzar my servant', and Deutero-Isaiah calls Cyrus,
who does not know the hand that girds him, 'the anointed of
Yahweh'.[1]

It is this theocentricity that alone explains the peculiar
detachment and consequent intensity of the prophets. They are
the outstanding example of the general truth that a man must
find a fulcrum outside himself in order to lift the world to
something higher than himself. They escaped from the narrow-
ing influence of egoism, of which the 'false' prophets are accused,[2] not so much through their concern for social morality—
that was effect rather than cause—but through the remarkable
degree of their theocentricity. We are apt to take their almost
inhuman detachment from self and representative identification
with God for granted, as they themselves do. Yet it is something
new in the world, as applied to history, and is as important a
change as that from Ptolemaic to Copernican astronomy. It is
one of the many services rendered to our understanding of
prophecy by Jeremiah's autobiographical poems that they
reveal the cost of this detachment and the intensity of this
passion to declare that God and God alone is the true centre of
the universe.

(b) We come to closer quarters with the actual history when
we pass from the theocentric principle to the constitutive—by
which I mean the constant incorporation of past, present, and
future events into that which claims to be a word of the ever-
living God. This also is something which we take for granted,
until we try to frame a philosophy of revelation, with the ever-
recurrent enigma of contingency set in the heart of the absolute.
At any rate, we may say here that it was this constitutive
method, this direct incorporation of human life into the
prophet's word, that has given to that word its perennial appeal
to the sons of men.

At first sight we may be surprised that the prophets do not
make more use of the past history of Israel, as it is known to

[1] Jer. xxvii. 6; Isa. xlv. 1.
[2] Jer. xxiii. 23, with Cornill's note; though verse 24 may point rather to the
repudiation of a locally limited God, as Peake argues.

ourselves; for it is true that they make comparatively little use of it in detail, and usually speak of it in sweeping generalizations. But two things must be remembered. The literary history as it lies before us in the Bible was for the most part written subsequently to the great prophets; reading, like writing, was a rare and professional art, and written documents would be a rare and costly possession. It was from oral tradition that men's knowledge of the past was chiefly or wholly derived. It must not be assumed that even a great prophet could necessarily read or write; in fact we find Jeremiah dictating his oracles from memory to Baruch after twenty years of prophetic activity. A prophet's references to past history would ordinarily depend on the common material of oral tradition,[1] such as the destruction of the cities of the plain,[2] the Exodus and the desert wanderings,[3] the crime of Gibeah,[4] the rebellion of Jehu.[5] The variety of the use made of such material is illustrated by the fact that in Amos David figures only as a musician or poet, whilst the only reference to David in Hosea is generally regarded as a later addition,[6] whereas Isaiah begins the national history with David, and emphasizes the central importance of Jerusalem, the city against which David encamped.[7] As may be expected the prophets have no antiquarian interests; they always refer to the past to point their message for the present. Naturally enough, they shape its presentation to their practical purpose. Hosea gives us a different impression of Jacob from that of the patriarchal narratives in Genesis.[8] Jeremiah refers to the destruction of the temple at Shiloh (of which we have no direct record)—

'Go ye now unto my place which was at Shiloh, where I caused my name to dwell at the first, and see what I did to it for the wickedness of my people Israel.' (vii. 12, xxvi. 6)

Here the past warns, but it can equally well encourage. Deutero-Isaiah (xliii. 16 ff.) refers to the ancient work of Yahweh in making a way through the Red Sea and in overthrowing Pharaoh, as the pledge and proof of the new Exodus from Babylon.

Naturally it is with contemporary affairs that the prophets

[1] This is shown for Amos and Hosea by J. Rieger (op. cit., pp. 112, 113).
[2] Amos iv. 11; Hos. xi. 8.
[3] Amos ii. 10, iii. 1, v. 25, ix. 7; Hos. xi. 1, xii. 9 ff., xiii. 4 f.
[4] Hos. ix. 9, x. 9.   [5] Hos. i. 4.   [6] Amos vi. 5; Hos. iii. 5.
[7] xxix. 1; cf. Procksch, *Isaiah*, p. 11.   [8] xii. 3 ff.

are most concerned. They were intensely practical; whether they proclaimed judgement or deliverance they were dealing with an actual situation. To it they applied the word of revelation, disclosing God at the centre of the situation; in it they believed that word to have operative power, and to inaugurate an ultimate decision and manifestation of God. To attempt to follow this out in detail would be to write a history of the creative centuries, covering both the social, moral, and religious conditions of Israel on the one hand, and political relations with other peoples on the other. Yahweh controlled the issues of both. So also in home affairs, there was no line of demarcation, such as we instinctively make between social and moral questions on the one side and religious on the other. Hosea, for example, can show us how intimately they were blended. It was 'the spirit of whoredom' within the heart of Israel which was the common root of the religious infidelity of Baal-worship and the sexual immoralities of both cult-prostitution and family life.

During the period which concerns us the horizon of Israel's foreign relations was constantly expanding, through the pressure of events.[1] But the prophets were equal to each new demand made upon their power to interpret the events. The broad principle applied was that Yahweh makes use of the nations around Israel to further His purpose within her, a purpose that will ultimately affect the whole world. Thus Jeremiah is made from the outset 'a prophet unto the nations'; he is made an overseer, the steward of God, 'set over the nations and over the kingdoms, to pluck up and to break down and to destroy and to overthrow; to build and to plant'.[2] This is an amazing commission, especially for a youth so little of the self-assertive type as Jeremiah. It reveals the enormous power of the theocentric conception. The working out of the commission is seen in ch. xxv, where the figure of the cup given to the nations to drink denotes the overwhelming power of Babylon, made irresistible by the will of God. Here, as in so many other oracles, the concrete details which we group as geography, history, ethnology, sociology are taken up into the single purpose of God. This is the constitutive or constructive principle of prophecy, which is never a word spoken in a vacuum, but always involves a strong grasp of actualities. The interpretation of these by the prophet is naturally very different from that

---

[1] Köhler, op. cit., pp. 63, 64.   [2] i. 5, 10.

which a member of one of these nations would have given, different indeed from that which some Israelite politician would have given. But since it deals with actual events, and entails a definite attitude towards them, it is inevitably a political judgement.

This raises the vexed question, how far ought the prophets to be regarded as politicians?[1] The clearest example of direct political activity is undoubtedly Isaiah. In the crisis of the Syro-Ephraimitic attack on Jerusalem he takes the definitely political action of opposing any resort to Assyria, though he fails to convince the king and his counsellors.[2] Towards the close of his career, in the time of Sennacherib, he definitely opposes any political alliance with Egypt.[3] To all intents and purposes, therefore, Isaiah must be reckoned a politician. On the other hand, his motives and standards clearly mark him off from the ordinary politician. He is no nationalist, even though he believes that Yahweh will bring the nation through its present troubles. Again, he is no pacifist, even though he consistently opposes Jingoism, for he constantly recognizes the place of military force in the divine Providence.[4] His motives and standards are drawn from the unwavering assertion of theocentricity. God is the supreme fact with which men must reckon, and He says the last word.[5]

(c) The third principle of the prophetic interpretation of history is a further application of the theocentric, and is indeed involved in the constitutive. It may be called the unifying principle, which acted like a magnet in evoking a pattern amongst iron filings. It created a pattern of history out of all its complexities, a pattern which disclosed the previously hidden purpose of God. This has been clearly described by Professor Porteous, and we may quote his statement of it:

'History . . . is the sphere of God's redemptive activity and a

---

[1] A useful review of this topic is given by K. Elliger, in 'Prophet und Politik', *ZAW*, 1935, pp. 3–22. He takes Winckler and Troeltsch as representing the two extremes of affirmation and negation, and argues from a study of Isaiah's prophetic experience that the prophets were given a real vision of the future by the Spirit of God, and that they accepted military as well as non-military and 'miraculous' agencies. Thus, though working with different means from those of ordinary politics, they were politicians, and did not sit by with folded hands as mere commentators.

[2] vii. 1 ff.   [3] xxx and xxxi.   [4] e.g. ix. 11.

[5] The relation of the prophets to the future will be discussed under 'The Day of Yahweh'.

certain group of historical events, the Exodus and Election of Israel as the Chosen People, the conquest and establishment of the monarchy under David, is taken as a kind of pattern of Yahweh's dealings with His people, which controls the prophetic view of God's subsequent activity and of the end to which all things are tending. We hear of a new Exodus, a new Israel after the spirit, a new covenant, a new occupation of the Holy Land and the sure mercies of David. . . . The unity of the Old Testament (and the unity of Hebrew prophecy) lies outside itself in God.'[1]

This general pattern is no inexorable prescription of detail, however sure in its final result. It is conditioned by the human response to the divine, the interplay of human freedom with divine control. We could hardly have a clearer statement of this than in the narrative of Jeremiah's visit to the potter's house.[2] Impelled to make the visit by divine inspiration, he discovers the purpose for which God has sent him thither only as he watches the potter at work. The rotating clay on the upper wheel is assuming a certain shape under the potter's hand; then, suddenly, he crushes the clay together and begins afresh on something else. Why is this? Because, perhaps, some fault in the clay makes the first design impracticable. This, says the divine revelation to the watching prophet, is God's way with the nations, and with Israel herself. The declared purpose of God is always conditioned by the response of the particular nation to it. The uttered prophecy of good or evil may be reversed, and the reason will lie in the obedience or disobedience of the nation to the will of God. The prophecy of good is meant to encourage goodness; the prophecy against evil to promote penitence. Thus, to the prophet, there is no weakness or inconsistency in an apparent change in the divine pattern; it means, in fact, a larger and richer revelation of God than any unswerving conformity to a fixed pattern could afford.

From this standpoint of conditionality we can understand the so-called pessimism of pre-exilic prophecy. In contrast with those who cried 'peace, peace' when there was no peace,[3] the great prophets before the exile were prophets of judgement, even though some of them could look beyond the judgement to the grace of which it was part, and make this explicit also.[4] But

---

[1] *Record and Revelation*, pp. 241, 247.   [2] xviii. 1–12.   [3] Jer. vi. 14, viii. 11.
[4] On both features, see J. Morgenstern, in *Hebrew Union College Annual*, vol. xv (1940), p. 302; the prophetic denunciation was the necessary complement to Israel's (unilateral) breach of the covenant.

it would be wrong to infer from this common feature that true prophecy is necessarily denunciatory. It is true that man as he is will always come under the judgement of the holy God, and that a superficial optimism is very far from Biblical religion. But we cannot deny the title of a true prophet to Deutero-Isaiah, with his message of comfort and restoration, nor can we deny as true an inspiration to the later part of Ezekiel's ministry as to the earlier. The deeper unity of inspiration can comprehend both denunciation and consolation as equally dependent on the prophet's relation to his own times and to the particular needs of his contemporaries.

The unity of the divine pattern is not conceived to spring from forces immanent in the substance of life. Yahweh indeed works from within as well as from without, and He is constantly represented as using or intensifying the latent capacities of men, so far as they can promote His aims. But there is never the suggestion that history achieves the divine purpose as the hands of a wound-up clock complete their circuit of the dial. The unity of history depends wholly on God and its consummation must be wrought out by Him. The Old Testament does not project this consummation to some supra- or post-mundane realm; nowhere in it (except for the quite exceptional destinies of Enoch and Elijah) is 'heaven' the goal of human life. Nevertheless, history does possess a goal, and this is to be found in a kingdom of God to be established on earth. Not all will attain to it, but the end of history will crown the work by an eschatological and divine act.

This future historical vindication of God to be accomplished on the earth is part, and a very essential part, of the prophetic interpretation of the time-process from the days of Amos onwards. We shall see this clearly when we come to consider the focal point of 'the Day of Yahweh'. But the fuller declaration of it was reserved for the apocalyptic into which prophecy developed by a natural transition. In the Book of Daniel, for example, we see the working out of the divine purpose in a series of stages, diversely pictured, yet always culminating in the final victory of God.[1] In apocalyptic the underlying and presupposed unity of history becomes explicit. The tangled web of human history is resolved into a clear pattern, and all that

[1] As in the interpretation of the image of Dan. ii. 36 ff., or in the 'animal' kingdoms of vii. 1–14.

seemed to challenge the divine purpose is now seen to be part of it, in the sense of adding to the glory of the final manifestation.

This, as we should always remember, is a new conception. Nowhere else in ancient literature can we find such a unity.[1] From the prophets the conception passed to the apocalyptists, and from them, when adopted by the Christian faith, it passed into our Western civilization. Here it has been applied in many ways and to many ends in which no religious purpose or presupposition is manifest, as in economic or political theories of history. Yet the idea of such a unity was born nowhere else than in the theocentricity of the prophetic teaching, and perhaps only there will it find full justification.

§ 3. History as Revelation

The interpretation of history of which we have reviewed the salient characteristics is both idealistic and realistic. It begins in the unseen and it makes the greatest assumption which the mind of man can make—the existence of God. But, granted this presupposition, the prophets are thoroughly realistic in their handling of historical events. They would have entirely concurred with the modern writer who reminds us that 'A fact is a holy thing, and its life should never be laid down on the altar of a generalization'.[2] Instead of such a sacrifice, they consecrated the life of their times by claiming it for the service of Yahweh. They were children of their own times as well as ambassadors of eternity. They are what they are through the impact upon them of all the moral, social, and political forces of their age, as well as of the biological and psychological factors which shape individual lives. Whatever the truth of the divine revelation made through them, it was shaped and coloured by what they themselves were. It is wrong as well as useless to try to detach the prophetic word from its historical context, until we are sure that we have understood it. We have to do with history becoming articulate through these prophetic voices which belong integrally to it. Thus we may say that

---

[1] Charles (*Daniel*, Introd., p. xxv) remarks that it was 'apocalyptic and not prophecy that was the first to grasp the great idea that all history, human, cosmological and spiritual is a unity—a unity that follows inevitably as a corollary to the unity of God as enforced by the O.T. prophets'. I should prefer to say that apocalyptic made explicit what was already implicit in prophecy.

[2] Nock, *Hibbert Journal*, July, 1933, p. 607.

history itself creates the values by which it is to be judged, by which in fact, it judges itself.

The revelation afforded by history is naturally of God in relation to the world. It is religious rather than metaphysical, even though all religion involves metaphysics. The revelation is of both judgement and grace, in the unity of an ultimately gracious purpose. There is no sense of antithesis between the two; Yahweh is 'a righteous God and a Saviour'.[1] The salvation belongs to the holiness of God as truly as the righteous judgement.

It is easy to dismiss the prophetic interpretation of history as too simple to explain its complexities. We have become much more aware of these than men could be then, but there is nothing new in the objection itself. It was the criticism raised by priests and prophets who were the contemporaries of Isaiah, for they said:

> Whom will he teach knowledge?
> And whom will he make to understand the message?
> Them that are weaned from the milk
> And drawn from the breasts?
> For it is precept upon precept, precept upon precept,
> Line upon line, line upon line,
> Here a little, there a little. (xxviii. 9-13)

Differing views can be taken of the exact meaning of the prophet's report of their saying, but the most likely one is that they were dismissing Isaiah's interpretation as 'the speech of the nursery',[2] mere babble. He replies by what is the only ultimate answer, by an appeal to history itself. They shall hear another 'babble', that of the unintelligible speech of an invader.[3]

Finally, we note that the literary record of history eventually assumes a new objectivity in becoming canonical and authoritative. As such it replaces the prophecy from which it drew its interpretation. The change from an oral to a literary revelation is influential in many ways, but chiefly because it introduces a certain fixity into the idea of revelation which did not attach to its original form of prophetic utterance. Revelation becomes static instead of dynamic. Both Jew and Christian have had to introduce the idea of a new interpretation, an oral tradition, administered by synagogue or Church, in order to make the

---

[1] Isa. xlv. 21.   [2] So Wade, in Westminster Comm. ad loc.
[3] Cf. Deut. xviii. 21, 22 for the explicit statement of this appeal—though it is modified by xiii. 1.

written revelation applicable to the needs of successive generations, and in so doing have often abandoned the historical meaning, whether for devotional or dogmatic ends. But graver still
is the loss of that sense of dynamic which belongs to the original
prophecy, the sense of a divine purpose at this moment in operation and of a real continuity between the prophetic oracle and
ourselves. The New Testament recovered this in its doctrine
of the Holy Spirit, and where this is lost there can be no vital
revelation of the living God. History in the making was always
dynamic, pointing beyond itself. The revelation that claims to
be historical will not less claim a double fulfilment—both in
further history, so long as the time-process endures, and also in
that larger and necessary complement of history, the eternal
reality which alone gives adequate meaning to the time-process.

X

THE DAY OF YAHWEH

ONE of the great themes of prophetic religion is that human history will culminate in a full and final revelation of Yahweh which will inaugurate His kingly rule upon the earth. The central phrase expressive of this inauguration is 'The Day of Yahweh'. It suggests the twofold character of the history as faith interprets it. On the one hand, it is implied that much of the history has been alien or contradictory to the purposes of the God of Israel. On the other, all this history is declared to be but the prelude to the triumphant vindication of God. There is much that rightly belongs to the theme in which the actual phrase does not occur, such as many passages introduced by 'In that day'. But a study of the actual occurrences of the phrase, of which there are some twenty-eight,[1] is the best introduction to the subject.

§ 1. THE GENERAL MEANING

From the earliest occurrence of the phrase, to be found in Amos v. 18, 20, and throughout its use, we note that it predominantly denotes 'darkness and not light', and that this is contrary to general expectation. The day will indeed usher in better things for 'the righteous remnant' of Israel,[2] but in itself is essentially for the prophets a day of *stern judgement*. That characteristic obviously implies that other days are not Yahweh's as they ought to be; His rule is not yet manifest, and therefore the day on which He does vindicate Himself will bring the penalties of judgement on those who have failed to make the other days His.

A second point to notice, again from the earliest reference and onwards, is that the judgement and the penalty will concern Israel as well as the Gentiles. It is true that the Day of Yahweh will bring the punishment of Israel's enemies, such as Egypt,[3]

---

[1] This includes slightly varied forms, such as *leYahweh* in place of the genitive. They are as follows: יוֹם י'' (16) Isa. xiii. 6, 9; Ezek. xiii. 5; Joel i. 15, ii. 1, 11, iii. 4, iv. 14 (ii. 31, iii. 14); Amos v. 18 (bis), 20; Obad. 15; Zeph. i. 7, 14 (bis); Mal. iii. 23 (iv. 5). לי'' (7) Ezek. xxx. 3; Isa. ii. 12, xxxiv. 8, lviii. 5; Zech. xiv. 1; cf. Isa. lxi. 2; Jer. xlvi. 10. With אַף or עברת (5) Ezek. vii. 19; Zeph. i. 18, ii. 2–3; Lam. ii. 22.

[2] Zeph. iii. 9 ff., &c.   [3] Jer. xlvi. 10; Ezek. xxx. 3.

Babylon,[1] Edom,[2] heathen nations in general,[3] and the apocalyptic Gog.[4] But the judgement falls also on Israel,[5] or the evil-
doers within her.[6] The capture of Jerusalem in 586 is regarded
as the Day of Yahweh,[7] and another capture of the city is
anticipated before Yahweh finally delivers her.[8] We notice
throughout that the Day of Yahweh concerns nations rather
than individuals; it is as nations that men are gathered into the
valley of (divine) decision.[9] On the day when Yahweh rises
to give judgement, He will gather nations and assemble kings.[10]
This is part of that corporate emphasis, which preceded the
(relative) individualism first discernible in Jeremiah and
Ezekiel.

A third feature of these references concerns the manner and
method of the administration of divine judgement. It is clearly
represented as a superhuman intervention in the affairs of history, not the term of a gradual evolution. Like the theophanies,[11]
it is sometimes accompanied by abnormal phenomena of Nature,
such as the darkening of sun and moon, and the quaking of the
earth,[12] changes in the contours of the earth,[13] or its devastation,[14]
or the abolition of the night.[15] Ordinarily, however, the punitive
work is done by the normal agencies of Nature, as by the plague
of locusts in Joel or by hostile armies, as when in the oracle
against Babylon of Isa. xiii, Yahweh says, 'Behold I am stirring
up the Medes against them' (verse 17). As S. R. Driver says,[16]
'The conception places out of sight the human agents, by whom
actually the judgement, as a rule, is effected, and regards the
decisive movements of history as the exclusive manifestation of
Jehovah's purpose and power'. But the Day of Yahweh is not
dependent on the operation of what are, after all, subsidiary
agencies. Two interrelated passages of Trito-Isaiah are here
relevant, viz. lix. 16:

When He saw with amazement that there was none to interpose,
His own arm helped Him,
His righteous might upheld Him,

---

[1] Isa. xiii. 6, 9.   [2] Isa. xxxiv. 8, lxiii. 4.
[3] Isa. lxi. 2; Obad. 15; Joel iii. 4, iv. 14 (Heb.).
[4] Ezek. xxxix. 8, 11, 13.   [5] Amos v. 18, 20.
[6] Isa. ii. 12 ff.; Zeph. i. 7, 14, ii. 2, 3; Joel i. 15, ii. 1, 11; Mal. iii. 19, 23 (iv. 1, 5).
[7] Ezek. xiii. 5; Lam. i. 12, ii. 1, 22.   [8] Zech. xiv. 1-3.
[9] Joel iii. 1-15.   [10] Zeph. iii. 8.
[11] Chapter I.   [12] Isa. xiii. 10 ff.; Joel iv. 15, 16 (iii. 15, 16).
[13] Zech. xiv. 4 ff.   [14] Isa. xxxiv. 8 ff.
[15] Zech. xiv. 7.   [16] *Joel and Amos*, p. 185.

and lxiii. 4, 5:

> For a day of vengeance was in my heart,
> And my year of redemption had come.
> I looked, but there was none to help,
> I looked in amazement, but there was none to uphold;
> So my own arm helped me,
> And my fury upheld me.

In such passages we see, as often, the double-sided implication of the day. It brings at one and the same time retribution for the wrong and deliverance of the right; the year of Yahweh's favour is also the day of His vengeance.[1] It is, in fact, the day of His activity,[2] in whatever direction that activity is needed to put wrong things right, and 'great will be His activity'.[3]

A fourth and last point to notice in the general significance of the day is its close proximity. Amos (v. 1, 2) utters his dirge over Israel as though she had already fallen. Isaiah (ii. 12) speaks of the day against all that is proud and high as something in the immediate future. Malachi emphasizes the surprise of the coming of the day:

> Suddenly to His temple shall come
> Yahweh whom ye are seeking. . . .
> Behold, He comes! (iii. 1)

In numerous passages the nearness of the day is explicitly declared: 'the Day of Yahweh is near.'[4] The immediacy of the day is but one aspect of its certainty, for it is already 'in the heart' of God,[5] that is, for Hebrew psychology, part of the purpose of God, a purpose that is pressing on to its fulfilment. Here, again, as in our study of the meaning of 'eternity' (*'olam*), we are lifted into a sort of timelessness, a point also illustrated in the use of the prophetic perfect. Thought is always pressing forward into action, and finds its expression most naturally for the Hebrew in the contemplation of the act as already performed.

Thus, the four characteristics of the day which are most likely to attract our attention are those of judgement, universality, supernatural intervention, and proximity. Further and more exact definition of its meaning for the subject of 'God and

---

[1] Isa. lxi. 2. Cf. Eichrodt, op. cit. i. 249, 250, who points out that this is characteristic for Israel's thought.
[2] Mal. iii. 17.   [3] Joel ii. 21: *higdil Yahweh la'ªsoth* (prophetic perfect).
[4] *ḳarob*; Ezek. xxx. 3; Isa. xiii. 6; Obad. 15; Joel i. 15.   [5] Isa. lxiii. 4.

History' must wait upon our view of the origin of the phrase, a matter much in dispute during the last generation, and still very much open to discussion.

§ 2. The Origin of 'The Day of Yahweh'

The most natural and direct explanation of the phrase regards it as one more example of the Hebrew characterization of time by its concrete content. Thus Job curses 'his day', by which is meant the day of his birth,[1] whilst an untimely death is described as one 'on not his day'.[2] The wage-earner is to be paid 'on his day' of work,[3] and David speaks of Nabal's sheep-shearing as 'a good day', a phrase used elsewhere of a festival.[4] In particular, the Isaianic phrase, 'the day of Midian', denotes the day of Gideon's victory over Midianite marauders,[5] whilst 'the day of Jerusalem' is that of its capture by the Babylonians.[6] Ezekiel refers to the same event when denouncing the prophets of Israel because 'they did not stand in the breach . . . in the battle, in the day of Yahweh'.[7] There are Arabic parallels to this use of 'day' for 'day of battle', and as W. R. Smith claimed, 'By taking the day of Yahweh to mean His day of battle and victory we gain for the conception a natural basis in Hebrew idiom'.[8] It was naturally assumed that the battle would be in Israel's favour, since Yahweh was the God of Israel. If, then, this was the conception attaching to the phrase in the time of Amos, we can understand his startling reversal of the current meaning (v. 18):

> Ah! they who desire the day of Yahweh!
> What use will the day of Yahweh be to you?
> It is darkness and not light.

That is to say, the day would be one of Israel's defeat, so bringing the penalty of her sins. Later prophets followed in the path thus opened by Amos.

What causes us to hesitate in accepting this apparently simple and straightforward explanation of the phrase? Chiefly, the fact that the contexts often seem to carry a much wider content of meaning than 'day of battle' easily affords. In such instances

[1] iii. 1.   [2] xv. 32.   [3] Deut. xxiv. 15.
[4] 1 Sam. xxv. 8; Esther viii. 17 (with *mishteh*).
[5] Isa. ix. 3 (4), cf. Judges vii. 9 ff.
[6] Ps. cxxxvii. 7, cf. Obad. 12; Lam. i. 12, &c.
[7] xiii. 5 (LXX).   [8] *The Prophets of Israel*[2], p. 398.

(including the much larger group of passages introduced by 'In that day'[1]) the 'darkness' may be not merely figurative, but an actual phenomenon of Nature. Joel, for example, links extraordinary physical phenomena with the Day of Yahweh, beginning with a visitation of locusts (iii. 3, 4, EVV ii. 30, 31):

> I will shew wonders in the heavens and in the earth,
> Blood and fire and pillars of smoke,
> The sun shall be turned into darkness
> And the moon into blood,
> Before the great and terrible day of Yahweh come.

The prophecy against Babylon in Isa. xiii certainly includes armed conflict (verse 2), but also goes far beyond it:

> 'The stars of heaven and the constellations thereof shall not give their light: the sun shall be darkened in his going forth, and the moon shall not cause her light to shine. . . . I will make the heavens to tremble and the earth shall be shaken out of her place, in the wrath of Yahweh of hosts and in the day of his fierce anger.' (verses 10, 13)

This cosmic and eschatological setting of the day, with its theophanic accompaniments—earthquake, storm, volcano, fire, and pestilence—led Gressmann in 1905[2] to look beyond the day of battle to the much larger conception of a world-catastrophe and a world-eschatology. This existed, he argued, long before such evidence for it, as we find in the prophets. It was of foreign origin, mediated, like other mythology, through the Canaanites, chiefly from Babylonia.[3] With this vision of judgement was linked a similar anticipation of the golden age which was to follow it. This thesis, in both respects following up Gunkel's *Schöpfung und Chaos*, was worked out by Gressmann impressively and has rightly received much attention. But it has been subjected to powerful criticism, notably that of Sellin[4] and Mowinckel.[5] Sellin declared that neither the Babylonians nor the Egyptians had an eschatological expectation, and that the texts to which Gressmann appealed are not to be understood in this sense.[6] Mowinckel claims that it breaks down in three

[1] e.g. Isa. ii. 11, where followed by the words, 'Yahweh of hosts hath a day'.
[2] *Der Ursprung der isr.-jüdischen Eschatologie.*
[3] Op. cit., pp. 150, 159 ff.
[4] *Der altt. Prophetismus*, 1912, pp. 111, 176, *et passim* in ii, 'Alter, Wesen und Ursprung der altt. Eschatologie': *Israelitische-jüdische Religionsgeschichte*, 1933, pp. 63 ff.
[5] *Psalmenstudien.* ii. 221 ff.   [6] *Religionsgeschichte*, p. 64 (1933).

ways: the Old Testament does not speak of a world-catastrophe in Gressmann's sense; there is no proof of the existence of such a theory in the ancient Oriental world; the theory offers no explanation of the uniqueness of Israel's eschatology.

Mowinckel's own theory of the Day of Yahweh might be described as the reverse of Gressmann's. Whereas Gressmann derived the day from the eschatology, Mowinckel derives the eschatology from the day. On the basis of his detailed examination of the enthronement Psalms—those marked by the phrase 'Yahweh has become king'—he argues against either an historical or an eschatological exegesis in favour of a cultic one. He claims that Yahweh's enthronement was celebrated every year as the high point of the autumnal festival known as the Feast of Tabernacles. The enthronement was the nucleus of an elaborate mythology, going back to the creation and symbolically initiating the New Year; the blessings which are sought are declared to be already given, and 'Yahweh has become king' is the characteristic cultic cry. The earthly king is the representative of the heavenly, and a principal channel of His grace. The New Year's Festival was borrowed from the Canaanites, and its fate as such was sealed by the exile.[1] The argument then proceeds to equate the phrase 'Day of Yahweh' with this New Year's Festival on the ground of alleged identity of content.[2] It is claimed that the Day of Yahweh so conceived gives the needed unity to the eschatological data of the Old Testament, which are so very fragmentary as they lie before us. The cult made them a present reality to the worshippers. It did not originally involve an eschatology,[3] but it ultimately supplied one, when Israel's adversities threw her hopes into the future.[4] 'The cult is the primary element, the eschatology the derived.'[5]

In passing judgement on Mowinckel's theory, we should distinguish three elements in it, calling for separate consideration, viz. (1) the alleged existence of a New Year's Festival in Israel, with the enthronement of Yahweh as king for its central feature, (2) the alleged identity of this festival with the Day of Yahweh,

---

[1] Cf. *ZAW*, 1930, p. 269, where he says that 'die Auffassung des alten Herbst- und Neujahrfestes als eines Thronbesteigungsfestes Yahwes erst in der Assyrerzeit unter babylonischem Einfluss aufgekommen ist'. After the Exile the Hebrews adopted the Babylonian calendar beginning the year in the spring instead of the autumn.

[2] Op. cit., p. 311.   [3] Op. cit., p. 313.
[4] Op. cit., p. 325.   [5] Op. cit., p. 231.

(3) the claim that this festival of enthronement was the source of the eschatology. The first of these is now accepted by many interpreters of the Old Testament.[1] There is no real difficulty in the way of such acceptance, although the festival is nowhere named amongst the three primary Hebrew festivals.[2] To postulate its existence, however, would explain the enthronement psalms better than any other theory, and also such survivals as 'the day of horn-blowing'.[3]

The second point is the alleged identity of this Enthronement Festival, if accepted, with the Day of Yahweh. Mowinckel seeks to prove this[4] by emphasizing the references to the kingship of Yahweh, central in the Enthronement Psalms, and also present in eschatological passages which he refers to the day.[5] It is certainly true, as he shows in much detail, that the eschatology (with its included mythology) is a common element in both, with very similar content. But, in the wide fields of eschatology, more than one allotment can be held and worked. The Enthronement Festival as presupposed in certain psalms would naturally be one part at which the fertility of those fields should be displayed. But the Day of Yahweh, construed according to the older view as the point of Yahweh's intervention, the triumphant manifestation of His power and purpose, would not be less likely to express itself in eschatological terms. Should we not be guilty of the fallacy of an undistributed middle term if we identified the Enthronement Festival and the Day of Yahweh because they are both of them capable of expression in eschatological terms? This seems to be the Achilles heel of Mowinckel's argument. It is noticeable that the passages to which he specially appeals for his proof of identity are *not* those in which the phrase 'Day of Yahweh' occurs. It is found, in fact, only in one of them, and in a modified form, i.e. in the obscure and difficult

---

[1] e.g. Gunkel, *Psalmen-Einleitung*, p. 111; Eichrodt, op. cit., i. 56; Sellin, *Religionsgeschichte*, p. 65; H. Schmidt, *Die Thronfahrt Jahves* (passim); Oesterley, in *Myth and Ritual* (ed. S. H. Hooke), pp. 122 ff.; T. H. Robinson, ib., p. 178; S. H. Hooke, *Origins of Early Semitic Ritual*, pp. 51 ff.

[2] Exod. xxiii. 14–17.

[3] Lev. xxiii. 24, cf. Num. xxix. 1. For a summary account of the Babylonian Festival, reference may be made to Gadd's essay in *Myth and Ritual*; for the documents, Gressmann, *ATAT*², pp. 295–343.

[4] Op. cit., pp. 230–44.

[5] Especially Mic. iv. 6 f.; Zech. xiv. 8–10; Isa. xxxiii and Deutero-Isaiah (*passim*). He regards Isa. lii. 7 ff. as an epitome of the Enthronement Festival, to which he also traces the 'processional' return through the desert.

apocalypse of Zech. xiv: 'Behold! a day is coming for Yahweh', which goes on to say that 'Yahweh shall go forth and fight against those nations, as on the day of His fighting, on the day of battle', which supports the older view rather than Mowinckel's. It is true that later on in the passage (verse 9) we have the words, 'Yahweh shall become king over all the earth'. But we cannot confine the kingship of Yahweh to the Enthronement Psalms, even if it forms a central element in them. The rest of the twenty-eight references to the Day of Yahweh[1] afford Mowinckel no primary material for his proof of identity. This fact suggests that they are used in a distinctive sense whilst sharing in a common eschatological content.

Equally unconvincing is the third claim, that the festival was the source of the eschatology. It is difficult to establish priority, but it may be claimed that a ritual does not (in the first place) create a mythology but is the concrete expression of one.[2] Once the ritual is established, it will doubtless find new interpretations from time to time, as well as serve to maintain the old. But the eschatology of Israel has unique qualities, which must be drawn from its unique faith in a unique God. It is, as Gunkel urges,[3] 'an achievement of the prophetic spirit', which flourished in the very time of adversity. That fact is not a psychological contradiction, as Sellin asserts,[4] but is one of the miracles in the history of Israel's religion. Her faith in Yahweh increased as her historical position decreased.[5]

We may instructively compare the relation of the eschatology to the Enthronement Festival with that between prophecy by word and the symbolic acts of the prophets.[6] These acts did not generate prophecy; they implied it and were part of it. They gave concrete reality to the prophetic word and were felt to be Yahweh's own initiation of His activity through the prophet. So also the concrete reality of the cult-drama, which Mowinckel has brought out so impressively, was an expression of the faith in Yahweh's kingship and reacted upon it, as all ritual is bound to do. The mythology which the ritual helped

---

[1] Zeph. iii. 14 ff. belongs to a source usually regarded as later than the 'Day of Yahweh' description in i and ii. The mention of the divine kingship in Obad. 21 is a natural climax, on any view, to the mention of the day in verse 15.

[2] Cf. Sellin, op. cit., p. 65.   [3] Op. cit., p. 115.

[4] Op. cit., p. 65.   [5] Hempel, *Gott und Mensch*[2], p. 42.

[6] *Old Testament Essays* (introd. by D. C. Simpson), pp. 1 ff. *Journal of Theological Studies*, xliii. 129–39.

to keep alive passed over into the eschatology of the later prophets. But in thus passing it was transformed through the power of a more spiritual faith, just as the symbolic magic underlying prophetic acts was itself transformed into acts of genuine religion within the prophetic service of Yahweh.

An interesting restatement of the view that the Day of Yahweh is that of His victory links it with earlier mythology, without claiming a specialized eschatological content. This is Julian Morgenstern's.[1] He traces back the day to the mythological victory of light over darkness, good over evil, which is seen in that of Marduk over Tiamat, of 'Al'eyan Ba'al over Mot, of life over death, which is a basic idea amongst agricultural Semitic people. He holds that it came to Israel in the time of Solomon from such sources as are represented in the Ras Shamra tablets, and that the day was originally linked with the orientation of Solomon's temple. In the time of Amos the larger world-outlook of Israel and the temporary decline in the power of Assyria had given it a political meaning in the popular belief. This is what the prophet was denouncing. It will be seen that, whether or not Morgenstern's speculation as to the mythological origin of the conception be accepted, he interprets the meaning in the time of Amos in accordance with the older view.

§ 3. RELATION TO REVELATION

Our general conclusion, therefore, as to the origin of 'the Day of Yahweh' is that the older view still stands as the best, and that it is adequate to explain the later history of the phrase. Prior to Amos, it denoted an extraordinary manifestation of Yahweh's activity on Israel's behalf, and in particular the victory of Israel in battle. Amos led the way in a prophetic reversal of this meaning, changing it into a day of Yahweh's judgement on Israel and on the world. For the prophets, the phrase did not denote any and every manifestation; it retained the special meaning evident in the use of it by Amos, the meaning of a final judgement.[2] With this meaning, it had a natural, and indeed an essential place in the prophetic eschatology, as this developed. But its popular use in the times of Amos does not prove, as Gressmann argued, the existence of an elaborate eschatology prior to that date, however true it be that much

[1] *Hebrew Union College Annual*, xv (1940), pp. 284 ff.
[2] Cf. Davidson on Zeph. i. 17.

of the material for this already existed in Babylonian mythology, mediated by the Canaanites as the Ras Shamra documents
suggest.

What, then, is the value for revelation of the Day of Yahweh
when so interpreted? In four principal ways it may be said
to give precision to our general conception of revelation. It
links up, on these lines, with the closely related theophanies and
also gathers up those ideas of Nature and man which we have
already studied.

(a) The conception of the Day of Yahweh brings to a focus
the manifestation of Yahweh's purpose in history. In Köhler's
words,[1] 'In the prophets the Day of Yahweh is the epitome of
history, seen from which the whole past and future runs together
into a significant unity'. Here we see the moral character of
Yahweh's government of the world brought out clearly in
judgement, and here, too, we see that the manifestation of
Yahweh's purpose is of the essence of that government. At this
point He comes unmistakably out of the clouds and darkness,
and shows Himself in power. At this point the ever-recurrent
problem of His apparent slowness to act is once and for all
time removed. At this point there begins a new period of history
in which the ways of God with the redeemed will be finally
apparent. Thus the Day of Yahweh might be called the pivot
even more than the goal of history. It provides the sure clue
to the meaning of that history and effectively declares its unity
under the control of God.

(b) Further, the character of the Day throws light on the
nature of revelation. It is the day on which Yahweh acts rather
than speaks; or rather we should say His acts are His speech.[2]
It is, in fact, so described, if we correctly render Mal. iii. 17:

'They shall be mine, saith Yahweh of hosts, on the day when I
act.'[3]

This day of action is declared to be a day of revelation in
Isa. lii. 6:

'My people shall know my name in that day, for I am He who
says, Here I am!' (lit. 'Behold me!')

---

[1] *Theologie des Alt. Test.*, p. 78.

[2] On a large view this characterizes all divine revelation; the *words* which
interpret it are a human contribution.

[3] Sellin, ad loc., rightly describes the clause as a paraphrase (*Umschreibung*) of
the 'Day'.

From the prophetic point of view it is immaterial whether the divine act be wrought through physical phenomena, such as earthquake and storm, or through human agency, such as that of Nebuchadrezzar or Cyrus, or through some mysterious means beyond man's knowledge and previous range of experience. The characteristic feature of the day is that God acts, and that He is thereby decisively revealed as the God of effective action, the living God, the God who will be that which He will be, in deed and not simply in word, as men contrast the two. Moreover, such action is from without, transcendent and not immanent, though God may act from within either Nature or man in the achievement of His purpose.

(c) A third feature of revelation which is illustrated by the Day of Yahweh is that He is shown to be victorious within the present world-order and on the stage of human history. Later apocalyptic enlarged its stage and developed a supra-mundane order. But, in the eschatology of the Old Testament Canon, the day is the triumphant consummation of human history on earth, whilst the heavens (with their host) are drawn into man's affairs, rather than affording his ultimate haven. Mythology is subordinated to history, in ways characteristic of the Old Testament. This is clearly apparent in regard to the angel-princes of the Book of Daniel,[1] and to the punishment of the powers on high for their misrule of the affairs of earth.[2] As we should put it, using more abstract terms, the final vindication of God is conceived to come within space and time. That such an aspect of the day would be reinforced by the parallel but independent Enthronement Festival is easily apparent.[3] 'The anger of Yahweh shall not turn until He has acted and until He has established the purposes of His will (*libbo*); in the end of the days (*b⁽aḥarith hayyamim*) ye shall fully discern it.'[4]

(d) Finally, and in continuation of what has been said, the Day of Yahweh ushers in a new era upon the earth, in which the divinely maintained justice, peace, and prosperity will be fully revealed. This new era is sufficiently illustrated for our purpose by the prophecy which is found both in Isa. ii. 2–4 and Mic. iv. 1–3, beginning, 'It shall come to pass in the end of the days that the mountain of Yahweh's house shall be established'.

---

[1] Dan. x. 13, 21; xii. 1 (Michael); viii. 16; ix. 21 (Gabriel).
[2] Isa. xxiv. 21.
[3] So Eichrodt, op. cit., i. 249. [4] Jer. xxiii. 20; xxx. 24.

Such a prophecy marks the limits of the eschatological outlook of the Old Testament which never advances to the timeless quality of 'eternal life' in the New Testament.[1] Yet, as we have seen,[2] the religious experience of the Old Testament at its highest enters into a relation to God which is implicitly, if not explicitly, above that of time and space, though as yet unable to articulate itself without their aid.

NOTE ON REVELATION THROUGH APOCALYPTIC

1. The chief reason (supplemented by considerations of space) which have prevented me from allotting a separate section to apocalyptic is that adequate consideration of it would cover so much that lies beyond the Old Testament (including the Apocrypha). The material offered by the beginnings of apocalyptic in later prophecy, and by Isaiah xxiv–xxvii and Daniel vii–xii, does not seem to justify more than a brief indication of the contribution made to our general subject.

2. Apocalyptic continues and develops further the prophetic interpretation of history. Whereas the prophets take more account of human agency under the divine providence, the apocalyptists tend to a much more deterministic view of history through their schemes of successive periods of time revealed in advance to the seer. The combined contribution to a conception of the unity of history (applicable in many other directions besides theology) has been highly influential.

3. The apocalyptists also share with the prophets the sense of the imminence of the divine intervention in the affairs of this world. The prophets urge this more directly; the apocalyptists often show it by bringing their foreseen periods of human history up to a time which is their own present; at this point the character of their knowledge of actual history naturally changes.

4. Because apocalyptic throws such emphasis on the divine intervention, it leaves little room for 'self-help', and the rather slighting reference of Daniel (xi. 34) to the Maccabean Revolt is characteristic of the general attitude. It is *God* who brings about the imminent change in human affairs for which the apocalyptists hope; there is no sense of a gradual development, still less of an immanent evolution towards better things, which has claimed so large a place in modern thought. But apocalyptists are no more consistent than are other men, and the Barcocheba Revolt (supported by Akiba) shows

---

[1] Howard, *Christianity according to St. John*, pp. 189 ff.; Dodd, *Apostolic Preaching*, pp. 158 ff.   [2] See above ch. VIII, 'Time and Eternity'.

that a doctrine of passivity can inspire energetic action in certain circumstances.

5. The chief contribution of apocalyptic to the revelation of God in history is that it amplifies and emphasizes the conception of the kingly rule of God as the goal and consummation of history. For that reason this note has been attached to 'the Day of Yahweh'.

6. Finally, it should be remembered that it is apocalyptic which provided the formula of resurrection for the nascent faith in something beyond death. We might have expected Wisdom to do this, but it may be that such a development required the enthusiasm of apocalyptic.

XI

THE ELECTION OF ISRAEL

§ 1. The Unity of the Old Testament

THE supreme and unifying theme of the Old Testament is
God, as Creator, Ruler, and Redeemer. Yet that obvious
truth would be incomplete and indeed misleading unless we
said, not only 'God', but 'the God of Israel'. The revelation of
God is bound up with a history, the national and individual
experiences of a particular people. As Marti long since reminded
us,[1] students of religion have not to ask the question how the
universal God became Yahweh, the particular God of Israel,
but how Yahweh the God of Israel became for Israel, and
subsequently for Christendom and for Islam, the one and only
God of the whole world. From the beginnings of the history
of Israel until it passes into Judaism, i.e. from the Exodus to the
nationalism of Ezra, whether we think of the war-God of Moses
or the land-God of David or the world-God of Deutero-Isaiah,
Yahweh is the God of Israel and Israel is the people of Yahweh.
One of the reasons for insisting on this national name 'Yahweh'
for God is to remind us of this.

There is nothing distinctive or characteristic of Israel in the
form of this belief in a national God. Ancient communities
usually thought of one or more gods as specially concerned with
their fortunes. Yahweh's relation to Israel as reflected in her
earliest literature is not easily distinguished from that which the
Moabite Stone reveals as existing between Chemosh and Moab.
Chemosh, like Yahweh, gives oracles for the guidance of a
military campaign, perhaps through prophets, though our evidence is only of priests of Chemosh.[2] The wrath or the favour
of Chemosh is as closely interwoven with the military fortunes
of Moab as is Yahweh's with those of Israel. Israelite captives
are put under the ban to Chemosh, just as are Moabite captives
to Yahweh.[3] The wrath of Chemosh, when kindled by the
costly sacrifice of Mesha's eldest son, could change Israel's
victorious advance into defeated withdrawal.[4] Moabite names

---

[1] *Geschichte der isr. Religion*, p. 150.
[2] Jer. xlviii. 7. The oracles of ll. 14, 32 on the stone may have been given
through a priest or diviner, by sacred lot; cf. 1 Sam. xxiii. 4, &c.
[3] 2 Sam. viii. 2.　　　　　　　　　　　　　　　　[4] 2 Kings iii. 27.

are compounded with the name 'Chemosh', as are Israelite names with that of Yahweh.[1] The Moabites are described as the sons [and daughters] of Chemosh,[2] as the Israelites are described as the sons of Yahweh.[3] The territory of the Moabites is the land of Chemosh as that of Israel is the land of Yahweh.[4] So far, then, as the mere form of the relation goes, there was nothing unique in the national consciousness of Israel that it was the people of Yahweh, fulfilling the purpose of its own God, as other peoples fulfilled the purpose of other gods. If there is difference—and there must be in order to explain the history— it must be found in the content of the belief, rather than its form, and the difference is likely to go back to the very beginnings of the national history. The place which the deliverance from Egypt assumed in the religious consciousness of Israel is the best and sufficient evidence of this. We shall discover what that difference is by thinking of the sharp antithesis to nature religion[5] which characterizes the religion of the prophets.

The antithesis is found in an act of redemptive choice, though we must not confine ourselves to the use of the primary verb, *baḥar*,[6] 'choose'. Not only does the general idea find expression in other verbs (such as *yada'*[7] and *ḳanah*),[8] but the whole idea of the covenant (*bᵉrith*) goes back to the divine initiative, God's choice of Israel. Thus in Neh. ix. 7, 8, we pass easily from the one to the other:

'Thou art Yahweh our God who didst choose Abram . . . and madest a covenant with him to give the land of the Canaanites,' &c.

The figures of fatherhood and of marriage employed by Hosea are ways of expressing election; Moses is commissioned to say to Pharaoh, 'Israel is my son, my first-born'.[9] If that were meant simply to express a quasi-natural relation, such as is found amongst other peoples in which the God is the husband of the land and the people are their children, there would be no 'election' in it. But when the relation is seen to be that of an 'adoption', as St. Paul describes it,[10] the natural relation is

---

[1] e.g. Chemoshnadab; see G. A. Cooke, *North Semitic Inscriptions*, p. 7.
[2] Num. xxi. 29.   [3] Deut. xiv. 1.
[4] Mesha's Inscription, *ll.* 5, 6; Ps. lxxxv. 1, &c.
[5] Cf. Eichrodt, op. cit., i. 10.
[6] Köhler seems to do this (op. cit., pp. 64–6) and consequently to minimize the importance of the idea.
[7] Amos iii. 2, &c.   [8] Deut. xxxii. 6.
[9] Exod. iv. 22.   [10] *uiothesia*, Rom. ix. 4.

spiritualized, and there is scope for a divine initiative, seen supremely in the deliverance from Egypt. That initiative is a constantly recurrent theme of the Old Testament, as when Ezekiel so realistically describes Yahweh's adoption of the desert-foundling.[1] To such divine grace, the only fitting human response is abiding gratitude,[2] expressing itself in loyal obedience. On the other hand, the consciousness of election could harden into externalism and the pride of prerogative. Thus the doctrine of election opens up into the whole development of Israelite and Jewish religion, and can be taken as the most comprehensive principle of unity in it, next to the primary emphasis on the unity of God.

§ 2. The Double Tradition

It is important to distinguish two different forms of the tradition of election, as was first done by Kurt Galling, in his monograph, *Die Erwählungstraditionen Israels* (1928). He rightly says that since the faith in election is the heart of Israel's religion, the history of the doctrine would really become a history of the people.[3] His special concern is with the difference between the deliverance from Egypt as an act of election and the promises alleged to have been made to the patriarchs. He shows convincingly that the appeal of pre-exilic prophecy is to the events of the Exodus, and not to the patriarchs, and that the Exodus appeal is the older of the two, as witness the edict of Jeroboam I, in the tenth century, which says of the golden bulls of Bethel and Dan, 'Behold thy gods, O Israel, which brought thee up out of the land of Egypt'.[4] He points out that in the older tradition represented by the prophets, the Sinai covenant falls into the background, and becomes a mere episode between the Exodus and the entrance into Canaan. The idea of the covenant, in fact, however important it subsequently became, is simply one form, and originally by no means the dominant form, of the tradition of the choice of Israel by Yahweh. On the other hand, the familiar references of the JE narratives carry back this divine choice beyond the Exodus to the ancestors of Israel. Thus the Elohist represents Joshua as saying, 'Your fathers dwelt of old time beyond the river, even Terah, the father of Abraham and the father of Nahor; and they served

---

[1] xvi *passim*; cf. xx. 5 ff., 'the day when I chose Israel'.
[2] Koeberle, *Sünde und Gnade*, p. 265.   [3] p. 68.   [4] 1 Kings xii. 28.

other gods, and I took your father Abraham from beyond the river.'[1] This was as natural a retrojection of election as was the later ascription of an elaborate tabernacle to the times of the wilderness. Both traditions agree in recognizing that divine initiative which is essential to election. But they bring out different conceptions of it, and different approaches to it. The patriarchal claim illustrates the principle of corporate personality. The nation is not only represented by, but is summed up in, its ancestors. To call Abraham is to call the race that springs from him. This is made explicit in the promise, 'I will make of thee a great nation, and I will bless thee and I will make great thy name, and it shall be a (word of) blessing . . . and by thee shall all the families of the earth bless themselves'.[2] The parallel passage[3] refers to Abraham's seed being as numerous as the stars of heaven. The unity of the race is thus emphasized in characteristic modes of thought. God deals with the race through its ancestor, and the time element falls into the background[4] in comparison with the real content, the election of Israel to a great destiny.

The appeal to the Exodus, which is the characteristic note of the prophets, is to an historic event in which the redemptive work of Yahweh established a new relation between Him and Israel, thereby constituting an election in which deed is more important than word. Thus Hosea represents Yahweh as saying, 'When Israel was young, then I came to love him and out of Egypt I called him for my son.'[5] With this we may compare 'I am Yahweh thy God from the land of Egypt' (xiii. 4). The prophets are silent as to an election of the patriarchs; the appeal to nomadic history and its ever memorable issue is their form of the divine election. So Jeremiah begins with the desert days (ii. 2 f.):

> I remember for thee the loyal affection of thy youth,
>   Thy bridal love,
> Thy journeying after me in the wilderness,
>   In an unsown land.

[1] Joshua xxiv. 2, 3.

[2] Gen. xii. 2, J; point *weḥayah* for the MT *wehyeh* (imperative) as the tense sequence requires; see Gunkel and Skinner, ad loc.   [3] Gen. xv. 5, JE.

[4] We may think of the unhistorical character of Rabbinical exegesis, with its principle that 'there is no earlier and later in the Bible' (Moore, *Judaism*, i. 245, citing Jer. Megillah 70 *d*).

[5] xi. 1; *libni* is peculiar, and the translation given would properly require the insertion of *lihyoth* (להיות), but the sense is clear.

Israel's disloyalty is due to her ungratefully forgetting that deliverance:

> they asked not,
> Where is Yahweh that brought us up
> From the land of Egypt (ii. 6).

'He found him',[1] recalls the Song of Moses (Deut. xxxii. 10), 'in a desert land.' 'In the day when I chose Israel . . . I lifted up mine hand unto them, to bring them forth out of the land of Egypt'; that is Ezekiel's dating of the election (xx. 5 ff.). So Deutero-Isaiah (xliii. 16 ff.) speaks of the ancient deliverance when Yahweh made a way through the sea for His people, in order to encourage the confidence that He will make a new way through the desert from Babylon. The historical psalms often follow this lead, as in cxiv. 1 ff.:

> At the going out of Israel from Egypt,
> Of Jacob's house from a people of unintelligible speech,
> Judah became His sanctuary,
> Israel His realm.

But the Psalms, true to their character of being an epitome of post-exilic religion in general, include also the appeal to an election of the patriarchs, as in cv. 6, with its:

> O ye seed of Abraham His servant,
> Ye children of Jacob His chosen ones.[2]

In course of time, and especially through the place given to the patriarchal narratives in the Pentateuch, the election of the patriarchs became the dominant view, though it could naturally include the other. But it was the 'Exodus' election which provided the most solid content for the faith of Israel in its pre-exilic and exilic periods. In this form of it we can see the doctrine being hammered out on the anvil of actual events.[3] How realistic its interpretation was may be seen from the contrast between 'Esau' and 'Jacob' with which the Book of Malachi opens, a contrast based on some recent invasion of the Edomite land, perhaps by the Nabataeans.[4] That is held to justify the

---

[1] Jacob.

[2] The enigmatic reference in Isa. lxiii. 16, 'thou art our father, for Abraham knoweth us not, and Israel doth not acknowledge us' has been explained from popular necromantism (cf. Jer. xxxi. 15); here abjured (so Duhm); but the reference might be simply to the larger corporate group of contemporaries.

[3] Whatever view we take of the historicity of Abraham, Isaac, and Jacob, they belong to a period for which we have only the most general evidence.

[4] Cf. Driver, *Century Bible, Minor Prophets*, II, p. 300.

principle, 'I loved Jacob, but Esau I hated'. Here, in post-exilic prophecy, as in the Psalms, the election of the patriarchs is virtually implied (as in the covenant with Levi, Mal. ii. 4 ff.). As between the two forms of the doctrine of election, later developments in Judaism justify us in saying that reliance on being 'sons of Abraham'[1] was more dangerous to true religion than that which appealed to the active presence of the redeeming God in the historical deliverance of Israel from Egypt. The patriarchal election lends itself to the static attitude; the 'Exodus' election was essentially dynamic, and capable of inspiring a more active faith in the living God.

§ 3. THE COVENANT

We have already seen that the idea of a covenant is closely related to the doctrine of election, especially in its patriarchal form. Indeed, some Old Testament theologians would subordinate the doctrine of election to that of the covenant,[2] and Eichrodt reconstructs and presents the whole theology of the Old Testament around the idea of the covenant. But, however important the covenant was, the importance is of formal expression rather than of independent idea. We shall be nearer the truth if we say of the covenant, with Galling,[3] 'It is in its ultimate basis not itself a redemptive act, but the expression or confirmation of one, the redemptive act being the Exodus. . . . The tradition of election is capable of complete detachment from the Sinai covenant, and finds its visible pledge in the fact that Israel stands on its own soil as a free people'.

We appreciate this distinction the more when we get rid of the false idea that the Old Testament covenant implied a bargain, the *do ut des* attitude typically illustrated in the Roman religion.[4] The word *b'rith* does not necessarily imply an agreement made between two or more people on an equal footing. Ahab imposed a *b'rith* on Benhadad after defeating him,[5] and God's covenants with men are virtually His commands. This agrees with the most probable etymology of *b'rith*[6] as 'something

---

[1] Matt. iii. 9.   [2] As does Köhler, op. cit., p. 66; cf. pp. 44 ff.
[3] Op. cit., p. 37.
[4] Though, as Warde Fowler points out (*The Religious Experience of the Roman People*, pp. 200 ff.), we may exaggerate even here.   [5] 1 Kings xx. 29–34.
[6] Accad. *beritu* means 'fetter'. This derivation is to be preferred to that which links the word with the root *barah*, so that it means a sacred meal (so E. Meyer, *Die Israeliten*, p. 558 n.).

binding'. A divine *berith*, therefore, becomes the revelation of God's will which is associated with some sacramental ceremony as its sign and seal,[1] and with an oath or its equivalent.[2] It should also be remembered that the Book of Deuteronomy, which is so strongly covenantal, is not less emphatic in asserting the *grace* of God in election:[3] 'Yahweh did not set His love upon you nor choose you because ye were more in number than any other people; for ye were the fewest of all peoples.'

There are three outstanding covenantal expressions of Yahweh's relation to Israel, each of which may be regarded as a further reinterpretation of the idea of election. The first is the Sinai covenant, usually associated with the Elohistic document; the second is the Deuteronomic; the third is the Priestly. At Sinai[4] Moses declares Yahweh's requirements and the people promise to fulfil them. The words are recorded, and a sacrifice of burnt-offerings and peace-offerings is made. The blood is sprinkled partly on the altar and partly on the people (a peculiar ceremony which incorporates the ancient conception of blood-kinship between God and man). The Deuteronomic covenant is located in Moab, and apparently regards the words of the Horeb (Sinai) covenant as covering no more than the Decalogue.[5] These are now extended into the Book of Deuteronomy,[6] or a substantial part of it. The essence of this new covenant is expressed in xxvi. 17–18:

'Thou hast avouched Yahweh this day to be thy God, and that thou shouldest walk in His ways . . . and Yahweh hath avouched thee this day to be a peculiar people unto Himself . . . and to make thee high above all nations which He hath made.'

This, then, was an election of Israel to obedience, and so, conditionally, to privilege, along the lines of the prophetic teaching which Deuteronomy incorporates. The appeal for obedience is still based primarily on the deliverance from Egypt, as is clear from the Shema in vi (though v. 10 refers incidentally to the divine oath to Abraham, Isaac, and Jacob):

'We were Pharaoh's bondmen in Egypt: and Yahweh brought us out of Egypt with a mighty hand.' (21)

---

[1] e.g. Gen. xxi. 22 ff., of the covenant between Abraham and Abimelech, the seven lambs corresponding to the seven wells.

[2] e.g. David and Jonathan, 1 Sam. xviii. 3, 4; xx. 8.

[3] The classical passage is Deut. vii. 6–10.

[4] Exod. xxiv. 3–8.　　　　　[5] iv. 13; v. 2, 22; ix. 9.　　　　　[6] xxix. 1.

This, then, remains the ground on which Yahweh is to be loved and obeyed.

The third great covenant is that of the priestly writings of the fifth century B.C. Here we note the characteristic post-exilic emphasis on the patriarchal election, especially the covenant with Abraham in Genesis xvii. The document P had already spoken of a preliminary covenant with Noah,[1] of which the rainbow was the sign. Here, with Abraham, the sign is circumcision and the promise is that of becoming a great nation. The view of P is that the whole content of the covenant, with all its institutions, was revealed at Sinai. God has promised to dwell among His people, the descendants of Abraham, who approach Him in this way. Thus the conception of the covenant has shifted from the divine *nature* to the divine *promise*,[2] with a resultant externalization of the whole idea of election. On the other hand, we must not overlook the remarkable emergence of the 'new covenant' in the thought of Jeremiah,[3] which has for its parallel, without the term 'covenant', Ezekiel's anticipation of the 'new heart' to be given to God's people.[4] These show a significant recognition of the failure of any external ceremony to achieve its end, and the need for an inner and drastic renovation of human nature, if it is to be capable of rendering the desired obedience. The combination is characteristic of Biblical religion, and is one of the secrets of its power. The 'pessimism' is not ultimate, but leads directly to a noble optimism based on God. Thus the spiritual logic of the doctrine of election carries it forward into the doctrine of grace which was to be central in Christian theology.

§ 4. TRANSFORMATIONS OF CONTENT

We have seen that the doctrine of election, as applied to Israel, brings out emphatically the divine initiative and the moral element in the relation between God and man. This means that any development in the conception of God will be reflected in that of His purpose, and so in the actual content of election, its practical meaning for Israel. It is instructive, there-

---

[1] Gen. ix. 9 ff.
[2] The contrast is Davidson's in HDB, i. 512–13. For an earlier form of the peril of religious pride, see the 'covenant with death' of Isa. xxviii. 15 (Galling, op. cit., p. 32). A reference here to magic (Procksch) does not seem probable.
[3] xxxi. 31–4.
[4] xxxvi. 26 ff. Cf. Sellin, *Theologie des A.T.*, p. 94.

fore, to glance at some of the transformations of this content within the Old Testament period, though we must not expect them always to mark progress. There can be no *a priori* reason why a prophet of the sixth century such as Deutero-Isaiah should not have reached a far higher idea of election than any subsequent writer of the Old Testament, or why the Pauline grasp of the Christian Gospel should not excel that of any of the Patristic writers. Yet we may say that some of the finest fruits of Old Testament religion come as a transfiguration of election.

(*a*) The most familiar of these transformations is the earliest, that which is implied in the words of Amos (iii. 2): 'you only have I known of all the families of the earth', which he proceeds to make the ground of a more searching condemnation of Israel's sin. Privilege, the prophet in effect argues, implies an increased standard of responsibility, here the responsibility for exemplary moral obedience. Failure to render it makes the imminent judgement all the more severe. In fact, we may say that Amos proclaims an election to judgement, instead of an election to privilege, the popular view. So we have one of the most concise and impressive statements of the recurrent theme of pre-exilic prophecy, viz. retributive judgement.

(*b*) A second and closely related transformation is that from self-aggrandizement to service. The divine choice of Israel, according to the teaching familiarized by Deuteronomy, ensured prosperity on the single condition of obedience. The death of Josiah and the political collapse of 608 B.C. must have shaken that doctrine to its foundations. The fall of Jerusalem in 586 completed its destruction, at least for the time being. It had to be rebuilt, partly on lines of greater individualism, but partly also on the transformation of election into something greater than the material prosperity of Israel. Ezekiel shows us the one; Deutero-Isaiah the other. His conception of Israel as the Servant of Yahweh carried with it the new thought that the highest national service would be through the nation's suffering. Israel was elected for an evangelism that would be world-wide, and her new and coming deliverance would exalt her, not as a warrior-nation, but as the prophet and priest of Yahweh, proclaiming His truth to the ends of the earth.[1]

[1] For other developments of this line of thought, cf. Isa. xix. 19–25; Mal. i. 11; Isa. xxv. 8, together with H. H. Rowley's *Israel's Mission to the World*. But note that 'Esther' remains as possible as 'Jonah'.

(c) A transformation of a different kind may be seen in the rise of the doctrine of a righteous remnant, from Isaiah onwards.[1] It marks the future transference of religion from a nationalistic to an ecclesiastical basis: such a group as that of Isaiah's disciples, carrying on the prophet's teaching, is virtually a Church.[2] We can trace such a group through the inner community of Mal. iii. 16, and the Ḥasidim of the Psalms and the Pharisees of the Psalms of Solomon down to those groups in which the religion of a new Israel began. The prophet of that new religion is represented as applying the doctrine of election to His own community: 'Ye have not chosen me, but I have chosen you,'[3] and indeed we may say with Schechter,[4] that 'it is difficult to see how any revealed religion can dispense with it'. Conscious obedience to divine command makes that obedience part of the divine purpose, and man 'a thought of God' to fulfil it.[5]

§ 5. PROBLEMS OF ELECTION

For the modern mind, any and every doctrine of election raises serious problems for both philosophy and theology. The philosophy of history, in particular, is faced by the cardinal difficulty of contingency, the correlation of the absolute and the particular, the eternal and the temporal, the rational and the casual—the difficulty expressed in Lessing's well-known dictum that 'contingent truths of history can never be made the proof for necessary truths of reason'.[6] This difficulty was, of course, not felt by the Hebrews, for whom the contingent *was* the necessary proof of the abiding purpose of God. Similarly, they did not feel, as we do, the difficulty of relating the divine foreknowledge and the (conditioned) predestination which the election of Israel implies, with the place given to human freedom and responsibility in the working out of God's choice of Israel.

For Israel the problem was religious and practical, viz. how to reconcile the divine election of Israel with the actual course of the history, so full of vicissitudes that seemed to contradict the doctrine. The reconciliation was sought by the prophets through the idea of moral retribution. But when this proved

---

[1] J. Morgenstern (*Hebrew Union College Annual*, xv, 1940, p. 300) emphasizes the originality of this doctrine, as marking Isaiah's advance beyond the direct influence of Amos.

[2] Cf. G. B. Gray on Isa. viii. 16 (ICC).   [3] John xv. 16.

[4] *Some Aspects of Rabbinic Theology*, p. 62.   [5] Duhm on Jer. i. 5.

[6] 'Letter to Schumann, 1777.

inadequate, as it did for the religious experience of the exiles, the purpose of God was reinterpreted along the lines of transformation just indicated, at any rate by Deutero-Isaiah. As for the more theoretical side of the doctrine of election, and especially the relation of Israel to other nations in the purpose of God, there is a striking reference in the 'Song of Moses' (Deut. xxxii), a poem probably of exilic date. The whole song might be called a philosophy of Israel's history, beginning with the deliverance from Egypt:

'Is not He thy father that hath begotten thee?' (verse 6)

and going on to say (verse 8):

> When the Most High gave to the nations their inheritance,
> When He separated the children of men,
> He set the bounds of the peoples
> According to the number of the sons of God.

This follows the preferable reading of the LXX 'angels of God', which is illustrated by the conception of guardian angels encountered (e.g.) in the Book of Daniel,[1] heavenly deputies of Yahweh to whom He assigned the fortunes of all but Israel. Hence we read in the next verse:

> But (LXX) Yahweh's portion is his people,
> Jacob is the lot of his inheritance.

This is the thought which ben Sira reproduces four centuries later:

> For every nation he appointed a ruler,
> And Israel is the Lord's portion. (Ecclus xvii. 17)

In 4 Ezra, especially in verses 23–30 of chapter 5, the old difficulty recurs, the contradiction between the election of Israel and its actual fortunes in alien hands:

'Why hast thou given this one people over unto many? . . . if thou dost so much hate thy people, they should be punished with thine own hands.'

In the Epistle to the Romans, we see the apostle grappling with the same difficulty and trying to meet it by the thought that Israel's rejection of its true Messiah has led, in the wisdom of God, to the wider dissemination of the Gospel amongst the Gentiles, though the apostle looks forward to a subsequent gathering in of Israel.

[1] x. 13, 20 f.; xii. 1.

Perhaps the most attractive approach to the election of Israel for the modern mind is through Israel's actual creation of moral and spiritual values which have become the permanent possession of the whole world. This is a matter of history and beyond question, and this manner of approach also leaves room for the recognition of other values created through other peoples, a recognition which our wider horizon demands. Such an approach, it is true, would lead us to base the authority of the revelation on the intrinsic worth of its content. But, as will be argued later, any really critical view of the history brings us to this. Israel remains an elect nation by virtue of the divine choice, and that choice is sufficiently vindicated by that which Israel's history has produced.

Our survey of the three great realms in which the revelation of God is conceivable, viz. Nature, Man, and History, brings us to the threshold of that interpretative process which we call 'inspiration', whether we trace this in the prophet, the priest, or the wise man. But before we pass to the closer examination of this process, so far as it is accessible to us, we should make up our minds as to what we may rightly and fairly expect to learn from it. The word of the prophet and the torah of the priest were ascribed by them, as we shall see, to psychological or physical processes, in which we can no longer find the ultimate explanation of revelation. Probably we see much more of the human activity than they did, whether in the prophetic vision or audition, or in the framing of the questions put to the sacred oracle. But over and above all this psychological analysis, there remains the larger issue. The divine revelation in Nature, Man, and History is through *acts*, which need to be interpreted through human agency to make them *words* in our ordinary sense. The spatial revelation through Nature, the temporal revelation through History, and the conscious response to these of the mind of man—none of these can be limited to oracles formulated in the Hebrew tongue. In essence they are universal, and their particularity in the Old Testament lies in their interpretation as a phase of the history itself. That view of them still leaves us free to make the loftiest claims for them as the revelation of divine reality. But it does again throw us back on the intrinsic character of the authority which has already been mentioned. If we are indeed dealing with the acts of God, no other authority than His own is conceivable.

PART IV

THE INSPIRATION OF THE PROPHET

XII

THE GENERAL FUNCTION OF PROPHECY

To reach an exact conception of the nature and function of Hebrew prophecy is no easy matter. In part, the difficulty is inherent in the subject, extending as this does beyond the horizon of human experience into the realm of religious and philosophical assumptions. To the limits of this horizon we can carry out some measure of psychological analysis, and apply the comparative methods of historical study with a reasonable hope of success. But, even if this investigation were much more complete than we can hope to make it, we should be left asking the most important question of all, the question as to the ultimate truth, the permanent and universal validity of the revelation which the prophet claimed to give by his 'Thus has said Yahweh'. That question is not to be answered by psychological analysis or comparative study. Its answer depends on our intuition of ultimate reality, and our general faith in religious values.

The difficulty of the subject, however, is partly due to historical, as well as to inherent, causes. The Hebrew prophets have so greatly influenced religion that they have become incorporated into it. Post-exilic Judaism subordinated them to its fundamental conception of a complete torah, revealed once for all to Moses on Mount Sinai. Christianity, by an intuition that unconsciously approximated to the historical truth, drew its noblest inspiration from that of the prophets (together with their disciples, the psalmists), thus restoring the prophets in some degree to their historical place, as the pioneers of Israel's higher religion. But Christianity, no less than Judaism, in assimilating the prophets to its later systematization of belief, and in employing them as an important element in its early propaganda, conventionalized their function, and made its exact historical interpretation more difficult. In fact, this conventionalism already dominated much of the New Testament use of Old Testament prophecy, such as we find in the Matthean 'fulfilments' and in Pauline rabbinism.[1] Whatever the value of these, they are not historical exegesis, and nothing but mischief results from their confusion with it.

In the two following chapters we shall consider first the psychological data, and second the theological validity, of prophecy. In this chapter, however, it may be profitable to take a more comprehensive view of the Hebrew prophet, in the light of our previous study of his historical setting within the triple environment of Nature, Man, and History. We have, of course, to recognize that what the prophet himself thought of his function may differ from the conception held by the people in general, or even by the official leaders of contemporary religion.[2] These conceptions, again, may differ from the interpretations most natural to ourselves, with a longer perspective of history open to our eyes, and with modern methods of psychological analysis.

§ 1

Our previous study of 'Revelation in the Old Testament' has shown three general realms in which it operates.

(a) The first of these was Nature, which to the Hebrew mind was alive even in those forms which we regard as inanimate, and much more directly dependent on God than our modern conceptions usually allow. Once this attribution of Nature to God was attained,[3] it clearly afforded a disclosure of God of the greatest importance. The prophet could point to the whole panorama of Nature, created, sustained, and transformed by God, as His constant activity, ever revealing His purposes. Thus the prophetic references to Nature are far from being merely the poetical embellishments of the declared word. They are argumentative appeals to that which Yahweh has already done and is ever doing, in proof of that further activity which is declared to be imminent. This is most notably evident in Deutero-Isaiah, for whom the eloquent description of God's control of Nature in ch. xl and onwards points to one basis of the confidence that He can overthrow every obstacle to the

---

[1] e.g. Matt. ii. 15; Gal. iii. 16.

[2] We may think of the first approach of Saul and his servant to Samuel (1 Sam. ix. 6 ff.), or of the view of the activity of Amos expressed by the priest of Bethel (Amos vii. 12), as illustrating popular or official views of the prophet's function.

[3] It does not seem to have become fully explicit before Deutero-Isaiah; see above ch. I.

restoration of His people.¹ But simply to speak of Nature as a revelatory activity of God is too external a way of speaking to express the Hebrew attitude. The divine activity in Nature is not only a theophanic background; it is itself in part constitutive of the revelation. It is through Yahweh's control of natural phenomena—locusts and drought, storm and flood, lightning and fire, earthquake and changes of the earth's surface—that He often actually accomplishes His purposes of judgement or deliverance. Of these purposes the prophets are the divinely commissioned interpreters.² In them, Nature becomes articulate. They stand over against it as its necessary complement, without which there would be no revelation. One important function of the prophet therefore was to be Nature's audible voice. For such a function it was essential that he should be in keen sympathy with Nature and her tragedies, and be not less conscious of the sympathy of Nature with human destinies.³

(b) The prophet is even more an interpreter of man, both in the individual and social aspects of human nature. The primary function of the prophet is to awaken the consciousness of Israel to the presence and power of God, and to evoke that inner spirit of obedience which alone gives reality to the ritual of worship. In the exercise of this function the prophet inevitably offers his own relation to Yahweh as the promise and potency of that of Israel. Thus there is nothing anachronistic in regarding Jeremiah as himself the revelation of the true Israelite, the man in whom human nature, in its Israelite form, finds fullest and truest expression.⁴ In fact, the best confirmation of this truth is the way in which the subsequent piety of Israel, as reflected in the Psalms, moulds itself on the pattern of Jeremiah's experience. In this closeness of individual relation to God human nature declares its highest privilege and touches its deepest source of power. The relation of human freedom to divine control here finds its most suggestive illustration, along the line of Tennyson's well-known words:

'Our wills are ours to make them thine.'

¹ The two others are drawn from history, especially the redemption from Egypt, and from the divine knowledge of the future, in contrast with pagan ignorance.
² meliz, Isa. xliii. 27 in the light of Gen. xlii. 23; Job xxxiii. 23. Cf. also Isa. xxix. 10, 'your eyes, the prophets'. ³ e.g. Jer. xiv. 2–6; Isa. xxxv. 1, 2.
⁴ This extends even to the exercise of prophetic functions, as we may see from Joel ii. 28, 29, compared with Jer. xxxi. 31–4. Note also Num. xi. 29. See further ch. XIII § 3.

On the other hand, the true social relations of men, as Israel conceived them, are even more emphatically made articulate in the prophet. He might be unconscious, at least before the 'New Covenant' of Jeremiah, that his own experience was to be in widest commonalty spread, and to be wrought into the general religious experience of men; but from the outset of Israel's prophetic religion (beginning with Moses) there is no question of the primacy of the great social values in the life and worship of Israel. We have already seen that justice and mercy, the moral accompaniments of the religious virtue of humility, went back to Israel's nomadic period for their essentially social basis. But it was in the prophets of the eighth century and onwards that the divine demand for them became most clearly explicit. No function of prophecy is more obvious than this; our modern tendency is indeed to divorce this social emphasis from its religious setting in the prophetic teaching, and thus to misinterpret, rather than to ignore it.

(c) In the third place, and most obviously of all, the prophet is the interpreter of history. Here prophecy found its chief material and from this derived its most significant content, which ultimately characterized the whole religion of Israel. The supreme relation of God to Nature, notwithstanding the impression made by the opening chapter of Genesis, was later in recognition than the relation of God to history. In principle also, the most characteristic revelation of God is that given through history, in which His redemptive purpose becomes most clearly apparent. Here the perspective of many generations, revealing a divine purpose and interpreted by the prophets, supplied the sanction to their utterances, the full harmony to the melody of their message. On the arena of history they struggled to vindicate God, not unconsciously like Job, but in awareness of a divine commission. Like St. Paul in his arena,[1] they bade men lift their eyes to see the invisible which was so clear to themselves. The changing events of political and social circumstance, always admitting a secular interpretation, were transformed by the prophets into firmly controlled activities of God. He was shown as often using human agencies, just as He used those of physical nature, in fulfilment of His purpose, yet also as ever able to pass beyond their instrumentality, in the exercise of His unlimited power and inexhaustible resources.

[1] The *theatron* of 1 Cor. iv. 9.

In this way prophecy avoided the Scylla of a remote and impracticable idealism and the Charybdis of mere political expediency and coarse materialism. So successful were the prophets in stamping their own methods of interpretation on the later writing of Israel's history that it is sometimes difficult for us to recover the actual course of events and the contemporary reaction to them. The history of Israel has to be critically reconstructed from a book largely written and dominated by the principles of prophetic religion, even in the legalistic elements which seem very remote from it. Thus, we are warranted in saying that in the prophet, history, like Nature and human nature, became conscious of its own deepest and highest meanings. Past, present, and future alike entered into this interpretation, and time became as nearly timeless as Hebrew realism would allow.[1] Thus the prophet's word gathers into itself the three realms of Nature, man, and history, which enter into the Old Testament revelation of God.

§ 2

In thus speaking of the prophet's relation to the three realms as that of interpretation, we must not, however, forget that we are explaining his function in a way more natural to ourselves than to him. Though he undoubtedly did discharge this function, it was for him absorbed into, and dominated by, the consciousness of being a direct spokesman of God to Israel and to the world. The emphasis falls where it fell in the very illuminating account of the relation of Moses and Aaron.[2] When Moses pleaded his inadequacy to be God's spokesman to Pharaoh, 'Yahweh said unto Moses, See, I have made thee a god to Pharaoh, and Aaron thy brother shall be thy prophet'. Whatever Nature, man, and history contributed to the content of revelation, the essential fact for the prophet was that his interpretation of them came to him as a word of God, to be proclaimed in His name, and with His full authority within it and behind it. Three important implications of this call for consideration.

(a) In every account of a prophet's call which we possess, the initiative is with God. Thus Amos speaks of himself as 'taken' out of his ordinary occupations to become the spokesman of

[1] See 'Time and Eternity', ch. VIII above, and note the 'prophetic perfect'.
[2] Exod. vi. 28–vii. 2.

God, and disavows any vestige of professionalism in his function. To get the full force of this, we must remember that the *n^ebi'im* with whom he contrasts himself *were* professional religionists, though of a much more erratic and unsystematized kind than the priests, and were probably not, like them, associated with, or at any rate closely attached to, particular local sanctuaries.[1] Again, in a very different experience from that of Amos, the divine initiative is no less recognized by Hosea. At the beginning of Yahweh's speaking to him Yahweh said, 'Go, take to thee a wife of whoredom and children of whoredom'.[2] The most natural interpretation is that in the light of subsequent events Hosea saw a divine purpose and a divine control running through his painful experience. Thus he could interpret his earlier love for Gomer and the continuance of this in the effort to reclaim her[3] as the divinely appointed means of revealing Yahweh's love for Israel. If Isaiah's voluntary offer of service ('Here am I, send me') seems to contradict what has been said, it is only because we forget that his offer sprang from an overwhelming vision of God, and that a profound conviction of his own unworthiness had first to be removed. The genuine prophet seems, in fact, very reluctant to become a prophet at all, and discharges the function only under protest and through a divine inward compulsion. This is brought out most explicitly in Jeremiah's experiences, from the day when he first pleaded the inadequacy of his youthfulness for so great a task until the days when he cried out against its intolerable burden. All the same, he submits to the inner compulsion, which is 'a burning fire shut up in his bones',[4] and makes it impossible for him to relinquish the task. The same kind of compulsion is intended when a prophet says, 'the hand of Yahweh was upon me'.[5] The divine initiative is further illustrated when we find that a prophet may have to wait for Yahweh's answer to a question, as Jeremiah waited for ten days.[6] The prophet himself may

---

[1] We may compare the similar phenomenon of the travelling 'prophet' of whom the *Didache* speaks. In the post-exilic period, however, prophets may have been affiliated to the temple personnel (see further, pp. 224 f).

[2] Hos. i. 2.

[3] Hos. iii. 1. On the relation of these two narratives, see my article, 'The Marriage of Hosea' in *The Baptist Quarterly*, vol. v, pp. 304–13.

[4] Jer. i. 6, xx. 9. Cf. xxiii. 9. Similar compulsion was felt by St. Paul (1 Cor. ix. 16).

[5] 1 Kings xviii. 46; 2 Kings iii. 15; Isa. viii. 11; Jer. xv. 17; Ezek. iii. 14, 22, viii. 1.   [6] Jer. xlii. 7.

grieve over the commission which he must reluctantly discharge.[1]

It is clear that all this sets the religion of the prophets in
strongest contrast to the aims of magic. Magic is essentially
directed towards the constraint of the supernatural that it may
execute or supplement the will of man. Prophetic religion, on
the contrary, submits the human will wholly to the divine.
Whatever resources the human will naturally brings with it,
they are put wholly at the disposal of God. As we have seen,
they constitute the material, from which the divine message
is framed. Yet that message acquires its peculiar quality of
'revelation' only because God is believed to have taken control
of the material. Like Habakkuk on his watch-tower,[2] the prophet must wait in patience for Him and His clear command,
whether this come through vision or audition or through some
inner consciousness, springing from the mysterious contact
between the human and the divine.

(b) This close and intimate association of the prophet with
God constitutes a second important aspect of his function. It
extends far beyond the occurrence of the formula 'thus hath
Yahweh said', or 'oracle of Yahweh'. Isaiah's 'Song of the
Vineyard' (ch. v) has no such formula; it begins simply as a lyric
poem composed and sung by the prophet about God. Yet (in
verse 3) it passes into the first person, and God speaks through
the prophet's artistry, saying 'Judge, I pray you, betwixt me and
my vineyard'. We constantly pass in this way to the incorporation of what *we* should call the prophet's own experience in the
divine revelation. We certainly cannot draw a line around the
prophetic oracles accompanied by the formula, and separate
them rigorously from those records from which it may be
absent. Thus the prophetic experience of Jeremiah often takes
the form of a dialogue between the prophet and God, and these
autobiographical poems[3] express the most intimate consciousness of the divine presence which we can find in the Old Testament.

In a not less intimate, though quite different manner, the
personal sorrows of Hosea become, as we have just seen, an

---

[1] e.g. Elisha's weeping over the prospect of what Hazael will do to Israel
(2 Kings viii. 11).

[2] Hab. ii. 1, cf. 2 Peter i. 21: 'No prophecy ever came by the will of man, but
men spake from God, being moved by the Holy Spirit.'

[3] Especially in chaps. xv and xx.

integral and inseparable part of his prophetic message. Such discovery of the divine purpose within a human experience, leading to the virtual identification of the human with the divine (for it is nothing less) is very remarkable, and ought to challenge our thought much more than it is apt to do. It certainly does not spring from any 'mystical' union of man and God. That would be quite alien to the genius of the Old Testament, which never loses its consciousness of the profound difference between them, and emphasizes the humility derived from the thought of this difference as the cardinal virtue of religion.[1] Any theory of the prophetic consciousness which postulates an essential merging of the human in the divine is out of harmony with the general trend of the Old Testament religion. On the other hand, we cannot be content with the purely external relation of a verbal command, such as a superior officer might give to a subordinate; the identification of the experience is much too close for that. The prophet's 'call' marked a definite beginning at a point of time, and his subsequent experience was punctuated by renewed revelations of God; but these imply some sort of permanent relation between God and the prophet, a conscious fellowship which was the inner warrant of the prophet's representation of God to man. This becomes explicit in Jeremiah, who carries back the very difference between true and false prophecy beyond all merely psychological tests to the intuitive intimacy of this fellowship:

> Who hath stood in the council of Yahweh, that he should perceive and know his word?

and he reports Yahweh as declaring:

> I sent not these prophets, yet they ran:
> I spake not unto them, yet they prophesied.
> But if they had stood in my council, then had they caused my people to hear my words (Jer. xxiii. 18, 21, 22).

This conception of the heavenly council of Yahweh, to which a true prophet is admitted, is highly suggestive, and deserves more attention than it usually receives. The word used, *ṣodh*, is much more than a figure of speech. Jeremiah uses it elsewhere[2] of a gathering of young men, or again,[3] of the human fellowships from which his prophetic mission has separated him:

---

[1] As in Mic. vi. 8 (*hazneaʿ lekheth*).
[2] vi. 11.
[3] xv. 17.

'I sat not in the assembly (*ṣodh*) of the merrymakers'. Ought
we not, *mutatis mutandis*, to take the heavenly assembly with as
much realism as we take the earthly group? Directly we do
this, a number of Old Testament passages come to illuminate
it. First among them stands the remarkable vision of Micaiah
ben Imlah,[1] in which, as he describes it:

'I saw Yahweh sitting on his throne and all the host of heaven
standing by him on his right hand and his left.'

Though the word *ṣodh* does not occur here, this is a deliberative
assembly of the heavenly places, in which Yahweh considers
how Ahab is to be led to his deserved doom. Different pro-
posals are put forward by members of the assembly; finally
Yahweh accepts the proposal of the spirit (of prophetic inspiration?) to become a lying spirit in the court prophets of Ahab.
Obviously, such a vision belongs to the time when the idea of
God has not yet been fully moralized, and that is a confirmation
of its genuineness. But it also means that we must take Micaiah's
vision quite seriously as a revelation of what was believed to
happen in the unseen world. We are naturally reminded of the
prologue to the Book of Job, which is again meant to be taken
seriously, as an explanation of Job's sufferings; Yahweh has to
be vindicated before the heavenly assembly, when the Adversary
has once raised the issue of Job's disinterestedness. We get other
glimpses of the heavenly assembly as in Ps. lxxxix. 7 (8):

A God very terrible in the council of the holy ones,
And to be feared above all them that are round about him.

So Eliphaz the Temanite sarcastically remarks to Job:

Hast thou listened in the council of God,
And dost thou monopolize wisdom to thyself? (xv. 8)

The mysterious plural of the first chapter of Genesis becomes
intelligible when we refer it to a divine utterance in the heavenly
assembly:

Let us make man in our image, after our likeness, (i. 26)

where the initial reference may well be to the heavenly bodies
of the sons of God (cf. vi. 2). We have also, in direct relation
to the prophetic mission, the words which Isaiah hears from out
of the cloud that veils Yahweh from his sight, 'Whom shall I
send, and who will go for us?' It is not fanciful to distinguish

[1] 1 Kings xxii. 19.

here the supreme control exercised by Yahweh who alone can 'send', and the corporately representative character of the person sent on behalf of the heavenly assembly, 'who will go for us?' Isaiah, whose purged lips now enable him to speak even in that august circle,[1] volunteers and is accepted; henceforth he can speak as the representative of Yahweh and as a fully qualified member of His assembly. Amos, again[2] using the word *sodh* of the decision which issues from such deliberation, says: 'Surely the Lord God will do nothing but he revealeth his counsel unto his servants the prophets.' We seem, therefore, to be justified in generalizing from the explicit statement of Jeremiah, and in thinking of the prophetic function and consciousness as that of one who had been admitted into a higher fellowship, of which he became the earthly representative.[3]

Such a view as this in no way deprives the prophet of that direct relation to God which we can see at its highest in the dialogues of Jeremiah with Him. It rather adds cosmic depth and meaning to our conception of the divine purpose as having all the collective wisdom and power of the heavens within it. Just as the host of heaven are conceived to be the agents of the divine activity in the later theology, so at this earlier phase which accompanied the work of the great prophets, they are associated with His counsels.[4] The conception of such a heavenly council does something to explain the standing miracle of Hebrew prophecy—that virtual identification of the prophet with God which enables him not only to say 'Thus saith the Lord', but constantly to pass into utterances on behalf of Yahweh without the stamp of this formula, even (cf. Hosea) to regard his human experience as a reflection of the divine, to hold, in fact, what we might call a general commission as well as one based on particular oracular revelations. Such a consciousness might easily be reinforced by the sense of 'corporate personality' with

---

[1] Note that the purging comes *before*, not after, his offer and his commission.

[2] iii. 7. His visions, e.g. ix. 1 ff., illustrate what this means.

[3] See further, Isa. xl. 1 ff.; Zech. i. 11 ff. for the angels as members of the heavenly council, to whom Yahweh speaks. In iii. 7 a faithful and obedient high-priest is promised access to God amongst הָעֹמְדִים, the *heavenly* attendants on God.

[4] Cf. *Henry IV, Pt. II*, Act IV, sc. ii, ll. 18–19:

       'To us the speaker in his parliament;
       To us the imagin'd voice of God himself.'

That this association was not allowed to challenge the clear monotheism of Deutero-Isaiah is seen from Isa. xl. 14, 'With whom took he counsel?, &c.' (נוֹעָץ).

the council of Yahweh, and through it with Yahweh Himself, as His adopted representative. Nothing could, of course, obscure the gulf between the human and the divine for the Hebrew consciousness. Man was flesh, God was spirit, and the 'sons of God' were conceived as sharing in the 'spiritual' nature of God.[1] But again, *mutatis mutandis*, to be conscious of an adoptive kinship was to give that wider range to the confidence with which a Hebrew prophet speaks in the name of God, as one, that is, over whom the name of God has been called in ownership.[2] Just as in the human relation of corporate personality,[3] there is an easy transition from the speaker to the whole group which he represents, and vice versa, so it was possible, for the prophet who believed himself to be a true member of the heavenly group, to speak freely in the name of Him whose will said the last word, but whose decisions were also those of the heavenly council.[4]

(*c*) A third important aspect of the prophet's function consists in the liberation of a word of God, which becomes objectively powerful far beyond the personal range of the prophet's activity. Once spoken and current, his word is, as we might almost say, depersonalized, and enters upon its own independent history. This is a specialized application of a familiar phenomenon—the ancient attitude to the spoken word, which we encounter in the widespread occurrence of blessings and curses. They depend for their power largely on the belief in their objectivity. A classical and well-known example is that of the father with his son meeting an enemy. The father thereupon threw his boy on the ground, so that the enemy's curses might pass over his head without harming him;[5] he treated the curses, in fact, just like the blast of a bomb. Naturally the word of a prophet as a 'man of God' has peculiar power beyond that of other men, when it is accepted as the word of God, 'which shall not return to Him void'.[6] A number of comparisons describe the objective power of such a divine utterance. It is a destroying fire, before which the people are but as fuel.[7] It is a hammer that breaks the rock

[1] Gen. vi. 1 ff.   [2] Jer. xv. 16.   [3] See above, pp. 70 f.
[4] It is interesting to remember that such a heavenly council, which absorbed all the other gods and powers of the world, goes back to the simple 'council' of Semitic nomads legislating on day-by-day affairs. God's rule is not conceived in the O.T. as that of a lonely tyranny or even as 'ethical monotheism'; it is nearer 'representative government' than we are apt to think (cf. Ps. lxxxii. 1 ff.; Isa. xxiv. 21; Dan. x. 13, 20, 21).
[5] Wellhausen, *Reste Arabischen Heidentums*[2], p. 139, n. 4.
[6] Isa. lv. 11.   [7] Jer. v. 14; cf. Hos. vi. 5.

in pieces.[1] In its permanence it is contrasted with the withering grass and the fading flower.[2] The word of the prophet is, in fact, like its frequently accompanying 'symbolic act', something *done* and not merely said. Its previous history, to be derived from our own analysis of the prophet's experience and our knowledge of his particular place in the course of events, now becomes negligible, for the word will be more or less detached from its human speaker, and become an independent event. This is a feature of prophecy which the modern student finds it hard to realize. Our contemporary interest is so largely psychological and historical that we do not think of the completeness of the prophet's detachment from his own word. Incidentally, this explains some of the difficulties of our literary criticism, difficulties made in part by its being too 'literary'. The ancient prophet was not, like a modern author, interested in questions of copyright. He was, as Yahweh said of Jeremiah, 'God's mouth',[3] and the utterance therefore entered into a far larger scheme of things than was covered by the prophet's immediate and personal concerns.

This detachment also helps to explain the unique position of the prophet in the political sphere. He is flinging into this realm something quite different from the necessary expediencies and compromises of the ordinary politician, and he is not concerned to show how his own contribution is to be incorporated with theirs. Yet, at the same time, he is so conscious of the real and effective power of the word of God that he can boldly enter with his sole weapon into the arena of 'Real-politik'. He is ready both to claim the service of the inferior weapons of the armies of the world, and to assert a superior power in the word of God which goes infinitely beyond theirs.[4] Here we may also notice a different kind of detachment of the prophetic word from its original environment. This is seen in the subsequent interpretations that may be given to it, beyond the historical meaning. Thus the 'Immanuel' prophecy of Isaiah[5] was probably not 'Messianic' in its original meaning, but belongs to the 'signs' implied in proper names. Yet in the (post-Micah) passage, Mic. v. 3, it seems to have been applied to a Davidic Messiah,

---

[1] Jer. xxiii. 29; cf. Eph. vi. 17; Heb. iv. 12. [2] Isa. xl. 8.
[3] Jer. xv. 19; cf. Ps. xlv. 2, 'grace is poured upon thy lips'.
[4] See the previous discussion of this point in ch. IX.
[5] Isa. vii. 14, on which see G. B. Gray, ICC, ad loc.

just as is done more explicitly in the New Testament.[1] Here
also we have a procedure which affects all notable literary
expression; subsequent generations read into it another and
possibly larger meaning, often with justification. The prophetic
oracle in particular lends itself to this treatment, which is legitimate enough if the spiritual continuity with the original meaning is maintained. This rules out much allegorization as purely
arbitrary.

At a later stage we shall contrast the function of the Hebrew
prophet with that of the other figure so often set over against
him—the priest. Both were concerned with *torah* or 'teaching'
in the sense of a divine revelation, and it will be argued that the
prophet consciously put his *toroth* in opposition to those of the
priest, as different both in content and in method of origin.
Whereas the priestly *torah* goes back to the sacred lot (as the
derivation of the word itself suggests), the prophetic oracle came
through the mediation of personal consciousness. Thus there is
a fundamental contrast of method, viz. that between physical
and psychical mediation,[2] corresponding to the contrast between
the contents of the two, that of the ritual rule and the moral
demands of Yahweh. The two distinct methods became the
authority-giving nuclei of much else that gathered round them
in the course of the generations. The priest was not constantly
resorting to Urim and Thummim, the typical method of divination. The prophet was not always carried out of his more
normal consciousness into the frenzy of the *nabi'*, when he
endorsed his message with 'Thus hath said Yahweh'. But the
characteristic difference remains and helps to explain the attitude of the prophet towards all forms of physical divination,
doubtless including that of Urim and Thummim.

[1] Matt. i. 23. The convenient German name for this further development of
meaning is *Nachgeschichte*; see BZAW, lxvi.
[2] For a fuller discussion of this important difference, as applied to the general
field of religion, see my *Redemption and Revelation*, Parts II and III, *passim*.

XIII

THE PSYCHOLOGY OF INSPIRATION

WE have already acknowledged that divine revelation will always elude our full comprehension, since it comes from a transcendent source and can be scientifically studied only from the point at which it makes contact with our experience. But from that point its activities do submit themselves to our analysis. The theology of revelation has for its counterpart, or rather for its necessary constituent, the psychology of inspiration.

§ 1

We can best approach this by considering the use and distribution of the term for 'prophet', viz. *nabi'*, with its related verb (*nibba'* and *hithnabbe'*) since etymology provides no clear help.[1] The noun occurs 312 times in the Old Testament, and its use falls chronologically into three distinct groups, more or less distinguished by differences of character, and showing important developments of usage. Thus, in the period prior to the eighth century, the term *nabi'* occurs 88 times, most (78) of which refer to the recognized prophets of Yahweh. But the phenomena of this earlier prophecy are not those which we have come to associate with the word. They are largely of the type commonly called 'ecstatic' (though we shall have later occasion to criticize the application of this term to Hebrew prophecy).[2]

---

[1] Robertson Smith (*Prophets of Israel*[2], p. 390, as note to p. 86) favours the meaning 'speaker', but does not claim that this can be established as the primary meaning. He points out that there is no Hebrew root in the historical period; the verbal forms are denominatives. The form of the word is that of a passive, so that as Stade says (*Grammatik*, p. 152) it should express 'das Beharren in einem Zustande', but it can be employed to express activity, as in *nagid* (leader) and *paliṭ* (fugitive). König (*Wörterbuch*, p. 260), citing these examples, refers the word to the Arabic *naba'a* (*nuntiavit*), so that it would mean 'announcer'. Guillaume (*Prophecy and Divination*, pp. 112 ff.) would explain the form to mean 'the passive recipient of something which is manifested in his condition as well as in his speech'. Albright (*From the Stone Age to Christianity*, pp. 230 ff.) stresses the passive form, and links the word with the Accadian root *nabu*, to call (cf. Delitzsch, *Assyrisches Handwörterbuch*, p. 441), and would explain *nabi'* as one who is 'called' (by God), i.e. one who has a divine vocation, but this seems to import too much 'theology' into what must have been a primitive term. On the whole, as Eichrodt (*Theologie des A.T.* i. 164) says, the meaning 'proclaimer' (*Verkunder*) is the 'überwiegend wahrscheinliche Bedeutung', though obviously it throws no light on the problems of actual usage.

[2] See § 2.

They frequently appear in groups, such as the company of prophets encountered by Saul, the 400 court prophets of Ahab, the 'sons of the prophets' of whom we hear in connexion with Elisha.[1] These do not essentially differ in the forms of their activity from the prophets of Baal and Ashera who appear on Carmel.[2] But there were also prophets of a more individual type associated with such groups, viz. Samuel, Elijah, and Elisha, whilst other prophets, like Nathan and Ahijah, have no such recorded association.

The second period, from 800 to 550 B.C., is that of classical and creative Hebrew prophecy; to this belongs the majority (168) of the instances of the term. Many of these, however, refer to the so-called 'false' prophets, towards whom Jeremiah and Ezekiel in particular stand in sharply conscious antithesis.[3] The most characteristic feature of the usage in this middle period is that those who were subsequently given canonical recognition as 'true' prophets are outstanding individuals whose message is emphatically ethical. The so-called 'ecstatic' features, though not entirely absent, are certainly removed from the centre to the circumference of the prophetic experience.

In the third period, that of the post-exilic literature, where there are only fifty-six instances of the term,[4] the use of it is largely retrospective, and we hear the complaint, 'There is no more any prophet'.[5] But the prophets of the past have already acquired an authoritative place, as we may see from Zechariah's reminder that the threats of former prophets have been fulfilled,[6] or from the Chronicler's reference to the seventy years of exile prophesied by Jeremiah.[7] But whatever the respect for the prophets of the past, those of the present, at any rate by the time we reach the Greek period, are no longer esteemed.[8] This then was the period of the decline and fall of Hebrew prophecy. In its really notable and important representatives it was confined to hardly more than a couple of centuries (750–550).

The general impression gained from this survey of the use of

[1] 1 Sam. x. 10; 1 Kings xxii. 6; 2 Kings ii. 3, &c.

[2] 1 Kings xviii. 19.

[3] We note that Deuteronomy, about this time, finds it necessary to offer tests of the distinction between the true and the false (xiii. 1 ff., xviii. 21, 22).

[4] Many of them refer to the Chronicler's alleged literary sources.

[5] Ps. lxxiv. 9.   [6] i. 4 ff.

[7] 2 Chron. xxxvi. 21; so also in Dan. ix. 2.

[8] Zech. xiii. 1–6. Already Nehemiah (vi. 12) shows a healthy suspicion of contemporary prophecy.

the noun is confirmed by that of the verb, which appears to be a denominative formation from the noun. The verb is found in two modal forms (the Hithpael and the Niphal) but any distinction in their meaning seems to depend on usage rather than on form, since they are sometimes used interchangeably without distinction of meaning.[1] In the first of the three periods indicated for the noun, both forms are used of the psycho-physical phenomena of possession. In the second, it seems true to say that the Hithpael retains this meaning, whilst the Niphal is differentiated from it to denote prophecy with a rational and moral content. In the third, both forms of the verb have acquired the meaning of 'prophesying' without any suggestion of abnormal psycho-physical accompaniments. This verbal development raises again the chief problem raised by the use of the noun, viz. the relation of the central type of prophecy to its earlier form. Was the classical *nabi'* a new and sharply contrasted figure, or was he a development, however remarkable, of the older kind of *nabi'*?

§ 2

The usage of both noun and verb has suggested to the majority of modern scholars a continuous development rather than a sharp antithesis. We may compare the somewhat similar phenomena of *glossolalia*, the 'gift of tongues' mentioned in the New Testament. St. Paul possessed it, and reckoned it amongst the genuine gifts of the Spirit; he thanks God that he excels the Corinthian Christians in the exercise of it, since they are inclined to make so much of it. Yet, he adds,[2] 'in the church I had rather speak five words with my understanding that I might instruct others also, than ten thousand words in a tongue'. We may fairly suppose that the Hebrew prophets from Amos onwards felt like this towards the abnormal phenomena of the more or less professionalized *n^ebi'im*. Amos, it will be remembered, told the priest Amaziah at Bethel that he was not one of them. We should be wrong to read into that disclaimer any necessary contempt for them, in view of the fact that he elsewhere[3] speaks of the nazirite and the *nabi'* as direct gifts of Yahweh to Israel. Amos himself received his essential message of judgement in the form of a series of visions, not to be distinguished in form from

[1] See the table in Jepsen, *Nabi*, p. 8.
[2] 1 Cor. xiv. 18, 19.   [3] ii. 11.

those of the earlier Micaiah. Yet it is clear that the classical prophets valued the intelligible content of their oracles far more than the abnormal phenomena of accompanying vision and audition, psychical compulsion and possession, which they shared, at least in some degree, with the typical *nabi'* of earlier times. This comes out most clearly in the attitude of Jeremiah to many contemporary prophets,[1] which will concern us at a later point.

Against this usual view of the relation of the classical prophets to the primitive *nabi'* as one of development from a lower to a higher level, the most elaborate argument in recent years has been that of Jepsen, in the lengthy monograph entitled *Nabi*. He regards the *nabis* as a professional order of Canaanite origin, consisting of men possessed by the Spirit of God, and distinct from either the soothsayer and the seer on the one hand or the true 'ecstatic' on the other. To this order belonged the 'false' prophets denounced by Jeremiah and Ezekiel. The classical prophets are *not*, he argues, to be regarded as a stage in the development of this professional order (p. 251), and the very name *nabi* does not properly belong to them; they lacked the psychical characteristics of the *nabi*. In order to make this sharp separation, it is soon apparent that Jepsen has had to deal drastically with the text, or, alternatively, to explain away what seems to be its obvious meaning. Thus he sets aside the reference of Amos to the *n^ebi'im* as being a gift of God; this, he says, is due to a later 'nebi'istic' redaction, to which also is due the insertion of the thirty-one instances in the present (Masoretic) text in which Jeremiah is called a *nabi'*, and also his references to the *n^ebi'im* as Yahweh's servants (p. 140). Jepsen's forced treatment of the evidence appears when he ignores the recorded visions of Amos in seeking to prove that he was quite unlike the *nābî'*, whilst he stresses the fact that Hosea records no visions, in order to prove the same thing (pp. 132–6). But he does not venture to reject the title of *nabi'* given to Jeremiah (i. 5), in the story of his call, or the two passages in which Ezekiel speaks of the divine vindication of his similar status as a *nabi'* (ii. 5, xxxiii. 33). Instead, Jepsen suggests that the term may here mean no more than the 'spokesman' (*Sprecher*) of God, without any relation to the social order of the *n^ebi'im*. But such an admission fatally weakens the whole thesis. If *nabi'* had already

---

[1] xxiii. See further on this attitude in pp. 187 f.

attained this modified meaning by the time of the classical prophets, and could be so used by them on occasion, this shows that they were not alienated by the term, but rather by the content of the utterances of the contemporary *nᵉbi'im*. It is quite true that the classical prophets did not regard themselves as a professional order; that is explicit from the words of the first of them, Amos. But their visions, their symbolic acts,[1] and their other abnormal experiences, most visible, of course, in Ezekiel, but not absent even from Jeremiah,[2] make apparent an affinity of form, however different the substance.[3] It is therefore much the sounder view to regard the classical prophets as the culmination of a long development, though the contrast between origin and result is here, as often in the history of religion, so marked.

In strong contrast with Jepsen stands Hölscher who, in his book of a generation back,[4] fully recognized the abnormal features present even in the greatest prophets. In view of the fact that he is often regarded as having unduly emphasized this aspect of their experience, some sentences of his may be quoted to show that, in principle at least, he admitted the subordinate character of these features. Speaking of the great prophets he says (p. 187):

'Before the clearness of their thinking the ancient nature of the ecstatic mantics more and more disappears. They are no longer involuntary fanatics who in their frenzy give details of information concerning the hidden purposes and whims of the deity, but serious and clear-thinking proclaimers of a great unified outlook. They do indeed feel themselves to be instruments of deity, seized by the Spirit and unconditionally surrendered to the will of God; in them also the old prophetic forms appear, though in a rationalized way; they give warning or advice in one instance or another through their

---

[1] It is significant that these are left out of account by Jepsen, though they are one of the most obvious of the links with primitive prophecy; cf. the use of horns by Zedekiah b. Chenaanah (1 Kings xxii. 11) and of the yoke by Jeremiah (xxvii. 2, xxviii. 10). Jepsen's only reference to this yoke (p. 209) is to cite the *breaking* of it by Hananiah as typical of the *nabi'*! But Jeremiah had to make it, before Hananiah could break it.

[2] xx. 9, xxiii. 9, describing psycho-physical convulsions.

[3] It is an impressive fact that the term *mᵉshugga'* (מְשֻׁגָּע) used of 'madman' (1 Sam. xxi. 15) and of the earlier *nabi'* (2 Kings ix. 11) is used of a prophet in Hosea's day (Hos. ix. 7) and even of Jeremiah himself by his opponents (Jer. xxix. 26, 27). In Arabic the root (شجع) denotes the 'crooning' of a pigeon or the chanting of rhythmical prose.

[4] *Die Propheten*, 1913.

oracles, but the particular instance is only part of their insight into the totality of the divine will. . . . Without being always inspired anew, they know what is the will of God.'

The general truth of this statement should be borne in mind against the claim that every utterance of a Hebrew prophet required an *ad hoc* inspiration.[1] Whilst we may be confident that some abnormal experience, such as the arresting voice or vision, was essential to the call of a prophet, and that such experiences were renewed from time to time, we are justified, as we have seen in the previous chapter, in thinking of the prophet as consciously and continuously one who might be summoned to Yahweh's council. This warrants the inference that he was potentially able to regard any thought, which came to him with sufficient intensity or impressiveness, as a divine word. What ultimate tests he applied in any particular instance is beyond our power to examine, but that it was no arbitrary decision is clear from the fact that Jeremiah had to wait ten days for a desired message.[2] In the last resort, conviction of any kind passes beyond rational analysis, if only because it is a reaction of the whole personality, and not simply intellectual in origin, or the product of purely inferential reasoning. But this does not mean that we cannot gain a partial understanding of the manner and method of the prophetic conviction, along the lines of Hebrew psychology.

§ 3

The primary question to be answered is, how did the prophet himself become convinced that Yahweh was speaking to him and through him? Many attempts have been made to answer it; perhaps the chief reason for the unsatisfactoriness of so many of them is that they do not begin with the actual conceptions of the Hebrews. Here we may note some of the most important differences between these and our own, viz. (*a*) the ready belief in invasive energies, (*b*) the attribution of psychical capacity to physical organs, (*c*) the objectivity assigned to such subjective phenomena as the dream and the vision. To these should be added some reference to (*d*) the symbolic acts of the prophets.

(*a*) Belief in the accessibility of human personality to invasion by some external spirit or energy is, of course, widespread in the

---

[1] As seems to be implied by T. H. Robinson, *Prophecy and the Prophets*, pp. 43 ff.
[2] Jer. xlii. 7.

ancient world, and can be copiously illustrated from the Semitic parts of it, e.g. from the Babylonians and Arabs.[1] The demonology, in fact, which springs from this belief is the usual explanation of any abnormal phenomena of the human mind and body. 'Inspiration', even at its highest levels, is genetically linked with such beliefs, as the development of the term *ruach* itself shows.[2] The fact that the demonology of the Old Testament is so scanty is easily explained. Anything that seemed to challenge the sole supremacy of Yahweh was not likely to survive into the later days, unless it could be neutralized by assimilation or by transformation. The lying spirit that misled the 400 prophets of Ahab, by the express commission of Yahweh, and the 'evil' spirit from Yahweh that caused Saul's homicidal madness, can be regarded as examples of agencies originally demonic and later brought within the circle of Yahwistic control. The inclusive term, *ruach*, for 'spirit', originally demonic or impersonal (as in Hosea's 'spirit of whoredom'), came to denote the energy of Yahweh Himself as in the Samson stories long before the conception of Him was fully moralized. Here we note a rather remarkable fact—the relatively small use of the term *ruach* by the classical prophets to explain their own inspiration. Most people to-day, if asked to define inspiration, would probably reply, 'the influence of the Spirit of God', and would expect to find this confirmed by the explicit claims of the classical prophets. Yet, so far as terminology goes, this would hardly be true. Hosea does use the term 'man of the Spirit' as an equivalent to 'prophet',[3] and Ezekiel frequently speaks of the Spirit as entering into him, falling upon him, lifting him up, transferring him. But we do not find such language in Amos, Isaiah, and Jeremiah. The explanation may well be that the term had become somewhat discredited through its long and close association with primitive types of prophecy, and with abnormal phenomena in general. Amos simply says of his call, 'Yahweh took me', and of his visions, 'Yahweh made me see'.[4] Isaiah describes the compulsive power of which he is conscious as 'the hand of Yahweh'.[5] Jeremiah is content to say, 'the word of

---

[1] Jastrow, *Die Religion Babyloniens und Assyriens*[2], i, c. xi; Wellhausen, *Reste Arabischen Heidentums*[2], pp. 148 ff.; Doughty, *Arabia Deserta*, Index, s.v. 'Jan'.

[2] Volz, *Der Geist Gottes*, p. 22.

[3] ix. 7; there is a doubtful reference also in Mic. ii. 7.   [4] vii. 14 f., viii. 1.

[5] viii. 11; cf. Ezek. i. 3, iii. 22, xl. 1, and note that 'the hand of Yahweh' in viii. 1 corresponds to 'the spirit of Yahweh' in xi. 5; both together in iii. 14, xxxvii. 1.

Yahweh came to me',[1] though he differentiates this from 'false' prophecy by making it conditional on admission to the heavenly council of Yahweh, which must imply conscious and intelligent fellowship with God. Thus the relative absence of 'Spirit' from the terminology of higher inspiration does not disprove the general development of prophecy from earlier and primitive types of possession. 'Possession' holds true of both higher and lower, whether or not 'Spirit' is conceived as the agency.[2]

'Possession', or some equivalent term denoting invasion, is preferable to the commonly used 'ecstasy', because the latter springs from a Greek conception of personality, which does not at all harmonize with Hebrew psychology. 'Ecstasy' ($\check{\epsilon}\kappa\sigma\tau\alpha\sigma\iota\varsigma$)[3] implies that the *psyche* can leave its usual earthly dwelling, the human body, and travel into other regions, as in the Shamanistic belief of Mongolia.[4] But the Hebrew *nephesh* is *not* conceived as such an entity, potentially independent of the body; it is no more than the animating principle of the body, and it is the

---

[1] i. 4, &c.

[2] Muḥammad's account of his own experience in the process of revelation is of interest as a parallel to that of the Old Testament prophets. In Surah liii. 1–12, we find (trans. by Bell, vol. ii, p. 540):

'1. By the star when it falls,
2. Your comrade has not gone astray, nor has he erred;
3. Nor does he speak of (his own) inclination.
4. It is nothing but a suggestion suggested.
5. Taught (him) by One strong in power,
6. Forceful; he stood straight,
7. Upon the high horizon,
8. Then he drew near, and let himself down,
9. Till he was two bow-lengths off or nearer,
10. And suggested to his servant what he suggested.
11. The heart did not falsify what it saw.
12. Do ye debate with it as to what it sees?'

We notice here the sense of divine compulsion as in Old Testament prophecy, the vision of Allah, with which we may compare that of Yahweh by Isaiah in the temple (though as Dr. Bell points out, the vision is usually taken to be that of Gabriel), and the statement of a direct communication of the message, without any further psychical explanation. D. S. Margoliouth says (*ERE*, viii. 874): 'The communications embodied in the Qur'an were, according to the tradition, made to the Prophet and uttered by him in trance; he would wrap himself in a blanket and perspire copiously at the time. . . . The form of the utterances at times approaches verse, *i.e.* a series of sentences in which the same quantity and quality of syllables are reproduced, the termination of each unit being marked by rhyme, whereas more usually rhyme only, and this of a somewhat loose character, is observed.'

[3] The distinction is explicitly illustrated by 2 Cor. xii. 2, 'whether in the body I know not (Hebrew) or whether out of the body (Greek)'.

[4] E. Bevan, *Sibyls and Seers*, pp. 134 ff.; Radloff, *Aus Sibirien*, ii, c. vi.

body which constitutes the real personality for the Hebrew. For this reason belief in any real life after death could not be held until belief in the resurrection of the body had been reached. The Old Testament offers no example of a disembodied 'soul' or 'spirit', however frequent that idea in the later apocalyptic, possibly through Greek influence. Thus the very word, 'ecstatic', as applied to the psycho-physical phenomena of Hebrew prophecy, helps to perpetuate a misconception.[1] The prophet's self does not leave his body. Ezekiel's visions suggest a (visionary) transfer of his *whole* bodily personality from place to place.[2] When the body is finally buried in the tomb or grave, it is the wraith, not the soul or spirit, which enters Sheol, i.e. the ghostly replica, corresponding more or less with the Egyptian *Ka*.

(*b*) In the second place, Hebrew psychology enables us to understand something of the manner of this 'possession' by invasive energy. The conception is facilitated by that of diffused consciousness or localized psychical function. The Hebrews knew nothing of the nervous system and of the psycho-physical function of the brain, which to them was no more than 'the marrow of the head'.[3] Neither did they know anything of the circulation of the blood from the heart as its central organ. In the absence of such unifying conceptions, they were left free, like other ancient peoples, to imagine that each part of the body was to some degree a self-contained entity. Of course this does not mean that there was no unity of consciousness, such as is supplied through the conception of the breath-soul, *nephesh*, and indicated by its very use as a personal pronoun. But each part of the body is conceived to have psychical and ethical as well as physiological functions of its own. This applies not only to the central organs, the heart, liver, bowels, kidneys, but also to the peripheral, the eyes, ears, mouth, hands, and indeed to the flesh and bones in general. It was therefore much simpler for the Hebrews than for ourselves to believe in 'inspiration'; an invasive energy could take possession of any one of these organs, such as the mouth and tongue, and use it in quasi-

---

[1] So rightly Jepsen, op. cit., p. 22, n. 1.

[2] Cf. viii. 3, 'by a lock of my head'.

[3] The word for 'marrow' (Job xxi. 24 מֹחַ עַצְמוֹתָיו) is used, in the corresponding formation of Aramaic, as well as in post-Biblical Hebrew, also for 'brain'. 'Of the Semitic languages it is only Arabic that has a word (*dimāgh*) for brain' (Toy, *Proverbs*, p. 33 n.).

independence of its owner.[1] It is this kind of conception that explains the reference to Jeremiah's mouth in the account of his call; his objection that he is too young to be made a prophet is answered by the hand of Yahweh touching his mouth and so making it His own organ: 'I have put my words in thy mouth'.[2] The prototype of this in the call of Isaiah is somewhat differently orientated, for the cauterizing of his mouth is, in the first place, to enable him to take part in the deliberations of the heavenly court, and so to make his offer of service. But both references illustrate the localization of function, and the consequently easier accessibility of human personality to divine inspiration. Many Old Testament phrases which the modern reader takes as simply metaphorical must have meant much more when they were first coined—the obedient ear, the tongue filled with joy, the eye satisfied or unsatisfied with seeing are examples. With or without the human owner's will, each separate organ could be controlled from outside himself. Thus the prophets, sharing as they did in the common beliefs of the Hebrews, could more readily believe that they were inspired of God. In vision their eyes were made to see, in audition their ears were made to hear, by Him to whom they had surrendered themselves. The thoughts of their hearts, the compassions of their bowels, the desires of their kidneys were realistically located in the same way, and each of them could be appropriated or stimulated by the direct action of Yahweh.[3]

(c) A third difference consists in our sharper distinction of psychical phenomena from those we regard as purely physical or 'objective'. Modern psychology (in the wider extension of the term) interprets the dream, for example, as wholly occurrent within the consciousness of the dreamer, whatever initiation or modification of its course may be due to external physical stimuli. The dream is substantially an involuntary product of sub-conscious data. We should similarly explain the occasional waking experience of hearing a voice where there is no visible speaker, or seeing an object or person out of all relation with the normal environment, as due to some abnormal psychological

---

[1] We may compare our own conception of the part played by the subconscious.

[2] i. 9. Here the 'laying on of hands' denotes ownership.

[3] See, for fuller details and references, my essay on 'Hebrew Psychology' in *The People and the Book*, ed. by A. S. Peake. A good example is that of 2 Sam. xxiii. 2:
רוּחַ יהוה דִּבֶּר־בִּי וּמִלָּתוֹ עַל־לְשׁוֹנִי׃

condition of the percipient. But these 'subjective' explanations
were not available, or available to the same degree, in the
ancient world, and certainly not amongst the Hebrews of
Old Testament times. The voice heard, or the thing seen, if not
explicable along familiar lines, would be ascribed to some supernatural source, and in some instances to Yahweh Himself. This
is instanced by the vivid dream of the youthful Samuel; the
voice heard in it is ascribed quite objectively to Yahweh. There
is no more impressive example of this 'objective' reference than
the explanation given for the optimistic utterances of Ahab's
court prophets, which are traced to an 'objective' spirit commissioned by Yahweh to mislead them. By the time of Jeremiah
the explanation might have been that of 'a vision of their own
heart'.[1] Jeremiah's phrase must not be taken, however, as meaning more than self-deception, or as if it were equivalent to a
modern psychological explanation. The phrase would be sufficiently covered by the wrong interpretation of some actual
object. Jeremiah's own vision of the almond tree in the first
chapter of his book was possibly based on the actual sight of an
external tree blossoming early; the whole significance of the
event lies in the interpretation given to it, by which it becomes
a divine revelation. The prophet would not distinguish, and
would not understand our interest in distinguishing, between
a visionary and an actually existent tree; in either instance the
sight of it was due to Yahweh and brought His revelation. If
we accept the modern evidence for telepathy and clairvoyance
as sufficient to prove their occasional occurrence, this would
simply extend the range of our psychological explanations. But
in Ezekiel's time, if clairvoyance is the proper explanation of his
visions of happenings in the temple,[2] the experience would
inevitably be ascribed to a supernatural revelation. There is,
of course, no reason why we also should not accept such happenings as ultimately due to divine activity; but we should do this
by positing the secondary mediation of psychical conditions,
effectively controlled by God for the purpose of revelation. As
we have seen, there is a close parallel in the Hebrew conception
of Nature when compared with our own.[3] In Nature also some

[1] 1 Kings xxii. 22, compared with Jer. xxiii. 16.
[2] Ezek. viii–xi. But on some modern views of the ministry of Ezekiel he was
himself in Jerusalem at the time; thus Bertholet, in his commentary of 1936.
[3] See ch. I.

of the secondary causes, the intermediate links, which our scientifically trained perception takes for granted, could not be present to the Hebrew mind. *We* may or may not share the faith of the Old Testament in the creative and sustaining work of God in Nature, but if we do share it, we certainly have to understand the divine activity as much more elaborate and indirect. The same thing is true in the psychical sphere of inspiration. Just because the Hebrew was not aware of many mental processes familiar to ourselves, he could more readily ascribe their products to the direct revelation of God. But there is no reason why we should not think of God as working through such activities, physical or psychical. They do not necessarily offer an alternative explanation of the event; they can equally well be a fuller and more adequate account of it than the Hebrew was able to give. Scientific knowedge can never invalidate religious faith, however much it may lead to the restatement of the ways and means of God. We may indeed regard the limitations of the Hebrew knowledge both of Nature and of man as part of the providential order of history. The fact that some generations have found faith to be (psychologically) easier to attain or maintain will then belong to the philosophy of revelation, which has always to find room, even in our own experience, for a beneficent 'ministry of illusion'.[1] The truth which at first seemed to owe its divine sanction to some peculiarity of its method of mediation will finally justify itself by its intrinsic content and by its recognized place in the world-order. The change of emphasis in the manner of proof does not discredit the validity of the message.[2]

A recent explanation of Hebrew prophecy which is primarily psychological, though intended to endorse its validity, is that of Abraham Heschel, in his book, *Die Prophetie* (1936). Summarily stated, it regards the prophetic consciousness as that of one who has been brought into such 'sympathy' ($\sigma\upsilon\mu\pi\acute{a}\theta\epsilon\iota\alpha$) with the divine *pathos* that it is able to reproduce this under the given historical conditions. The strongly emotional element in Hebrew prophecy makes Heschel's statement attractive, though he has burdened it with the over-elaborate trimmings of a modern psychology instead of getting back to the Hebrew point of view,

[1] Plato's reference to the value of mythology supplies an ancient parallel (*Republic*, 382).

[2] This is more fully discussed in the following chapter.

as the true *Sitz im Leben*. But two considerations should prevent
us from accepting Heschel's theory as adequate. The first is that
the differences between Hebrew psychology and our own, here
neglected, must form an essential factor in any explanation. The
second is that the emotional element in both human and divine
personality as presented in the Old Testament is not the most
fundamental for the religion of Israel. This is beyond question
the volitional; the prophet is above all else a man of God under
orders to utter and perform the *will* of God. It is the prophet's
will, rather than his emotions, which reproduces the divine.[1]
We may apply to him the words of the Prophet of Nazareth:
'If any man willeth to do God's will, he shall know of the teaching whether it be of God.'[2] Some confirmation of this emphasis
may be seen in the symbolic acts of the prophets.

(*d*) No theory of Hebrew prophecy which neglects its symbolic
acts can be regarded as satisfactory, for they are characteristic
of it. The prophet is essentially a man who knows himself to
be under orders to *do* that which Yahweh wants done. To the
prophet it is of no account whether his doing be in the realm
of speaking or acting, since speech is itself an act.[3] Thus the
prophet believes himself to be under orders to go to a certain
place to utter his testimony, as did Amos to Bethel, or to enter
into such personal relations as did Hosea with Gomer, or to bind
himself by a legal bond as did Jeremiah for the family property
at Anathoth, or to walk about Jerusalem in the garb of a captive
as did Isaiah, or to enact the role of a fugitive from Jerusalem
as did Ezekiel.[4] All these acts are words, significant words with
a meaning deeper than lies on the surface; they serve to initiate
the divine activity amid human affairs by performing in miniature that which Yahweh is performing on a larger scale, from
the first utterance of His judgement to the final overthrow of
His city. Through the prophet, as through none other, the will
of Yahweh is done. 'Would God that all the Lord's people were
prophets!' says Moses,[5] and Joel[6] foresees the time when prophecy itself shall be democratized. Jeremiah's 'new covenant'
is virtually the extension to every Israelite of the prophet's own

---

[1] This emphasis is often hidden from the reader of the English Bible, because he
is unaware that the term 'heart' is the volitional, rather than the emotional, centre
for Hebrew psychology.   [2] John vii. 17.

[3] The Hebrew for 'word' (*dabar*) also denotes 'thing'.

[4] Amos vii. 10 f.; Hos. i. 2; Isa. xx. 2; Jer. xxxii. 6 ff.; Ezek. xii. 3 ff.

[5] Num. xi. 29.   [6] ii. 28 ff. (Heb. iii. 1 ff.).

obedient relation to God. Thus Hebrew prophecy takes its true place as the supreme achievement of Hebrew piety. In contrast with all lower forms of communication, such as the dream and the vision, God is represented as saying to Moses,

'With him will I speak mouth to mouth, even manifestly and not in dark speeches; and the form of Yahweh shall he behold.' (Num. xii. 8)

That may be regarded as a later idealization of an experience which less direct means of communication and their 'dark speeches' more imperfectly mediated. To see the face of Yahweh was the goal of true worship, fulfilled in the vision of Isaiah; to will the will of Yahweh in word or in deed was the very core of the prophetic consciousness for Isaiah and his fellows. Both belong to the ideal of the devout Israelite, as it is reflected in the Book of Psalms.[1]

[1] Note how often the worshipper passes to the thought of himself as proclaiming Yahweh's deeds, i.e. as prophet of Yahweh.

XIV

THE THEOLOGICAL VALIDITY OF PROPHECY

WE have considered the general nature and function of prophecy within the religion of Israel, and we have tried to
penetrate a little way into the psychology of the prophetic
consciousness, where lies the last secret of personal religion, the
ultimate contact of God and man. It remains to raise the
theological question, much like that put by Jesus in regard to
the mission of the last of the prophets, 'the baptism of John, was
it from heaven or from men?'[1]

Naturally enough, similar questions arose in much earlier
days, if only because prophets did not speak with unanimous
voice. The court prophets of Ahab prophesied victory; Micaiah
ben Imlah defeat. His explanation[2] of the discrepancy was that
Yahweh was inspiring in the court prophets a false oracle.
When such an explanation became impossible through higher
conceptions of Yahweh, the problem became how to distinguish
between inspired and uninspired prophecy. We have evidence
of this towards the end of the seventh century. The Book of
Deuteronomy says that non-fulfilment of the sign given dis-
credits the prophet, but also that even the fulfilment of the sign
does not warrant acceptance of his teaching if it forsakes the
national religious tradition.[3] The fullest discussion of the difficulty is found amongst the oracles of Jeremiah, in the same
period.[4] He condemns contemporary prophets on four grounds.
They are men of immoral character: 'they commit adultery and
walk in lies, and they strengthen the hands of evil-doers'. They
seek popularity through an unconditional promise of immunity
from disaster: 'they say continually unto them that despise me,
Yahweh hath said, Ye shall have peace; and to every one that
walketh in the stubbornness of his own heart they say, No evil
shall come upon you.' They do not distinguish their own dreams
from the prophetic 'word': 'the prophet that hath a dream, let
him tell a dream: and he that hath my word, let him speak
my word faithfully'. Finally, they are plagiarists: they 'steal
my words every man from his neighbour'. On these grounds,

---

[1] Mark xi. 30.   [2] 1 Kings xxii.   [3] xviii. 20–2; xiii. 1 ff.
[4] xxiii. 9 ff., on which see Skinner, *Prophecy and Religion*, ch. x.

Jeremiah is ready to say that these men 'speak a vision of their own heart, and not out of the mouth of Yahweh'. But he does not tell us directly how he himself recognized the true word of Yahweh to himself.[1]

If we consider the whole question from our own point of view (whilst taking into account the Hebrew reasons for the acceptance of prophecy), we may usefully notice four aspects of the subject, viz. (1) the anthropomorphism and anthropopathism which inevitably attach themselves to Israel's conception of divine personality as they do indeed to all human conceptions of God ; (2) the psychological parallels to prophetic inspiration which may be found in artistic creation and scientific discovery ; (3) the part taken by intuition in the process of revelation ; (4) the confirmation of prophecy to be derived from the whole pattern of history, of which we have so much longer and wider a view.

§ 1

The Hebrews were not troubled by what is to the modern man perhaps the greatest of all difficulties in regard to revelation—the haunting doubt whether our so-called knowledge of God may not be, after all, the mere projection into empty space of our fondest hopes and most cherished desires. The problems of anthropomorphism were not theirs; it never seems to have disturbed them, as it did some amongst the Greeks,[2] that God was pictured after the same pattern as themselves, made in their own image and likeness. But ought it to disturb *us*, seeing that if we are to think at all, it must be with such means as we possess, necessarily conditioned by our human experience? If personality is to be ascribed to God, the conception must be drawn from the experience of it in ourselves, emotional, intellectual, or volitional. We may try to raise the conception to a higher plane, by thinking away all that seems defective in human personality, and may ascribe to the divine a range of power, knowledge, purpose, infinitely beyond that of any human being. But still such enlarged conceptions of God are built up

---

[1] Ezekiel's parallel denunciation (xiii. 1–16, cf. also Mic. iii. 5–12; Isa. xxviii. 7–13) adds nothing material to the greater detail of Jeremiah. The false prophets by their superficial optimism whitewash an unsound wall; they see a vain vision and speak a lying divination, without warrant from Yahweh.

[2] e.g. Xenophanes, as quoted by Clement, *Strom.* v. 14 (*ANCL*, p. 285 f.); cf. Ritter and Preller, *Historia Philosophiae Graecae*, § 100, for text.

on what we know of man. If we reduce the human element to a thin conception of 'supra-personality', then either that term becomes vague and unintelligible, or else it must be interpreted through the human experience, so that it still fails to escape from some degree of anthropomorphism. All human thought and language, in fact, has to be symbolic when directed to that which lies beyond the horizon of our actual experience.

We get the same result when we approach the problem from the Godward side. God in Himself must for ever be beyond the reach of human comprehension, or He would not be God: 'God is great and we know Him not.'[1] The only way in which we can know Him is by His willing entrance into our human experience, i.e. by some form of activity or manifestation which we *can* know. This is one of the cardinal truths of revelation as asserted in the Old Testament, i.e. that the initiative is with God. He creates that which can be a revelation of His unseen glory and so a sacramental bond between man and Himself. We have kept before us three great realms in which this is brought about, viz. Nature, Man, and History. Revelation always means an appeal to something drawn from one of these three, something which is both natural and supernatural, natural as product or event, supernatural in its interpretation. There must be the actual event to be the nucleus of the interpretation and of faith in the divine revelation. In this sense, therefore, God must anthropomorphize Himself in order to be known by man.

The Hebrew prophets, of course, do not argue in this abstract way. They simply take for granted that the event does reveal God, and that He may be effectively and sufficiently known through it. In all simplicity of conviction they do not hesitate to use the most daring language of God, and to ascribe to Him what might be called a human constitution, with heart, soul, eyes, hands, &c., though in substance this constitution is spirit, and not flesh, like man's.[2] They speak of Him as sorrowing and rejoicing, loving and hating, pleased and angry, purposing and then modifying or changing His purpose, and they are surely justified in so doing, for in no other way could they have conveyed their meaning. It is a travesty of that meaning to try to transform it into the Greek philosophic pattern, as Christian theology has often done. The God of the prophets, on whom depends the whole truth of revelation, is no changeless and

[1] Job xxxvi. 26. [2] Isa. xxxi. 3.

impassible being, but a living Person, revealed through His
activities as sufficiently like man to be known by him. They are
not consciously using 'symbolism' in the weakened modern sense,
as something arbitrary and a mere metaphor; they are saying
what they believe to be actually true of God, however great and
inaccessible in Himself as the Holy One. Can we justify their
simplicity? If we deny its validity, then we have struck at the
very roots of revelation as it grows in the Old Testament.

We can assert its validity only if we are ready to admit that
there is a real kinship between God and man, a kinship which
makes possible both sympathy and understanding, the kinship
which Hosea describes as that of Husband and of Father. Man
is presented in the Old Testament as a spiritual being, and as
such he is, notwithstanding all limitations, akin to God who is
Spirit. The greatest of those limitations, the most serious of all
the barriers between man and God, is again and again declared
to be moral evil. If men persist in it, there can be no knowledge
of God in them, no revelation of Him to them. But this does
not mean, as some theologians down to our own times have
asserted, that the kinship of God and man has been broken by
the sin of the first man for all his descendants. There is no
exegetical warrant for reading back into the story of Eden the
Christian dogma of 'original sin'. Man may individually sin
himself away from the very capacity to know God, but there
is no such inevitability and personal irresponsibility in this
result as the dogma of original sin implies. Both the word which
the prophets declare and their frequent appeals for obedience
to it imply the capacity of man to understand and to obey. The
kinship of God and man means that Yahweh is the kind of God
who does reveal Himself to man, and that man is the kind of
being that is capable of response to the revelation. Such a
divine nature and such a human capacity implies the common
ground which is expressed by 'kinship', and we are fully justified
in using the anthropomorphic and anthropopathic language of
the prophets, even though we are more conscious than they
could be of its ultimate inadequacy.[1]

[1] On the whole subject, see E. R. Bevan's very valuable discussion, *Symbolism
and Belief*. It lies beyond the scope and purpose of the present discussion to enter
into such important theological topics as the use of analogy by St. Thomas Aquinas,
on which see the brief but illuminative account given by G. B. Phelan (the Aquinas
Lecture, 1941), *St. Thomas and Analogy* (Marquette University Press, Milwaukee,
1941).

§ 2

In the second place, some of the essentials of revelation are forcibly expressed through the Hebrew psychology of inspiration, in spite of what seems to us its crudity and its obvious ignorance of the true facts of physiology. Their psychology no more satisfies us to-day than does their mythological account of creation or their moralistic way of writing history. Yet it is a mistake to reject a result because the method of reaching it seems to us to be faulty. People once believed that a poker set upright before a fire kept away the devil by its sign of the Cross and allowed the fire to burn; many still believe that it creates a draught which makes the fire burn better. The fire often does burn better, but just because the poker is temporarily out of action and the fuel gets a chance of burning. So, when we wish to evaluate some ancient conception we do well to consider what those who held it were seeking to express, besides the degree of accuracy to which their explanation of it could attain. That is particularly true of the psychology of the Hebrews shared by the prophets, through which they interpreted the process of inspiration. Both their psychology and the physiology which is so closely linked with it are impossible beliefs for us; even the most thoroughgoing Fundamentalist would not like his doctor to treat him strictly by Scriptural methods. But this same system of beliefs which doubtless made it easier for the prophet to believe in his mission, and so had its place in the providence of God, also serves to express fundamental and permanent essentials of revelation, which some of our up-to-date theories of mind and body may easily obscure.

Amongst these essentials we may set first of all the truth that all revelation must begin from God. The conception of an invasive energy which may enter and control a prophet, of a divine hand laid irresistibly upon him, does bring out the cardinal truth of the divine initiative. Revelation implies that, depends on that. It is not simply man's discovery of truth, however much that factor may enter into it. Revelation is divine activity, that which God does. So again the appropriation of some human organ, such as the mouth or hand, which the prophet believed to be made instrumental to that divine activity, does not correspond to our own ideas of the unified control of the body by the brain and nervous system. But it does emphasize the necessary completeness of the surrender and the divine control of the result. This word my mouth utters, this deed my hand does, are God's, and they have so far ceased to be mine. Such a view of the result is essential to the right understanding of revelation. We may be so occupied with the psychological process that we forget the most important fact of all, that God in His own way, whatever that was, has brought to birth by human travail a truth which man needed to know. Further, that truth once uttered or enacted becomes objectified, and enters upon a history of its own. That fact remains true for us, though we no longer explain it, as did the ancients, as being like the quasi-magical power of their blessings and cursings. The spoken word, the accomplished deed, are henceforth detached from their speaker or doer, who falls into the back-ground. God has spoken; that is the vital fact, and what He has said will take care of itself.

In our modern world the psychological processes most often suggested as a parallel to those of ancient prophecy are seen in artistic creation or scientific discovery. In these realms we can certainly find some striking resemblances to the phenomena of religious inspiration. There is notably the consciousness of a much larger body of truth or beauty already existent behind and above the particular product of the scientist or artist. This as yet unseen reality is often thought of as a compelling force to which the artist or discoverer must yield. Again, the creative work is always shaped in terms or within the scope of a particular personal endowment, in order that it may body forth the unseen, and receive 'a local habitation and a name'. We may instance Shelley's classical statement of this truth in his *Defence of Poetry*, especially the words:

'Poetry is not like reasoning, a power to be exerted according to the determination of the will. A man cannot say, "I will compose poetry". The greatest poet even cannot say it; for the mind in creation is as a fading coal, which some invisible influence, like an inconstant wind, awakens to transitory brightness.'

The comparison of prophecy and poetry is perhaps the most suggestive of all, if only because the prophetic oracles were so often given in poetic form. That fact alone suggests the underlying consciousness of congruity between poetic creation and prophetic utterance.

In the realm of science a well-known example is Sir W. R.

Hamilton's discovery of quaternions. He was walking and occasionally talking with his wife when:

'An electric circuit seemed to close and a spark flashed forth, the herald (as I foresaw immediately) of many long years to come of definitely directed thought and work, by myself if spared, and at all events on the part of others if I should ever be allowed to live long enough distinctly to communicate the discovery.'[1]

Of the two examples given, Shelley's words emphasize the poet's consciousness of an external compelling power, whilst Hamilton's bring out the intuitive completion of a long process of preparation. But we may safely say that in every such experience both compulsion and intuition are integrated, just as they were in that of the Hebrew prophet. It is worth noting also that Hamilton was moved to do something that brings him into an even closer resemblance to the prophet. He could not, he says, resist the impulse then and there to cut his famous formula on a stone of the bridge he was crossing, just as a prophet was often moved to the 'symbolic act' which expressed and also initiated the larger activity to come. This instinct to make visible the invisible probably belongs to all creative work, and goes deep down to the very object of divine creation, to bring forth in a new realm and category something that already exists but is not yet revealed to men.

In the modern world the artist or discoverer does not necessarily or to-day even usually regard his experience of such creation as due to the revealing act of a personal deity. Reference to the divine is likely to be in terms of immanence rather than of transcendence. The artist and man of science is also much more conscious than was the prophet of the training which has prepared for his achievement and made it possible. But his experience does contain some of the essential qualities of the prophetic, and so far helps to explain it. In both activities there is inevitably a point at which all explanation fails, and 'inspiration', whether of poetry or prophecy, brings with it the consciousness of some 'Beyond' which does not abide our question.

On the other hand, we ought not to be blind to the important differences between aesthetic or intellectual inspiration on the one hand and that of the prophets on the other. The cardinal recognition of the divine Person which belongs to prophecy

[1] Letter to his son dated 5 Aug. 1865; as given in *The Times* of 12 Oct. 1943.

gives to it a peculiar and intense note of authority. The prophet's concern is not to give pleasure or impart information, but to get something done. The 'word' he brings from God may have rhythmic form and it certainly involves some intellectual activity, as in the interpretation of contemporary history, but it belongs immediately to the moral and religious realm; it is concerned with the relation of God to men, and of men to God and to each other. With what scorn does Ezekiel repudiate the treatment of his oracles as a mere occasion of aesthetic interest, 'as a very lovely song of one that hath a pleasant voice and can play well on an instrument'![1] The prophetic emphasis, as we have seen again and again, is volitional. It is impossible to 'know' Yahweh without obeying Him. The prophet calls men to enter into the same relation to God as gives him his own prophetic knowledge. Morality is thus integrated into religion and made inseparable from it.

§ 3

In the third place, there is what may be called the intuitional character of prophecy, which looks like its weakness but really proves one aspect of its validity. 'Intuition' is a difficult and suspect term, as every student of psychology, ethics, and philosophy knows. But it does serve to bring out the ultimate *immediacy* of personal judgement which we have found to belong to prophecy, from its first reception by the prophets down to our own response to the record of it. Intuition is not taken here to beg the question of validity, but simply to mark that subjective feature of prophecy, and indeed of all religion, which we have again and again found to be present.

The clearest and most explicit statement of its presence is, as we might expect, to be found in some words of Jeremiah, who so often takes us into the very heart of the prophetic consciousness by his frank disclosure of his own heart. In the course of one of his dialogues with Yahweh he hears the words, 'If thou wilt take the precious from the common, thou shalt be as my mouth' (xv. 19). In that value-judgement, as we should call it, we reach a psychological ultimate, and we cannot expect to go farther. Whatever the psychological conditions or accompaniments of prophecy, the prophet feels himself divinely directed to exercise his own judgement on all the medley of

[1] xxxiii. 32.

thought and feeling which is his. God says in effect that His word will carry an intrinsic and self-evidencing authority which will be its final and sufficient guarantee.

An intuitional value-judgement of this kind clearly involves a response of the whole personality, emotional, intellectual, and volitional. It means an active participation of all these in the process of revelation and the result will bear the stamp of all that we may know of the prophet's personal characteristics. This is exactly what we find when we think of Elijah's condemnation of Ahab over Naboth's vineyard, or the visions of destructive judgement which Amos saw, or the sense of Yahweh's loyalty to Israel which came to Hosea, or the experience of the holiness of God which constituted the call of Isaiah. The participation may often have involved a personal struggle as severe and costly as that of Jeremiah himself, an agony of the spirit into which we can hardly enter, which foreshadows the struggle of the prophet of Nazareth in Gethsemane. At any rate, the inner loyalty to the 'word' as personally received was essential. In this connexion we recall the strange story of the man of God who prophesied at Bethel, yet disobeyed the command given to him because another prophet claimed divine authority to cancel it, and for his disobedience was brought to an evil end.[1] We have always to remember in our study of the prophets that there was for them no ultimate court of appeal in a written Scripture. They were pioneers, with little more than the ancient nomadic tradition to guide them, and this by word of mouth.

We find that the inclusion of the prophets in the ultimate Canon of Scripture also depended on an intuitional judgement. Jewish theories, centred in Ezra, have considerably antedated the formation of anything that can be called a Canon. The process of that formation was continued down to the first and even the second Christian centuries, when certain books of the Old Testament were still open to Rabbinical discussion and dispute. So far as we can see, one of the chief factors in the gradual collection of the Scriptures and the ascription of authority to them was the use and wont of the synagogue, just as the use and wont of the Christian Church later on was one of the chief factors in the formation of the Canon of the New Testament. But such use and wont means a series of intuitional

[1] I Kings xiii. 11 ff.

value-judgements exercised by the community. In regard to both Testaments, the Canon was not decided by conciliar authority, which did little more than to recognize a *fait accompli*. Once more it was the response of the hearer which recognized authority in the record.

So it continues down to our own times. There is a striking passage of Origen's which shows that the appeal to an intuitional value-judgement is no device of yesterday, invented by Coleridge when he said, 'whatever *finds* me bears witness for itself that it has proceeded from a Holy Spirit'.[1] In the third century Origen had said:

'He who with diligent attention reads the words of the prophets will from his very reading experience a trace and vestige of inspiration in himself, and this personal experience will convince him that these are no compilations of men, which we are firmly persuaded are the words of God.'[2]

We may fairly claim that this continued demand for an active response to the record of revelation is a divinely established guarantee of its continued vitality. The current must flow without break of contact from the generating power into the receptive spirit, whatever the intermediate links. So it is that every man reading the prophets creates for himself a Scripture within the Scriptures; the prophets speak to him effectively in several parts, and not through all that is ascribed to them. Whatever may be said of the use of anthologies of Scripture instead of the Bible as a whole, it is certainly true that every Bible-student does in effect make an anthology of his own. Yet it would not be true to say this subjective element robs the Scriptures of their real authority. We must combine with it the objective features which form our final argument for the theological validity of prophecy, and see their objectivity in its relation to the intuitional response.

§ 4

Europeans and many Americans have been born into a tradition on which the prophets of Israel have exercised a great formative influence. This may be the interpretative tradition of Roman Catholicism, based on the ecclesiastical emphasis of the Council of Trent, which explicitly gives to the Church the

[1] *Confessions of an Enquiring Spirit*, Letter I.
[2] *De Principiis*, iv. 6; Gwatkin's trans. in *Selections from Early Christian Writers*, li A.

authority to interpret the Bible. Or, again, it may be the tradition of Protestant evangelicalism, however modified by influences later than the doctrines and systems of the reformers, which professedly gave to the Bible an authority superior to all ecclesiastical tradition, whilst creating a less formal and explicit one of its own. Such far-reaching traditional influence is in itself no proof of validity, but, as part of history, it should command respect. It begins within the Old Testament itself, where prophecy has shaped much of the literature—that of the historical books, the Psalms, the Wisdom books, much of the Pentateuch, in particular Deuteronomy. It extends over the New Testament, where the appeal to prophecy and its fulfilment constitutes the chief argument. In varied forms, many of them no longer cogent, this appeal has always characterized Christian apologetics.

The pattern of history in which the prophets of Israel occupy so prominent a place is, for the modern man, seen to be vastly greater in both length and breadth than it was for the ancient European world. But the prophetic interpretation of history as being under the control of God to beneficent ends can still be applied to this larger area and include India and China as well as Greece. It was, indeed, from the prophets and their successors the apocalyptists that the very conception of the unity of history was derived. The conception of that unity as based on the ultimate control of God can still maintain itself, in spite of all apparent contradictions of what in our human judgement that control should be. Is there any better interpretation that can displace it? Or are we to believe that human history has no meaning at all, and is but 'a tale told by an idiot, full of sound and fury, and signifying nothing'?

If prophetic intuition is indeed the key to unlock the door of history, then we have a parallel to it in that interpretation of Nature which the physicist of to-day offers to us—the recognition of the working of mind without, as well as within. The prophet on whom rests the hand of God in revelation thereby sees that same hand resting on Nature and on other men in other ways till His purpose is accomplished. It is in the combination of the event with its interpretation that we get the stereoscopic synthesis which is the reality we seek. The authority of the religious fact so constituted is neither purely subjective nor purely objective; it is both subjective and objective, and in that duality lies its continual validity. There are secondary and delegated authorities in religion, with which we cannot dispense, and such are the Church and the Bible. But in the last resort, it is in the prophetic consciousness and its continuance in personal religion that there is found the ultimate sanctuary in which the voice of God is still heard, the sanctuary in which the ancient Scriptures are still transformed into His living oracles.

PART V

REVELATION THROUGH THE PRIEST

XV

THE MEANING AND DEVELOPMENT OF *TORAH*

INTRODUCTION

IN the study of revelation it is natural that the prophet, rather than the priest, should arrest our attention. The prophet looks forward, and is the pioneer of the future; the priest backward as the guardian of tradition. The identity of the priest is usually merged in the continuous life of a hereditary and corporate body; the classical prophet stands before us as an individual, with characteristic personal qualities written large on his message. In the prophet we can trace the work of inspiration active in a living present, whereas the priest refers us to a remote past, in which a whole corpus of ready-made law, now largely of antiquarian interest, is alleged to have been verbally communicated by God to one man, Moses.

One result of these and other differences has been to obscure and to minimize the work of the priest in revelation, by contrast with that of the prophet. But closer attention will show, not only that the priestly contribution is important,[1] but that it by no means depended on a 'once-for-all' disclosure of the divine will, as was maintained by later Jewish tradition. Critically studied, this contribution shows a psychological process not without its own interest, and extending over a much longer period. Prophecy of the higher kind belongs to little more than a couple of centuries. Priesthood endured from the earliest days of Israel's national history down to the close of that history in A.D. 70, and even Herod had to pay it lip-service, whilst it supplied the political form under which the Hasmoneans maintained their rule. Thus, long after prophecies had ceased, the priestly office flourished, and the shaping of the forms under

---

[1] The actual bulk of the Pentateuch, which is so largely concerned with the priesthood and its duties, is little less than that of all the prophets together. As the basis of Judaism, the Pentateuch (*Torah*) won a permanent place, never assigned to the prophets.

which the Old Testament has come down to us lay in priestly hands, even though the interpretation of the Scriptures was to pass to the scribe and the Rabbi.

§ 1. THE EARLY HISTORY OF THE PRIESTHOOD

This is inseparable from the difficult problems arising in connexion with the alleged 'tribe' of Levi. Was there ever such a tribe, in the sense of a group of kinsfolk sprung from a common ancestor? In the Song of Deborah, Levi's name is not mentioned. In the Blessing of Jacob,[1] Levi is a purely secular group, accused with Simeon (also absent from the Song of Deborah) of violence,[2] and destined to be scattered. In the Blessing of Moses,[3] Levi is a priestly group, but primarily characterized by the possession of the sacred oracle, Urim and Thummim, and the teaching function, and only secondarily by the offering of sacrifice.

If there seems to us no adequate reason why the scattered members of a secular tribe should adopt the professional role of priests, it is open to us to suppose, with Mowinckel,[4] that the term 'Levi' originally denoted a professional priest, and that a tribal origin was assigned to the whole group of priests (as to the very mixed group of Judah) as a natural explanation of their existence. This supposition is not without evidence. There are Minaean inscriptions[5] in which the term $l(a)w(i)$ denotes a cultic official, just as 'Levite' came to do, and the two terms may well be etymologically related. In the Old Testament we note that Samuel, who was attached to the temple at Shiloh, was an Ephraimite,[6] and that Micaiah's Levite was a Judahite,[7] elsewhere described as 'the son of Gershom, the son of Moses'. This points to an original connexion between the Levites and Moses, for which there is other evidence.

Whatever decision, if any, we ultimately reach on this vexed question, it is clear enough that the earlier form of the priest-

---

[1]. Gen. xlix. 5, 6.

[2] This is usually explained by the Shechem tradition of Gen. xxxiv. 25, 30.

[3] Deut. xxxiii. 8–11. The references to Massah (Exod. xvii. 1–7) and Meribah (Num. xx. 2–13) throw no light on the 'proving' of Levi.

[4] *RGG²*, iii. 1601–2. Cf. Gressmann, as quoted by Gray, *Sacrifice*, p. 246.

[5] Found at El-Öla in N. Arabia, though written in a South Arabian dialect and alphabet. See the account and discussion of them in G. B. Gray's *Sacrifice in the Old Testament*, pp. 242 ff. Prof. H. H. Rowley, in *JBL*, 1939, pp. 116 ff., rejects the theory that there was no secular tribe of Levites.

[6] Gray, op. cit., p. 253. But Gray holds that the tribal evidence is too strong to be dismissed as theory.   [7] Judges xvii. 7, cf. xviii. 30.

hood in Israel differed greatly from that which it assumed in the post-exilic period. Whilst sacrifice was not at first confined to the priest, but was normally carried out by the head of a family group, the priest was regarded as the administrator of the sacred oracle,[1] and consequently as a teacher. As we have just seen from Deut. xxxiii. 8–11, Levi is primarily characterized by his possession of the sacred oracle, the Urim and Thummim. He teaches Israel Yahweh's *mishpaṭim* and *toroth*, and his sacrificial function is named last. Through the prophet Hosea Yahweh says to the priest (iv. 6), 'Because thou hast rejected knowledge, I have also rejected thee, that thou shalt be no priest to me, seeing thou hast forgotten the *torah* of thy God'. According to Malachi (ii. 6), even in the fifth century the true priest is depicted as a teacher, not as a sacrificial expert: 'The *torah* of truth was in his mouth and perversity was not found in his lips; in well-being and straightforwardness he walked with me, and many did he turn from iniquity.' So again it is said to Aaron and his sons (Lev. x. 11), 'Ye shall teach the children of Israel all the statutes which Yahweh hath spoken to them by the hand of Moses'. Even Ezekiel, concerned as he is to emphasize the priest's specialism in the technique of ritual, also shows us the other and earlier function. The priests teach men to discern between holy and common, clean and unclean, and to observe feasts and sabbaths; they also constitute, as we shall see more fully, a general court of appeal: 'in a controversy they shall stand to judge: according to my judgements shall they judge it'.[2] [At an earlier period the sacred oracle which they administered had been the supreme court of appeal, and so it became the nucleus and pervasive sanction of all priestly law, to which it lent its name (*torah*).]

§ 2. PRIESTHOOD AND DIVINATION

The truth of the statement just made will become apparent when we study the original meaning of the term *torah*, which

---

[1] Mention may be made here that *kohen* (כֹּהֵן), the regular word for 'priest', is the etymological equivalent of the Arabic *kahin*, denoting a seer and so a diviner (cf. Kur'an, lii. 29).

[2] xliv. 23, 24. Begrich, in BZAW, lxvi, seems to me to confine the function of the priest much too narrowly to the detail of distinctions in ritual practice. Whatever be the precise application of the ritual *torah* which Haggai (ii. 10 ff.) elicited from the priests, there is no adequate ground for the inference that all their *toroth*, even in post-exilic times, were of this nature (cf. Mal. ii. 6 above).

was destined to acquire so extensive a range of application that it virtually came to mean 'revelation'. First of all, it seems to have denoted the casting of the sacred lot,[1] by which the will of the deity was ascertained.[2] This widespread practice was carried out in Israel by means of Urim and Thummim, which yielded a divine 'yes' or 'no' to the questions submitted to Yahweh.[3] Thus the term *torah* acquired the general meaning of any particular revelation of the divine will, and any instruction

[1] The verb *yarah* is used in the Ḳal of casting the sacred lot (Joshua xviii. 6), and in both Ḳal and Hiph'il of 'shooting' arrows, &c. The participles of both formations denote 'archers'. The sense of 'teaching' is found in the Hiph'il in 51 instances (out of 83 for the whole verbal use), e.g. the teaching of God (Job xxxvi. 22), of the priests (Deut. xxxiii. 10; Ezek. xliv. 23), of Wisdom (Prov. iv. 4). Isaiah (ix. 14) speaks of the prophet who teaches lies, and Micah (iii. 11) of the priests who teach for hire and the prophets who divine for money, as if teaching and divination could be synonymous. Ancient place-names preserve the memory of ancient oracles by incorporating the root, e.g. *gib'ath hammoreh* (Judges vii. 1), 'the hill of the giver of *torah*', and *'elon moreh* (Gen. xii. 6), '*torah*-giver's terebinth' at Shechem, cf. Deut. xi. 30. In two instances only is the verb *horah* used of the higher prophetic teaching, viz. 1 Sam. xii. 23 (later than the eighth century) and Isa. xxviii. 9, where the prophet is quoting the scornful words of his opponents, priestly and prophetic, who say, 'Whom will he teach knowledge (*de'ah*), and whom will he make to discern the thing heard (*sh^emu'ah*)?', i.e. they are rejecting his *toroth* as false. In no instance is the verb used by a prophet of his own teaching, which suggests that it was originally a priestly term like the noun, *torah*.

[2] Other methods were those of the oath before the altar (1 Kings viii. 31), on which see Pedersen's *Israel*, p. 407f., and the ordeal, of which we have a striking example in Num. v. 11–31.

[3] This is clear from the LXX of 1 Sam. xiv. 41 (on which see S. R. Driver, *Notes on the Hebrew Text of the Books of Samuel*, ad loc.), which justifies us in restoring as the original text, 'Why hast thou not answered thy servant to-day? If this guilt is in me or in Jonathan my son, O Yahweh, God of Israel, give Urim, and if it is in thy people Israel, give Thummim'. In 1 Sam. xxviii. 6 the sacred lot is called simply Urim, and is named with 'dreams' and 'prophets' as a mode of the divine answer to inquiry. We have already seen in Deut. xxxiii. 8 that Urim and Thummim are linked closely with Torah (Professor G. R. Driver, in a private communication, says, 'Urim, I feel sure, is connected with an Acc. *u'uru*, "to give an oracular response"', but does not think that *u'uru* ever refers to casting lots). Eleazar the priest (in P) is to inquire for Joshua by the judgement of the Urim (Num. xxvii. 21; cf. Exod. xxviii. 30; Lev. viii. 8, where we find Urim and Thummim as part of 'the breastplate of judgement' worn by the high priest; the ephod was used for divination at an earlier period, 1 Sam. xxiii. 6ff., xxx. 7). But the alleged inclusion in 'the breastplate of judgement' is merely a traditional survival, for as we may see from Ezra ii. 63 and Neh. vii. 65, decision by this means was no longer available in the post-exilic period. We have no certainty as to the meaning of the two names, which prima facie suggest 'lights' and 'perfections', but the Arabian custom of divination by headless arrows before an image of deity may suggest the probable procedure (cf. Ezek. xxi. 26, 27 (21, 22)). The names of the alternatives may have been inscribed on the arrows. The Arabic *istiḳsamu* describing the procedure is from *ḳasama*, 'divide', 'share', cognate with the Hebrew *ḳaṣam*, denom. from קְסָם 'divination'.

or teaching given by God, and ultimately came to be applied
to the Pentateuch as embodying the fullest and most authoritative statement of that will.

In an instructive passage Jethro advises Moses to delegate the
ordinary routine of his judicial work to others, whilst personally
obtaining a divine decision on special controversies: 'be thou
for the people to God-ward, and bring thou the causes unto
God'.[1] So, elsewhere,[2] Moses is represented as saying to the
'judges' or sheikhs, 'the judgment is God's: and the cause that
is too hard for you ye shall bring unto me, and I will hear it'.
These passages show us how the whole system of law and justice
could be conceived as under divine sanction and its decisions
as divine revelation. This is unaffected by the fact that the
nucleus of this conception became more and more remote in
the course of the development, and that the elements which
were absorbed from sources other than a divine oracle were
greatly preponderant. The point from which a development
begins is important, not so much in itself as in the way it directs
the whole subsequent course of things, even when itself lost to
sight. The Urim and Thummim by which God was approached
in the early days of Israel's history was a particular form of
divination by physical means. In later days all such forms of
divination were regarded as 'heathen', and put under taboo.
This is seen most clearly in a passage which enumerates nine
different forms of divination and magic,[3] and goes on to substitute for them the promise of a succession of prophets, 'like
unto Moses'. The contrast admirably brings out the ultimate
difference between priest and prophet without any intention
to do so. As Buchanan Gray rightly says:

'prophetic revelation comes unsought, varied in its manifestation in
the different individual prophets; but priestly revelation that comes
in response to seeking rests on a craft.'[4]

The administration of Urim and Thummim constituted such a
craft. It was essentially a form of divination by mechanical

---

[1] Exod. xviii. 19. The (Levite) Moses is to some extent represented as priest (on
this see G. B. Gray, op. cit., pp. 194 ff.).   [2] Deut. i. 17.

[3] Deut. xviii. 9–14; cf. Exod. xxii. 18 (17); Lev. xix. 26, 31, xx. 27.

[4] *Sacrifice*, p. 206; I have ventured to suppose that Gray's difficult script has been
wrongly deciphered in the posthumous printed text as 'manipulation' which makes
no sense here; examples of such wrong decipherment are not infrequent in the
book, and quite understandable to anyone who has struggled with Gray's hand-
writing.

means, though sublimated by its absorption into Yahwism. But unabsorbed divination, if not the sacred lot by Urim and Thummim, naturally incurred the polemic of both priest and prophet in the later religion. The prophetic polemic is most explicit in Deutero-Isaiah, who sarcastically contrasts even divination by the stars, so cherished in Babylonia, with that true knowledge of the future which Yahweh alone possesses.[1] Hosea may be condemning even Urim and Thummim, when he says, 'my people ask counsel at their stock (lit. "wood") and their staff declareth unto them'.[2] Isaiah of Jerusalem condemns those who practise divination by resort to ghosts and 'familiar' spirits. In opposing all this, the prophets were virtually reject-ing the ultimate sanction of the priestly oracle, for they had found a higher mediation of revelation in the living, personal consciousness. They more or less consciously opposed their own *toroth* to those of the priests,[3] not only in content but perhaps also consciously in form. It is certain that the contrast of the psychical with the physical mediation is of real significance. Revelation through personality is potentially as much higher than divina-tion by the sacred lot as the dynamic conception of Yahweh the living God transcends all kinds of necessarily static idolatry.

---

[1] Isa. xliv. 25, xlvii. 13, xlviii. 5 ff.　　　　[2] iv. 12; so Sellin, ad loc.

[3] Amos and Micah do not use the noun *torah*. Hosea has three instances of it, of which two (viii. 1, 12) are not very clear, whilst the third (iv. 6) accuses the priests of forgetting the (true) *torah* of God. Isaiah has four explicit instances (apart from ii. 2–4, cf. Mic. iv. 1 ff. and the apparent gloss of viii. 20, 'to the Torah and the Testimony!'). In i. 10 the true *torah* is social righteousness. In v. 24 the rejec-tion of the true *torah* is seen in contemporary immorality. In viii. 16, xxx. 9, we have the characteristic demand for faith in the prophetic *torah* or in the condemna-tion of those who will not listen to it. Jeremiah contrasts the inner *torah* of the New Covenant with all outer expressions of it (xxxi. 33). The true *torah* is that the people should tread the old paths in contrast with the new ways of an elaborate cultus (vi. 19) or with the worship of Ba'alim (ix. 12 f.), or of 'other gods' (xvi. 11). The prophet's biographer in xxvi. 4, 5 identifies the true *torah* with 'the words of my servants the prophets', whereas the priests are 'they who handle the *torah* without knowing Yahweh' (ii. 8; is this a scornful reference to the manipulation of Urim and Thummim?). In viii. 8, cf. xviii. 18, the 'wise' claim to possess the *torah*, on which claim the prophet's comment is that 'the false pen of the scribes hath wrought falsely', meaning in the formulation of *toroth* which the prophet repudiates. Thus Jeremiah makes explicit the general attitude of the prophets and their claim to possess the true *torah* of Yahweh, in antithesis to the claims of the professional classes, whether priests (xviii. 18), wise men (ib.), or the prophets whose oracles he rejects (v. 31, vi. 13). The priests in particular were Jeremiah's enemies (see vi and xxvi, and Skinner, op. cit., p. 236). Provided that we remem-ber to translate *torah* by teaching (chiefly oral) at this time, we have some ground for asserting that the great prophets are deliberately using the term with a new content.

§ 3. THE INTERPRETATION OF LAW AS REVELATION

Amongst the Hebrews, as elsewhere, the casting of the sacred lot or something equivalent has become the nucleus of a much wider legislation. It is easy to see why this should have happened. In an ancient society the local sanctuary was likely to be the most permanent of institutions, and the priest, especially when he was the hereditary guardian of the sanctuary, the most permanent of officials. It was natural, therefore, that the sanctuary should become the place at which to deposit law-records, and that 'judgments' of whatever kind should be recorded by a succession of priests. So Samuel is said to have written the *mishpaṭ* of the kingdom, and to have laid it up before Yahweh.[1] Thus judgements of many kinds, whatever their origin, might come to be regarded as under the protection of the deity, and indeed inspired by him. As J. M. P. Smith points out:

'This was quite a general attitude in the ancient world. The Cretans attributed their laws to Jupiter; the Spartans to Apollo; the Romans said that Numa wrote their laws at the dictation of the goddess [Egĕria]; the Etruscans claimed to have derived theirs from the god Tages; and for the early Sumerians the laws were conceived as coming from the god and goddess Hani and Nisaba.'[2]

In the Semitic field the most familiar example is that of Hammurabi, who is depicted as receiving his Code of Laws from the sun-god Shamash. He himself explicitly claims this, though we know that he is actually incorporating an earlier code.

In the actual development of Hebrew law, as recorded in its successive codes, we can trace the process by which what we should have called 'secular' law, that of the sheikhs or local judges (largely based on tribal custom), was brought under the conception of divine revelation, and subordinated to the authority of the priests as constituting the final court of appeal. In the first of these codes, that known as 'The Book of the Covenant' (Exod. xx. 22—xxiii. 19) we note the distinction made between the 'judgments',[3] i.e. the decisions of the judges in particular cases, and the 'words' or positive commands,[4] now combined

[1] 1 Sam. x. 25; cf. Deut. xvii. 18.   [2] *The Origin and History of Hebrew Law*, p. 12.
[3] Exod. xxi. 1–xxii. 17 (so S. R. Driver and McNeile, ad loc.).
[4] Exod. xxiv. 3. But, as Alt points out (*Die Ursprünge des israelitischen Rechts*, p. 59, n. 2), it is doubtful whether this general term, or even the more suitable *ḥok* (חֹק) of Lev. xx. 8 has a technicality similar to that of *mishpaṭim*.

with these, dealing with morality and religion, and formulated differently from the customary 'judgments'. Moses, as we saw, referred cases of special difficulty to the decision of God. In the law-codes we see similar references from time to time, e.g. in the transformation of temporary into permanent servitude, where a memorable ceremony was thought necessary, or in disputes about property which could be best clarified by the solemn oath.[1] The use of the oath in settling disputes illustrates the incorporation of social issues under religious sanctions. The oath is originally a solemn invocation of the Deity, appealing to His decision; it is, in fact, the verbal equivalent of the ordeal, which brings the divine sanction into immediate operation.[2] But the formal curse also is supposed to bring God into action, sooner or later, as we may see from the curses appended to the Deuteronomic Code,[3] and to the Code of Holiness.[4] Alt, in his important study of the beginnings of Israelite law,[5] shows clearly the distinction in form as well as in content between the 'judgements' and the 'words'. The judgements (case-law) were more or less common to the international tradition, seen in Babylonian, Assyrian, and Hittite Codes also, which the Israelites found already operative in Canaan. It is the other kind, including the Decalogue, which illustrates Israel's own specific contribution. This springs, of course, from the conception of Israel's God as concerned with moral conduct as well as with religious observance. Alt refers to the scene at the sanctuary at Shechem (described in Deut. xxvii) as typical of the method of publication of the Yahwistic law, which was ultimately to assimilate to itself the Canaanite tradition of judgements delivered by the elders of Israel. As he says, we are not to think of the priests as taking part in the local administration of justice, i.e. apart from the sanctuaries; the priests had no part in the hereditary land-interest of the elders.[6] The priests come into action through

---

[1] Exod. xxi. 6, xxii. 8–11.

[2] In Num. v. 11–31, we may suppose that the pregnant woman guilty of adultery might give premature birth through the psychical shock of the ceremony; this seems to lie behind the purposely obscure terms of verses 22, 27.

[3] Deut. xxvii. 15 ff.   [4] Lev. xxvi. 14 ff.

[5] *Die Ursprünge des israelitischen Rechts* (1934).

[6] 61 n. Cf. Deut. xviii. 1 ff. In the exceptional case of untraced homicide (Deut. xxi. 1 ff.) the local elders act and the priests appear only at an advanced stage of the proceedings, perhaps because the killing of the heifer was regarded as a quasi-sacrificial act, or possibly to preserve their ultimate authority (see verse 5).

the sanctuary court of appeal, as is made explicit in Deut. xvii. 8f.:

'If there arise a matter too hard for thee in judgment . . . thou shalt come unto the priests the Levites and unto the judge that shall be in those days; and they shall enquire (LXX) and they shall shew thee the sentence of judgment.'

Elsewhere[1] it is said that to stand before the priests and judges is to stand before Yahweh. As distinct from the priests, the local lay tribunals are mentioned in Deut. xvi. 18:

'Judges and officers shalt thou make thee in all thy gates . . . and they shall judge the people with righteous judgment.'

The reference to 'the judge that shall be in those days' (Deut. xvii. 9) who is associated with the priests at Jerusalem has been taken to mean the king; more probably it indicates a separate official.[2] The king seems to have had little, if anything, to do with the local tribunals and their case-law.[3] Even Ahab and Jezebel secure Naboth's vineyard by secret influence exercised through the local elders, not through a royal edict or overt act of tyranny.[4] Later on, the king's power was no doubt systematized and incorporated. This is possibly reflected in the Chronicler's ascription to Jehoshaphat of the institution of a supreme court.[5] This is said to have consisted of both spiritual and lay judges, with the chief priest as president in sacred cases and a representative of the king in secular. Of course, we must not forget that a sacred or quasi-sacred character attached to the king as the anointed of Yahweh, and 'supernatural' powers of discernment could be ascribed to him.[6]

The Book of Deuteronomy as a whole is the most striking example and proof of the assimilation of the 'judgements' to the comprehensive revelation of '*Torah*'. It incorporates much of the 'Book of the Covenant' containing those judgements, and its humanitarianism in particular shows the influence of the

---

[1] Deut. xix. 17; Ezek. xliv. 24 (where the priestly decision in controversy is mentioned amongst their other duties).

[2] So Galling, *Die isr. Staatsverfassung*, p. 40f.

[3] Alt, op. cit., p. 29, n. 1. Pedersen (*Israel*, p. 409), after referring to the appeal of the woman from Tekoa to David, remarks, 'There is no formal relation between the various judicial powers applied to, because they are natural authorities', by which I suppose him to mean that they grew up independently.

[4] 1 Kings xxi. 8 ff.   [5] 2 Chron. xix. 8 ff.

[6] 2 Sam. xiv. 17, xix. 27; cf. 1 Sam. xii. 3, &c.

eighth-century prophets. But it is ultimately dominated by the centrality and increasing power of the priests, and of their distinct conception of revelation.

§ 4. THE ASCRIPTION OF *TORAH* TO MOSES

However obscure may be some of the details and uncertain the precise stages of the long development of the law literature, there can be no rehabilitation of its traditional ascription to Moses, for those who have learnt to weigh evidence critically and impartially. But one question which arises and does create difficulty for many concerns the good faith of those who made Moses the one channel of the revelation of Torah. How can we defend that good faith? There are several considerations which go far to explain the ascription as a perfectly natural process of the times, like the parallel ascription of Wisdom to Solomon and of psalmody to David.

(*a*) In the first place, we have to remember the marked difference of the Hebrew time-consciousness from our own, which was brought out in an earlier chapter.[1] Israel acquired great traditions, but these were not controlled by a long and precise historical perspective. Hebrew concern was not with the chronology of successive periods, but with the content of separate portions of time, its quality rather than its measured quantity. The Torah of the priest, like the Word of the prophet, was timeless. Consequently, its successive phases could the more easily be gathered up and put into the hands of some one outstanding figure fitted to sustain the particular quality in view. Thus there could be the tradition of an oral Torah, actually the product of generations of interpretation through a long succession of rabbis, yet equally ascribed to Moses together with the ultimately closed written Torah.[2] Doubtless the rabbis felt that they were but bringing out from the written Torah that which was already present there, at least implicitly or germinally. But prior to the completion of the written Torah there had been another long period of partly oral transmission in which the original nuclei accumulated around them much later material.

[1] See ch. VIII.
[2] Cf. Maitland, *Why the History of English Law is not written* (as quoted by Butterfield, *The Englishman and his History*, p. 35: 'That process by which old principles and old phrases are charged with a new content, is from the lawyer's point of view an evolution of the true intent and meaning of the old law; from the historian's point of view it is almost of necessity a process of perversion and misunderstanding.'

Whatever the actual amount of genuine Mosaic *toroth*, the figure of Moses established as the unique lawgiver was bound to act as a magnet.

(*b*) This was helped by the Hebrew methods of recording and writing history. The tendency to retain the *ipsissima verba* of the written record or records, so far as possible, meant a very real link with the past, even when there was revision and restatement. The old material was there by the side of or underneath the new, constituting a genuine contact with the past. In every code of law there is much which has its roots in the past, buried from our view. In the absence of that literary documentation which belongs to modern historical method, that which was of yesterday soon acquired the flavour of antiquity. Indeed, antiquity, real or supposed, is one of the most prolific creators of authority, so long as it is not tested by historical criticism. But authority, for the Hebrew, meant the authority of a commissioned agent, the role which Moses filled beyond any other. The intervening generations and the long process of accretion from them dropped out of sight, and the result of it all was thrown back to him in whom the process had begun.

This is wholly in accord with the whole genius of Israel's mode of thinking, as shown in its literature. The Hebrew is always more interested in result than in process. His metaphors often seem to us to be 'mixed', just because he is not thinking of what may be the strongly contrasted means, but of the identical end.[1] This may often be seen in the poetry of the prophets. Here is a striking and fourfold example from Isaiah (xxx. 27 f.):

'Behold, the name of Yahweh cometh from far burning with his anger and in thick rising smoke: his lips are full of indignation and his tongue is as a devouring fire and his breath is as an overflowing stream that reacheth even unto the neck, to sift the nations with the sieve of destruction; and a bridle that leadeth astray on the jaws of the peoples.'

Water—fire—sieve—bridle are very mixed metaphors; they are unified only in their common goal, here destruction. The same psychology may be seen in the emphasis on the Torah as something given once for all in its entirety, regardless of the process, so making more natural the ascription to Moses. The result is all that really matters.

[1] See R. H. Kennett, *Ancient Hebrew Social Life and Custom as indicated in Law, Narrative and Metaphor*, pp. 3 and 92.

(c) It is also highly probable that the spirit inspiring the ancient lawgiver was actually thought to rest on those who succeeded him and to operate through them. It was thus a revelation made through him, though implemented by them. We may think here of the 'spirit' which was upon Moses and was imparted to the seventy elders.[1] Similarly, Elisha asks that an elder son's portion of Elijah's spirit may be inherited by himself; the narrative shows how realistically this petition is to be taken.[2] The same sense of continuity underlies the important passage already mentioned, in which Moses is represented as promising a line of prophets like unto himself, and with his authority.[3] There was a much greater sense of this continuity than we usually recognize. It is a particular application of that emphasis on corporate personality, which we have seen at work again and again. In the priesthood the corporate sense was especially strong; one could there speak for all, and all could merge their individual consciousnesses in one. The apocalyptic fondness for pseudonymity is probably to be explained in this way; it could very easily be felt that the spirit of Enoch or another from the past could inspire his successor in the present. We dismiss as literary fiction what should rather be regarded as the product of a psychology different from our own.

Altogether, therefore, we may claim that the priestly formula 'Yahweh spake unto Moses' which introduces so many groups of successive *toroth* is in several respects parallel to the prophetic formula, 'Thus hath said Yahweh', or 'oracle of Yahweh'. The differences in the nature of the material and in the actual process are great and important. Yet for both the final emphasis falls on the intrinsic content of the two bodies of revelation, rather than on the persons who became their historical media. If prophecy had not been too closely embedded in history to be detached from it, we might have had the successive contributions of the prophets all ascribed to some one outstanding figure of the past, such as Elijah. If priestly laws had not been impersonal by their intrinsic character, we might have had, in place of the ascription of all *Torah* to Moses, the assignment of successive strata of it to their actual compilers.

[1] Num. xi. 16 ff.   [2] 2 Kings ii. 9.   [3] Deut. xviii. 15.

XVI

REVELATION THROUGH THE LAW

IF the prophet supplied the soul of Israel's religion, the priest created its body. The successive codes of law, in their ultimate setting of priestly history, constitute the main element in the Torah and laid the foundation for Jewish faith and practice. Yet the prophetic influence is manifest in the writing of that Torah. This is seen, moreover, in its legal as well as its non-legal elements. To some extent, at least, the body becomes the servant of the soul, which animated it, and to which it was necessary.

We are here concerned with the law literature primarily as a revelation of God, and it is not possible or necessary to discuss it on either its literary or its antiquarian side. But before we turn to the revelation reflected or implied in the Codes, it is important to remember that the very form of revelation by divine law gives to a religion a characteristic impress. Whatever the historical origin of particular laws, their ultimate ascription to deity, *when taken seriously*, sets the divine *will* in the foreground. The volitional aspect of the ethics and religion of Israel, which is so strongly marked a feature of them, is thus wholly congruent with revelation by the method of divine law. This characteristic is explicitly claimed in the introduction to the Deuteronomic law (iv. 8):

'What great nation is there, that hath statutes and judgments so righteous as all this law, which I set before you this day?'

Here, as in so many other passages of the kind, God is brought near to Israel, and in a distinctive way, as the beneficent lawgiver. The difference from the stark emphasis on the will of Allah, which characterizes Islam, is not so much in the emphasis itself as in the larger and richer conception of divine personality attributed to Yahweh, and the activity of that personality throughout a long and continuous history. In the same chapter of Deuteronomy from which we have just quoted (iv. 34 f.) the redemptive work of Yahweh is summarized, to point the conclusion:

'Unto thee it was shewed, that thou mightest know that Yahweh He is God; there is none else beside Him.'

Here again we may see the influence of the prophets through their interpretation of the history. But it was the work of the priests that has given the final character to Judaism, through their embodiment of the religion of Israel in legal form. This is the more apparent when we contrast the result with the gradual and not less characteristic divorce of law and religion in Roman and Greek history.[1]

§ 1. The Book of the Covenant (Exod. xx. 22–xxiii. 19)

This falls to be noticed under 'Revelation through the Priest', even though much of its content did not originate in priestly circles. But this, the earliest of the Codes that have come down to us, has certainly been incorporated by priestly compilers and historians as part of the divine revelation, and it is closely related to the next in order of the Codes, the Deuteronomic, in which the priestly emphasis is more apparent. Part of the revelatory significance of the Book of the Covenant lies for us in its comprehension of ordinary, everyday life, as being within the divine control. Here and there this becomes explicit. Thus, of what we might call a chance meeting, we read (Exod. xxi. 13):

'If a man lie not in wait, but God deliver[2] him into his hand, then I will appoint thee a place whither he shall flee.'

Less picturesquely than in the stories of the patriarchs, yet to the same effect, this code shows God in intimate relation to the lives of ordinary men. Though little is said directly of Him other than that Yahweh alone is to be worshipped, and that He hears and will avenge the cry of the oppressed,[3] the inclusion of this code in the Torah means that Yahweh is behind all the just decisions of the local tribunals. Legal acts are to be ratified before Him.[4] He is to be honoured through the offerings and observances of Israel,[5] and every approach to Him requires an offering: 'none shall appear before me empty'. Even the first-born of Israel's sons are His,[6] which may indicate human

---

[1] On this see my essay on 'Law and Religion in Israel', in *Law and Religion* (ed. by E. I. J. Rosenthal), pp. 48 ff.

[2] The Hebrew verb is the Pi'el of *'anah* (אָנָה) and means 'cause to meet'; an unplanned meeting is thus represented as in the hand of God.

[3] Exod. xxii. 20–4, cf. xxiii. 13.

[4] Exod. xxi. 6, the permanent incorporation of the slave in the household; xxii. 8–11, the oath of purgation under accusation.

[5] Exod. xxiii. 14 ff.   [6] xxii. 29.

sacrifice at an earlier time. Of God Himself there must be no representation by an image, not even in the costliest metal.[1]

If we compare the Book of the Covenant with the Babylonian Code we shall probably agree with J. M. Powis Smith that 'it was in most of its regulations far ahead of the Code of Hammurabi, so far as religious and humanitarian qualities go'.[2] This is due to the conception of God which is behind it, the God revealed in it as Yahweh the righteous and merciful God.

§ 2. DEUTERONOMY

Both in inception and content, the Book of Deuteronomy is both prophetic and priestly. Prophet and priest collaborated in introducing it to Josiah,[3] and we may well suppose that both groups were represented amongst the reformers who compiled the book sometime during the dark days of Manasseh. The chief evidence, however, is to be found in the prophetic spirit in which many of the laws of the actual code are expressed (xii–xxvi, xxviii) and the historical introduction (i–xi) and the conclusion (xxix, xxx) are written. In both elements of the book, viz. the historico-hortatory and the legislative, the prophetic work of the previous century is apparent.[4] On the other hand, the Code is itself an expanded edition of the Book of the Covenant, and its concentration of all worship in Jerusalem[5] is a measure which must have appealed strongly to the priests of that city. The essential compromise of the result can be easily seen in ch. xviii, of which the first part defines the priestly status and dues (distinguishing the priests of the capital from those of the country sanctuaries)[6] and the second part refers to the succession of prophets who will replace Moses as the agents of revelation.

The conception of God is that of the prophets. Yahweh, who

---

[1] xx. 23. (The injunction in xxii. 28, 'thou shalt not revile God', interrupts the context and is perhaps a later insertion.)

[2] Op. cit., p. 37. He goes on to point out that the claims made by Hammurabi for philanthropic qualities and deeds, and the religious spirit manifested in the Prologue and Epilogue to the Code do not find expression in the Code itself to any extent.

[3] 2 Kings xxii. 8 ff., cf. verses 14 ff.

[4] For the detailed proof the commentaries must be consulted; I have summarized the chief evidence in the *Century Bible Deuteronomy*, p. 33 f.

[5] The reason is that an ordered worship (xii. 8 ff.) may be established, from which the evils of the local sanctuaries, notably those of xxiii. 17 f., will be eliminated.

[6] For other references to the priests see xix. 17, xx. 1 f., xxiv. 8.

alone is to be worshipped, is the righteous God, 'which regardeth
not persons nor taketh reward; He doth execute the judgment
of the fatherless and the widow, and loveth the resident alien
(*ger*) in giving him food and raiment'.[1] The example of Yahweh
is made the direct incentive to a like humanity on the part of the
Israelite, with the particular remembrance of Israel's own lot
in Egypt. The characteristic humanity of the book may be seen
by comparing the law of the slave in xv. 12–18 with its previous
form in the Book of the Covenant (Exod. xxi. 2–6); we find now
the addition of an injunction to give the departing slave a liberal
provision 'out of thy flock and out of thy threshing-floor and out
of thy winepress'. Even to animals kindness is to be shown.[2]
In both the Introduction and Conclusion to the Code, and in
the Code itself, the retributive righteousness of God is strongly
and repeatedly emphasized. He is:

'the faithful God which keepeth covenant and mercy with them that
love Him and keep His commandments to a thousand generations,
and repayeth them that hate Him to their face, to destroy them.'
(vii. 9, 10)

Therefore,

'that which is altogether just shalt thou follow, that thou mayest live
and inherit the land which Yahweh thy God giveth thee.' (xvi. 20)

'See, I have set before thee this day life and good and death and
evil.' (xxx. 15)

Israel's relation to Yahweh is that of sonship, and this unique
relation should constitute it a holy people. The very appeal is
thus a combination of prophetic and priestly conceptions.[3] The
holiness is not simply that of moral obedience, as it essentially
was for Isaiah and Jeremiah; there are also rules for its attainment such as those of the list of animals, clean and unclean, to
which nothing in the earlier code corresponds.[4] The unique
relation of Israel to Yahweh depends not on its merit or magnitude; it is wholly due to the divine grace seen in the redemption
from Egypt.[5] Here we come to the great recurrent theme which
underlies the appeal for obedience, and goes so far to remove

---

[1] x. 17 f.
[2] xxii. 1–4, 6 f.; xxv. 4. Even if such rules go back to primitive ideas, their
humanitarian interpretation here is significant.
[3] Hos. xi. 1 and Lev. xix. 2, &c.
[4] xiv. 3–20; but this may be later than D; see Lev. xi. 2–23.
[5] ix. 5, vii. 7; see above ch. XI, 'The Election of Israel'.

the obloquy of 'legalism' from the Old Testament: 'Thou shalt love Yahweh thy God.'[1] The paradox of this command to love is explained by the subsequent answer to a son's question: 'We were Pharaoh's bondmen in Egypt, and Yahweh brought us out of Egypt with a mighty hand.' So in the liturgy of thanksgiving[2] the explicit motive for the offering of the basket of produce is the vision of all that divine providence in history which began with the wandering and solitary Aramaean, Jacob. These two passages take us to the heart of the Deuteronomic religion, and display the great evangelical motive of gratitude which is always the secret of the deepest obedience. To know aright the divine redemption is to be inspired with a love that makes obedience natural and easy, and turns God's statutes into man's songs in the house of his pilgrimage. Thus once more we see the co-operation of prophetic interpretation and priestly ritual.

§ 3. The Law of Holiness

We enter a different though not unrelated realm with the 'Law of Holiness', substantially found in Leviticus xvii–xxvi. The name is derived from the repeated emphasis in this Code on the holiness of Yahweh, and of the consequent requirement of holiness in priests and people. This is expressed in words which may be taken as the keynote of the Code: 'Ye shall be holy: for I, Yahweh your God, am holy.'[3] In its original sense, 'holiness' seems to have denoted 'separation'.[4] This is seen most clearly in the demand for separation between clean and unclean which is so prominent in this Code. Thus[5] 'ye shall be holy unto me; for I, Yahweh am holy and have separated you from the peoples, that ye should be mine'. In particular, the priest is to be 'made holy', since he offers 'the food of God'; 'he shall be holy unto thee, for I, Yahweh, which make you holy, am holy'.[6] The insistence on the divine 'I' in this Code is remarkable,[7] especially in the characteristic phrase repeated nearly fifty times,[8] 'I am Yahweh', which is naturally meant to carry with it the sense of His holiness elsewhere made explicit.

---

[1] vi. 5; cf. verse 20 f.   [2] xxvi; cf. viii. 10.   [3] Lev. xix. 2.

[4] See pp. 53 ff.; note the root *badal* (בדל) 'separate' in Lev. xx. 26, in close connexion with *ḳadosh*.

[5] xx. 26; cf. xviii. 24 ff., xxii. 4, &c.   [6] xxi. 8.

[7] Driver, *Introduction*[9], p. 49: 'the divine "I" appears here with a prominence which it never assumes in the laws of P'.   [8] So Driver, loc. cit.

This conception of God as holy, with the accompanying demand for a ritual of separation which shall enforce it, naturally corresponds to a deepened sense of the divine transcendence. This is a valuable gain, but it brings its own perils. One of them is seen in the great ethical chapter (xix) which in moral scope and depth is worthy to rank above the Decalogue, whilst incorporating part of it. This is the chapter containing the words which Jesus set in a new and larger horizon, 'Thou shalt love thy neighbour as thyself' (verse 18). It is clear that in the meaning of Leviticus 'neighbour' does not include Gentiles; the nations of the land are to be cast out because they have made it unclean.[1]

A further and even more marked limitation in the revelation of God is that no distinction is drawn between His ritual and moral commands, which are mingled in ch. xix and throughout as though they were on the same level of importance. This is the gravest defect in the revelation through the law, for it obscures and may come to contradict the chief truth for which the prophets strove, viz. that Yahweh desires mercy rather than sacrifice. Thus even bodily defects disqualify for the priesthood, and the profanation of the holy 'Name' may spring from chance incidents of a wholly non-moral kind, such as accidental contact with a dead body.[2] So the revelation of the divine holiness falls below the level reached by the insight of Israel's finest spirits, which is partly expressed in the earlier 'Deuteronomic' conception of Exod. xix. 6: 'ye shall be unto me a kingdom of priests and an holy nation'.

This is the most suitable place in which to refer to the legislative material in the last nine chapters of Ezekiel, which is clearly related in some way to the Law of Holiness. There are both similar phraseology and similar ideas.[3] For example, Ezekiel's insistence on the honour of God corresponds to the demand of the Law of Holiness for the fuller recognition of that holiness. No clear critical conclusion as to the precise relation has been reached, but the general opinion of the majority of scholars is that the Law of Holiness is the earlier.[4] On the other hand, the assumption throughout the present form of the Law of Holiness

---

[1] xviii. 25.   [2] xxi. 17 ff.; xxii. 2 ff.

[3] For details see *The Hexateuch*, by J. E. Carpenter and G. Harford-Battersby, i. 147 ff.

[4] e.g. J. M. P. Smith, op. cit., p. 71; Eissfeldt, *Einleitung*, p. 274.

that sacrifices are to be offered only at one (central) sanctuary seems to date it after Deuteronomy. Thus it is a stage on the way to the priestly legislation, though, like P, it is largely based on ritual practices of much earlier date.

§ 4. THE PRIESTLY LEGISLATION

There remain for consideration the conceptions underlying the priestly legislation as a whole. Here we have to remember both its complex origins (seen in the inclusion of smaller bodies of law within it, such as that just reviewed) and also the fact that its account of the religious institutions in which it is specially interested is incorporated in a continuous (priestly) narrative. We may easily forget this latter feature when we come to such large bodies of legislation as the instructions for making and serving the tabernacle (Exod. xxv–xxxi) or the whole Book of Leviticus. There is the further complication that the account of the wilderness tabernacle and of its ritual is an idealistic retrojection from the second temple and its worship, not less visionary than the programme for the second temple itself which closes the Book of Ezekiel. A similar, though less obvious and extensive, idealization of the past is seen in the later work of the Chronicler. In his case, however, we are able to check the version of ancient history which he reconstructs with the earlier documents on which he chiefly depended.[1]

It is not easy to describe briefly material so extensive and comprehensive as the final *corpus* of the priestly work. All we can do in a limited space is to single out certain features which characterize its subject-matter, notwithstanding many diversities and inconsistencies of detail.

(*a*) First of all, we may note the importance ascribed to the actual performance of the ritual, as affecting the relations between God and man. The holiness of God, as our glance at the incorporated Code of Holiness has shown, requires these particular forms of sacramental mediation. So important is the daily offering that a specially grievous aspect of famine is the enforced suspension of its meat- and drink-offering.[2] 'Not even at the very capture (of Jerusalem by Pompey in 63 B.C.) whilst

---

[1] The stock example is the account of the bringing of the ark to Jerusalem in 2 Sam. vi. 12 ff. compared with the Chronicler's description of how it ought to have been done (1 Chron. xv, xvi).

[2] Joel i. 9, 13, cf. Lev. ii. 1; 'das Band mit Gott war dadurch durchschnitten' (Sellin on Joel, i. 9).

they (the priests) were being slaughtered around the altar, did they abandon the ordinances of daily worship.'[1] Such insistence on the *act* shows the importance attached to precise conformity to the divine commands, a conformity not confined to the priests, but observed by the devout in such matters as the keeping of the Sabbath with meticulous care. Clearly, even in such observance, the stress may largely fall on the *moral* quality of obedience, that 'hearing the voice' of Yahweh,[2] which replaces the earlier observance of mere taboos on what we should call superstitious grounds. This 'sublimation' operates even when the practice has had a different origin from that ascribed to it in the Torah and was not confined to Israel, e.g. circumcision. Thus Yahweh reveals Himself as a God who first and foremost requires obedience to His revealed will. To remember and do all the commandments of Yahweh is to be holy to Him.[3]

(*b*) The primary service rendered by the priests in the systematized worship of the post-exilic period is that of making 'atonement' for 'sin'. The ritual culminates in the Day of Atonement.[4] An earlier chapter[5] has dealt with the conceptions of Holiness and Sin. Here we must emphasize the fact that the atonement described is of a highly ritualistic character, corresponding indeed to the generally ritualistic conception of sin in the priestly legislation. There is a sharp distinction between intentional and unintentional disobedience to the commands of Yahweh, and atonement is confined to the latter. Of the former it is said:

'The person who acts with a high hand (*bᵉyadh ramah*), whether a native or a resident alien, blasphemes Yahweh, and that person shall be cut off from the midst of his people.' (Num. xv. 30)

Such 'cutting off' denotes either death or excommunication.[6] On the other hand, priestly atonement deals with breaches of the law committed 'unwillingly' or 'in error',[7] which further reminds us of the importance attached to the precise act, without regard to motive.[8] The word translated 'atone' (*kipper*) is

---

[1] Josephus, *Jewish War*, I. vii, § 148 (Loeb trans.). So, during the siege of A.D. 70, the Tamid (morning and evening offering) was maintained even in the extremities of famine.   [2] *Shamaʿ bᵉḴol*, from Deut. and Jeremiah onwards.

[3] Num. xv. 40.   [4] Lev. xvi.   [5] Chapter IV.

[6] e.g. Lev. xvii. 10 and Num. xix. 20.

[7] *bishᵉgagah*, Num. xv. 27, 29; Lev. iv. 22, &c.

[8] This, of course, operates throughout the religion of Israel (cf. Uzzah) and far beyond it.

more probably to be regarded as meaning 'wipe away' than 'cover'.[1] In usage, the term denotes 'expiation' rather than 'propitiation'; as Buchanan Gray puts it:

'since in the Priestly Code the Hebrew verb is sometimes construed with an accusative of the thing that is in a state of sin, but never with God as an object, it is more probable that "to make expiation" is the most adequate rendering of *kipper* used in its technical sense and without a direct object.'[2]

Thus we have to think of priestly atonement as the divinely appointed method of removing 'unholiness', and so restoring a broken relation to God. In the atonement for the altar, the blood of the sin-offering is smeared upon its horns, and it thereby becomes 'holy' again.[3] Atonement is therefore a proof of God's grace in dealing with that which interferes with His relation to men and theirs to Him, by impinging on His holiness. The atonement is made not only, though especially,[4] by the blood of the sin-offering, for it can be effected e.g. by the burnt-offering,[5] or by the half-shekel tax;[6] indeed, the whole ministry of the priests is a work of atonement for Israel.[7]

At a later point more will have to be said of the philosophy of sacrifice; here it is sufficient to say that the revelation of God is necessarily that of one who acts within the given system of contemporary and unchallenged ideas. To ask why blood should atone is to be thrown back on the previous question, why contact with death or childbirth or leprosy should forbid access to God. It was enough for the men of that day to believe that the atonement 'wipes away' or expiates the breach of taboo. In every theology, as in every philosophy or science, something is accepted as the starting-point, which raises no question in the minds of contemporaries, though it may do for successors.

(c) The priestly technique naturally occupies a central place in the priestly legislation. Yet we should get an altogether false impression of the religion which centred in this technique and of the revelation which it implies, if we did not take also a larger view, warranted by statements of the law literature, and especially of the religion of the psalmists, so largely based on the temple worship. The whole of Israel's life is brought into rela-

---

[1] See the full discussion by G. Buchanan Gray, *Sacrifice in the Old Testament*, pp. 67 ff. He accepts the Accadian root, *kaparu*, 'wash away' (with a liquid), as the original meaning.

[2] Op. cit., p. 74.   [3] Lev. viii. 15.   [4] Lev. xvii. 11.
[5] Lev. i. 4.   [6] Exod. xxx. 15, 16.   [7] 1 Chron. vi. 34 (49).

tion with God by means of the far-reaching principle of *representation*. As Kautzsch has stated it,[1] 'all directions regarding holy places, times, persons and actions have ever in view the *one* aim of realizing the idea of a God-consecrated people, the fact of its absolute dependence upon Him, and the necessity of ever renewed surrender to Him'. Thus a peculiar holiness attaches to the 'tabernacle' (*mishkan*) as the earthly 'dwelling-place' of Yahweh (made after the heavenly pattern), wherein His 'glory' dwells,[2] yet the whole land belongs to Him. He commissions Joshua to divide it amongst the tribes,[3] and Ezekiel's idealistic redistribution is based on the same principle, that the central portion on which the temple is to stand is itself an 'oblation' (*t'rumah*)[4] which represents the whole. From earlier times individual tenure was subject to the condition that the land was to lie fallow in the seventh year for the sake of the poor.[5] Now, however, that year is a Sabbath to Yahweh,[6] whilst the (probably theoretical) jubilee of the fiftieth year marks a general return to the original family tenancy:[7] 'the land shall not be sold in perpetuity; for the land is mine'. Similarly all the property of the Israelite belongs to Yahweh, and this is expressed in the offering of first-fruits and tithes,[8] and indeed of the sacrifices in general. The most general conception of these is that of a *gift* to Yahweh, even though they may be further differentiated by special intentions and occasions.[9]

Sacred seasons, again, the sabbaths and the festivals, are representative of the whole life of an Israelite as belonging to Yahweh. This is marked by the representative prohibition of all forms of secular work at these times.[10] Finally, the theory of the separation of priests and Levites from the rest of Israel as being specially 'holy' persons springs from the same principle of representation. Thus the Levites are explicitly declared to be set apart in place of the first-born among the Israelites.[11]

---

[1] HDB, v. 722; details in pp. 717–22.

[2] Exod. xxvi. 33, xl. 34 ff.   [3] Joshua xiii ff.   [4] Ezek. xlv. 13 ff.

[5] Exod. xxiii. 10 (E): 'that the poor of thy people may eat.'

[6] Lev. xxv. 4 ff.   [7] Lev. xxv. 23.   [8] Num. xviii. 12, 21.

[9] G. B. Gray, op. cit., p. 32: 'while what are called Jewish sacrifices were all of them certainly gifts and felt to be such, some of them were also something more'.

[10] See the repeated injunctions in the festal calendar of Lev. xxiii.

[11] Num. iii. 44 ff. As the number of Levites fell short of the number of the first-born by 273, a special tax of 5 shekels apiece was to be exacted from the excess number, a provision which shows how realistically the principle of representation was taken.

These, then, are the general conditions on which Yahweh is conceived as dwelling amongst His people within His land. The focus of His presence is the *kapporeth* (rendered 'mercy-seat' in our English versions), the golden slab covering the ark of the testimony, on which stood the two golden cherubim. From between them Moses is said to have heard the voice of Yahweh in the tent of meeting.[1] There Yahweh meets with Israel in its appointed representative, and the tent is made holy by the 'glory' of His presence.[2] Thence was proclaimed by the priest the resultant blessing which so finely epitomizes the faith of Israel:

Yahweh bless thee and guard thee,
Yahweh cause His face to shine upon thee and shew thee favour,
Yahweh lift up His face towards thee and appoint thee welfare.
(Num. vi. 24–6 (Gray's trans.))

[1] Num. vii. 89; cf. Exod. xxv. 22, xl. 34; Ps. xxvi. 9 (8), &c.
[2] Exod. xxv. 22, xl. 34 f. Note the impressive ending of the Book of Ezekiel: 'the name of the city . . . shall be, Yahweh is there', and cf. Exod. xxix. 45.

XVII

PRIEST AND PROPHET

IN our summary view of 'revelation through the law' we have already seen something of the way in which the prophetic influence asserted itself from Moses onwards in shaping the records of priestly tradition.[1] The very first page of the Old Testament offers one of the best examples. Without the lessons of prophecy the story of the creation by a transcendent God would not have been written as it there stands. Comparison with the Babylonian parallels brings out a moral and religious quality which is unique, due to the assimilation of prophetic truth by priestly writers. Apart, however, from such general influence there are special features of the relation of prophet and priest which call for some notice, viz. (1) the relation of the prophet to local sanctuaries and to the temple, (2) the interpretation of sacrifice, (3) the written Torah and its further exposition.

§ 1. PROPHETS AND SANCTUARIES

The first of these was brought to the front by Mowinckel,[2] as part of his general thesis that 'with very few exceptions our Biblical psalms were composed as cultic psalms'. For him the prophetic elements in the Psalms are not a liturgical imitation but an actual product of prophets participating in the cult. He argues that even the earlier pre-exilic prophets had already an official connexion with one or another of the sanctuaries, as we may see from what is said of Samuel. He was brought up as an assistant to the priest of Shiloh. Later on, we hear of him as taking the leading position at a high place 'in the land of Zuph',[3]

---

[1] Jewish scholars often complain that Gentiles give to the prophets a disproportionate attention in comparison with the Torah. This does not, of course, refer to literary analysis or to antiquarian research, but to the religious evaluation of the Law. So far as the complaint is justified, it is easily explicable. In the eyes of critical scholarship, chiefly in Gentile hands, the prophets are the great originators and pioneers in the higher religion of Israel, and hence of Judaism itself. Christian interest is much more closely linked to the prophets than to the Torah. Yet we cannot hope to understand the revelation of God in the Old Testament without putting the work of the priest alongside that of the prophet.

[2] *Psalmenstudien III*: *Kultprophetie und prophetische Psalmen*, esp. pp. 1–29. He has recently been followed, with further detail, by A. R. Johnson in *The Cultic Prophet in Ancient Israel*, so far as the present application is concerned.

[3] 1 Sam. ix. 5 ff.

so that the guests at a sacrificial feast wait for him to come and give the blessing, which is a priestly office. He is described as a seer, and Mowinckel argues for the original identity of priest and seer, comparing the *baru* priest-seers of Assyria. Moses also was priest and seer and the guardian of the tent of revelation.[1] David had a seer amongst his officers,[2] and often obtained oracles through a priest-seer (הכהן).[3] The *nᵉbi'im* were not indeed priests, but they appear in connexion with sanctuaries,[4] in the times of Samuel and of Elisha. According to Jer. xxix. 26, the *nᵉbi'im* were under the control of temple priests. Jeremiah and Ezekiel were both priests and prophets.

These are the chief data to which Mowinckel appeals to prepare us for his claim that the liturgy of the temple included prophetic oracles, and that these are still to be discovered in many of the psalms. Thus in Ps. cxxxii, which represents David as installing the ark in Jerusalem, and asking for Yahweh's continued presence and help, we are to hear God saying (through a temple-prophet):

Of the fruit of thy body will I set upon thy throne. . . .
This is my resting-place forever. . . . (verses 11–18.)

At the end of the ninety-first psalm, which assures the worshipper against a long list of perils, comes the direct oracle (14–16)

Because he hath set his love upon Me, therefore will I deliver him,

confirming the faith of the psalmist or user of the psalm. In the 20th psalm, after the expressed hope that Yahweh will hear the king's prayers comes (verse 6) the assertion of confidence:

Now know I that Yahweh saveth His anointed,

which suggests that some interpretation of the accompanying sacrifice—such as inspection of the liver of the victim or observation of the movements of the rising smoke—has warranted the declaration. To such realistic interpretations Mowinckel refers Ps. lxxiv. 9:

We see not our signs,
There is no more any prophet.

He would find such temple-prophets chiefly amongst the Levitical singers. He admits that such oracles might in time

---

[1] Exod. xxxiii. 7 (כל מבקש יהוה יצא אל אהל מועד אשר מחוץ למחנה:).
[2] 2 Sam. xxiv. 11 (here *ḥozeh*, not *ro'eh*).
[3] 1 Sam. xxiii. 9 ff., xxx. 7 ff., &c.
[4] 1 Sam. x. 5, xix. 19; 2 Kings ii. 3, 5, iv. 38.

become a fixed part of the formal technique, just as for us in the Anglican liturgy the priestly absolution comes after the General Confession.

How far is this convincing either as a history of the development of priesthood and prophecy or as an interpretation of the psalms? First in regard to Moses and Samuel, we must remember that they were outstanding personalities who would naturally, either in actual fact or treasured tradition, take a leading place in regard to any sanctuary with which they might be even temporarily associated. As for priestly functions, sacrifice was not at first confined to a distinct professional class as later; the head of family or group offered the sacrifice of his group. The sanctuaries at Rama, Bethel, Jericho, Gilgal would very naturally be the centres near which groups of n^{e}bi'im would be found in the days of Samuel and Elisha, but this does not prove any official connexion with the sanctuaries. This applies also to the Jeremianic reference[1] which Mowinckel regards as 'unquestionably' proving that temple-prophets were a recognized institution. In fact, the passage suggests opposition rather than organized incorporation:

'Yahweh hath made thee (i.e. Zephaniah) priest in the stead of Jehoiada the priest, that ye should be officers in the house of Yahweh, for every man that is mad (m^{e}shugga') and maketh himself a prophet, that thou shouldest put him in the stocks and in shackles.'

This really tells against Mowinckel's argument, for Zephaniah is being summoned by Shemaiah to do his official duty against Jeremiah, as Pashhur did it, when he put Jeremiah in the stocks on another occasion (xx. 1 f.). But if the prophets were mere underlings of the priests, they could be dismissed when disobedient to their masters. Who can imagine Jeremiah in the role of a temple-prophet? No doubt there were contemporary prophets who sided with the priests, but this does not make them into officials of the cult. It does not seem, therefore, that there is sufficient evidence to warrant us in accepting a pre-exilic order of temple-prophets. A prophet might naturally choose the crowd at a sanctuary festival for his audience, as Amos may have done at Bethel; but Amos repudiated the suggestion that he belonged to any professional order of prophets.

When we come to the post-exilic temple, the conditions are

[1] xxix. 26.

somewhat different. Here, as we have already seen, and as the Book of Psalms amply shows, the assimilation of the prophetic contribution to Israel's religion had proceeded to a very marked extent. There would be nothing strange in the appearance of divine oracles as part of the liturgy. The priests as such had the tradition of their ancient oracular methods, and that tradition, adapted to the substance of prophetic truth, would supply a natural form of assurance to anxious worshippers, seeking an answer to their sacrifices and prayers. We may think that Mowinckel has exaggerated the number of such oracles, as of the cultic element generally in the Psalms. Even so, there are numerous passages which do suggest the incorporation of prophetic *forms* of utterance in some of the temple-liturgies. It seems much more doubtful whether we can posit a special class of officials charged with these utterances. If there had been such specialization of Levitical function, we should have expected some clearer evidence of it than seems to exist, either in the later Scriptures or in the Mishnah. Mowinckel does appeal to the Chronicler's account of the Spirit coming upon a Levite in the midst of the congregation,[1] and moving him to prophesy deliverance to Jehoshaphat.[2] But does such an isolated occurrence, even apart from its questionable source, justify him in regarding it as 'typical'? On the whole, then, it is safer to confine ourselves to recognizing some assimilation of prophetic form as well as much of substance, without admitting the necessary establishment of any separate order of temple-prophets. The ancient priestly oracle, and the official position of the priests, provided sufficient warrant for the assimilation of prophetic forms in the liturgy.

§ 2. The Interpretation of Sacrifice

From the beginning to the end of Israel's religious life, as recorded in the Old Testament, sacrifice was an indispensable part of it. Sacrifice is not, of course, characteristic of Biblical religion alone, as is often assumed by those not acquainted with its place in other religions. All over the ancient world the approach to God was normally accompanied by some gift supposed to be acceptable to Him, such as the gift brought to an earthly superior to win his favour. The analogy of the earthly and the heavenly was sufficient in itself to justify sacrifices

[1] 2 Chron. xx. 14 ff.   [2] Mowinckel, op. cit., p. 21.

and offerings, and no further theory was deemed necessary.
The only question in the worshipper's mind was whether what
he brought would prove to be acceptable to God. The need
to get this question answered fostered an elaborate priestly
technique, through which the worshipper would find assurance.
Apart from the details by which this assurance was given,
resembling those of divination and indeed a consecrated form
of it, the general conviction would grow that this and this were
commanded, and would therefore be efficacious. The particular
intention of a sacrifice would naturally vary with the occasion.
Thus the well-known pre-exilic sacrifices of the so-called 'peace-
offering', an act of blood-communion with the deity, and of the
whole burnt-offering, the most complete form of gift, were
extended in the post-exilic period by the development of the
sin-offering and the guilt-offering which marked a deepened
sense of alienation or remoteness from God. In the priestly
legislation the expiation of ritual offences claimed a central
importance, as we saw when dealing with 'atonement'.

The attitude of the classical prophets to the sacrifices of their
times has been repeatedly discussed, and differing conclusions
have been reached. At first sight it might seem that they
rejected all sacrifices in favour of the moral relation to God on
which they so vigorously insisted. 'Was it sacrifices and offerings that ye brought me in the wilderness for forty years?' asks
Amos,[1] and his rhetorical question expects a negative answer.
'To what purpose is the multitude of your sacrifices unto me? . . .
bring no more vain oblations' is God's word through Isaiah.[2]
Through Jeremiah God says, 'I spoke not unto your fathers, nor
commanded them in the day that I brought them out of the
land of Egypt, concerning burnt-offerings or sacrifices'.[3] All
this is good evidence against the ascription to Moses of an
elaborate system of sacrifice such as we find in the priestly
legislation. But it does not deny *any* legitimate place to an
offering when accompanied by the right moral and spiritual
attitude. It is difficult to conceive how these prophets would
have devised a worship wholly without sacrifices. They were
attacking a false and non-moral reliance upon them, rather
than the expression of true worship through a eucharistic gift.[4]

The interpretation of sacrifice can usefully be approached

---

[1] Amos v. 25.   [2] Isa. i. 11 ff.
[3] Jer. vii. 21 ff.; cf. vi. 20.   [4] So G. B. Gray, *Sacrifice*, p. 89.

through the symbolic acts of the prophets, to which reference was made in a previous chapter.[1] These acts were clearly held to be more than merely dramatic illustrations of the prophet's spoken word. They were part of it, indeed the more intense part, which initiated the divine action in miniature, and thus helped towards the fulfilment of what was foretold. Genetically, they spring from the widespread practice of symbolic magic, but the prophets have transformed them into religion by assimilating them to the will of God. In a similar way we may think of the sacrificial act performed by the priest. It is in miniature the actual renewal of a relation. In the fundamental conception of sacrifice as a gift, seen in the whole burnt-offering, acceptance of it restores some previous relation which has been broken, or reinforces one which exists. This relation extends beyond the visible and tangible world, but realistically includes its visible and tangible elements, because what is done here is done there also. The peace-offering works to similar ends by different means. Here the meal eaten by the worshippers and the blood poured out for the deity upon the altar, coming as they do from the same consecrated animal, realistically unite the worshippers and their God. The sin-offering with its special manipulation of the blood primarily cancels what the anthropologist would call a broken taboo, figuring as a ritual offence. The guilt-offering centres in the necessity to make reparation for offences of wider range, such as theft, in addition to restitution. Yahweh's will as well as man's right has been infringed; the offering, if accepted, restores the broken relation to Him.

One way of expressing all this would be to say that sacrifice establishes or renews the covenant,[2] as is suggested by the words of a psalmist:

Gather my saints together unto me;
Those that have made a covenant with me by sacrifice. (Ps. l. 5)

True as that is, it does not serve to bring out the realistic and 'symbolic' function of sacrifice. If we learn to think of it as being parallel with and of the same order as, the symbolic acts of the prophets, we get closer in both forms of action to the actual thoughts and feelings of the worshipper. Given his general outlook on the world, no other interpretation of sacrifice was necessary to him. Sacrifice actually did (in part) that which

[1] See p. 171. See also my article, 'Hebrew Sacrifice and Prophetic Symbolism', in *JTS*, July–Oct. 1942 (xliii. 171–2). [2] See above pp. 153 f.

had to be done. Obviously, he might stop there, and not go
on to do the rest, i.e. to accompany the sacrifice with that
obedience to Yahweh's other commands which was required of
him. So far as he regarded the sacrifice as a sufficient substitute
for this, he would fall under the stern condemnation of the
prophets; their attack on sacrifice was mainly directed against
this aspect of it. In theory at least, the better type of priest in
the later system would have fully agreed, as did the rabbis still
later.[1] But the perils of all professionalism in religion are
familiar, and one of them is to exaggerate the value of the
technique and to divorce it from the living world.

The interpretation of sacrifice as a 'symbolic' act thus brings
it within that realism which we have had frequent occasion to
notice. Of course, 'symbolic' is not to be taken in the loose,
modern sense of mere suggestiveness. The ancient symbol is an
effective part of that which it represents. Sacrifice is an efficient
act. On this view of it, the world of time is closely correlated
with the world of eternity, and the value of this world to God is
emphasized. We see why the ancient mind felt that no further
explanation of sacrifice was necessary.[2]

§ 3. The Written *Torah*

In what has been said, we have had in view the ritual of the
second temple as a working system, with its daily public offerings, its festival sacrifices and other observances, and the many
private offerings which gathered around these. We get many
glimpses of all these as a whole through the eyes of the Chronicler, though his setting for them is often unhistorical, and they
really reflect the usage of his own times; e.g. in regard to
Solomon's burnt-offerings:

'Even as the duty of every day (*bid^ebar yom b^eyom*) required, offering according to the commandment of Moses, on the sabbaths, and
on the new moons, and on the set feasts, three times in the year, even
in the feast of unleavened bread, and in the feast of weeks, and in
the feast of tabernacles.'[3]

[1] Moore, *Judaism*, i. 504, 505: 'A false reliance on the efficacy of sacrifice of
itself is condemned in the spirit of the Scriptures . . . while the temple was still
standing the principle had been established that the efficacy of every species of
expiation was morally conditioned—without repentance no rites availed.'

[2] This opens up the right (exegetical) line of approach to the New Testament
sacraments, and to the conception of the death of Christ as a sacrifice.

[3] 2 Chron. viii. 13; expanded from 1 Kings ix. 25, where confined to the three
set feasts.

So again, after the reformation of Hezekiah, there is an account
of the sacrificial ceremonial suited to a great occasion in the
times of the Chronicler (2 Chron. xxix. 20 ff.).

We have been endeavouring to see what conception of God
and of His relation to Israel underlay this system in its successive stages of development, prior to the reduction of its ordinances to a written revelation. The priestly literature is partly
of the nature of technical memoranda for the priests (often set
out at greater length and with fuller details in the Mishnah),
and partly in the form of a priestly history of Israel, which
incorporates accounts of some of its institutions at what were
regarded as nodal points. Hardly before the middle of the
fourth century was this literature combined with earlier documents (JE and D) to form the written Torah,[1] and thus to
inaugurate a new and highly important phase of the development of revelation. The outstanding figure in the transition to
this appears to be Ezra 'the priest, the scribe'.[2] But it is as
difficult to be confident as to the exact form and extent of his
activity as in regard to those of Moses; later legend has obscured
both of these impressive personalities. Ezra probably arrived
in Jerusalem in the seventh year of the *second* Artaxerxes, i.e.
in 397, half a century later than Nehemiah.[3] His law-book is
probably to be regarded as consisting of part of the priestly Law
(including the Law of Holiness), and not the whole Torah.[4]
The exposition of that which was publicly read is also associated
with him and his fellows.[5] It was natural that the professional
'scribe' should also in the first place be the expounder. In due
course from such a beginning came the long line of rabbinical
discussion and expansion, which is recorded in the Mishnah and
Talmud. Somewhere between the completion of the Torah (say
by the middle of the fourth century) and the Maccabean Revolt
(in which the destruction of law-rolls figures prominently),

---

[1] The Samaritan schism is rightly regarded as the *terminus ad quem* for the
completion of the Torah, but unfortunately we cannot date this schism with any
certainty, and as Moore says (*Judaism*, i. 25), the date must be sought in the fourth
century rather than the fifth. See further my article in the *Expository Times*, on
'Canonicity and Inspiration', vol. xlvii, no. 3, pp. 119–23, and ch. viii ('The
Canon') in my book, *The Old Testament, its Making and Meaning*.   [2] Ezra vii. 11.

[3] On the history of this dating of Ezra, see H. H. Rowley, *Darius the Mede*, p. 49,
n. 7, giving references to the authorities.

[4] Cf. G. B. Gray, 'Law Literature', in *E.Bi.* 2741 (vol. iii).

[5] Neh. viii. 8; the verse seems to imply this, whatever be the precise meaning we
attach to m\u1d49phorash.

we must suppose that great transfer of emphasis to have been effected which (after A.D. 70) enabled the Torah to replace the ritual of the temple as the basis of Judaism. That meant the passing of the priest in favour of the rabbi, and the replacement of the lost temple by the synagogue, of which we first hear definitely towards the end of the third century, B.C.[1]

Thus we face a new conception of the mode of divine revelation, by way of the written record instead of by cultic acts. It is difficult to overstate the importance of this change into a book-religion. This is written large on the whole subsequent development of Judaism. The fixation of the tradition in written form had the inevitable result that it became continuously necessary to adjust the now stereotyped Torah to ever new needs and conditions by a constant process of reinterpretation. So grew up the new tradition of an oral law handed down by Moses through a long succession of trustees which gave authority to the ultimate decisions of the rabbis.[2] Some such claim is always likely to be made when authority is derived from an ancient book. It is to be seen in the decisions of the Council of Trent, making the Church the ultimate interpreter of Scripture, and therefore the supreme authority. The Torah was regarded as existing prior to the world, and indeed it provided the pattern for the creation of the world.[3]

In much of this later reinterpretation, grossly unhistorical as it so often is, we may see a continuation or revival of the living religious spirit which had found its finest expression in the great prophets. The continued growth is seen in both Halakhah and Haggadah,[4] i.e. in the discussion of the Law and its new applications and problems, and in the embroidery of the ancient material with all the adornments of pious fantasy and moral exhortation. Rabbinical Judaism did indeed refuse to include in its Canon of Scripture most of the apocalyptic which was the direct continuation of prophecy, and as a whole Palestinian Judaism stands with the priest rather than with the prophet. That was very natural, since the priest had had so large a share in shaping the religion of Judaism. In the revelation of God to Israel and so to the world, the priest was the necessary complement to the prophet.

---

[1] In Egypt (Elbogen, *Der jüdische Gottesdienst*[3], pp. 446 ff.).

[2] *Pirke Aboth*, i. 1.   [3] Moore, op. cit., i. 266 ff.

[4] The most convenient sources for the Gentile reader are the translation of the Mishnah by Professor Danby and *A Rabbinic Anthology*, by Montefiore and Loewe.

PART VI

REVELATION IN 'WISDOM'

XVIII

WISDOM, NATIVE AND INTERNATIONAL

BY the Wisdom literature of Israel we mean chiefly the three canonical Books of Proverbs, Ecclesiastes, and Job and the two post-canonical Books of Ecclesiasticus and the Wisdom of Solomon. In addition to these there are less familiar writings, such as 4 Maccabees, inculcating the control of life by devout reason,[1] and portions of books, such as the admonitions of Tobit to his son (ch. iv).[2]

Broadly considered, this literature consists of two main types, viz. anthologies of epigrams with practical advice about life and conduct, such as the canonical Proverbs and the post-canonical Ecclesiasticus, and (at later stages) discussions of the problems of life as raised by experience of it, such as Job, Ecclesiastes, and the Wisdom of Solomon. The appeal to 'experience' is throughout characteristic of Wisdom, and differentiates it from both Prophecy and Law, whilst reducing it to a lower level of authority by ascribing to it a less direct origin as 'Revelation'. The classical statement of the differences is afforded by Jer. xviii. 18:

'*Torah* shall not perish from the priest, nor counsel from the wise man (*ḥakam*), nor word from the prophet.'

Here the counsel (*'ezah*) of the wise seems to be the practical advice[3] on the conduct of life given by a special class in the community. Such advice would naturally be sought from the 'elders', i.e. those of long experience,[4] and this is made explicit in the parallel statement of Ezek. vii. 26:

'They shall seek vision from prophet and *Torah* shall perish from priest and counsel from elders.'

---

[1] Here belong also the Mishnic tractate, 'Sayings of the Fathers', and probably the New Testament Epistle of James.

[2] Cf. also 1 Esdras iii. 1–iv. 63, Epistle of Aristeas, §§ 187–293, Baruch iii. 9–iv. 4. Some of the canonical Psalms (e.g. xxxvii, xlix, lxxiii) can be classed as 'Wisdom'.

[3] Cf. 2 Kings xviii. 20; Isa. xix. 3.

[4] 'Much experience is the crown of old men' (Ecclus. xxv. 6). Gressmann, in *ZAW*, 1924, p. 292, reviews the different ways in which this experience could be employed.

From amongst the elders (the heads of family groups) the local 'judges' would be drawn. They are warned not to accept gifts, 'for a gift doth blind the eyes of the wise'.[1] But the 'wise men' are not to be identified with the judges as such, though forming like them a specialized class in the community, a class which as we have seen could be ranked with priest and prophet as a channel of the revelation of the divine will.

§ 1. The Development within Israel

How far back can we trace the existence of this special class? The difficulty in answering that question is that the meaning of a term will change with successive generations, especially of such terms as are involved in the changes of social life, i.e. the changes of its officials and organs. Joab employed a 'wise woman' to influence David,[2] and was himself influenced by one of Abel-beth-maacah, when he was besieging it.[3] It is said of Ahithopel that his counsel 'was as if a man inquired of the word (*dabar*) of God'.[4] The ascription of outstanding wisdom to Solomon[5] belongs to that later tradition which made him the copious composer of songs and proverbs, a very different kind of 'wisdom' from that practical sagacity as a judge which is illustrated by the early story of the two women brought before him.[6] But we can well understand how the earlier reputation might become the nucleus of the later, just as happened with the later ascription of the law-codes to Moses and of many psalms to David, and of many anonymous prophecies to one of the better-known prophets, such as Isaiah. The general scope of Wisdom is described in the opening verses of our Book of Proverbs (i. 1–6). Wisdom gives discipline (*muṣar*) in wise dealing and imparts prudence (*'ormah*) to the simple and knowledge

[1] Deut. xvi. 18, 19; the official appointment of such 'judges' was made necessary by the destruction of the local sanctuaries, and the removal of their priests (who had previously given oracle-judgements when necessary as a final court of appeal). The judges continue the role of the nomadic sheikhs, by a natural process of development.

[2] 2 Sam. xiv. 1–21, cf. Jer. ix. 16 (17).

[3] 2 Sam. xx. 15 ff.; the place is said to have been renowned as a home of Israelite tradition (see Driver, *Hebrew Text of Samuel*, on verses 18–19).

[4] 2 Sam. xvi. 23; i.e. it had genuine prophetic quality. The opposite of such effective counsel is 'foolishness' (2 Sam. xv. 31).

[5] 1 Kings iv. 29–34.

[6] 1 Kings iii. 16–28.

and discretion to the inexperienced. The aim is the attainment
of sound counsels:[1]

> To understand a proverb (*mashal*) and an interpretation (*mᵉlizah*),
> The words of the wise and their riddles (*ḥidoth*).

Here some of the more or less technical vocabulary of Wisdom
is employed, such as *muṣar* (discipline), *mᵉzimmah* (discretion),
leḳaḥ (learning, as something 'received'), *taḥbuloth* (guidance),
mashal (rendered 'proverb', but much wider in scope; perhaps
'comparison'), *ḥidah* (riddle). Some of these, it will be seen,
refer to content, others, like the 'comparison' and the 'riddle'
to the form. Elsewhere, we have the fable, as in that of Jotham[2]
which would doubtless come under the general heading of the
mashal, as does the more extended collection of aphorisms on the
same topic, amounting to a short poetical essay, which we frequently find in Sirach. As an example of the riddle, the best
known is probably that ascribed to Samson:

> Out of the eater came forth meat,
> And out of the strong came forth sweetness. (Judges xiv. 14)

The distinction between the earlier (oral) and later (literary)
kinds of 'Wisdom' should be kept constantly in view, or we may
easily be tempted to antedate some of the actual Wisdom literature of Israel.[3] It is true that the canonical Book of Proverbs
shows by its six subordinate titles of sections that it draws upon
earlier collections, and that these doubtless contain some pre-
exilic material. We know that there were proverbial sayings
from early times, such as 'Let him not boast who fastens his
girdle as he who loosens it',[4] the reproof of the boastful Benhadad before the battle, or 'Is Saul also among the prophets?'[5]
used to express astonishment at some surprising change of
conduct. But the popular creation of such sayings, which may
be found all over the world, is one thing; their literary selection, expression, and classification is quite another. One of the

---

[1] The word *taḥbuloth* seems to be connected with that for 'rope', and to refer to
steering.

[2] Judges ix. 6 ff.

[3] As is done, I think, by Gressmann, *ZAW*, 1924, pp. 272–96, and by O. S.
Rankin, *Israel's Wisdom Literature*, e.g. p. 164, cf. p. 14, where he claims that
'Israel's wisdom writers' preceded and influenced the prophets. Wisdom, yes;
Wisdom writers, no.

[4] 1 Kings xx. 11 (four words in Hebrew): אל־יתהלל חגר כמפתח׃ :

[5] 1 Sam. x. 12, xix. 24.

sub-titles of Proverbs to which appeal is made for an early date
of the collection which follows is:

> These also are proverbs of Solomon, which the men of Hezekiah
> king of Judah copied out. (xxv. 1)

But unfortunately for such an appeal the Hebrew word for
'copied out' is one which belongs to the post-canonical period,[1]
and is not found anywhere else in the Old Testament.

We cannot prove the early date of literary Wisdom in Israel
from the existence of 'scribes' in the times of David and Solomon.[2] A secretary of state is one thing;[3] the scribe eulogized
and indeed typified by Jesus ben Sira[4] is quite another. Identity
of name (*sopher*) here as so often conceals a changing connotation. It was, however, natural enough that the professional
'writer', the master of the art of using a pen, should develop
into the later 'scribe', and one passage in Jeremiah connects the
scribe with the wise man (viii. 8, 9):

> 'How do ye say, We are wise and Yahweh's Torah is with us?
> But, behold, the false pen of the scribes hath wrought falsely. The
> wise men are ashamed, they are dismayed and taken: lo, they have
> rejected Yahweh's word; and what manner of wisdom is in them?'

The precise reference here is not as clear as we could wish, but
whether the newly discovered law-book (Deuteronomy) is in
view, as seems to be probable, or some other document is
intended, the wise are here scribes in the earlier sense of professional writers, who also claim to be competent exponents of
Yahweh's Torah in opposition to the oral 'word' of Yahweh
through Jeremiah. Ezra, at any rate, in the conception of him
presented by the Chronicler,[5] is already a scribe in the later
sense of an interpreter of the Torah of Moses.

On the whole, therefore, the use of the term 'wise man' agrees
with that of 'wisdom' in showing a not unnatural development.
In the earlier days it derived its meaning from individual men
and women, whose counsel commanded respect through their
long experience or their personal qualities. At a later stage it

---

[1] he'tiḳu (הֶעְתִּיקוּ). Oesterley, *Proverbs*, ad loc., rightly says that 'The
occurrence of this word stamps this title as belonging to a much later time', whereas
in the Introduction, p. xxviii, he inconsistently says: 'The nature of this title stamps
it as belonging to the time when the collection was made.'

[2] As does Humbert, in *RGG²*, v. 1806.

[3] 2 Sam. viii. 17, xx. 25; 1 Kings iv. 3; 2 Kings xii. 11 (10), xviii. 18.

[4] xxxviii. 24 ff., li. 13 ff.   [5] Ezra vii. 6, 10, 11.

describes a semi-professional class, less official than the priests, but more stabilized than the prophets, whose itineracy reflects their irregularity of utterance. To this development the idea that professional *writers* possess wisdom (or at least knowledge) would contribute. By the closing decades of the seventh century the scribe was ready to concern himself with anything in the past of which a record seemed worth while, and the exile accentuated the need for a record of Israel's 'wisdom'. But it was chiefly after the exile that the literary activity of the scribe displayed itself in the compilation of anthologies of wise sayings, and in the discussion of religious problems. The argument of Gressmann and others that Wisdom *literature* existed in Israel long before the exile is largely based on its undoubted existence in Egypt and Babylonia from early times. But such an argument is quite inconclusive. Knowledge and culture, especially in ancient times, advance very unequally in different communities; only when we can prove dependence by positive evidence of connexion and influence have parallel developments any weight. Now evidence of this kind points to such dependence only in or after the exile.

§ 2. THE RELATION TO EGYPTIAN AND BABYLONIAN WISDOM

The second question which we encounter on the threshold of any study of the Wisdom literature of Israel is that of its relation to the similar literature of Egypt and (in a much less degree) of Babylon.[1] Here we are fortunate in having a clear proof of contact between Hebrew and Egyptian Wisdom through such a detailed comparison of Prov. xxii. 17–xxiv. 22 with *The Teaching of Amenophis* as has been made by Professor D. C. Simpson.[2] As one example of many close parallels we may take Prov. xxii. 24:

> Do not associate to thyself a man given to anger;
> Nor go in company with a wrathful man;

[1] See the admirable study by J. Fichtner, *Die altorientalische Weisheit in ihrer israelitisch-jüdischen Ausprägung* (BZAW, lxii, 1933). The chief Egyptian documents can be seen in Erman's *The Literature of the Ancient Egyptians* (Eng. Trans. by A. M. Blackman), pp. 54 ff.; cf. also Ranke's trs. in Gressmann, *ATAT*, pp. 33–46. Selections from the Babylonian are given by R. W. Rogers, *Cuneiform Parallels to the Old Testament*, pp. 164 ff.; cf. also Ebeling's trs. in *ATAT*, pp. 284–295. See also the useful Excursus (I) to W. O. E. Oesterley's *Proverbs* (1929).

[2] *The Journal of Egyptian Archaeology*, vol. xii, pp. 232–9 (Oct. 1926). The study is based on the preceding (pp. 191–231) translation of the Egyptian document by F. Ll. Griffith.

to which the corresponding lines of the Egyptian document are:

> Do not associate to thyself the passionate man,
> Nor approach him for conversation. (xi. 13, 14)

The general view of scholars is that the compiler of this section of the Book of Proverbs was dependent on *The Teaching of Amenophis*, and this is confirmed both by the order of the thought and by the striking fact that the thirty chapters of the Egyptian book seem to have been reduced to thirty sayings in the Hebrew compilation. Moreover, this has explained the obscure Hebrew word in xxii. 20, rendered by the A.V. and R.V. as 'excellent things' without much warrant, a word of which the re-pointed consonants yield the numeral 'thirty'.[1]

The particular instance afforded by 'Amenophis' is confirmed by a wider comparison of Israel's Wisdom with that of other peoples.[2] This supports the generalization that Israel drew on an international stock of Wisdom common to the countries of the Near East. In that wider literature there are extant both of the main types of Wisdom found in Israel to which reference has been made, viz. collections of gnomic sayings like those of the Biblical Proverbs and discussion of the problems of life, such as we have in the Book of Job. One of the oldest Egyptian collections is known as *The Instruction of Ptahhotep*, purporting to be the counsel of an aged vizier to his son. Thus to teach fidelity in the deliverance of messages we find:

> 'If thou art one of the trusted ones, whom one great man sendeth to another, act rightly in the matter when he sendeth thee.' (Erman, p. 58.)

This is to the same effect as Prov. xxv. 13:

> As the coolness of snow in the heat (LXX) of harvest,
> A faithful envoy to those that send him.

As an example of the second kind of Wisdom, the discussion of the problems of life, we may take the Egyptian writing known as *The Dispute with his soul of one who is tired of life*, of which the general tenor recalls well-known passages of the Book of Job, such as those expressing a longing for death, and contrasting present adversity with former prosperity.

Of the Babylonian parallels, the best known is the so-called

---

[1] Point *sheloshim* (with Erman) instead of the Kethibh, *shileshom*, or of the Qere *shalishim*. See Gressmann, *ZAW*, 1924, pp. 273, 285 (cf. Griffith, op. cit., p. 191, and Simpson, p. 236).   [2] Such as has been made by Fichtner, op. cit.

Babylonian Job[1] where the author complains that the gods give him no answer in his troubles, though he has never neglected their worship. He asks 'Who can understand the counsel of the gods in heaven?' Some of his complaints suggest corresponding details in the Book of Job, e.g.:

In the middle of the night, he lets me not breathe for a moment,[2]

with which we may compare Job ix. 18:

He will not suffer me to take my breath. (הָשֵׁב רוּחִי.)

Greek parallels also come into discussion, more particularly in regard to Ecclesiastes. Dr. H. Ranston, after a careful examination of all the possible Greek sources for this book, reaches the conclusion that:

'Koheleth, in his search for suitable proverbs (ix. 9 f.) moved for a time in circles where the minds of the people were stored with the wisdom-utterances of the early sages mentioned by Isocrates as the outstanding teachers of practical morality, Theognis being the most important.'[3]

In accepting the general dependence of Israel's Wisdom on a common international stock—a dependence which was doubtless exerted through oral tradition much more than through literary borrowing—we encounter yet another example of Israel's capacity to assimilate material from a different tradition, and to set on it her own characteristic stamp. We have already seen this illustrated in the realms of mythology,[4] and of law[5] and it can be found also in psalmody by, e.g. a comparison of Ps. civ with the well-known hymn of Ikhnaton to the sun-disk.[6] There was both a native nucleus and a foreign contribution in the case of Israel's Wisdom. But the controlling principle was the belief in Yahweh and the new emphasis and values which this belief ultimately gave to all that was appropriated from without. The general trend of the development is well illustrated by the final identification of Wisdom with Torah, which was reached by ben Sira. Wisdom, he says, had sought entrance into many nations, but finally, by divine commandment, her peculiar home was to be Israel:

All these things are the book of the covenant of the Most High God, Even the law which Moses commanded us for a heritage unto the assemblies of Jacob. (xxiv. 23.)

---

[1] Rogers, op. cit., pp. 164–9.   [2] Op. cit., p. 168.
[3] *Ecclesiastes and the Early Greek Wisdom Literature*, p. 150.
[4] See ch. I and X.   [5] See ch. XV.   [6] Erman, op. cit., pp. 288 ff.; see also p. 8.

The development may be set out diagrammatically:

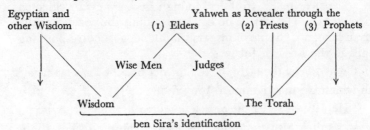

In our study of the ethics and the theology of the Wisdom books we shall see the effect on the contents of Wisdom of its incorporation within Yahwistic faith. But we must first take account of the distinctive quality of Wisdom which accrues to it as fundamentally an appeal to experience.

§ 3. THE APPEAL TO EXPERIENCE

In the well-known passage which ascribes to Solomon a wisdom exceeding that of Egypt and of the Near East, special emphasis is laid on his concern with Nature:

'He spake of trees, from the cedar that is in Lebanon even unto the hyssop that springeth out of the wall; he spake also of beasts and of fowl and of creeping things and fishes.' (1 Kings iv. 33 (Heb. v. 13))

Wisdom was certainly interested in natural objects as well as in the behaviour of men. Whatever may have been historically true of Solomon as the nucleus of the legendary material which eventually gathered round him, it is at least true that Wisdom showed a real curiosity and interest in Nature, though this interest was subordinated to the moralistic use of natural history. Nature could easily be made to teach useful lessons, e.g. the industry of the ant,[1] or the folly of presumption on the part of the worthless, illustrated by Jotham's fable of olive and fig and vine and bramble.[2] It was a later and very important extension of this pedagogic aspect of Nature to see in it the revelation of God's wisdom and power as in the Yahweh speeches of the Book of Job, or Sirach's eloquent description of 'the mighty works of God's wisdom'.[3]

The supreme interest of the wise men, however, was in human nature, more especially in its individuality. The Wisdom

[1] Prov. vi. 6–8, xxx. 25.   [2] Judges, ix. 8 ff.   [3] Ecclus. xlii. 15 ff., xliii.

writers do not concern themselves with history as such, probably because this realm had already been appropriated by
prophecy, and already incorporated into the presentation of
revelation in the Torah. When Sirach gives his review of past
history, 'Let us now praise famous men',[1] it is clearly based on
a written literature that lies before him, and is very different
from those creative interpretations of contemporary history
which we owe to the prophets.

When the common wisdom of human experience, native or
foreign, was brought into relation with Israel's God, the conception of Wisdom was profoundly affected. One of the most
important of the changes may be seen in the doctrine of divine
retribution as the ultimate sanction of Wisdom. It was one
thing for the Israelite to believe, with other peoples, that the
conduct of life had definite consequences, that wisdom brought
success and that folly brought failure; that truth was sufficiently
obvious to anyone who, with open eyes, went by 'the field of
the slothful and the vineyard of the man void of understanding'.[2]
It was another thing to say:

> Divers weights and divers measures,
> Both of them alike are an abomination to Yahweh (Prov. xx. 10),

for that meant that a deeper sanction of commercial honesty
had been found, a sanction that drew on the faith of which the
prophets were the pioneers. Wisdom on the level of mere
prudence is thereby transcended, and a wise man who believes
in Israel's God will say:

> The horse is prepared for the day of battle,
> But Yahweh's is the deliverance. (Prov. xxi. 31)

The doctrine of divine retribution which endorses all the Wisdom of Israel in its present literary forms is applied, as was said
a little earlier, to the individual, not to the generations of history,
where its limitations are not so obvious. In fact, the chief problem of Israel's religious thought, that of reconciling the suffering
of the individual with the declared righteousness of God, could
hardly have arisen at an early date. The doctrine of divine
retribution according to righteousness is usually and rightly
traced to the work of the great prophets of the eighth century,
and is especially proclaimed in the Book of Deuteronomy and

applied to the history in Judges, Samuel, and Kings. But the marked emphasis on the relation of the individual to God does not appear before Jeremiah, and is first explicitly taught by Ezekiel. When we find, therefore, that the Wisdom literature of Israel characteristically and strongly emphasizes the doctrine of individualized retribution, it becomes very difficult to date that literature before the exile. Further we have the evidence afforded by the discussions of the problems of life, such as we find in Job and Ecclesiastes and certain psalms. Such critical discussions of divine individualized retribution imply the previous existence of such a doctrine (as represented, e.g. by the friends of Job), but hardly its existence from times immemorial. It was relatively easy to believe in the justice of divine retribution when the proof of it was to be drawn from a series of generations or from the fate of a nation, for here the strong sense of 'corporate personality' overcame and absorbed the problems raised in individual experience. It was much more difficult, indeed it ultimately proved impossible, to maintain that doctrine absolutely, when the individual life was considered in its distinctive claim for justice, the claim illustrated by Job. Yet, if men appeal to experience, to experience they must go, and put up with the consequences. The court of appeal speaking through some of its ablest writers refused to confirm the more superficial verdict. We cannot suppose that this refusal began very long after the doctrine had been individually applied and logically developed, but it is difficult to see how it can be placed earlier,[1] i.e. how it can be assigned to the pre-exilic period.

[1] These remarks are directed in particular against the argument of Gressmann, ZAW, 1924, pp. 288 ff. His further argument from Proverbs in the same place that the absence of any reference to retribution beyond death is yet another proof of its pre-exilic composition 'since it was otherwise after the exile' seems a curious use of his data, for it might equally prove that Sirach was pre-exilic.

XIX

THE ETHICS OF WISDOM

HEBREW Wisdom is perhaps the best historical example of ethical experience interpreted as revelation. It is well documented, even though the precise dating of the documents is not always as definite as we could wish. The documents are widely distributed over the post-exilic centuries and into the Christian era. We can study the separate origins of both, since the close union of religion and ethics in Israel has a prior history visible to us, in which they were not yet so united, a history to be traced in the general literature surviving from the pre-exilic period. Further, in relation to the future, the ethical contents of Hebrew Wisdom stand in genetic relation to the morality of both Judaism and Christianity; it is much easier therefore for us to sympathize with, and to understand, the ethics of Israel than that of Confucius or the Buddha.

We naturally turn to Hebrew Wisdom for the most ordered and complete statement of Hebrew ethics in general. Yet it is, as we have seen, not Wisdom but Prophecy which is the main shaping factor of the moral ideas. Prophecy alone explains the characteristic qualities and the theocratic emphasis of Israel's Wisdom over against the qualities of the international Wisdom (not itself without relation to various types of religion of a very different kind from that of Israel). We may, in fact, define the Wisdom of Israel as *the discipline whereby was taught the application of prophetic truth to the individual life in the light of experience.*

§ 1. A School of Instruction

It was a discipline which gave instruction in the art of living. One of the favourite words to describe the course and method of instruction was *muṣar*, which we may render 'discipline'. The word is significant as showing the practical, indeed, the pragmatic nature of the instruction. The typical form of address is 'My son' spoken by teacher to pupil. The teacher may be the actual parent instructing his own children, after the pattern of Deut. vi. 7 in regard to the commandments of God:

Thou shalt teach them diligently[1] unto thy children,

[1] The Hebrew word is the intensive form of a root which means 'sharpen' (from

or the wise senior standing figuratively in a paternal relation
to his pupils, e.g. Prov. v. 1:

> My son, attend unto my wisdom;
> Incline thine ear to my understanding.

Egyptian Wisdom is often put into the same conventional form,
as when the vizier Ptahhotep, retiring from office in his old age,
is represented as instructing his son how best to fill his place.[1]
In speaking of Wisdom as providing a school of instruction we
must, of course, avoid ascription of the systematic work of the
synagogue school, the *beth hammidrash*, to the pre-exilic period,
or indeed even to the early post-exilic days. The prerequisite
for this was the completion of the Torah, and the rise of the
synagogue itself. There are good grounds for believing that the
Torah was not completed until the middle of the fourth century.[2] The earliest evidence for the existence of the synagogue
comes to us from Egypt, and from the third century B.C.[3] The
earliest reference we have to the *beth hammidrash* is found in the
closing chapter of ben Sira's book, in which he has described
his own eager search for the Wisdom of which he is now a
teacher:

> When I was yet young, before I wandered abroad,
> I desired her and sought her out.
> In my youth I made supplication in prayer,
> And I will seek her out even to the end.
> . . . Turn unto me, ye unlearned,
> And lodge in my *house of instruction*.[4]

Earlier in his book (vi. 34–6) he has urged resort to the wise:

> Stand thou in the assembly of the elders,
> And whoso is wise, cleave unto him.
> Desire to hear every discourse
> And let not a wise proverb escape thee.
> Look for him that is wise and seek him out earnestly,
> And let thy foot wear out his threshold.[5]

We are to think of experienced teachers as gathering around
them, at first more or less informally, a group of eager young
men to whom they imparted their knowledge (orally). It was

which 'tooth' is derived). Perhaps 'inculcate', i.e. 'tread' in, best expresses the
Hebrew in English; the sequel describes the discipline necessary to do this.

[1] Erman, op. cit., pp. 55 ff.　　　　　　　[2] See p. 229.

[3] Elbogen, *Der jüdische Gottesdienst*, pp. 446 f.

[4] Ecclus. li. 13, 14, 23; trs. by Oesterley and Box in Charles's *Apocrypha*, pp.
515 ff.　　　　　　　　　　　　　[5] Op. cit., p. 337.

in a more established group of this kind that the youthful Jesus was found by his parents.[1]

We naturally think of the Greek Sophists as the most familiar external parallel to the teachers of Wisdom in Israel. The Sophists also gave instruction to young men which covered the art of living, though specially concerned with a successful public career, in which fluency of speech and efficiency in debate were of the first importance. Their positive instruction seems to have covered the whole field of knowledge, and their earliest representatives have contacts with the primitive Greek philosophers. But the lack of any unifying conception in their teaching and its subservience to their own careers marks them off sharply from the wise men of Israel. As a scholar who has written about the Sophists reminds us, their degeneration corresponds to that of the name they bore:

'the paid teacher became the needy adventurer, the incompetent pretender, the charlatan or trickster, the last implication being firmly embedded in our modern words "sophism", "sophistical", "sophistry" '.[2]

Whatever the faults of Israel's wise men, there is nothing in them to correspond to such degeneration; their devotion to the Torah inspired personal loyalty to a high purpose, and the lineage of the future rabbis lies through them.

We do better to turn to ancient Egypt and Mesopotamia in our search for parallels. The collections of material offered by Fichtner and by Dürr[3] are sufficient to show this. In all these areas the method seems to have been that of oral repetition and of learning by heart, with plenty of catechism of the pupils by the teachers. But in Egypt at least, we meet with the instructor's order, 'Write with thy hand and read with thy mouth'.[4] Chanting or singing was one of the methods of repetition.[5] In

---

[1] Luke ii. 46. We are reminded of Hillel listening at the window in the snow to the rabbis within (Montefiore and Loewe, *A Rabbinic Anthology*, p. 146, trs. from Talmud Babli, *Yoma*, 35a).   [2] R. D. Hicks, in *ERE*, xi. 692a.

[3] Fichtner, op. cit., is concerned with the content of the international Wisdom in order to bring out the kinship of the Israelite Wisdom with that of Egypt and Mesopotamia. L. Dürr, *Das Erziehungswesen im alten Testament und im antiken Orient* (1932), describes the general characteristics of Wisdom and of the relevant religion as something to be taught, together with the methods of teaching. Like others, especially those influenced by comparative study, he tends to date Israel's literary products in this realm too early.

[4] Dürr, p. 22; cf. Erman, op. cit., p. 189.

[5] Dürr, ib., and for Assyria, p. 72.

Mesopotamia the wise men were identified with the priests,[1] as was natural when the instruction to be imparted was so often concerned with ritual. In Egypt, as in Israel, Wisdom became, as we have seen, in particular, a concern of the scribes.[2]

§ 2. THE TRIPLE CHARACTER OF THE TEACHING

The common content of the instruction in Wisdom given in Israel, Egypt, and Mesopotamia can be classified under the three heads of prudence, morality, and piety.[3] By prudence is meant the rules for life drawn most directly from the experience of good and evil as the consequences of following these rules or of turning from them. Counsel of this kind is therefore frankly utilitarian. There is nothing either moral or religious, but simply worldly wisdom, in ben Sira's advice (xiii. 9):

> If a mighty man invite thee, be retiring,
> And so much the more will he invite thee.

A man of any type of morality or religion, or of none, might give us such advice as one of the secrets of getting on in the world. It pays to behave like that, according to the experience of the counsellor. As an example of *moral* teaching we may take the words of one of the sages of Proverbs (xxii. 28):

> Remove not the ancient landmark
> Which thy fathers have set.

To interfere with the established rights of property in this way is definitely an anti-social act, which a wise man will not perform. As part of Jewish Law also, the act is forbidden in the Deuteronomic Code, and one of the closing curses of Deuteronomy also protects the boundary stone.[4] In the passage quoted from Proverbs no penalty or protector is named. But the next chapter (xxiii. 10, 11) offers a good example of the way in which such purely social morality, necessary to the welfare of any ordered society, can be taken up into religion. Here the injunction is repeated, but this time with a religious sanction added to it:

> Remove not the ancient landmark;
> And enter not into the fields of the fatherless:
> For their redeemer is strong,
> He shall plead their cause against thee.

---

[1] Dürr, p. 60.   [2] Dürr, p. 19.

[3] So Fichtner, whose terms are *Lebensklugheit*, *Sittlichkeit*, and *Frömmigkeit*.

[4] Deut. xix. 14; xxvii. 17. A curse is not necessarily religious, though it may become so (as here) in a religious setting.

As an example of the purely religious motive to wise action we may take Prov. xxi. 2 (cf. xvi. 2):

> Every way of a man is right in his own eyes;
> But the weigher of hearts is Yahweh.

Such teaching obviously brings the whole of life under the judgement of God, for the heart is the seat of volition. We have only to turn over the pages of Proverbs or Ecclesiasticus to see how wide is the range of application. Wisdom, in its religious aspects, comprehends all the relations of the life of the family, the business world, and of society in general, as they involve the individual.

Even when the advice given seems purely prudential, or at the most, moral, we are not to suppose that Wisdom is neglecting or ignoring the appeal to piety as its ultimate motive and sanction. The principles by which a man lives, whether explicit or implicit, were and are always worked up into a concrete complex, a unique kind of life and of outlook on life, which is brought to a focus of intensity in the aim and motive of the moment. Who could say, for example, how far a man, then or now, is restrained from removing his neighbour's landmark (or its modern equivalent) by a motive that is prudential or moral or religious? In most instances the restraint is a blend of all three, no longer admitting of exact analysis.

This, then, is the proper reply to the charge of 'utilitarianism' which is sometimes brought against Hebrew morality and religion. There is a strongly pragmatic element in both, but that is their strength as well as their weakness, if it be a weakness. In the long run, both morality and religion have to prove themselves, on the one hand by the intrinsic worth of the good or the intrinsic badness of the evil as seen in result, on the other, by the degree of completeness with which the doctrine of divine retribution is seen to justify itself. On short-term views both may be obscured, and the religion of Israel could not, until nearly the end of the Old Testament period, look to a life beyond death which would adjust the observed inequalities or injustices of this present life. But we must not forget the finer strain also present in the religion of Israel, which could give all to God and ask for no reward, confident of fellowship with Him. That is the triumphant note on which end the 73rd Psalm and the Psalm of Habakkuk; that is the motive of Job's piety, as

depicted in the Prologue, the motive of a disinterested loyalty
to God, which finds its own reward in serving still.

We are not to think that a religious motive did not enter also
into that international Wisdom with which Israel's was so
closely connected. The difference is not so much in the presence
or absence of religion as in the kind of religion, and especially
in the degree to which the ethical was taken up into the conception of God and made integral to it, as it was in Israel. An
Egyptian can say, 'My heart never demands to do anything
which the great God forbids'.[1] All are familiar with the Egyptian
concern with the life after death, and its retributive dependence
on the divine judgement of the earthly life. The Babylonian
outlook here resembles the earlier Hebrew, and there is little
thought of any retribution beyond death.[2] But both Egypt and
Babylonia lack anything to correspond to Israel's prophetic
faith in Yahweh, the righteous God whose righteousness shines
forth in His saving acts. It is the consciousness of *this* God which
gives to Hebrew Wisdom its really distinctive quality and makes
it a revelation of Him in its own characteristic manner.

Hebrew Wisdom is consciously based on the revelation given
through the other channels of Prophecy and Law. That is
summarized most clearly in the saying which meets us at the very
outset of the Book of Proverbs, and has been described as its motto
(i. 7): The fear of Yahweh is the beginning of knowledge.

Towards the close of the nine chapters which form the Introduction (ix. 10) this recurs in the form:

The fear of Yahweh is the beginning of wisdom.

Reverence for God is in fact the keynote of the whole poem
constituted by these chapters, the keynote on which it begins
and to which it returns. As one commentator[3] has put it:

'The idea of the Hebrew sage is that he who lives with reverent
acknowledgment of God as lawgiver will have within his soul a
permanent and efficient moral guide . . . his purpose is to emphasize
the one principle of reverence as paramount, and he identifies the
man's own moral ideal with the divine moral law.'

§ 3. THE INSPIRATION OF THE SAGES

How far, we may ask, did the teachers or writers of Wisdom
regard themselves as divinely inspired? In the earliest passages

---

[1] Dürr, p. 30.   [2] Jastrow, op. cit.   [3] Toy, *Proverbs*, p. 10.

naming them,[1] they appear in the company of the priests and prophets, as a source of revelation. Ben Sira says of the student of the sacred books (xxxix. 6):

> If it seem good to God Most High,
> He shall be filled with the spirit of understanding,
> He himself poureth forth wise sayings in double measure.[2]

In the Book of Job, Eliphaz, a typical representative of the wise men, claims that the truth of man's sinfulness before God was revealed to him by a supernatural voice.[3] In one striking verse of Proverbs (xx. 27) we seem to come nearest to an identification of man's moral consciousness with an inner divine revelation:

> Yahweh's lamp is man's breath,
> Searching all the chambers of the belly.

To understand this we have to remember that the body, with all its parts, is the essential personality.[4] Thus, the verse says that human consciousness enters into the knowledge of the whole inner life, all that the body comprises, and serves as a lamp in its dark corners, by which tribunal of conscience (as we should say) God is revealed. We have an interesting use of the same metaphor of the lamp in regard to prophetic revelation in the Second Epistle of Peter (i. 19):

> 'We have the word of prophecy made more sure; whereunto ye do well that ye take heed, as unto a lamp shining in a dark place until the day dawn and the day-star arise in your hearts.'

We may usefully bring those two passages together, not only because they employ the same metaphor, but because they complement each other by their description of the outer revelation of the sacred book over against the inner revelation of what we call the 'enlightened' conscience. The same God who kindled that light that shines through the prophets has lit a lamp in every man that reveals the man to himself. Yet we

---

[1] Jer. xviii. 18; Ezek. vii. 26.

[2] i.e. that received by tradition and his own (loc. cit.), unless there be an echo of 2 Kings ii. 9 (cf. Deut. xxi. 17), the eldest son's portion, which Elisha asked as a parting gift from Elijah. The same phrase is used in the Syriac of both passages. Cf. Oesterley and Box, op. cit., p. 456.

[3] Job iv. 12 ff.

[4] So also for the Egyptian conception; see Erman, op. cit., p. 87 n.: 'The body is to the Egyptian the seat of thought.' Cf. Prov. xviii. 8:

> A backbiter's words are greedily swallowed,
> They go down to the chambers of the belly.

must not press the statement to the point of making it assert the general immanence of God in the spirit of man. There is no such immanence (in any proper use of the term) in the Old Testament; God is always transcendent, revealing Himself by His Spirit on particular occasions and through particular people, not by any universal presence. This holds even of such passages as Proverbs viii, though this was doubtless written in a period in which Greek conceptions of immanence were beginning to affect Hebrew thought, as they did so much more fully in the Wisdom of Solomon and in the writings of Philo. As we shall see, the figure of Wisdom in Proverbs viii is no more than the means of the divine direction of human life, as in the words (14, 15):

> Counsel is mine and efficiency,
> I am discernment, mine is might,
> By me kings reign and princes decree justice.

Wisdom inspires right decisions in Solomon or another, just as the makers of Aaron's garments are said to have been filled with the spirit of Wisdom.[1] They were made inspired tailors *ad hoc* in order to make sanctifying garments; they were 'wise-hearted' because temporarily possessed by divine skill. Thus we have an exact 'Wisdom' parallel to the references to the Spirit of God or to the Hand of God as coming upon the prophets.

An interesting 'Wisdom' passage occurs at the close of Isa. xxviii, in which we find those same two terms of the Wisdom vocabulary as in Proverbs viii, viz. 'counsel' and 'efficiency' (verse 29). The whole passage in Isaiah (verses 23–29) describes the agricultural methods of the times (no doubt taken over by the Israelites from the Canaanites), and the description is given in order to bring out their variety, and thus to illustrate the variety of the divine method with men. Its bearing on our present theme is that this right way of treating the soil, this agricultural skill, is traced to divine revelation, so that it can be said of the farmer (verse 26):

> His God doth instruct him aright and doth teach him,

whilst the passage ends:

> This also cometh forth from Yahweh of hosts,
> Who is wonderful in counsel and excellent in efficiency.[2]

---

[1] Exod. xxviii. 3, cf. xxxi. 1 ff. (Bezaleel).

[2] The two outstanding technical terms to which reference was made (עֵצָה and תּוּשִׁיָּה).

If instruction in agricultural efficiency, the right way to treat the earth, can thus be ascribed to the inspiration of divine Wisdom, much more easily could human ethics, the right relation of man to man, right conduct in all the circumstances of life, be so ascribed.

One more passage may be cited, viz. that in which the youthful Elihu definitely claims inspiration for his correction of the alleged Wisdom of the friends of Job (xxxii. 6 ff.):

> there is a spirit in man,[1]
> And the breath of the Almighty giveth them understanding.
> It is not the great that are wise,
> Nor the aged that understand judgment.

Such passages corroborate the general view here taken that Wisdom is regarded as the product of divine inspiration. Thus even the passage from which we began (Prov. xx. 27), 'Yahweh's lamp is man's breath', is to be interpreted of the manner of Yahweh's occasional working, rather than of any permanent and immanental indwelling of man's conscience or consciousness.

We see, therefore, in what sense we are to understand such a claim as is made in Prov. ii. 6:

> Yahweh giveth Wisdom,
> Out of His mouth knowledge and understanding.

Even though the sage, like the prophet or the priest, is the intermediary, the Wisdom which the sage imparts comes ultimately by divine inspiration. To that end God uses man's whole experience interpreted in the light of his moral nature, itself a divine creation, and under the guidance of the divine Torah in its later development, that Torah to which all the precepts of Wisdom will conform.

It is this comprehension of the whole of experience within itself, without any separation of natural and supernatural, that gives to Wisdom its characteristic quality over against the ultimate Torah of the priest and the *dabar*, the 'word', of the prophet. As we have seen, this comprehensiveness extends beyond man's behaviour to Nature and Nature's ways. We may see it illustrated in what we should call the natural human instincts, such as regard for parents, which in the Decalogue appears as a divine command, and often recurs as one of the applications of Wisdom.[2] The three kinds of revelation which we have reviewed—

[1] So in verse 18, 'the spirit of my belly constraineth me'.
[2] Cf. Dürr, op. cit., p. 132.

prophecy, law, Wisdom—frequently overlap, since they must all draw their content from the same three realms of Nature, Man, and History, with widely varying methods and emphases.[1] This comprehensiveness alone is a convincing argument against the early dating of the *literature* of Wisdom.

[1] Thus the same forbidden act is in view when all the three kinds of revelation together with piety itself, are focused upon it. To remove a landmark is forbidden by prophecy (Hos. v. 10), law (Deut. xix. 14, xxvii. 17), Wisdom (Prov. xxii. 28), piety (xxiii. 10, 11). To consider one such example as this is to be warned against trying to draw hard-and-fast lines between the sources of Wisdom and Wisdom itself. We can also see how wise men could sometimes claim material derived from the other realms, as when we find attached to the closing chapter of Hosea the words:

> Who is wise, and he shall understand these things?
> Prudent, and he shall know them?

XX

THE THEOLOGY OF WISDOM

THE consciousness of divine inspiration found in the Wisdom writers is itself theological. At least three other topics claim notice under what may be called the theological, as distinct from the ethical, aspects of Wisdom. The three are (1) the general relation of religious faith to that *experience of life* on which Wisdom characteristically builds; (2) the problems raised for Wisdom by the assertion of *divine retribution* completed within this present life; (3) the extent to which the *personification* of Wisdom advances towards becoming a mediating *hypostasis* between God and man.

§ 1. FAITH AND EXPERIENCE

We have frequently had occasion to speak of Hebrew 'realism', and here again it meets us as fundamental for Wisdom. Of course, all thought is, in the last resort, drawn from experience and must appeal to it as a final court of appeal, however much it may try to conceal this reference—as in *a priori* philosophical reasoning or in the religious dogmatism that claims to build on either the decrees of the Church or the revelation of Scripture. But the faith of Israel is realistic in a more direct sense. According to its own tradition, its vital conception of Yahweh depended on experience of a divine act of redemption accomplished at the exodus from Egypt. This is the great example of Hebrew realism; in this experienced event the true nature of Israel's God was realized, on which future generations might build. Here we see on the largest scale the realistic quality which is seen in miniature in the particularism of the Hebrew vocabulary and syntax.[1] There is here nothing *a priori*, and all the subsequent piety of Israel continues in the same strain. What can be more familiar in it than the repeated motif of the Psalms:

I love the Lord because He hath heard
  My voice and my supplications;
Because He hath inclined His ear unto me,
  Therefore will I call upon Him as long as I live. (cxvi. 1, 2)

---

[1] See *The Bible in its Ancient and English Versions*, pp. 3 ff.

It is this realism of Hebrew piety which gets so close to the ordinary experience of ordinary men. This it is that has invested that piety with its catholicity of appeal, and made it the finest vehicle of the most glowing idealism which the world contains.

Hebrew Wisdom (like international Wisdom) builds on the firm conviction that experience in general will bear out its teaching. But this experience naturally includes for Israel faith in Israel's God. Behind the ethical aphorisms, as we have already seen, there is almost always present a confidence that Yahweh is active in man's life. This confidence does not find such constant expression as in the prophets who proclaimed it, or as in the psalmists who responded to it. But Psalms and Proverbs largely belonged to the same community and represent different aspects of the religion of the same people. Two[1] mutually related questions at least are relevant to this confident faith, viz. how far the distinction between good and evil is held to be intrinsic, and therefore existent before we take account of the divine control of life, and further, how far the righteousness of God is held to be dependent on the will of God.

(a) As to the first of these questions there can be no doubt that many of the precepts of Hebrew Wisdom ultimately appeal for their verification to the intrinsic nature of life as men come to know it, without regard to any further sanction, e.g. Prov. xii. 24:

> The hand of the keen shall bear rule,
> But slackness becomes tributary.

That is true of any social order; industry tends to bring a man to the top and laziness sends him to the bottom. Similarly, it is always intrinsically true of the individual life, whatever its moral quality, to say (Prov. iv. 23):

> Above all guarding, watch thy heart,
> For from it are the issues of life,

especially when we remember that the heart is for the Hebrew the seat of volition. The admonition says in effect, 'A man is what he wills to be'. One of the classes of the Hebrew vocabulary of sin describes it by what it is in itself;[2] some of these

---

[1] See my essays on 'The Inner Life of the Psalmists' and 'The Social Life of the Psalmists' in *The Psalmists* (ed. by D. C. Simpson).

[2] See my *Christian Doctrine of Man*, p. 43, and Eichrodt, op .cit., iii. 83.

terms recur in the Wisdom literature, as when lying is characterized (in parallelism) by its 'emptiness' (*shaw*' שָׁוְא). The frequent references to the 'folly' of evildoing in Proverbs are familiar.[1] But, as was said in the previous chapter of the intimate blending of motives drawn from prudence, from morality proper, and from religion, analysis is exceedingly difficult. It would usually be impossible to say where the prudential motive ends as proved by experience and the religious faith in the retributive action of God begins. The safest thing to say in general is that Hebrew Wisdom accepts aphorisms largely and originally drawn from experience and interprets or reinforces them by the faith (when this eventually arose) that God vindicates them through His control of life.

(*b*) The second question, as to the priority of God's righteousness or of God's will, may be illustrated by the dialogue between God and Abraham as to the fate of Sodom and Gomorrah,[2] which is intended to bring out the deeper meaning of the words of verse 25, 'Shall not the Judge of all the earth do right' (*mishpaṭ*)? That way of putting the relation between the divine will and the divine character holds for Hebrew religion in general. The greatest problem which arose for it was not as to the existence but as to the righteousness of God. This means that there is a standard to which He is expected to conform (*zedek* צֶדֶק), just as there are standard weights and measures to which the tradesman ought to conform. But it does not mean that there is an abstract righteousness existing 'in the air'; the will of God is felt to be supreme. Faith wrestles hard to maintain its conviction that the divine will is fundamentally and intrinsically righteous, even if, in its higher ranges, sometimes incomprehensible by our human standards of righteousness.[3]

R. W. Dale's words are quite true of the Old Testament conception of God:

'In God the law is *alive*; it reigns on His throne, sways His sceptre, is crowned with His glory.'[4]

---

[1] On this see Excursus XI in Oesterley's *Proverbs*, pp. lxxxiv ff., dealing with the *pethi* (simpleton), the *keṣil* (dullard), the *'ewil* (fool), the *lez* (scorner), the *nabal* (churl).　　　　[2] Gen. xviii. 16–23.

[3] So that we may compare the religious with the ethical blending; good and evil work out as good and evil by what they are in themselves, though they are reinforced by divine retribution; the nature of God works out as what it is, though it is not left to be automatic but is reinforced or rather expressed in His will.

[4] *The Atonement*, p. 372.

We must not expect the Old Testament to face the philosophical questions that arise when we try to translate the concrete and personal into the abstract and impersonal, for that is something which Hebrew thought never tried to do.[1] Nor must we expect from it consideration of the further question—whether there ever can be ethics without implicit religion, whether every moral demand does not ultimately imply some faith in God. That is an issue beyond our present scope.

§ 2. The Problem of Suffering

From these more general questions we turn to the central religious problem for Israel, viz. the challenge raised by the actual experience of life to the faith in God's righteous government of the world. This challenge the Hebrew Wisdom thinkers (as contrasted with its anthology makers) were sooner or later bound to face, just because of Wisdom's appeal to experience. But they combine with it faith in the active providence of God. The problem became the more acute because there could be no resort to any belief in life after death which would balance off the retributive inequalities of this life.

Four different attitudes towards the problem are exhibited by the Wisdom literature: (a) there is the apparent unconsciousness that any problem exists, or the belief that any emergence of it is temporary and will somehow be adjusted before death. This is the attitude shown by Proverbs[2] and Ecclesiasticus and by some of the psalmists. (b) The Book of Job restates this orthodox belief through the friends of the hero, only to disprove it by the experience of Job. But as a whole the book reaches the conclusion, through the speeches of Yahweh and Job's responses, that man cannot hope to comprehend the ways of God, though there *is* a divine purpose in the suffering of the innocent (Prologue). (c) Thirdly, we have the direct denial that any theodicy can be constructed; experience shows in fact that God does not rule the lives of men in righteousness. This is the attitude of the author of Ecclesiastes (i.e. Koheleth, the pseudo-Solomon). (d) Finally we reach the method adopted by the author of the Wisdom of Solomon, i.e. to proclaim a life

---

[1] The nearest approach to it, in the earlier Rabbinical periods, might be found in the conception of the Torah (the expressed will of God) and of God's premundane relation to it. Cf. Moore, op. cit. i. 266.

[2] Except by the words of Agur xxx. 1-4, which rank with the scepticism of Ecclesiastes.

beyond death in which the injustices of this life will be 'ironed out' and God's righteous government of the world will be vindicated.

(*a*) It may seem strange to us that any collection of sayings professedly based on experience could ignore the glaring inequalities of life and its frequent failure to show the active presence and present activity of God. The difficulty is accentuated by the fact that the teaching of Wisdom is so markedly individualistic, and is not, like that of the prophets, largely addressed in nationalistic terms—to Israel and only indirectly to the Israelite. It was much easier for the prophets to assert their common doctrine of divine retribution, since they were usually dealing with whole groups of men, such as Israel or the Assyrians, for whom retribution could be carried on from one generation to another, and all of them together treated as a unit.[1] That which the father escaped could be inherited by his son and his son's son. But we might have expected that as soon as the divine retribution was associated with the conduct of the individual and self-contained life, the contradiction would become apparent. The answer lies, no doubt, in our universal habit of turning our attention to particular aspects of life and either consciously or unconsciously ignoring the rest, from which spring the varieties of social, political, and ecclesiastical life. We see, in fact, only what we want so see. Nothing short of this could explain such a statement as that of a 'Wisdom' psalm:

> I have been young and now am old;
> Yet have I not seen the righteous forsaken,
> Nor his seed begging their bread. (Ps. xxxvii. 25.)

What impartial or critical observer of life to-day would venture to say that? Yet many similar sayings are found in Proverbs, e.g.:

> Yahweh will not leave hungry the appetite of the righteous. (x. 3.)

> The righteous eateth to the satisfying of his appetite,
> But the belly of the wicked shall lack. (xiii. 25.)

Ben Sira, whose horizon is as much confined to this earth as

---

[1] On the rare occasions on which an individual is addressed, it may be as the representative of a party or policy. Thus Shebna, 'who is over the house', is to be deposed and expelled, and replaced by Eliakim, 'who shall be for a throne of glory to his father's house' (Isa. xxii. 15–25).

that of the various writers of Proverbs, no less decidedly asserts complete retribution within this life for each individual, as in xvi. 13, 14:

> The sinner shall not escape with his plunder,
> And the patience of the godly shall not be frustrated. . . .
> Each man shall find according to his works.

No student of ben Sira would deny that he is a shrewd observer of life; yet he can commit himself to a generalization such as this, under the influence of doctrinal orthodoxy.

(b) The first critic of this individual retribution, so far as we know from the extant literature, was the author of the Book of Job. His own observation or personal experience has proved it false as a complete explanation of suffering, which does not mean that he denies the general doctrine of retribution. That which the hero of the poem denies is that the doctrine adequately explains his own personal suffering, which is beyond all his deserts. So he advances to his final challenge of the righteousness of God, since he knows no reason beside retribution for human suffering.[1] The challenge is answered by Yahweh's panorama of Nature as beyond the power of Job to create or maintain. Thus Job is reduced to the characteristic Hebrew virtue of humility and to the confession that he is not competent to criticize the ways of God with men. So far the majority of the interpreters of the book are agreed. If we go no farther, then the writer's attitude to the problem is that of reverent agnosticism. But this seems a weak climax to such a debate and indictment of God. Moreover, it takes no account of the prose Prologue and Epilogue. The Epilogue can be explained as necessary to vindicate Job in the eyes of men, seeing that the book has definitely dismissed (ch. xiv) any thought of life after death, to which the vindication might have been relegated. The Epilogue was also necessary to make explicit that the friends of Job were wrong and that Job was right, in spite of all his wild speech, on the major issue of retribution. Job's suffering was *not* retributive. Then what was it? The answer is in the Prologue. When this is taken seriously, it

---

[1] The Elihu speeches (xxxii–xxxvii) are not to be regarded as an original part of the poem; they emphasize the disciplinary value of innocent suffering (xxxiii. 14 ff.) whilst maintaining the doctrine of retribution (xxxiv. 11, xxxiv. 31 ff., xxxvi. 11 ff.). The value of disciplinary suffering had been stated, though not strongly emphasized, by Eliphaz (v. 17).

provides a new and noble explanation of the suffering of the innocent, worthy of the supreme qualities of the Book of Job. The Prologue explicitly declares that Yahweh may permit a righteous man to suffer in order that he may demonstrate the reality of disinterested religion; thus and thus alone can he vindicate God against the Adversary. In other words, Job is a 'martyr',[1] a witness-bearer by suffering, though knowledge of the divine purpose is withheld from him. It *had* to be withheld from him, in order to make his vindication of God valid, for Job is depicted as one who would have rejoiced in a direct commission to serve God in this way at whatever cost to himself. But it had to be revealed somehow to the readers of the book in order to convey the author's belief in a divine purpose in suffering which would justify it even when non-retributive. So he used the conception of a divine council held in heaven,[2] which is not to be dismissed as a mere literary device, original or adapted from a folk-lore story that was traditional. If it is old in content, as it is certainly archaic in form, the author has charged it with a new meaning in its new context. In any case, some introduction to the poem was essential, and if we take the Prologue in the sense here suggested, the noblest book of the Wisdom literature of Israel will not culminate in agnosticism, however reverent, but will make a real contribution to theology in its own characteristic fashion. That which has hindered interpreters of the book from seeing this is probably the fact that they have not taken the heavenly council of Yahweh seriously, as part of the genuine faith of the Old Testament.

(*c*) Instead of the almost unbroken orthodoxy of Proverbs,[3] and the substitution for that orthodoxy of another explanation of the suffering of the innocent in Job, we have in Koheleth unashamed heterodoxy which springs from a thoroughgoing dissatisfaction with life. True, there are scattered gleams of conventional doctrine and pious exhortation,[4] to which the

---

[1] J. Hempel, *Althebräische Literatur* (1934), pp. 175–9. So also in my little book, *The Cross of Job* (1916, pp. 51–4; 2nd ed. 1934, pp. 64–9). It is quite in harmony with Job's role as martyr that he should be called upon to intercede for his mistaken friends (xlii. 8).

[2] On the realism of this, see my article, 'The Council of Yahweh', in *JTS*, July–Oct. 1944, vol. xlv, pp. 151 ff., and cf. 1 Kings xxii for the nearest parallel in the Old Testament. See pp. 167 f.

[3] Except for the enigmatic words of Agur xxx. 1–4.

[4] ii. 26, viii. 11 ff., xi. 9, xii. 1, &c. The most likely explanation of such remarks which contradict their present context is that they are pious glosses and corrections,

book owes its preservation in the Canon, if not altogether. Apart from these, the book is a stern and sombre denial that God's government of the world is righteous. He is indeed beyond our comprehension, but the moral drawn is not that we should trust when we cannot understand, but that we should make the best of what is, after all, the bad job of living. All is emptiness and weariness (i. 2, 8, 14, &c.); nothing satisfies (ii), and though the wise excelleth the foolish, 'one event happeneth to them all' (ii. 14, ix. 2) on this treadmill of time (iii. 1–9), where there is nothing to distinguish men from beasts in ultimate destiny (iii. 18–21). Better dead than alive; best of all unborn (iv. 2, 3). Even to God, let thy words be few (v. 2). Injustice is everywhere (v. 8); eat and drink and enjoy what good you can (v. 18). God's administration of the world is inscrutable (vii. 14, viii. 17). Wisdom profits, yet often fails of its reward (ix. 16 f.).

It was fitting enough that such an un-Hebraic philosophy of life should reach its climax in an eloquent but sombre picture of death (xii).[1] The book has indeed the smell of the tomb about it. The writer has no perspective of past history, and no apocalyptic vision of the future to inspire him. His book is one of sheer individualism, deprived of all that might have been its inspiration. Its teaching lies rather in being so complete a contrast to the Hebrew *joie de vivre* than in making a positive contribution to the theology of Wisdom.

(*d*) Finally, we have the Wisdom of Solomon, which under Greek (Alexandrian) influence adopts a solution which is new for Hebrew thought. This is the definite doctrine of a life beyond death, explained not by the genuinely Hebrew conception of resurrection (first reached by the Apocalyptists)[2] but by the Greek doctrine of immortality. Here it is said explicitly that righteousness is immortal (i. 15). God created man for incorruption, but 'by the envy of the devil death entered into the world, and they that are of his portion make trial thereof' (ii. 23 f.). It is nowhere said that they are annihilated; 'death' means that they receive their deserts (iii. 10) in being excluded from true life (xvii. 21). On the other hand, the souls of the

not that they represent the author's 'divided heart', which would have required a different scheme.

[1] Worked out in the interwoven double allegory, of the house left tenantless and the body reduced to its original dust.

[2] Isa. xxvi. 19; Dan. xii. 2, 3.

righteous are in the hand of God (iii. 1); in this world they may suffer (iii. 5), but hereafter they enter into rest (iv. 7, 17; v. 1 ff.) and live for ever (v. 15).[1] Thus the problem of the present suffering of the righteous finds its solution in the faith that another world will put right the wrongs of this, and full retribution will vindicate the ways of God.[2]

It was natural that the Wisdom writers of Israel should face the problem of suffering, for they are Israel's thinkers and contribute the element most nearly approximating to a philosophy. The variety of their attempts at a solution is significant, and its series is one of the most interesting and illuminative amongst the developments of the Old Testament. But it is also significant that there is no interpretation of human suffering as sacrifice. Nowhere does Wisdom attain to the height of Isaiah liii, where the suffering of Israel is regarded as sacrificial. The nearest approach to this is in the Prologue to Job, which is not unworthy to be named next after Deutero-Isaiah's interpretation of suffering. But, though Job is a martyr-witness, and in the loose modern usage, a sacrifice, whilst unconscious of being one, in the stricter ancient usage of the term we should not call him this. In the Prologue (i. 5) he offers sacrifices, without himself being called one; in the Epilogue, his mistaken friends sacrifice (xlii. 8) and Job becomes an intercessor for them. Isaiah liii profoundly influenced the New Testament, whereas it is difficult to trace any direct influence exerted by the Book of Job. Yet this admits of easy explanation, for the archaistic form of presentation in the Prologue was transcended, and left behind. But the figure of the martyr-witness was to reappear in the Maccabean times, and has been prominent throughout the history of both Judaism and Christianity. From him will always come the supreme proof that men will still serve God for naught that the world of things seen can give them.

§ 3. THE FIGURE OF WISDOM

There remains our third topic in the theology of Wisdom, viz. the degree to which the figure of Wisdom advances from a personification to a hypostasis, i.e. an entity conceived to

[1] We may compare the similarly positive conception of eternal life in the New Testament, which says much less about those who do not receive this gift.

[2] This solution is nowhere found in the Old Testament; Job xix. 25, 26 is no exception (see the commentaries), and the apocalyptic hope is highly specialized and varies greatly from book to book.

exist in independence of man's thought and to mediate between
God and man. There are three test passages which at once
come to mind, and up to a point their testimony is clear enough,
viz. Proverbs viii, Ecclesiasticus xxiv,[1] and Wisdom of Solomon,
vii. 22 ff.

The crucial passage in Proverbs viii begins at verse 22:

> Yahweh formed me as the beginning of His way,
> The first of His works of old.

Through this primeval creation of Wisdom were made heaven
and earth and all that they contain (30):

> I was beside Him as trusted artificer ('*amon*).[2]

Clearly this is a strong and remarkable personification of
Wisdom, probably much indebted to the Greek influences
which were beginning to be felt by the third century B.C., to
which these chapters probably belong. But is it more than a
personification in the familiar Hebrew way of making vivid
individualization replace our abstract thought? Wisdom here,
after all, remains a divine attribute, characterized and manifested in the creative work of God. For thought, it helps to
mediate the relation of God to the created world, but this is not
ontological mediation. Wisdom is not an entity in its own right,
though this poetical description depicts it as having an independent existence.

In Ecclesiasticus (xxiv) Wisdom is again personified as seeking entrance everywhere amongst the nations, but finally
obedient to Yahweh's command to find her inheritance in
Israel, where she reaches concrete expression in the divine
Torah (23):

All these things are the book of the covenant of the Most High God,
The law which Moses commanded us for a heritage unto the
    assemblies of Jacob.

This identification is as clear and definite as we could expect.
The revelation of Sinai is the supreme manifestation of Wisdom;
her mediating role is handed over to that concrete expression
of God's will, and reverence for the God so known is the
beginning, the fullness, the crown, the root of Wisdom.[3] There

---

[1] With which ch. i should be compared.

[2] The word '*amon* is difficult to render; the view taken above connects it with
a root meaning 'firm, trustworthy', and so a trusted assistant, a clerk of the works.

[3] i. 14, 16, 18, 20.

is here, then, no hypostasis, but a characteristic transformation of Wisdom into the most cherished possession of Israel.

In the Wisdom of Solomon, which contains so much that is Greek rather than Hebrew, the conception of Wisdom is much more advanced, and she is certainly described as an immanent divine presence (vii. 22 ff.):

'more mobile than any motion; yea, she pervadeth and penetrateth all things by reason of her pureness, for she is a breath of the power of God and a clear effluence (ἀπόρροια) of the glory of the Almighty . . . an effulgence (ἀπαύγασμα) from everlasting light, and an unspotted mirror of the working of God and an image of His goodness . . . from generation to generation passing into holy souls, she maketh friends of God and prophets.'

Here, then, Wisdom remains an 'effluence' and 'effulgence' of God, always dependent upon Him, and cannot be called a hypostasis in any proper sense of the term, though it is easy to see how such conceptions could contribute to the Logos-synthesis of Philo and the recapitulation of all things in Christ.

As we review the whole conception of Wisdom and note its very real contribution to the divine revelation in the Old Testament, we must not overlook one conspicuous lacuna in it, which seems inherent in the humanism of all the ages. It does not bring out the heart's need for a divinely wrought renewal, a regeneration, such as we find promised in prophecy. Both Jeremiah[1] and Ezekiel[2] are led to a point at which their one hope is in divine grace—for Jeremiah the grace of the New Covenant, for Ezekiel the grace of the substitution of a heart of flesh for a heart of stone. There does not seem to be anything in the Wisdom literature which really corresponds to this deeper note.[3] If there are aphorisms in plenty to suggest the words of Jeremiah (xvii. 9):

The heart is deceitful above all things and it is desperately sick,

what have we to recall:

I will put my law in their inward parts and in their Heart will I write it?

---

[1] Jer. xxxi. 31–4. [2] Ezek. xxxvi. 26.

[3] Naturally Wisdom is represented as a divine gift (e.g. by ben Sira i. 10) and so comes (with all inspiration) under a wider definition of grace. Cf. Koeberle, *Sünde und Gnade*, pp. 621 ff.

PART VII

THE PSALMISTS

XXI

THE RESPONSE OF THE PSALMISTS

§ 1. Introduction

'THE Psalms . . . are responsive, not creative. . . . It was for the prophet to find God, for the Psalmist to praise Him; in prophecy God speaks to man, in psalmody man sings to God. . . . In Religion the message of Israel was truth about God; in Art the lyric response to that truth.' These words from Israel Abrahams's lecture, *Poetry and Religion*,[1] may well serve as our point of departure in considering the relation of the Psalms to the material previously studied.

(a) In the ordinary use of the Old Testament (both by the Jew and by the Christian) the Book of Psalms would be cited as part of the divine revelation, without any attempt to distinguish it from the contribution of prophet, priest, and sage.[2] Yet, as soon as we think about the precise nature of the Psalms, we see that important differences characterize them. They do not claim the direct inspiration of the prophet's word or the priest's *torah* and they are more conscious of the aesthetic element in their composition than are the prophet and the sage. They can be described in general as responses of varying kinds to the revelation of divine grace along the lines of Nature, Man, and History, and in the temple ritual as ordained of God. The Hebrew name of the book, *t^ehillim*, i.e. 'praises', may not comprehend all of them, but it does fitly suggest the praise of God as a response to the manifestation of His grace. The Greek name, *psalmoi*, from which comes our 'Psalms', represents the Hebrew *mizmor*, the title of many individual psalms, which describes them as sung to a musical accompaniment, and may serve to remind us of the aesthetic aspect of these lyrics. We recall that the prophet Ezekiel repudiated those who listened to him on aesthetic grounds, as a singer gifted with an attractive voice, or as the skilful player on an instrument.[3] This does not,

---

[1] pp. 54, 58, 80.   [2] e.g. the reference to Ps. cx in Mark xii. 36.
[3] xxxiii. 32.

of course, mean that poetic form was absent from the prophets' utterances in general; the simple rhythms of Hebrew poetry were the traditional form in which a divine revelation was couched. It is a question of emphasis, and we can safely say that the psalmists were much more conscious of poetic form than were the prophets, even whilst form was always subordinated to substance in their products. Thus they can pray that the words of their mouths, as well as the thoughts of their hearts, may find acceptance,[1] or that they may be equipped with the skill of a ready writer.[2] They approach the task of composition with a declared purpose:

> I will incline mine ear to a parable,
> I will open my riddle to the lyre. (xlix. 4, cf. lxxviii. 1 f.)

A praise-song is appropriate to God in Zion,[3] and as definitely an offering as the performance of a sacrificial vow. Moreover, it is ordered praise, not a casual ejaculation:

> I cried unto Him with my mouth,
> And a lofty hymn was (already) under my tongue.[4]

Yahweh, in the morning thou shalt hear my voice,
In the morning will I array (my offering) for thee and look out.
> (v. 4.)

Here the term for 'array' ('*arakh*) could denote either the ordered prayer or the accompanying sacrifice; it is a sacrificial term, which sets the prayer[5] within the cult. The whole worship, including the musical accompaniment of the praise or prayer, is conceived as an offering to God, and it must be made as worthy of Him as possible:

> I will also praise thee with the psaltery . . .
> Unto thee will I sing praises with the harp. (lxxi. 22.)

The following verse shows that lips and tongue are regarded as instruments of praise. A psalmist summons all his faculties to the work of blessing Yahweh, as he does all the instruments of his orchestra in the closing psalm.[6]

(b) Another characteristic feature of the response of the

---

[1] Ps. xix. 14; cf. civ. 34.   [2] Ps. xlv. 1.   [3] lxv. 1 (2); cf. xcii. 1–3.
[4] lxvi. 17; so Cheyne, but the text is somewhat uncertain here.
[5] Note '*ethpallal* in v. 3. Prayer as well as praise is based on the experience of divine grace, and can be regarded as a response to it.
[6] cl. On the musical instruments of the Hebrews, see the valuable appendix to Wellhausen's *Psalms*, in the 'Polychrome Bible'.

psalmists is that it is largely corporate. The prophet was a highly individualized channel of revelation, so far as the 'classical' prophets were concerned. Both priest and sage were more conscious of belonging to larger groups, the priest officially by his lineage in the successive generations of the 'sons of Levi', and by his ministering participation in Israel's central institution, the temple, the sage as the spokesman of a whole group of the observers and interpreters of experience, both within and without Israel. But, in the reception of revelation, both were consciously individualized, the priest in the casting and interpretation of the sacred lot, the sage by his personal perception of the applicability of a general truth to particular circumstance. It might be said, of course, that the psalmist was an individual composer of lyric poetry, and that those who used his composition were individual worshippers, though assembled together. That is true enough, but it ignores the peculiar quality of the response, which has gone so far to make the Psalms the outstanding expression of congregational worship. This is its representational character, the constant awareness of the larger group for whom the psalmist speaks, whether that group be the circle within Israel to which he is most intimately allied (e.g. the *hasidim*), or Israel as a whole, or even the widest group of all, that of mankind (as in the 8th and 90th Psalms). In this representation the operative principle is best described as that of 'corporate personality', the sense of a unity which comprehends all the individuals belonging to it, so that there is fluidity of transition from the one to the many and from the many to the one.[1] This is the best explanation of the frequent changes from a plural to a singular, and vice versa, and indeed of the much-discussed 'I' of the Psalms. Does it refer to Israel or to an Israelite? The true answer seems to be that it refers to both, and that either (according to the context) can become uppermost in the thought and language of the psalmist, without explicit indication of the change, since his own consciousness includes both. Here, too, is the reason of the remarkable fact that there are no intercessory psalms—the one main type of prayer absent from the catholicity of the Psalter. There are no such psalms because all the psalms are potentially intercessory, being fundamentally corporate and representational. We must always be ready to recognize this corporate character in the

[1] See pp. 70 f. and my essay in BZAW, lxvi.

response of the psalmists, without specific warning. It is there, like the pedal notes of the organ, ready to give body and substance to whatever be the melody.

(c) It was said at the outset that the Psalms, though strictly a response to revelation, have become for us a part of it. This could be amply justified by the very fact that they *are* a response, a response which helps to interpret that which stimulated it. It is a common experience that we enter into full possession of a truth only when we have taught it to others, and have seen in their faces the kindled gleam of that truth, what it is and what it can do, as we could never see it in ourselves. It is the experience which F. W. H. Myers ascribes to St. Paul (in his poem bearing that title), when making him say of the response of Damaris to the message of the Gospel:

> Then I preached Christ: and when she heard the story,—
> Oh, is such triumph possible to men?
> Hardly, my king, had I beheld Thy glory,
> Hardly had known Thine excellence till then.

It can safely be said that without the Psalms much of the effect and meaning of the Old Testament would be absent from its revelation. They show us, in intense and profound, yet in simple and universal expression, what revelation is by what revelation does. Without prophecy the Psalms as we have them could not have been written; but without the Psalms we should not have known the full greatness of the prophets. The Psalms show us the majesty of God not so much by what they say directly about it (rich and copious as this is) as by showing us the worshippers prostrate before Him in the courts of the temple.[1] The Psalms show us His 'loyal love' (*ḥeṣed*) towards His people, not simply or chiefly by the string of epithets attached to His name, but by the way in which men are drawn to cast themselves, in their sins and sorrows, their frail and brief tenure of life, their utter dependence, on that which they believe God to be. The prayers of the Psalms echo, often in the same terms, the promises of the prophets. How fine an example of this can be seen in the promise of Deutero-Isaiah (xlvi. 4):

> Even to old age I am He,
> And even to hoar hairs will I carry you,

---

[1] See *Christian Worship* (ed. by N. Micklem), ii, 'The Old Testament Background'; also *The Bible and Worship* (B. & F. Bible Society), both by the present writer.

which is transformed into a prayer on the lips of the psalmist
(lxxi. 9):

> Cast me not off in the time of old age;
> Forsake me not when my strength faileth!

The earthly praises of the Psalms constantly remind the worshipper of the heavenly praises of the higher temple, of which
they are the echo. We realize those mighty acts of God which
the psalmists recount when we listen to the 'new songs' of those
who have been redeemed by them. Thus, in its own right, the
response of the psalmists claims a permanent place in divine
revelation, a place to which the liturgies of both Synagogue and
Church bear fullest witness.

§ 2. THE KEY-WORD 'TRUST'

It was said by a distinguished exegete of the Psalms that the
single word which best gathers up and expresses their piety is
baṭaḥ, which we may render as 'trust'. It occurs in them forty-
six times, and a brief study of its use is amply repaying. This
use can be classified in a fivefold way, viz. (*a*) what it is, (*b*)
what it does, (*c*) its particular response to the divine *ḥeṣed*,
(*d*) the contrast with unworthy objects of trust, or with trust in
men, (*e*) trust as constituting a ground of appeal to God.

(*a*) *Baṭaḥ* is a synonym of Isaiah's word for faith (*heʾᵉmin*),[1]
though it is more suggestive of a personal relation and of
expectancy.[2] This personal trust is the very opposite of fear.[3]

(*b*) Such trust brings the confidence that Yahweh will withhold no good thing from the trustful, that His active protection
encompasses the life entrusted to Him, bringing deliverance and
security and the fulfilment of petitions, that He is a help and
a shield,[4] covering all the occasions of life and providing a sure
refuge:

> In thee, Yahweh, have I trusted;
> I have said, Thou art my God.
> My times are in thy hand. (xxxi. 14, 15.)

We should notice the completeness and comprehensiveness of
the scope of this trust, covering as it does the whole of life.

(*c*) The special characteristic of Yahweh to which *baṭaḥ*

---

[1] Isa. vii. 9, xxviii. 16; cf. Ps. lxxviii. 22.

[2] xxxiii. 21, xxv. 2, xl. 4. [3] xxvii. 3, lvi. 5, 12 (4, 11).

[4] lxxxiv. 13 (12), xxxvii. 5, xxii. 5 (4) (bis), xxxvii. 3, cxii. 7, cxxv. 1, cxv. 9–11,
xxviii. 7, xxxi. 14, 15, lxii. 9 (8), xci. 2.

appeals, and by which the trust is awakened and maintained, is His *ḥeṣed*, which brings joy and security and surrounds the trustful.[1] The point here is the fidelity of Yahweh,[2] which is made explicit in ix. 11 (10):

> They who know thy name may trust in thee,
> Since thou, Yahweh, dost not forsake those who seek after thee.

(*d*) In contrast with this trust in Yahweh, men often rely on false aids, such as material resources, wealth, oppression of others, weapons of war, idols.[3] Or, they may seek refuge in man, though even the most influential or the most intimate may fail them.[4]

(*e*) Such personal trust becomes a sure ground of appeal, for it puts God on His honour when His word is trusted.[5] In fact, He leads men on to trust Him.[6] Trust is the something more that goes beyond all sacrifices:

> Sacrifice due sacrifices
> And trust in Yahweh, (iv. 6, (5)),

the something more of personal relation which sacrifices have but partially expressed; such trust will not be put to shame.[7] It should be noted that such trust does not exclude legitimate, indeed necessary, confidence in one's own integrity:[8]

> Judge me, Yahweh, for I walk in my integrity (*bᵉthummi*)
> And in Yahweh have I trusted, without wavering.

In fact, it is the righteous (as opposed to 'men of blood')[9] who are characterized by their trust in Yahweh.

It will be seen how wide an expanse is covered by this single word, and at the same time how deep are its implications. Of course, there are many psalms of trust which do not actually use the word *baṭaḥ*, and yet illustrate its meaning from beginning to end; these are significantly amongst the favourite and best known of the Psalms, as e.g. xxiii, xci, ciii. But *baṭaḥ* in the Book of Psalms is a master-key which opens many locks and

---

[1] xvii. 7, xxi. 8 (7), xiii. 6 (5), lii. 10 (8), cxliii. 8, xxxii. 10.

[2] See what is said on *ḥeṣed* as the 'loyalty' of Yahweh which is the kernel of the *bᵉrith* (covenant); pp. 57 f.

[3] xlix. 6, lii. 9 (7), lxii. 11 (10), xliv. 7 (6), cxv. 8, cxxxv. 18.

[4] cxviii. 8, 9, cxlvi. 3, xli. 10 (9).

[5] cxix. 42, lxxxvi. 2, lvi. 4; cf. the force of such an appeal even to an enemy, recorded in Doughty, *Arabia Deserta*, i. 63–4 ('I am thy suppliant').

[6] xxii. 10 (9) (Hiph'il Part.). [7] xxii. 6 (5).

[8] xxvi. 1; cf. Job's final appeal. [9] lv. 24 (23).

admits us to the very heart of the response of the psalmists to God's revelation of His grace.

§ 3

The response of the psalmists is made to the revelation of God in each of the three realms—Nature, Man, and History, and also to that which is the combination of these, the products, of the centuries, such as the Torah and Wisdom. We have already drawn on the Psalms to illustrate the interpretation of these realms as media of revelation, and few further examples are necessary. First, in regard to Nature, we have the outstanding example of Ps. civ, the poetical version of the first chapter of Genesis. A comparison of the two versions shows, better than any description, the difference between the straightforward prose narrative (however high the dignity of the rhythmical prose which befits the story of creation) and the lyrical praise of God in view of the achieved result. In the narrative God says, 'Let there be light': in the lyric we have, 'who coverest thyself with light as with a garment'. In the narrative God says, 'Let there be a firmament in the midst of the waters'; in the lyric, 'who layeth the beams of His chambers in the waters', and so on. Naturally, there is more detail in the lyric, as in the singing of the birds among the branches of the trees where they nest, some of which detail has doubtless come through that Egyptian love of Nature which is enshrined in the Hymn to the Sun, the model of this psalm.[1] But the total effect is clear; it is to show how the revelation of God's power and wisdom in Nature can stir men to responsive praise and thanksgiving. Thus the psalm sets its seal upon the divine self-disclosure, and completes the full circle of revelation and response in this realm.

We have also seen that Revelation includes a new conception of Man in his relation to God. True to their responsive character, the Psalms bring no new discoveries, such as that of a destiny extending beyond death, a discovery which we owe to the apocalyptic doctrine of resurrection. But they do show deep consciousness of the frailty of the tenure of human life (xxxix), of the mystery of God's dealing with the successive generations (xc), of man's apparent insignificance, yet actual exaltation over against the starry hosts of heaven (viii), and of that relent-

[1] Erman, op. cit., pp. 288 ff.

less pursuit of him by God which is inspired by a love that will not let him go (cxxxix). It is in the abiding consciousness of these truths that the foundation of true and deep piety consists.

The retrospect of history and the prospect of its glorious and triumphant vindication of righteousness give occasion for another kind of response. God has wrought great deliverances on the larger scale of Israel's history (cxiv) and in smaller groups (cvii), for which there must be praise and thanksgiving. The retrospect has shadow as well as light upon it, not least the shadow of Israel's infidelities (cvi), but God, at any rate, has been faithful and more than faithful:

> O Israel, hope in Yahweh,
> For with Yahweh there is loyal love (*ḥeṣed*)
> And with Him is plenteous redemption. (cxxx. 7.)

Similarly, a number of psalms rejoice concerning that future when Yahweh shall manifest Himself as King over all the earth: 'Yahweh reigns'.[1]

It will be seen that all these illustrations of response are equally illustrations of personal trust (*baṭaḥ*). It is this trust which is able (with the pioneer guidance of the prophets) to interpret the revelation of God in these various ways and to respond to it. Because of this comprehensive variety the Book of Psalms is not only the living and passionate utterance of Israel's piety at its highest, but also supplies the data for an epitome of Old Testament theology.

The centre at which the consciousness of revelation and the instinct to respond to it found amplest expression was the temple at Jerusalem. Here with all the material expression which the times allowed, whether of site, architecture, or ritual, here where men were brought together in their manifold varieties, here where historical memories went back through the long line of Davidic kings to the great David himself, the devout Jew was especially brought 'to see the face' of Him who used all these ways to manifest Himself. Here, too, was the richest elaboration of response known to Israel, the response of sacrifice and the more articulate response of the accompanying psalms. We need not wonder at the enthusiasm which the temple with its ritual so constantly evokes from these lyricists,[2] for it was the concrete embodiment of so many other means of

---

[1] xlvii, xciii, xcvi–c: see ch. X ('The Day of Yahweh').
[2] e.g. in Ps. lxxxiv.

revelation. Their love of Yahweh's house was in fact a response to the whole revelation of His grace in Nature, Man, and History.

§ 4. THE URGE TO TESTIFY

One other feature of the response takes so large a place in the Psalms that it is not likely to be missed by anyone. This might be called the duty and privilege of witness-bearing, or the urge to evangelism. It is indeed one aspect of the corporate character of the worship. Others, as well as the speaker or singer, must be called to join in the same song of praise and must be moved to vicarious gratitude. This motif is clearly expressed, for example, in xl. 10, 11 (9, 10):

I have proclaimed glad tidings of righteousness[1] in the great congregation;
Behold, I will not refrain my lips,
O Yahweh, thou knowest.
I have not hid thy righteousness within my heart;
I have declared thy faithfulness and thy salvation:
I have not concealed thy lovingkindness and thy truth from the great congregation.

But it is constantly recurrent,[2] for 'the Bible knows nothing of solitary religion',[3] i.e. of religion content with an individual experience of it. It is as natural, indeed, as inevitable, for the psalmist to sing of his deliverance or of the confidence that he will be delivered,[4] as for the prophet to utter the word of God committed to his charge. Even where there is no explicit mention of those who are to hear the testimony, its expression in a psalm, by social implications or cultic use, will show that the relation to others is consciously in the background. In this obligation to testify, which runs on into the faith of the New Testament with not less intensity, and is one of the causes of the earliest dissemination of that faith, the response to grace is seen to be an integral part of the experience of grace. The absence of the impulse to 'evangelize', to make others sharers in the good things God has revealed to ourselves, casts doubt on our own participation in them.

[1] i.e. Yahweh's deliverance; the verb is *bissarti*, used in Jer. xx. 15, &c.
[2] e.g. ix. 1, 2, 11; xviii. 49; xxii. 22 ff.
[3] J. Wesley's *Journal*, i. 469 note; cf. Moore's *Life*, i. 162.   [4] xiii. 5, 6.

XXII

CONCLUSION

§ 1

W HAT are the general impressions to be drawn from this survey of the methods and material of revelation in the Old Testament? One of the most obvious is of the diversity of the methods. Revelation is mediated through prophet and priest and sage, to say nothing here of the historians, the psalmists, and the other writers who have contributed to the Old Testament literature. The method varies with the varying agents, as for example the 'word' of the prophet through his God-consciousness, the *torah* of the priest, originally through the sacred lot, the counsel of the sage, through his common-sense analysis of ordinary experience. It is clear that we must not look for the test of genuine inspiration in any one external or internal form of mediation, with exclusion of the rest.

We get a similar warning from the unlimited extent of the material on which revelation draws for its content, viz. the three vast realms of physical Nature, human nature, and the history of the successive generations of men. Together they are exhaustive of the data of human life itself. In their combinations and mutual reactions they open up the possibility of new data for revelation to an unlimited degree. It is only by arbitrary abstraction from the kaleidoscopic variety of life that we can say, 'There is nothing new under the sun'; it would be much nearer the truth to say, 'There is nothing old' in the events befalling an individual life. Each birth is a new kind of beginning, in which the elements are mixed as never before. Each death leaves a unique life face to face with the question-mark of eternity. All this variety of material provides the potential data for revelation, in the hands of the living God. To stereotype it and Him is to caricature both.

By the very unity of man's self-consciousness, however attained, he is compelled to seek a unity within and behind all this diversity. He may attempt this along the line of the beauty it manifests, as did, for example, the poet Keats. For him, the ultimate truth of things and men lay in their beauty, as is expressed in his best-known lines:

> Beauty is truth, truth beauty,—that is all
> Ye know on earth, and all ye need to know.

This, of course, implies a philosophy, but it implies much more. For Keats the resultant expression of that truth must be in the poetic forms of beauty. An ugly expression of the ultimate beauty of the universe would be self-contradictory.

In contrast with the poet (or other artist), the philosopher abstracting from life an intellectual formula of ultimate reality often seems to neglect the manner in which his conception of truth is expressed (which partly explains why so many philosophic works are dull or unreadable). But the philosopher, of all people, ought to be the master of a perfect prose style. He claims to have reached clarity of thought; if this clarity is not reflected by the language in which he speaks or writes, we may gravely doubt whether his thinking has itself attained clarity. His concern is to interpret life through intellectual formulae, and a formula that is not precise is as self-contradictory as poetry that is not beautiful.

In strong contrast with the artistic creator or the intellectual analyst stands he who finds the ultimate unity (within and above the diversity of experience) through divine revelation. Much that is ugly must be incorporated into his data, nor can those data be completely reduced to satisfying intellectual formulae. He is concerned with men as men; not with their aesthetic or intellectual capacities taken apart but with personality as a whole, and in all its activity, including its partial freedom. The unity to which (consciously or unconsciously) he aspires does not lie in this world at all, even in principle; it depends wholly on the divine Reality beyond this world. On the activity of that Reality within and through the realms of Nature, Man, and History depends the restoration of the world to its true pattern. The revelation is of this restoration; the restoration is achieved through the revelation only in part.[1]

Here, then, we see the premises from which our study of revelation in the Old Testament has been conducted. The comprehensive data of life (Nature, Man, and History) have been compelled to pay tribute to a remarkable and varied

---

[1] This is the theme of my book, *Redemption and Revelation*.

succession of prophets, priests, and sages, whilst the psalmists who respond to this revelation constitute a new type of revealers by reflecting the products of the old. It is this total interpretation which has eventually constituted the Old Testament, and entitles it to be called 'Revelation'—or, more exactly, it is in the interpretative interplay of event and faith together constituting the religious fact. There is much in the Old Testament which, taken by itself, would never be accepted as a revelation of God; it has been superseded. But this does not mean that it can be detached from the historic record. It will have its permanent place there, when properly understood. To select certain portions of the Old Testament as Revelation and to reject others is to make the anthologist the inspired voice of God. In a very secondary sense, he may be this, by calling his contemporaries to those parts of Scripture which make contact with *them*. But it is plain that the 'authority' of the anthologist has no finality, since the choice of one generation will not necessarily be that of the next. We must find authority in Revelation, for authority is its hall-mark. But that authority cannot be something conferred by our own choice, even though our convinced response is part of the whole process of revelation.

§ 2

The vast majority of believers find the authority of revelation in some form of external guarantor, notably the Church or the Bible. They do not usually raise the further necessary question, Who guarantees the guarantor? If they did, they would reach a point like that in the theistic argument from a First Cause, as it is popularly and erroneously conceived. The point is that at which the chain of tradition breaks off—and both Church and Bible illustrate this in their different ways. In the history of their development a value-judgement had to be made by someone or other, which changes the character of the appeal, just as the argument from causality alters its nature when it appeals to the necessity for an 'uncaused Cause' at the beginning of things. The value-judgement may be that of the prophet trusting his own intuition of God's word, or of the priest trusting the truth of the tradition as being 'Mosaic', or of the simple-minded worshipper in synagogue or church who comes to regard a particular body of literature or a particular group of men as vested with a divine authority. The process is usually veiled in obscurity; doctrines of inspiration or conciliar decisions come in simply to register the *fait accompli* that something has been accepted long enough to acquire the warrant of antiquity.[1] But careful examination of the process of revelation will always bring us back to some form of this intuition, however combined with other factors, as essential to the process. So far as the Old Testament goes, we have seen the presence of the value-judgement along each line of inquiry. How could we expect to eliminate it, since personal agents or recipients are concerned with a personal God, and have to be personally convinced of the authority of the truth imparted to them? The intuition of a value-judgement, therefore, is exactly what we ought to expect when personal Reality reveals itself to persons. Tradition and reason will more or less co-operate, either to introduce or to confirm, but the ultimate basis of the conviction will have to come in this way, involving all the faculties of personality.

In the Law and in the Prophets the revelation is usually described as 'spoken' by God to man.[2] This externalization of the process was inevitable, with the given psychological limitations, in order to express the authority of the revelation. But the historic form of the event, the actual way in which it came about, must have been much more intimate than an external voice in order to secure the necessary nucleus of conviction. Even if an external voice was sometimes 'heard' by the prophet (as is quite possible), this would not dispense us from psychological analysis of the constituent experience, which would bring us back to the same point of an unconscious intuition. Whatever the precise method, as it might have been reported by the percipient, the authority of revelation was secured by a personal conviction, because this was an essential feature of the authority with which the prophet himself clothed his message. That authority was intrinsic in the original 'inspiration' and

---

[1] McNeile, *Introduction to the New Testament*, p. 294, writes of the formation of a New Testament in similar terms: 'We take our stand, then, at the beginning of the second century, and during, roughly, the first three-quarters of it we find the conception of a Canon being formed, i.e. the separation of a group of apostolic writings from all other Christian writings to be reverenced on a level with the Old Testament. The Christian writings were of four main kinds: Gospels, Acts, Epistles, and Apocalypses; in the case of all four classes some being rejected, most of them decisively from the first, but some after hesitation and sporadic use as Scripture.'

[2] The history and the varied writings of the third part of the Hebrew Canon have been assumed to be written by inspired persons.

made the divine 'word' recognizable as such. That which comes from God will need no external testimony, necessarily lower than its source and nature as divine truth.

The original reception of revelation gives us the clue to the exercise of continued authority (in a secondary sense) by the Bible and by the Church. The way in which the 'inspired' were convinced that the very truth of God had come to them is still the way in which their conviction becomes ours. Without tradition we could not attain to knowledge, but without personal conviction that knowledge could not be assimilated as revelation. When we listen to a symphony with genuine appreciation, some degree of musical capacity is presupposed in us, though it falls far short of that of the composer of the symphony. So also, when we respond to the revelation of God as recorded in the Bible or as proclaimed by the Church, a certain degree of faith is presupposed and of capacity for more faith, though it never reaches the intensity of faith in the original prophet. This leaves us, it is true, with another problem—why some believe and some reject, with equal honesty. There is no present solution of it. Indeed, it might be said that to explain it completely would be to explain faith away, for the exercise of personal freedom involved in faith can never be stated in terms of scientific causality.

It should also be noticed that the reasons given as the intellectual explanation of faith may vary from generation to generation and usually will. Given the nucleus of sympathetic intuition, there will quite naturally gather round it the contemporary methods of understanding and expression. But this means that they will necessarily change with the changing generations.[1] Our own is predominantly psychological and scientific in its interests. We therefore try to analyse both the subjective aspects of faith and the data of its objective documents, and may easily forget that their synthesis in living personal conviction involved, as it still involves, something more, and something that must be taken as a new unity.

For this unity we may claim quite as much 'objectivity' as can attach to any theory of revelation making Bible or Church its final court of appeal. It is sheer camouflage to take refuge behind Bible or Church as though the decrees of a Council or the collection of a literature were sufficient to give the desired

[1] See the notable statement of this in Robert Browning's *A Death in the Desert*.

stamp of authority. A further theory is needed, such as that of the guidance of the Holy Spirit, to give the required authority to our alleged authority. But directly we have supplied this theory, the alleged 'objectivity' and independence of ourselves which Bible and Church seemed to possess is lost. However important, they are ultimately links in a chain, which hangs from nothing less than God Himself, and becomes visible to us only at the point at which He chooses to enter into our consciousness.

There is a useful parallel in the interpretation of scientific data. These may seem independent of the observer to a degree never possible with the data of religion, and so far as they are in the physical realm they are easier to observe and record than psychical data can ever be. Yet the seeming independence is only relative. From the first observation of some material phenomenon and the first perception of its details, there is a psychical element at work, which becomes increasingly apparent as larger combinations or perceptions are built up into an interpretation of the physical universe. The simplest perception is already in some degree an interpretation, and nothing in the universe can make contact with us except through our consciousness. If we venture to use those notoriously dangerous words, every element in that consciousness is both 'subjective' and 'objective', and science has no prerogative of objectivity over religion. The Old Testament shows us God making use of both physical and psychical data in order to convey His revelation, but both have to be combined with the personal reaction of the agent or recipient of revelation. It is in the combination of a particular capacity to respond with some particular occasion that we should think of the real focus of revelation. There is just as much an opportunity for the divine initiative in such combinations as there would be in the dictation of a verbal message, or even the infusion of some superhuman quality. The outcome may be the same, but the procedure seems much worthier of a God who calls man into collaboration with Himself. If man claims all for himself, and fails to recognize God's major part, it may be due to the misfortune of his prejudice or the fault of his pride.

§ 3

The first cardinal truth, therefore, brought home to us concerning Revelation by the Old Testament is that the divine authority attaching to it is intrinsic and inherent. It is not to be sought through any testimony other than itself, whatever be the legitimate place of the secondary and subsidiary authorities by which God may make contact with ourselves. Here the second cardinal truth is found, viz. that God is known through the known.

The Spencerian type of agnosticism, so popular in the last century, relegated religion to the dim realm beyond the brightly lit circle of scientific knowledge. This naïve division was supposed to leave everybody happy. The scientist could work unchallenged in the ever-growing circle of the known; the religionist could give free scope to his imagination everywhere else.[1] Whilst no competent thinker would defend such a dualism to-day, there is always a risk of repeating its error within religion itself, and of counting a 'dim religious light' as more reverent than the realism of a historic revelation. The Old Testament has nothing to do with that sort of division. God indeed is great, so great that in all His majesty we know Him not. But God is also merciful, stooping to the needs of the world, entering into its comprehension by actual events and their interpretations, by agents whom He commissions, by the innermost thoughts of men's hearts. It is His 'secret presence' which, in James Martineau's fine words,[2] is 'the soul of every blessing, the solemn look of every duty, the healing anguish of our contrition, and the life of all that is not dead within us'. The unknown God becomes known in the sphere of that which man *can* know.

But such a conception of Revelation should be clearly distinguished from any theory of immanence, and God's presence in His world is not to be explained (according to the Old Testament) by any type of pantheism. God remains transcendent, and only by His own will does He so accept the limiting conditions of the known as to become Himself known. Never is He unable to detach Himself from even His most cherished agents or instruments. His people are a chosen people, which means that they can become a rejected people, as the prophets constantly remind them. But whilst and where God is present, He is known by His activity, known in His reality, known

[1] Herbert Spencer, *First Principles*, Pt. I, *passim*; cf. p. 84 (1904 ed.): 'it is alike our highest wisdom and our highest duty to regard that through which all things exist as The Unknowable.' [2] *Home Prayers*, p. 11.

through that which is part of the whole truth about Him, because it is His activity. That which is known may be the merest fragment of the whole, yet it is, like the Christian's present experience of the Holy Spirit, a true ἀρραβών, being 'a payment on account' of the same kind, however far short of the capital amount.[1]

It is plain that everything which exists can acquire a twofold significance for Revelation. Since it must depend at last on God as Creator and Upholder, it reveals His activity, and therefore in some degree it reveals Him. But it can acquire a further meaning, as part of some more complex pattern of His purpose. An event in the natural order, for example, reveals God in being what it is, but it may also reveal Him by being taken up into the web of human life and history.

This would hardly be conceivable if God had created Nature to be independent of Himself; there would have to be far too much appeal to providential coincidences, or far too much 'interference' with a fixed order. But if Nature be conceived as alive through its continued maintenance by God, it is responsive to Him in all its elements, and there is no reason why this responsiveness should not correspond to a related responsiveness in his human agents of revelation. Whilst we have insisted on the place of man's interpretative activity in Revelation, we have also to remember that our mental dualities cannot exist as such for God. For Him there is a unity of responsiveness, which has been finely expressed by one poet characterizing another. This is what Francis Thompson has said of Shelley:[2]

'He had an instinctive perception (immense in range and fertility, astonishing for its delicate intuition) of the underlying analogies, the secret subterranean passages between matter and soul; the chromatic scales, whereat we dimly guess, by which the Almighty modulates through all the keys of creation.'

The division we make between physical and human nature is indeed transcended in our own bodies, as the Hebrews rightly (though instinctively) felt through their conception of a diffused consciousness.[3] We cannot tell where matter ends and spirit begins. As the hand that writes is incorporated into the mind that thinks, so we might imagine a prophet making his own the

---

[1] 2 Cor. i. 22, v. 5; cf. Eph. i. 14.
[2] 'Essay on Shelley' in *The Works of Francis Thompson* (Prose), iii. 25 (ed. of 1913).
[3] See pp. 71 ff.

famous words of the *Theologia Germanica*,[1] 'I would fain be to the Eternal Goodness what his own hand is to a man'.

The symphony of Nature, Man, and History which the Old Testament supplies witnesses to the unity of Revelation amid all its diversity. That unity is found in God, and in Him alone, since all goes back to Him at last. He is known in and through these realms of the (partially) known though He always transcends them. Yet the knowledge of Him which they afford is real knowledge, given by His gracious activity, and not by the mere play of our imagination upon the uncontrolled events of human life.

§ 4

The third characteristic of Revelation in the Old Testament is that God is known through personal fellowship. We should beware of taking this as an obvious general description of the relation of God as Person to men as persons, and then dismissing it as commonplace. Equally must we avoid dismissing it as impossible, on the ground that God is more than any form of personality yet known to us. We cannot here enter into the problems for theistic philosophy of any anthropomorphic conception of God. It must be sufficient to recall what our examination of the different lines of Old Testament revelation have suggested as the essential relation. The prophetic consciousness in its highest forms was quite clearly a relation with God conceived as personal. To be admitted into 'the council of Yahweh' was to be brought into the vividly imagined circle of those who knew His purposes and were swift to further them by service. It has been urged that this conception has to be taken quite realistically, to do justice to the Hebrew thought. Thus taken, it expresses as intensely as anything could the reality of the fellowship between God and man which underlies the prophetic consciousness. As truly as God meets and converses with the superhuman beings of His heavenly court, does He meet and converse with man when He wills so to do.

From the mountain-peak of Hebrew prophetic experience we can look both backwards and forwards; backwards to the idyllic days of the patriarchs, when God drew so near to man, and took so intimate a share in his affairs, and forwards to such developed piety as is recorded in the Psalms. It is in the

[1] p. 32 of *Golden Treasury* ed. (trans. by Winkworth).

response of the psalmists to the whole previous revelation of God, especially as gathered up into the cult of the temple, that we see how intense the piety of Israel could be, how full of the sense of God's nearness and intimacy, notwithstanding all His majesty and awfulness. So even in the more generalized consciousness of the Wisdom writers, we saw that God could come very near to man in his daily life, not only as retribution from without, but also as inspiration and motive from within. One measure of the intensity which the fellowship could reach may be seen in the passionate agony of Job, when the consciousness of it had been lost (xxix. 1–5):

> Oh, that I were as in the months of old,
> As in the days when God guarded me!
> When his lamp shone upon my head,
> And by his light I walked through darkness;
> As I was in the ripeness of my days,
> When the fellowship of God was by my tent;
> When the Almighty was yet with me,
> And my children were about me.

Here the word rendered 'fellowship' is *sodh*, which has been rendered elsewhere (in other contexts)[1] as both 'council' and its outcome in 'counsel'. No Hebrew word could better describe that gracious personal fellowship out of which revelation comes, in all its pregnant series of activities; from the high council of God, through the privileged admission of His prophets to it, down to the prerogative of ordinary piety, to share in and live by the declared purposes of God.

If we seek a physical metaphor (inadequate as the physical must of necessity be as a parable of the psychical), we may think of Coleridge's

> hidden brook in the leafy month of June
> Which to the sleeping woods all night
> Singeth a quiet tune.

But here and there the regular murmur of the brook will be modified by the little pile of stones or by the growing weeds or by the shaping constraint of the banks. So may we think of the revelation that comes through human fellowship with God. The things that seem trivial or accidental in a human life, as well as the obviously 'merciful constraints' of divine Providence,

[1] See pp. 166 ff.

enable something to be said that had to be said, whilst the capacity to say anything at all comes through the regular flow of the stream of personal fellowship with God.

It follows that revelation through such means will not be in a series of propositions *about* God, but a disclosure of God Himself, so far as the event can disclose Him. This event may be cataclysmic on the grand scale or like most of what constitutes human life, trivial and apparently accidental. There, in the event, men may 'see His face' and so come to know Him in His own degree of revelation. With the reflection of the light of this knowledge of God, man's face also will shine, as did that of Moses coming down from the mount. There will be a revelation of man, again not consisting in a series of propositions declaring his depravity or dogmatizing on his immortality, but showing him both in his remoteness from God and in his capacity for God, in his need of God and in the changes wrought in him by fellowship with God.

To realize what all this means we must learn to live in the atmosphere of the Old Testament, and of its sequel, the New Testament. Probably the necessity is more fully recognized in regard to the New Testament, where the fellowship of Jesus with His disciples sets a pattern of daily fellowship with the divine. In the Old Testament revelation is imparted in more external forms of communication according to the record, whilst the New Testament brings us into a life of fellowship (κοινωνία) as the avowed product of the faith it describes.[1] But it is just as true for the piety of the Old Testament as for that of the New that the generating experience of its revelation is that of a fellowship between God and man.[2]

As for the content of the revelation (in distinction from its form), it is inevitable that we should state this in a series of propositions to constitute a 'Theology of the Old Testament', even if they are arranged in historical order, and called a 'History of the Religion of Israel'. If they are stated topically, and not chronologically, as a 'theology' requires, they become still more abstract and remote from the once-living, vibrating, and dynamic religion of Israel. Let us constantly remind ourselves that this religion, like any other, can be understood only

---

[1] 1 John i. 3: 'That which we have seen and heard declare we unto you also, that ye also may have fellowship with us.'

[2] The conditions for being Yahweh's 'guest' are set forth in Pss. xv and xxiv.

from within, or through a sympathy that makes us its 'resident aliens' (*gerim*).

Such a theology naturally requires a volume to itself. It will have to be rewritten in each generation, for each has different needs and each will interpret the past in its own characteristic way. But it will have its inevitable poles around which all else turns. Over against each other are God and man, and all that lies between can be conceived as belonging to the Kingdom— the active kingly rule—of God. The Jew will find the beginnings of that Kingdom in the increasing obedience of man to the divine Torah. The Christian sees it as already begun in the life, death, and resurrection of Jesus the Messiah. But both, in their different ways, depend on that religion of Israel which is neither Judaism nor Christianity but the mother of them both.

SCRIPTURE INDEX